PATHWAYS TO PEOPLE

Pathways to People

LEONARD W. DOOB

New Haven and London, Yale University Press, 1975

Library of Congress catalog card number: 74–29716
International standard book number: 0–300–01843–6

Designed by Sally Sullivan
and set in Palatino type.
Printed in the United States of America by
Vail-Ballou Press, Inc., Binghamton, N.Y.

Published in Great Britain, Europe, and Africa by
Yale University Press, Ltd., London.
Distributed in Latin America by Kaiman & Polon,
Inc., New York City; in India by UBS Publishers'
Distributors Pvt., Ltd., Delhi; in Japan by John Weatherhill,
Inc., Tokyo.

To acquaintances and friends
wittingly or not
they have given
one or more essential ingredients
to me and this book
above all themselves
as well as
peace, affection, stimulation, vision
in places variously located
two universities, Yale (U.S.A.) and Legon (Ghana)
two South Tyrolean kingdoms, Mölten and Brunnenburg (Italy)
next to Knocknarea (Ireland)
an island approaching ghastly tragedy (Cyprus).
With gratitude
I offer advice.
Dare I
Do they need it
Should they listen?
I wonder.
August 1974

Contents

You never really know what the other person is doing or thinking, you never really know what he is like. Almost always he is wearing a mask; he keeps changing the mask; he does not tell you which mask he is using, he may not know, you certainly do not know. He is separated from you, and you cannot get inside him. You observe him for years— and you think you know him as well as you know yourself or better, but suddenly he surprises you, and you are pleased or not. You have similar, often more provoking, problems with groups of persons when their behavior belies your anticipation.

But you, my companion throughout these pages, are quite aware that you cannot survive when you are ignorant of others, and you would be bored or anxious if they continually caught you off guard. At home or in the market you must know the identity of the persons you meet, the kinds of behavior they are likely to display, the ways in which they react to you and you to them. Most of the time you structure and categorize people; they cannot remain vague, fuzzy, and unlabelled the way plants and trees are largely ignored by those with little interest in botany, or the way stars and constellations are unobserved by eyes intent upon the ground. A policeman in your community, you assume, speaks the same language as you; the woman who cheats you now is not to be trusted in the future; a laughing child must be happy and a crying child sad; the exotic foreigner may—or may not be—an evil man. In addition, although it is sometimes sufficient to know what a person has done, is doing, will do, you usually seek to understand why his behavior has taken one form and not another; you would, I suppose, also discover what is going on within him. Immediately in the

privacy of your own reverie you acknowledge that you are solipsistically encased, that everybody is similarly detached from everybody else,
that complete understanding is never, never possible—or may be undesirable. You carry on, nevertheless. Again and again your judgments
agree with others, though the agreement may mean simply that you
use the same words as they. Your judgments frequently are not in error
because in fact you have pathways to people, the people you must
characterize and evaluate, the people whose actions you must more or
less successfully predict.

Are you satisfied with these pathways, the ones you choose to tread,
are you satisfied that they enable you to judge others correctly? Your
reply cannot be a blunt yes or no. For you believe you understand some
persons and not others, or you grasp a particular individual on some
occasions but not on others. If you were omniscient, you would not be
carrying on discussions with me in a book having the title this one
bears, and I would not be struggling with it: you would be too perfect
or imperfect, too much of a success or a failure to be able to pause to
consider the problem, and I would not dream of troubling you. I admire you for not being smug, and of course I am not smug. Thus we
begin happily by acknowledging that at least we share the trait of
non-smugness, a good reason to rejoice but not to relax.

Who are you, the you with whom I speak in written words? You
are a real person in my imagination and therefore, in addressing or
describing you, I use whatever knowledge of you I choose to think I
possess, and I ascribe to you the traits you have or in my opinion those
you ought or ought not to have. A conscientious reader, if he is patient
and so inclined, can perhaps extract the references to you and emerge
with a complete, one-sided portrait. Often, it will be evident, you are
my devil's advocate, you raise difficult or rhetorical questions I ignore
because I have no immediate answer; but they trouble me and eventually, though not always, I try to reply. You keep pointing to the
persisting, perennial problems which, quite correctly sometimes, you
assume I tend to neglect just because they are so persistent and
perennial.

Whenever you address me directly, or when I think you do, I shall
place your words in italics. *Why use italics and not inverted commas?*
You mean quotation marks, I suppose. Like you, the I referring to you
is also real, rather most of the time I believe I am real, though obviously I cannot prove that this is so to your satisfaction or mine.

In our discussion you may be able to contribute your experience and especially your intuition, and I shall do the same. In addition, however, I have a laborious role to perform which I would have you carefully understand at the outset. Before and while writing this book, I have surveyed some, but obviously not all, the systematic evidence concerning the ways in which we actually or allegedly judge and appraise other persons. *Why do that?* As I report the fruits of this drudgery, I shall try to avoid two hazards. First, the studies are so numerous and diverse that I am not even tempted to try to summarize and synthesize them, even if I had the time, ability, and valor to do so. No, this is not my task for many reasons. Others more qualified than I have already made the attempt, in rare instances quite satisfactorily. The topic of what is called person perception is being hotly pursued by an army of researchers who appear to be far from their goal, however quickly they inch forward. Also, if I may whisper the thought here before shouting it later on, I consider the goal unattainable: no study or series of studies on the subject has ultimate value. *A very bold statement: what will your colleagues think of you?* I do not care, I think I do not care.

The second hazard involves a variant of what is called the naturalistic fallacy in philosophy: deriving an ethical or prescriptive principle from conditions as they exist in the here-and-now among imperfect human beings or their society. I do judge you thus, hence I should judge you so. Surely you would not assert that we, being prejudiced, should follow our prejudices. The converse of the fallacy, however, is also to be eschewed: disregarding knowledge of the status quo that might be utilized to overcome present defects. Indeed some of the studies indicate fairly directly how improvement might be attained.

Many of the so-called scientific studies, therefore, are mentioned at the end of each chapter where other parts of the conversations between you and me are also relegated under alluring, though arbitrary, headings I call, with supreme originality, "Postscripts." *A crude way to submerge the less significant?* Yes.

Now for the sake of intelligibility and compatibility, permit me to standardize our vocabulary:

Ego: any person passing judgment upon another person: the judge, observer, assessor, critic, psychiatrist, psychologist, parent.

Alter: the person being judged.

Ego-expositor: the person judging why and how Ego judges Alter. Awkward perhaps, but not neologistic.

Group Alter: the interacting, functionally related persons being judged.

Halt—must you deal with Group Alters too, are you not being a trifle megalomaniacal? No, I do not think so, for a number of reasons I consider compelling (Postscript 0.1: Group Alters).

> *Naturalistic pathways:* Ego's modes of judging Alters determined on the basis of systematic evidence. They are naturalistic only in the sense that they have been, are being, or will be employed by Egos; they are not natural in a genetic or biological sense, for they contain—perhaps always—cultural ingredients.
>
> *Professionals* (not hereafter capitalized): the social scientists, psychiatrists, and psychologists who in the role of Ego-expositors systematically collect the evidence.
>
> *Advisable pathways:* recommended modes of judging others derived from naturalistic pathways; *positive* ones should be traversed, *negative* ones avoided.

Two questions occur to me immediately. The first: just how are advisable pathways "derived from naturalistic pathways"? The derivation is based upon a value judgment, usually that of accuracy, and the reasoning is really not cumbersome. If we wish to read signs more accurately at a distance, we are advised to use eye glasses or binoculars. Similarly, you begin with the naturalistic fact, add the value judgments, and there you are. *The analogy is much too simple; moreover, what do you mean by accuracy when you refer to judging people?* I provide no easy reply right now—our discussions will touch upon this question again and again, I promise—but I would say that the reference is to Alter's internal state (his feelings, his ideas, his motives) or his overt behavior. Often, however, only my very best guess will enable me to leap from a naturalistic onto an advisable pathway, which you then are free to applaud or decry.

Your second question. *How does one obtain "systematic evidence" to discover naturalistic pathways?* All of us, whether professionals or laymen, are Egos trying to comprehend many Alters in our daily life, less frequently are we Ego-expositors. Why is the patient anxious? Why did the defendant allegedly commit a crime? Why can't the student study for his examinations? Is the man qualified for the job? Is the woman trustworthy? We usually have ready if not necessarily valid ways to reply to such questions: these are our naturalistic pathways. The professionals, however, try to approach the same problems with more or less systematic theories and with specified techniques for gathering information, in order to discover both kinds of pathways. The

Freudian view that slips of the tongue, dreams, or free associations may reveal, more often than not, core motives or frustration is an example of a theory that has diffused from psychoanalytic circles to the wider society of writers, artists and ordinary men and women. Formal or informal interviewing and testing—the pompous call them instruments—are the blatant devices used to elicit information; in addition, straightforward or concealed observation of behavior as well as oral or written reports or documents can also supply relevant data. Diagnosis is often only a first step: prognosis and therapy attempt, respectively, to predict future behavior and to intervene by promoting constructive changes in the individual. Of course this quick portrayal of the professional is idealized—most professionals are willing to admit, if only privately, that they cannot often function without a huge dose of commonsense.

Without disparaging their skill and ingenuity, I must immediately say that, more often than not, clinicians and experimenters in their role as Ego-expositors perforce achieve very circumscribed results. Their choice of Egos, of measurement modes, and of situations in which Alter is observed or tested must be limited if precision is to be attained; consequently, it is always uncertain whether a solidly based conclusion or generalization can transcend the investigation from which it is derived. A good study, however, makes some contribution to knowledge, actually or potentially, just as the examination of a single case history is said to aid "fundamental clinical psychological research" (Shapiro, 1961). *How, then, can you possibly report a generalization about a naturalistic pathway without misleading me or your readers?* Suppose, let me say, one study indicates that all its Egos with russet hair jumped more quickly to conclusions concerning Alters than did Egos with dark hair. The most conservative and accurate mode of reporting would be to say just that. But we are really interested in the generalizability of the conclusion beyond the present subjects (who may have been coeds in a small college in the Middle West of the United States), or the present procedure (judging photographs on color slides by means of ratings). Changing "jumped" in the conclusion to "jump," as is so often done by professionals in scholarly journals, is obviously reckless and unwarranted, for we have no way of knowing whether russet- and dark-haired damsels in Finland behave similarly when they see young lads upon the green during the approach of the summer solstice. As I report the result of investigations, usually in Postscripts, I shall resort to a compromise enabling me both to have and eat my cake without causing you or me to suffer. Russet and dark females or males, I shall say, *may* react in that manner, or *perhaps* they do. The *may* or *perhaps* will always be in italics to serve as a danger signal—*ugh, more italics*. The conventional reference in parentheses—author or authors and date of publication, sufficient to identify the complete reference in the list at the end of the book—will be preceded by two bits of non-bibliographic information when they do not appear in the text itself: the name of the country in which the study was conducted and the status of the subjects or informants. These two facts must serve as an additional warning against illicit generalization. So many investigators, alas, have been Americans and have dragooned easily obtainable college students as subjects that, instead of repeating "U.S.A., college students" again and again, I shall use the word *Usual* to indicate those two facts. Another vital datum affecting generalizability, the investigator's method, cannot be described concisely as I could do in connection with the problem of time (Doob, 1971, p. 23); and so let me say once and for all that almost every conclusion depends upon the method employed and probably would have been different if another method had been followed.

How have you selected the references that suggest naturalistic pathways? I have used two criteria. First, I cite those I believe the most illuminative and provocative. *Subjective?* Yes, but how else would you have me choose? Then, since we perhaps profit from past mistakes and sometimes improve our predecessors' findings, I give priority to recent books and articles. Like you I treasure the classics, but some progress in scholarly pursuits is, I guess, discernible. *Are you sure?* No, of course not. Some perspective is provided, I hope, by sporadic references to the pathways of non-Western or traditional peoples, sporadic because, regretably, little anthropological spice seems to be available.

A personality theory lurks behind the investigations of professionals as well as the judgment of laymen—the latter point is elaborated in Postscript 0.2 (Lay Theories of Personality). For this reason alone we must dig deep into Ego if we are to understand how and why he passes judgment and if we are to find advisable pathways to improve his judgment. *Good, I admire thoroughness.* Actually every writer on person perception offers a series of steps through which the process may be analyzed, stretching from the input of information to the output which is the culmination of the judgment (Sarbin et al., 1960, p. 45). My own proposal is embodied in the chart nearby. There I would

suggest concisely and simply—*Concisely and simply do you say?*—
I suggest what Ego does when he judges Alter or what an Ego-expositor
does when he would explain Ego's judgment concerning Alter. Look at
it. *Ah me, it seems so complicated, so needlessly complicated; is that
what we really do when we decide whether a person is a hero or a
rogue, must we glide through all those circles, don't we usually quickly
come to a decision?* Some decisions are speedily made, others are more
deliberate. Perhaps months pass before you come to think you understand a new acquaintance. After centuries critics and spectators continue to speculate about Hamlet's character. We are uncertain why
some persons commit suicide or genocide. And, like a computer, in a
moment's time we can integrate a vast and complicated process. The
chart, consequently, would embrace the intricate and the simple. It is
modestly Faustian in its effort to include everything, yes, at least the
outline of absolutely all that we would know about Ego and his reactions to Alter. *I am skeptical.* So am I, but let us continue this part
of the conversation in Postscript 0.3 (The Omniscience of the Chart).
I would, however, call attention to the arrows on the chart: some go
in only one direction, others in both directions. The latter are especially
important: they signify that one factor affects the other, that the two
have a relation that is indeed a spiral (Pathway 4.b). Examples of
spirals appear at every corner: Ego affects Alter, Alter affects Ego, and
the spiral goes on and on until something mysterious or mundane
emerges. Admittedly we all have trouble with spirals, but the only
way to avoid them would be to provide a one-sided treatment, and
that we must never, never do. *Of course not.*

Our struggle to find naturalistic and advisable pathways is organized around the chart. Chapter headings and subheadings follow its
roman or arabic numerals and letters: they are the principal naturalistic
and sometimes also the advisable pathways. The appearance of other
pathways is signalled by indented headings with two numbers (the
first denoting the chapter, the other the order within the chapter).
Cross references to all pathways are made by citing the symbols in
parentheses, but—lest the exposition become too choppy—only when
this seems necessary or particularly desirable. An appendix lists them
all in one place. I hope you find this system useful and not too cumbersome. *I wonder, I admire pedantic orderliness only distantly.*

Unquestionably the allocation of some pathways to one place in
the chart and in our discussion rather than to another is arbitrary. The
difficulty, however, resides not within the exposition but within us all:

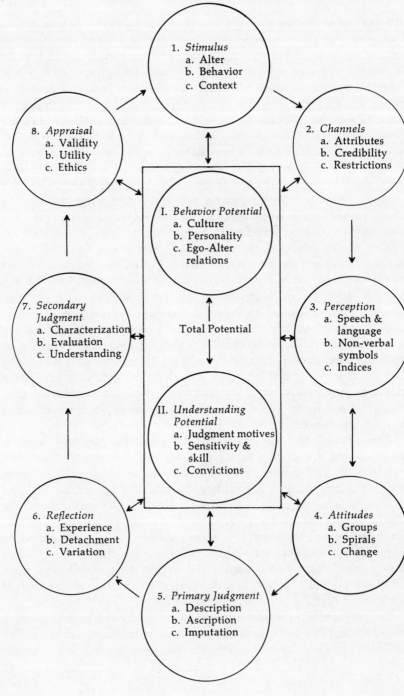

1. *Stimulus*
   a. Alter
   b. Behavior
   c. Context

8. *Appraisal*
   a. Validity
   b. Utility
   c. Ethics

2. *Channels*
   a. Attributes
   b. Credibility
   c. Restrictions

I. *Behavior Potential*
   a. Culture
   b. Personality
   c. Ego-Alter
      relations

Total Potential

7. *Secondary
   Judgment*
   a. Characterization
   b. Evaluation
   c. Understanding

3. *Perception*
   a. Speech &
      language
   b. Non-verbal
      symbols
   c. Indices

II. *Understanding
    Potential*
   a. Judgment motives
   b. Sensitivity &
      skill
   c. Convictions

6. *Reflection*
   a. Experience
   b. Detachment
   c. Variation

4. *Attitudes*
   a. Groups
   b. Spirals
   c. Change

5. *Primary Judgment*
   a. Description
   b. Ascription
   c. Imputation

we are human beings and hence we jump about so variously that our reactions cannot be eternally pigeonholed. What I have done is to try to be chronological. Ego judges Alter—let us observe the temporal sequence with the major pathways indicated in parentheses. First, we must try to understand Ego in general (I) and his way of judging other persons (II). After that, we are ready to look at Alter (1) and the channel (2) through which he is perceived (3) by Ego in whom certain attitudes are functioning (4). Ego arrives at some kind of judgment (5) which upon reflection (6) he may revise (7) and eventually appraise (8). The fact that at any given moment this wondrous sequence may be interrupted is symbolized by the arrows on the chart and by frequent cross references during our discussions in the text.

The very first pathway to be mentioned springs out of the chart. Obviously, as you have said, that chart is very complicated, too complicated in fact to be an accurate reflection of the naturalistic pathways an Ego-expositor follows when he analyzes an Alter or of the advisable pathways an Ego should seek when he would comprehend an Alter. But here at least we have in one place an inventory of the factors each should take into account as he goes about his task. The chart is an idealized version of reality; in the language of our day it is

0.1 *Ideal Model*

a model that can serve as an inspiring and hopefully not a paralyzing guide. Again and again we shall meet these unrealizable models enabling Ego-expositors and Egos alike to appreciate their own imperfections and then to struggle to approach a little more closely the utopia that is thereby glimpsed.

Postscripts

0.1 Group Alters

The question being posed is whether it makes sense to speak of a Group Alter. The term may refer to a nation, and why not? For an Ego who is its ruler, a member of the opposition, or a political scientist may set himself the legitimate task of determining whether a revolution is about to take place. That problem does involve a judgment more complex than one made by Ego—though perhaps not qualitatively different—when he tries to decode the expression on a single Alter's face. Now obviously I cannot pause long enough to provide a treatise on revolution even if I had the necessary knowledge, which of course I do not. In fact, you and I find it easier to focus upon more encompassable Group Alters such as small groups. Most of the time a lone Alter or Ego-expositor is our target. Still—and here is the point worth driving in with a sledgehammer—any kind of judgment is made by a human Ego who therefore utilizes whatever cues he can, and he is affected by whatever dispositions reside within him, whether he is confronted with a revolution or an incipient smile. *In this instance I agree with you: although I realize that calling a person honest or crafty is different from using the same adjectives to describe a group or nation, the fact of the matter is that I use identical or at least similar criteria in passing both judgments.* I must say, nevertheless, that the bases for the two judgments and the problem of their validity are not the same, however laudable it is to seek common pathways to the one and the many.

0.2 Lay Theories of Personality

Laymen assess normal and abnormal persons but usually less formally or self-consciously than most professionals (Holt, 1969, pp. 591–615). They have their own psychological assumptions which investigators have labelled somewhat contemptuously . . . . *Why contemptuously?* Their labels are "naive psychology," "commonsense psychology, "implicit personality," and a host of other fancy words (Cronbach, 1955, p. 186; Heider, 1958b, pp. 5–7). Perhaps, for example, they believe that groups are more likely to be stable and to behave consistently than specific persons and hence they *may* predict more confidently the behavior of groups than of persons (Lindskold et al., 1974) because—well, perhaps you can supply the reasons. *I cannot, I believe quite the opposite.* Obviously, too, laymen gather data concerning Alters and, although they do not consider their data-gathering devices "instruments," they believe in their infallibility with a passion frequently as strong as the clinician's faith in an intelligence test or in the symbolic meaning of an overt act. Similarly, lay prognosis or therapy is generally much less structured than that of professionals, and the diagnostic goal may be not to assist Alter but to smother or exploit him. *Are not these lay theories better than those of professionals?* Perhaps in some instances, but we must continue to hope that professional investigations can yield new insights. *A matter of faith.* Obviously.

One aim of our analysis, in fact, is to suggest that some aspects of professional psychology can or should be absorbed by laymen to improve their own psychology. This is not an overly ambitious objective, you must agree, when you consider Freud's effect upon ordinary persons in the West; persons who have never read a word of his use the expression "Freudian slip." *Are you not forgetting that the theories of some professionals serve them poorly in their ordinary existence, for with all their sophistication they may make a mess of their own lives or maltreat those close to them?* What you say is relevant and distressing.

0.3 The Omniscience of the Chart

You may reject the chart if you wish—I am your guide, and I am a philosophical anarchist who tries not to proselyte—but, before you do, permit me to point to its advantages. It purports to indicate the factors, the variables, that may affect the kind of judgment Ego passes concerning Alter. *But surely the chart does not include every possible factor; what about gestures and facial expressions?* They are there; within the circle of Perception they are called "Non-Verbal Symbols." *What about the schemas others have offered?* All right, consider the finding that "recognition of emotion seems to be an example of complex information processing" which, according to the writer of this assertion, can be described only by means of a "flow diagram" containing thirteen "subprocesses" (Frijda, 1969, pp. 213–17). After serious and prolonged concentration I have convinced myself that the subprocesses in his diagram have different names and are combined differently than in my chart and hence that both of us are plowing the same field; whether you prefer his or mine is a decision for you to make. *What about Ego's mood that induces him to take a rosy or a jaundiced view of Alter?* A more abstract concept, "Personality," is to be found within what I call the Behavior Potential. *Are you not thus pushing too much into the concept of personality?* That charge I consider unfair, for the essence of systematic thought is abstraction: the ability to group together phenomena which, though diverse, share some common attribute. In this instance mood belongs to personality because, like any trait, ability, or bit of temperament, its locus is not within Alter or the milieu but within Ego. *Carry on.* You might well wonder, if you were a professional, about a so-called psychophysical method by which Ego judges Alter on a scale of his own devising. He first constructs the scale by imagining a "best liked" person at one end of a line, a "least liked" one at the other, someone else halfway in between, etc. (Rudin, 1959). On the chart such a judgment belongs to the category of secondary judgment derived from a very specialized form of skill within Ego's understanding potential.

The chart does not demand that all variables always be considered in order to uncover a pathway. If you read *Hamlet*, you are stimulated by what the chief character says and what he does, you have no clue to the third factor on the chart labelled "Stimulus." But in a theatre you may be affected by symbols provided by the actor playing the role, and surely you cannot deny that in everyday life somehow you are influenced by gestures and posture. I maintain, in brief, a fairly simple thesis: in some situations each of the factors portrayed on the chart may, but need not, be consulted; yet those that are neglected are the very ones to be declared "equal" before a generalization can be squeezed out of a given observation or piece of research. *What can you say about an Alter on the basis of the hyperboles he promiscuously and boringly employs on too many occasions?* In this case one factor, that of language, is being pounced upon, and it can be pounced upon only by assuming that the other factors affecting Ego's judgment are not interfering with language "as such"; for example, we must believe that the Alter being judged is not personally detested by Ego. In real life or in research, consequently, the relation of two or more of the factors on the chart may become the central problem, and thus we know under what conditions the emerging induction can be utilized in the future. To say that a principle has limited utility or applicability is a bit of realism, not an insult.

All right, then, I admire not the chart's content but its aesthetic symmetry; how did it come into existence? I went into the wilderness and found it there; then an internal spirit instructed me to pass it on to eager you. The wilderness has been the research with which I have become acquainted during too many years, the opinions I have exchanged with persons like you and others I truly respect and trust, the experience I have had when I have been the Ego passing judgment or the puzzled Ego-expositor. Most important of all, the chart is really another version of ones I have used to analyze communication (Doob, 1961, p. 11), nationalism (Doob, 1964, p. 23), and time (Doob, 1971, p. 31); thus I would unify within myself and, hopefully, within you and others seemingly diverse phenomena. *But will it really help me?* Again I say that you must be the judge. The analysis will not be a pleasant hike through a virgin forest but a long, long trek through the chart which often crosses barren, dull flatlands. We must be patient and cheer each other along—and I immediately offer some cheer by promising to avoid tedious metaphors like the one in the last sentence. *Bravo.*

The first and most enduring pathway to Alter
1.1 Self-knowledge is Ego himself, and instantly a classical, advisable
pathway is forthcoming: know thyself before
you would know others. *But surely Ego can look at Alter and judge
him without thinking about himself.* He may not deliberately think
about himself, but that self is somehow involved. Furthermore, Ego
often judges Alter deliberately by referring to himself: Alter likes me,
I shall surely like him. *Or be bored by him?* Accurate self-knowledge
is needed if the comparison is to be. . . . *Is to be what?* Patience, this
pathway must puzzle us again and again later on (Pathways 6.b, 7.c).

Need I remind you that the world out there, whether you are considering Alter or his footsteps, the shadows on the wall of the cave or
the echoes inside of it, exists for you only when you perceive it? Perception is the outcome of a struggle or a collision between the world
and you, the two components are always present in varying degrees.
What you hear depends not only upon the wind and its velocity but
also upon the depth of your reverie. If you had been fully occupied,
you would not have noticed the noise. *Obviously.* Similarly a saint is
judged with malice by a rogue and with reverence by a true believer.
Enough, enough, let us consider Ego. Yes, his behavior potential.

I.a Culture

If the professionals or we were permitted to have only one bit of
information about Ego—or about Alter for that matter—the choice
would be knowledge about the culture in which he is embedded. We
all live and share with other men of our society common modes of
behaving, feeling, and thinking which are the culmination of a stagger-

13

ingly complicated series of events in the past involving a people's adaptation to their physical environment, to themselves, and to imposed or self-imposed changes. *Of course.* Yes, that is the difficulty: many of us use the word "culture" so frequently and glibly that we have come to overlook the significance and pervasiveness of the social forces the concept summarizes. Since you are not an anthropologist whose craft requires you to find the best description of the modal behavior, beliefs, or values of a society, you often are unaware of cultural influences. What is required to achieve such awareness is "culture shock," the sudden experiencing of a culture quite different from your own.

I have had that experience many times. Yes, I know, yet we must review the more pressing aspects of culture that lead to Ego and to the pathways he uses in judging Alter. Every society. . . . *I note the breathlessness of your transcultural phrase.* Every society requires considerable cooperative behavior which begins in the family and eventually includes an occupational group. People must coordinate many of their efforts to attain efficiency and tranquility. Whether they grunt in unison as they haul in a dugout canoe or whether they hurl stereotyped phrases about in parliamentary debates, they must comprehend the intentions and responses of the Alters with whom they interact. For this reason they are taught and they must learn how to interpret one another. A smile can have many meanings aside from joy—among the Zande, an inferior person smiles when he is snubbed by his superiors in the presence of others (Larken, 1926–27, pp. 86–87)—and joy can be expressed in many ways other than by smiles. *You are pointing out the pathway of relativity?* Yes, I am, and in theory. . . . *What do you mean by theory?* In theory we must ever appreciate the fact that Ego carries within himself his society's values and beliefs. As a consequence
he is likely to judge Alters in terms of those
I.2 *Ethnocentrism*   values and beliefs, and hence to tread the naturalistic pathway of ethnocentrism, the advisable
pathway of which is negative: avoid ethnocentrism, beware of the tendency to impose your own standards upon others. *Advice that is easier to give than to follow?* Yes, and that is true of all advisable pathways: we poor mortals are. . . . *I know.* The task, moreover, is particularly difficult in the case of ethnocentrism (Postscript I.1: The Perils of Ethnocentrism).

The more we know about his culture and his subcultures, the more we are likely to know about Ego and the naturalistic pathway he may be doomed to follow. Also, the closer we come to the specific situations in which we find him, the more we know about him. So let us examine him per se, which is a graceful way to introduce a discussion of personality. *Graceful? I call it forced.*

I.b Personality

Although conceptions of personality are as numerous as stars on a clear summer's night, virtually all of them call attention to the individual's more or less unique set of traits and their equally distinctive relationship, organization, or integration. The mathematical possibilities resulting from the interaction of countless different genetic structures and countless different nuances in milieux are de facto without limit, for the millions and millions of combinations embodied in the human race have not yet, or so we believe, produced two completely indistinguishable persons. Even identical twins, reared together in the same family, come to be somewhat dissimilar, presumably because parental favoritism or what is recklessly called chance has subjected them to minutely different environmental pressures. Individuality is writ large. . . . *So large that ought you really not abandon the quest for pathways? For if we begin with a unique Ego and end with a unique Alter, how can we expect any kind of satisfactory meeting between the two?* This pertinent question pushes me toward a solipsistic problem I would not, cannot, and eventually will not gainsay. *Why do you cause yourself grief by facing the problem of personality, a subject worthy of treatment in its own right?* A fair question this time; but except for a pragmatic reply in Postscript I.2 (Reasons for Postulating Personality: Illustrations), I shall defer the exposition until later. *Don't put off onto another pathway what. . . .* I must, I am trying to be systematic.

Personality and personality traits are the outcome of another long series of events in the past and hence can be fully comprehended only by noting their genesis and development (Postscript I.3: Roots and Fruits). Ego's judgment concerning himself, his self-esteem, *may* be shakily related to the way in which he has been treated by his parents and the resulting identification or lack of it (Usual; Hollender, 1973). The brave, true, but banal thesis concerning the relevance of life history, however, is unfortunately seldom honored, in large part for practical reasons. Most professionals or Egos ordinarily cannot afford the time and energy or do not have the patience to investigate the past if they are to discover, respectively, how Ego judges Alter or how

Alter is to be judged. We all are limited by a lack of data, a difficulty that confronts us again and again and that con-

I.3   Limitation   stitutes a potential danger if or when judgment is passed on the basis of inadequate information. The advisable pathway, partially positive, partially negative, takes the form of another warning to be cautious: nobody, no matter how smugly confident, is ever omniscient or omnipresent.

Ego's personality, like his culture, affects his judgment of Alter. *Proof?* This time you cannot be serious when you challenge me. An abnormally aggressive Ego surely observes Alter through lenses that make him also appear aggressive if he projects, or non-aggressive if he compensates. *But when will he project, when will he compensate?* I assure you that these pages will overflow with illustrations of the naturalistic pathway of egocentrism. The advisable

I.4   Egocentrism   pathway, however, is clear-cut and negative: avoid egocentrism if you can. *I cannot, I will not.* Do note that ethnocentrism is a special case of egocentrism: Ego's egocentrism is ethnocentric when the differences between him and Alter are cultural rather than personal. The line between the two is frequently indistinct or unimportant. Does it really matter whether the false judgment of a traditional African stems from the fact that the Alter being judged comes from a different tribe or, though of the same tribe, has been educated by missionaries?

It is insufficient merely to call Ego egocentric. His personality must be described in order to specify the precise ways in which he projects or compensates. For the first but not the last time, therefore, we are face-to-face with the ahistorical problem of designating concepts. To describe is to state or half-state a proposition containing a concept allegedly applicable to a person, object, or event. For example: the man is honest, the leaf is green, the battle is fierce. As you know better than I, we could return to the ancients who would tell us that such descriptions are useful: the concepts call attention to particular attributes of the man, the leaf, and the battle, yet they are also arbitrary and incomplete because each subject has other attributes not specified in the propositions. *And must you not also say whether each proposition is true or false?* Or partially true or partially false. In any case conceptualization has far reaching implications; it is both necessary and dangerous; and therefore it offers a pathway, always naturalistic, potentially advisable (Pathways 5.a & 7.a). For better or worse, Ego-expositors must choose concepts to understand Ego per se and his judgment of Alter, and that is not an easy task (Postscript I.4: Choosing and Losing Concepts).

Fine, but is there no way out of this morass? The problem has been attacked in three ways. First, investigators have attempted to determine the concepts actually employed by persons in their own society; this approach is useful in locating the specific concepts Ego applies to Alter but is of dubious value in analyzing Ego himself—and so it will be appraised on Pathway 5. Secondly, logical schemas have been suggested; for example, concepts for both Ego and Alter can be thrown into three types, those referring to persons in general, to persons in a given category (such as occupation), and to one specific person (Warr & Haycock, 1970). An arbitrary distinction of this sort may be useful, but it does not necessarily help us find the concepts we need. While it is true that tightrope walkers must be judged in terms of the agility and balance associated with their occupation and while we may generously neglect the fact that the rest of us are also agile to some degree and have a sense of balance, we end up without an infallible guide enabling us to select the attributes in the first place. Actually most of the schemas are not very logical, for in connection with a specific type of investigation, such as the description of emotions, each investigator tends to prefer anarchy and to devise his own pet concepts that subjects are instructed to use in recording their judgments (Frijda, 1969, pp. 187–88). And thirdly there is a sophisticated technique called factor analysis which, though likely to be comprehensible only to those skilled in the use of statistical methods, can function advisably as a very specialized ideal model (Pathway 0.1) for conceptualizing knowledge concerning personality (Postscript I.5).

And now I challenge you: after being so critical, can you as an Ego-expositor be positive; can you suggest concepts that might serve as a basis for comprehending Ego and then for evaluating his judgment concerning Alter? The challenge, though just, is difficult to meet. You may have guessed that I am not all-wise. . . . *Ah, yes.* And I freely admit being tempted to welcome every new concept I come upon, no matter where or even from whom, provided it is not merely ostentatious jargon and provided it seems to promote an innovative observation or investigation. I squeeze out a very, very eclectic list: (1) intelligence; (2) sociability; (3) style (which is meant to include readiness, abstraction proneness, and organizing ability); (4) sense of responsibility; (5) temporal orientation. If you wish definitions and details, turn to Postscript I.6 (Parameters of Personality).

I have now read the Postscript, and I do not find your list of concepts very impressive, I must say; I would rather follow the concepts of the ancient philosopher, Galen. Let the argument continue sub rosa (Postscript I.7: The Endless List of Categories). *How do you expect me to pay attention to the text when you keep telling me to turn to postscripts?* Fair enough, I'll stop for a while. In the meantime, I would neither weep nor apologize, for we now have at least a foundation for describing Ego; the rest of the structure takes shape as each new situation demands. *Flabby?* No, I enthusiastically endorse this kind of eclecticism, which can be called situational empiricism, for it would

I.5 Situational Empiricism

seem to be a valuable advisable pathway to follow: analyze each situation as it arises, try as hard as you can to use concepts proven to be useful in similar or somewhat similar situations in the past, but always anticipate some distinctive feature.

Since you are using common sense. . . . I deny this. *You might as well consider the most obvious aspect of Ego that you have so far neglected: he is more than a collection of traits and impulses.* Traits and impulses are interrelated so that Ego is indeed more or less consistent whether we consider his internal beliefs, attitudes, and goals, or his external behavior. Even an infant during the first two years of life *may* reveal a distinctive and consistent pattern of behavior to observers who view him carefully and continually (U.S.; Thomas et al., 1963, pp. 57–61). In the clouds of theory, consistency may be difficult to define or discern, but on the practical ground it can be conceptualized in terms of centrality. Some traits, values, goals, etc., exert a greater influence than others; those that are central rather than segmental reflect the organization of personality and produce behavior that is similar or congruent in a variety of situations at a given moment or in various situations over time (Postscript I.8: The Case for Centrality).

I.6 Centrality

Centrality, I maintain, is a valuable, positive, advisable pathway: if we know an individual's central tendencies, what seem to be discrete bits of behavior may turn out to be consistent, and hence intelligible and predictable.

I.c   Ego-Alter Relations

Another approach to personality can be introduced here more appropriately than elsewhere: Ego is what others think him to be, attractive or unattractive, smart or stupid, honorable or dishonorable. Sociologists espousing this viewpoint are ever inclined to emphasize forces in the milieu affecting behavior. And so, as perhaps the most influential of them has asserted, "the self... is essentially a social structure, and it arises in social experience"; self-consciousness is "an awakening in ourselves of the group of attitudes which we are arousing in others"; the "me" is "the organized set of attitudes of others which one himself assumes"; and hence of critical significance is "the generalized other" defined as "the organized community or social group which gives to the individual his unity of self" (G. H. Mead, 1934, pp. 140, 154, 163, 175). *Rubbish, such a framework misses most of Ego's subtleties, provides little insight into him.* I agree. Like you and me, Ego may have a brave or cowardly facade to conceal many impulses and therefore from a deity's point of view his peers really do not know him. Being aware of his reputation, however, may offer an advisable pathway to him since, after all, he must frequently have been brave or cowardly to have given others that impression. All information about an individual is potentially useful, none should be sacrificed even when it is one-sided or startlingly sociological. *Clear?* *No.* Suppose Alter is generally considered cheerful by his peers, although he also feels frequently depressed. Ego could probably predict much of his behavior from a knowledge of that reputation. But, I immediately add, he would be better able to anticipate Alter's deviation from the modal behavior if he also had insight into Alter's depressions, indeed he could more adequately understand the reason for the apparent cheerfulness if he could trace the connection between Alter's internal feelings and external actions.

On a less global but more useful level, the relation between Ego and Alter (or several Alters) has a fleeting or enduring effect upon Ego in most situations. For central to all interactions is a judgment. Ego, while driving along a road, sees a man beside a car, metal container in one hand, trying to thumb a ride with the other. Will the driver stop because he thinks the man is out of gasoline and wants to be driven to the nearest station; or will he ignore him because the stranger may be a rascal wanting to rob him if he stops? Ego's decision may depend not only upon what he perceives but also upon his judgment of Alter based upon clothes, hair, skin color, and sex. His evaluation of these attributes in Alter in turn may be affected by whether or not he himself has similar or dissimilar attributes; an American male with short hair *may* be more inclined to help an Alter with short rather than long hair

(U.S., adults; Graf & Riddell, 1972). Both Ego and Alter contribute to Ego's decision, and both are affected by it: Ego drives on or stops, Alter gets a ride (perhaps also robs Ego) or does not.

More generally, although the reciprocity between Ego and Alter can be variously described (Sarbin et al., 1960, pp. 216–23), especially useful are distinctions based upon the direction and quantity of influence which, in political terms, means power. One may dominate the other as a result of the situation (Alter is the host and Ego the guest) or of personality characteristics (either Ego or Alter suffers from logorrhea and dictates the conversation). Ego may have no effect upon Alter when Alter is unaware that he is being observed (e.g., by a professional through a one-way vision window or by another patron in the same restaurant), or when Alter is dead and being judged on the basis of reports or documents. The power may be more or less equally divided (a lively give-and-take between two persons of similar status). The effect may be virtually zero when there is a minimum of interaction (two strangers seated side-by-side in a public hall).

Knowledge of the specific relation between Ego and Alter should be able to provide lay and professional Ego-expositors with a naturalistic pathway suggesting the kinds of judgment Ego is likely to pass and to offer Ego an advisable pathway along which he can correct whatever distortion results from the relation. But first of course that relation must be known and, secondly, its judgmental consequences must be appraised. There can be no universal guides, inasmuch as cultural, subcultural, and individual factors are involved. You have been silent; why? *I have been thinking: what good does it do to realize that the Ego-Alter relation affects Ego's judgment unless its precise effects are known?* The answer is annoyingly simple: we anticipate effects, although the details are not immediately forthcoming. Digging is necessary (Pathway I.5), the anticipation at least alerts us to the problem (Postscript I.9: The Limitless Relations of Ego and Alter).

Let us spare ourselves no complication: Ego's effect upon Alter may be quite unconscious or unintended. The relatives and friends of schizophrenics *may* employ various devices "to drive the other person crazy," while being quite unaware of these efforts, in fact ready to deny them if challenged (presumably U.S., patients; Searles, 1959). The professional clinician unwittingly affects the patient as a result of his appearance, mannerisms, or present mood. If he wishes to know whether Alter is suggestible or not and if, furthermore, suggestibility depends in part, as I think it does, upon the prestige of the person giving the suggestion, an Ego with great prestige is likely to think of Alter as being most suggestible; and the judgment may be reversed when Alter is the one with prestige. Suggestibility, in brief, is not ascertained in the abstract; it is affected by the Ego-Alter relation. The unastonishing conclusion applies not only to a live Ego facing an Alter but also, if to a lesser extent, to a surrogate of Ego, which can take the form of another person, a paper-and-pencil or laboratory exercise, or a tape-recorder when Ego may be present only in Alter's imagination.

On this pathway references have been made again and again—whether the discussion has concerned culture, personality, or the relation between Ego and Alter—to variability from

I.7 Normality   some norm or modal tendency. Herein, I would now suggest, we find both a naturalistic and an advisable pathway involving the criterion of normality which in turn assumes some degree of quantification. Normality is a statistical abstraction inevitably implying deviations. There is continuity in behavior: we behave not in an all-or-none manner but in varying degrees. *I do not agree; surely an individual is either honest or dishonest, there are no in-betweens; a person is a good or a bad poet; everybody wears clothes, nobody goes out naked when the temperature is below freezing.* Let me pedantically consider each of the instances. In terms of some specific criterion, such as stealing, Alter may be either honest or dishonest, I agree, but the degree and frequency of his thefts—if he is dishonest—can certainly vary. Still, I admit, the leap from no thefts whatsoever to one or more does represent a considerable shift. Characterizing a poet as good or bad must mean that you have no room in your standards for someone who is mediocre or for a good poet who sometimes writes bad poetry or for a bad one who has written one good poem. Here the difficulty lies in the standards: on the continuum of poetry, where do you place a given person? *I admit there are very, very few good poets; and if a poet is not good, he must be bad. On second thought I agree; I know many, too many, mediocre poets.* As for clothes in subfreezing weather, you are merely saying that no one in our society—unless insane or addicted to peculiar fads—goes about naked, though you could, if you had the patience, grade each person on the quantity and quality of his clothes. This fascinating give-and-take leaves our respective positions unchanged except that I now freely concede that a slight quantitative shift along a continuum can make a whale of a qualitative difference. *I am willing to abide by the principle that, within admittedly qualitative limits, there can be quantitative differences.* I care very little whether the distribution of behavior or judgments is, as postulated, "normal"—you emerge with what is called a bell-shaped or gaussian curve—provided the fact of variability is admitted. Wherever we turn, we are confronted with individual differences which, though a delight to you, to all humanists, and to scrooges like me, make the task of comprehending a particular person especially difficult. Both the professional and the Ego, therefore, must know the norm against which they pass judgment and the deviations embodied in the person they would judge.

Postscripts

I.1   The Perils of Ethnocentrism

Ego may not be surprised when children from different countries in the West, such as Finland and the United States (Britton et al., 1969), have both similar and dissimilar values or when adolescents in scattered societies, such as Peru and Japan (Loh & Triandis, 1968), express identical and divergent values. He is sorely tempted, nevertheless, to employ ethnocentric standards whenever he is confronted with another person who, after all, is a human being like himself. Or he may be aware of the dangers of ethnocentrism but lack adequate information. Would you say, for example, that Ego, an American Ego, has the belief or delusion that he himself is more likely to take risks than one of his peers is? We have scraps of information on this point (Usual; Willems, 1969), but variability from person to person is too great for any generalization based on a necessarily limited sample to be very useful. The mere fact that two persons come from different cultures does not enable us to know in advance that they will differ in certain specified respects. Would you or would you not expect secondary-school children in the Netherlands to be similar to American high-school and college students with respect to their ways of judging one another or noting differences between their parents and teachers as they grow older (Fiedler & Hoffman, 1962)? So salient and compelling are ethnocentric categories that they *may* be applied almost as rigidly to peers in the same society as to strangers from elsewhere (Usual; Passini & Norman, 1966). Another complication: the reality of culture is normally experienced within the significant groups of a society, such as those based on sex, age, kinship, talent, occupation, etc. It is not sufficient, therefore, for Ego to know the standards of his culture as a whole, he must also try to grasp those within the subcultures to which he belongs. It has been persuasively alleged, for example, that all of us in the West tend to participate in lonely crowds and are likely to be concerned not with traditional or even with our own values but with the impression we make upon others (Riesman, 1950, pp. 19–25). A valuable pathway? *Nonsense, my values are more important than the impressions I create.* Are you sure?

Perhaps Ego is less prone to use the naturalistic pathway of ethnocentrism as the distance between Alter and himself increases. For he can quickly apprehend that the distinctly different person differs from himself, whereas he is tempted to believe that someone similar to himself in one or more respects is similar in many other respects. If Alter dresses like you and speaks your language, he must be similar to you and your friends. . . . *But I may be wrong.* We cannot detach ourselves completely from the chains that bind us.

I.2 Reasons for Postulating Personality: Illustrations

I instantly acknowledge the existence of professionals, both young and not-so-young Turks, who argue that ascribing traits does not really help us understand or predict Ego's behavior. Better, they say, to talk of the role requirements of each situation. *I do not fully understand.* It seems to me self-evident that some aspect of Ego, however small and however named, whether personality or personality trait, almost always intrudes when Ego judges or investigates Alter. Individual differences and variability cannot be overlooked, and they must be traced to the person exhibiting them. In a very simple laboratory situation, for example, the evaluation of a pratfall *may* depend not only upon the nature of the blunder that Ego perceives more or less directly, but also upon his status and the competence he attributes to the blunderer (Usual; Mettee & Wilkins, 1972); that attribution clearly involves Ego's personality. The degree to which Ego's judgment concerning Alter's attractiveness is affected by prior knowledge concerning Alter or by Alter's apparent consistency or inconsistency *may* depend upon Ego's sex and a general tendency to view events and persons in simple or complex ways (Usual; Frauenfelder, 1974)—again Ego's opinion reflects the kind of person he is. Even a change in mood produced simply by recalling an experience from the past *may* interfere with Ego's ability to utilize previously perceived information concerning facial expressions in photographs (U.S., uncertain; Kissen, 1968). Latent hostility *may* exert a more powerful influence on Ego's judgment than a recent frustration, but its effect *may* also depend upon Ego's sex as well as his momentary judgment concerning the similarity between Alter and himself (Usual; Kaufman, 1966). In all these diverse instances you cannot understand Ego's reactions only from knowing the situation, you must also know something about Ego and his personality. *Yes, I agree.* Good for you.

I.3   Roots and Fruits

The relation betwen early childhood experiences and adult personality traits is exceedingly complicated not only because roots give rise to diverse fruits but also because during socialization and thereafter we continue to be affected by ongoing experiences. Which of these experiences turn out to be critical, those with parents of the same or opposite sex, those before or after weaning, those involving affection or toilet training? Without too much skill or perseverance it is possible to ferret out one or more studies that focuses upon, and emphasizes the significance of any imaginable socializing factor. The associations between the past and the present established by formal or informal research, moreover, are usually either anecdotal or correlational. If anecdotal, they apply only to a single case. If correlational, they stem from many persons or many cultures and, even when reaching or exceeding the magnitude required to be statistically significant, they are far from perfect. In compiling a life history moreover, there is no standard formula to follow, not even a semi-universally acceptable schedule to complete, such as the kind provided by an agency to its social workers for interviewing new clients. Professionals, biographers, autobiographers, novelists, dramatists, poets, all have their own way of assembling and presenting the details of an individual's past. *I know, I have tried to push together the pieces of my own life, so far.* Although you have given a sensitive description of how you experienced the cultures in which you were reared, you know better than I that you have pounced upon the sections of the past you thought might be either revealing or interesting. You omitted incidents and views you considered indiscreet or legally objectionable. Also you have, I daresay, unwittingly repressed information that is better forgotten. When in one striking instance we observe how much of a life story may *not* be uncovered even after three days of innumerable measurements and after patient and skillful interviewing (U.S., one graduate student; Barron, 1955), it is difficult not to feel discouraged: all we can do is acknowledge the inevitability of this negative pathway, a limitation both naturalistic and advisable (Pathway I.3). You, I, even the professionals, however, can console ourselves with a thought expressed throughout the ages, whether we turn to Aristotle's *Metaphysics* or the writings of a modern critic: "any beginning" must always be "arbitrary," inasmuch as "chains of causality reach back in time forever" (Kenner, 1962, p. 65). Consolation, yes, but this leaves unanswered the choice of the beginning point.

Utilizing the roots of Ego's life history has become fashionable only recently in Western society, particularly as a result of psychoanalysis. Elsewhere quite different explanations may be invoked, especially with reference to mental illness. An Apache Indian was thought to have gone insane because he did not follow the restrictions placed upon him —a taboo on hitting a horse with a stick and on eating certain foods— after being treated for rheumatism (Opler, 1943, p. 17). A Navajo woman was said to have been cured of amnesia following an appendectomy by the following method: first she was put into a trance and then informed that "a portion of her mind was still 'empty' "; that portion was "filled up" with a long prayer she memorized during a special ceremony (F. J. Newcomb, 1940, p. 17). In neither instance is there a reference to an unhappy childhood or a traumatic adolescence. *More power to the Indians.*

I.4   Choosing and Losing Concepts

The choice of concepts is difficult. *You mean impossible?* First, we are confronted with an embarrassingly rich vocabulary from which to choose: in English, a dictionary count once revealed 17,953 words then available with which to describe human beings (Allport & Odbert, 1936). Then the professionals are of little help: they have not agreed upon the crucial variables to be examined and hence their vocabularies have not been standardized. They are chemists without a periodic table of elements; they allow their own interests of the moment to determine whether they use very general or specific concepts (Allport, 1958); they invent new trait terms, utilize them for a few years, and ignore them like last decade's dress or hair-do. A generation or so ago "extroversion" and "introversion" were the rage; recently "rigidity" and "locus of control" have become fashionable (Rokeach, 1960; Rotter, 1966). *Why not, as I shall say in the text, use the four temperaments (sanguine, phlegmatic, choleric, and melancholic) which Galen in the second century derived from Hippocrates' four elements of the human body (air, water, fire, and earth) and their corresponding substances (blood, phlegm, yellow bile, black bile)?* My reply: new concepts call attention to different aspects of human behavior which the ancients may have overlooked or under- or overemphasized. Freud's concept of the unconscious can be found in Plato, I agree, but it was Freud and not Plato who showed in detail the significance of a wide variety of unconscious processes. I could go on and on and say that propositions containing changing concepts, if they are truly scientific or even if merely pseudo-scientific, are at least testable, whereas those of philosophers may be brilliant and stimulating but often lead us nowhere. "It is impossible for us, in effect, to conceive of ourselves as not existing, and no effort is capable of enabling consciousness to realize absolute unconsciousness, its own annihilation" (Unamuno, 1954, p. 38); true enough, perhaps, but then what? *Stop, you are displacing your own feeling of futility upon philosophy; surely there are other less compelling reasons for the changing fashions in concepts besides an advance in knowledge.*

Right. The professionals and laymen, too, resort to many different techniques to judge Alter—a generation ago no less than 52 were noted, categorized, and neatly diagrammed (Allport, 1937, p. 370)—and each almost inevitably seems to require its own peculiar vocabulary. The reverse may also be true: new concepts demand new methods. In contrast with small, closed, traditional societies in which undoubtedly concepts for judging Alters did not change appreciably from generation to generation, our own society may retain a few descriptive terms like "bravery" for men and "beauty" for women from ancient times, while demanding new words to apply to changing values and goals. "Rigidity," as I have said, is now in vogue probably for reasons related to a penchant for progressive education, a rebellion against the discipline required by powerful regimes, a dislike of the dogmatism and authoritarianism fostered by fascism, a tendency to experiment in all fields, and perhaps even a renewed emphasis on personal and social freedom: make note of the common attribute, give it a name, measure it, banish it if you can. The truly great—again Freud, also Pavlov and Darwin—label their discoveries and theories, and the names diffuse to the rest of us. Think of how concepts such as sadism, conditioning, and survival have sharpened our perceptions. Lesser men seek a fleeting immortality by inventing neologisms or fancy words like. . . . *No, better not be nasty.* They then try to foist their words upon us by using them again and again and by training students to do so. *And you call that not being nasty?* In a sense we are again rendering homage to the non-rigidity of professionals and laymen when we note that our concepts are not invariant and are altered to respond to all kinds of change.

I.5   Factor Analysis

Let me briefly describe the technique of factor analysis—and pain-lessly, I hope. A sample of individuals is given a questionnaire con-taining a variety of items more or less related to what the investigator considers personality or personality traits. With the aid of a computer the interrelations ("correlations," in a technical sense) of the replies are calculated. Usually but not always some cluster significantly to-gether (are highly correlated) and others are not. Inspecting the clusters that do appear then suggests to the investigator basic processes or traits they seem to reflect; he assigns them a number, letter, or an actual name, such as adaptability, neuroticism, or intelligence. So-called multidimensional analysis varies the technique: instead of items, a sample of individuals is asked to decide to what degree each pair of persons within that sample, including the respondent himself, is "very different" or "very similar"; and these comparisons are correlated with known attributes of the individual, such as perceived friendship, age, and intelligence (Usual; Jackson et al., 1957). In either case, the labels assigned to the clusters are arbitrary and hence are "descriptive cate-gories rather than underlying entities" (Mischel, 1968, p. 52), but the clusters giving rise to them spring out of the human data and are thus not completely dependent upon the investigator. It is encouraging to know that factor analyses of groups as diverse as female prisoners in Australia and male prisoners in America, unmarried mothers, and patients diagnosed as anxious, obsessional, psychosomatic, psycho-pathic, and hysteric have elicited two pairs of factors, the continua of stability-instability (or normality-neuroticism) and of extroversion-introversion (Eysenck & Rachman, 1965, p. 21). I must also note, with utter kindness I hope, that I see no signs of professionals flocking to these or other studies to find there a Rosetta stone for deciphering personality. *Why?* Aside from the labels themselves, other aspects of the procedure are also arbitrary: the choice of the sample responding to the questionnaire or making the comparisons; the items on the questionnaire; and the way in which the correlations have been manipulated (viz., "rotated").

I.6   Parameters of Personality

1. *Intelligence:* the ability to learn, to profit from past experience, and to find solutions to pressing or trivial problems. This is one of the very few concepts that have survived in some form for centuries within

our own tradition and that are useful outside the West. Closely related
is memory which markedly affects Ego's ability to comprehend Alter.
For the pathways to Alter can be more easily traversed when techniques already employed are recalled; when previous judgments of the
same Alter or similar Alters are not forgotten; when his face or other
physical features and when his name and other significant and non-
significant information about him are readily remembered. This kind
of memory, a component of the behavior potential, is linked to other
aspects of the personality and also glides into the understanding
potential: the abilities associated with personality facilitate or inhibit
the skill associated with comprehension. Intelligence, moreover, even
when measured by conventional tests, may affect the nature of Ego's
judgments; for example, the higher the intelligence, the greater the
tendency *perhaps* to hold other Alters, whether public figures or close
associates, in relatively low esteem (Usual & high school; Quereshi
et al., 1974).

2. *Sociability:* the ease of establishing contacts with other persons
and the satisfactions derived therefrom. The direction of sociability is
often indicated by the terms *extroversion* and *introversion,* concepts
that originated with Jung and that have become so useful that they
have survived for many decades.

3. *Style:* the different ways in which the individual perceives and
reacts to the external world, the most promising of which may be:

a. *Readiness:* the tendency to welcome or resist new information.
Everyone on occasion protects himself selectively from perceiving the
unpleasant, which obviously, however, must also be noted if danger
or disaster is to be avoided. The defense is stronger in some persons
than in others. You are open-minded about topics of a scientific nature,
but less receptive to new humanistic values; does your receptivity to
persons you call scientists and humanists similarly vary?

b. *Abstraction proneness:* the tendency to perceive similarities or
differences in events or situations. Some individuals more than others
seek to discover common elements amid diversity. They immediately
note or can be made to note identical attributes in a motor car and a
glass of beer: both objects can be moved, both bring pleasure, both
cost money, etc. They try to find the common interests of Alters coming from different milieux. In contrast are persons who emphasize
peculiarities and idiosyncrasies. They point out that no two motor cars
are exactly alike even if they have come off the same assembly line on

the same day. Two members of the same monastic order, they quickly observe, not only look different but also hold somewhat different beliefs with respect to unimportant matters. *Such proneness is also a facet of intelligence?* Yes.

c. *Organizing ability:* the tendency to store and organize varying amounts and kinds of information. Some Egos, for example, judge others by means of a limited number of black-white categories: Alter is either good or bad, useful or useless, attractive or unattractive—and nothing more needs to be known about him. Others prefer a multitude of categories so loosely organized that they are only utilized piecemeal, such as a so-called double standard regarding the two sexes or members of the in- or outgroup (cf. Pathway II.1).

4. *Sense of responsibility:* the tendency to ascribe responsibility for events either to the self or to external sources outside that self (locus of control). *You mean that, unlike you, I am convinced my destiny is largely determined by external forces over which I have little or no control; it is pointless to plan too fully?* Yes.

5. *Temporal orientation:* the tendency to look, modally at least, toward the past, the present, or the future as well as to prefer immediate or delayed rewards.

I.7   The Endless List of Categories

You say you are not very impressed with my list and still incline toward Galen. Well, then, keep Galen but add my list to his. *And of course I myself could make some additions. What, for example? Ego's goals.* I agree, for I may know the languages you speak, the values you treasure, the kind of person you are, without being able to say what your ambitions are. But then we need a list of goals, don't we? *Why?* For the same reasons we advance when we would conceptualize personality traits. Professionals and the rest of us may agree that there are basic drives—hunger, thirst, sex, respiration, excretion, etc.—but the strong cultural component in almost all of them prevents us from specifying in satisfying detail the behavior to which they give rise in a particular person. *I have also noted your "etc.," which shows that even this list is incomplete.* The goals associated with secondary or learned drives, moreover, are even more complicated, so that no atlas seems feasible. Think of the varied ambitions human beings possess and display. Or what do leaders and their adherents seek internationally in the modern world? I find it useful to say their goals are security, power, prestige, and—and then I add whatever goals seem necessary for the problem at hand. I weakly recommend such a schema, but not for a millisecond do I expect any friend, foe, or neutral to adopt it.

I.8   The Case for Centrality

Central traits involve what Ego himself or his associates consider his philosophy of life or the values he seeks to attain; they come close to being his individuality; for many professionals they are those traits that are highly correlated with other traits so that from their presence or absence a syndrome can be anticipated. Segmental traits are less important, and are likely to be salient when the individual is discharging roles he considers peripheral to his main interests. Being divinely discontent until a task is finished is central within you, being icily polite to persons you consider inferior is a segmental if consistent strain.

Some consistency is needed in everyone and everywhere, otherwise none of us would know what to expect from one another and from ourselves. Emerson's sneer about consistency is not applicable to normal social life; consistency is deservedly downgraded only with respect to creativity. Ego may deliberately seek to be consistent, as when he follows a philosophy inspiring him to treat all men like brothers; or he may be unwittingly consistent, as when his overt bodily movements reflect deeper, central layers within him of which he is not conscious. *Do you think the seriously insane are organized consistently around a central core?*

Centrality in fact is so important that it appears again and again under various guises in our own speech and in the jargon of the professionals. The most overworked term is "type" (Cattell, 1965, pp. 53–55). When centrality is thus emphasized, typologies may use the same concepts as those designating traits [you are an introvert]; or when socially significant beliefs or behavior is the referent, non-trait words may appear [you are a conservative. *No, not always*]. More often than not the writer or speaker resorts to a simple dichotomy [you are either an introvert or an extrovert, a conservative or a radical], or he may emerge with an assortment of labels, like the following: Ego's "dominant direction" can be described as economic or utilitarian; political or power-oriented; theoretical or devoted to truth; aesthetic or leaning toward beauty and harmony; social or inclined toward people; *or* religious, which is either self-explanatory or beyond my reach (Spranger, 1928; Allport et al., 1951). You yourself have suggested a difficulty admittedly inherent in types: you are "not always" a conservative. For the tendency indicated by the type may be quite central; but not completely so, hence we and Ego do not end up by being omniscient when, respectively, we type him and he types Alter. In addition, neither Ego nor Alter can always be typed by means of only one of the categories selected from an assortment: your strongest component may be aesthetic, but you also have more than a touch of the social and religious.

Other words in the language suggest the total or almost total organization of the personality: *outlook, philosophy, disposition, principle, frame of reference,* and—of course—*Weltanschauung.* When a person is evaluated from an ethical standpoint, reference may be made to his *character;* according to the word's ordinary connotation, someone with character does not succumb to his own impulses and instead pursues ideals considered lofty. There is *temperament:* the individual's modal manner of expressing his emotions, including especially the ease or difficulty with which they are aroused and also their intensity after being aroused. Finally, there is *style,* which refers, it would seem, to the entire person, his way of thinking and acting, or commanding and responding—*le style est l'homme même*—and judging and being judged. Most of these concepts, like trait names, go through cycles of popularity and unpopularity in the language of professionals and laymen. Each of them, moreover, has the virtue of referring to the individuality of the person, but thereby poses rather than resolves the brute problem of determining the precise details of that individuality. Consider the global term *adjustment,* which certainly suggests something central about Ego or Alter: in what respects might the adjusted differ from the maladjusted in their judgments? *Perhaps* American college students classified as maladjusted on the basis of their responses to Rorschach blots (a) believe that there is a greater discrepancy between what Alter "appears" to be and what he "really" is and (b) have more confidence in their judgments in this respect than do those called adjusted on the same dubious basis; whether the maladjusted or the adjusted judge the "real" traits with more or less certainty *may* depend on what they know about Alter (Matkom, 1963). Did you anticipate these astonishing, cosmic differences? *I did not, still I do not think they tell me very much.*

I.9 The Limitless Relations of Ego and Alter

I am not being nihilistic but realistic when I heavily emphasize the obvious: the factors determining the relation between Ego and Alter are for practical purposes limitless in number. Even an apparently simple phenomenon, such as whether Ego feels that he is the observer or the observed when he is in direct contact with Alter, *may* be dependent on antecedent experiences as well as on the social and physical nature of the situation (England, students & children; Argyle & Williams, 1969). A broad survey of the ways in which an Alter in one society may react to an interviewer from another society uncovers a multitude of factors that can affect the reaction: Alter considers Ego rude; he believes he knows the answer to every question; he tries to give Ego the answer he guesses Ego wants; he pulls Ego's leg; he misinterprets Ego's purpose; he talks too much or too little; he tries only to make a good impression; he is disturbed by Ego's higher or lower status; he is perplexed or worried when Ego belongs to a different ethnic group; or he may wish only to respond in the presence of his peers (Brislin et al., 1973, pp. 68–72). Within a society, of course, all sorts of reactions may exist, many seeming exotic from an outsider's viewpoint. Among the Tallensi in West Africa, for example, a husband becomes very anxious and suspicious when his wife visits her parents for more than two or three days: the view prevailing there is that all women are "fickle and gullible; a plausible suitor can seduce any woman" (Fortes, 1949, p. 85). In our own society, some mothers reject their children and others are pathologically devoted to them. We appreciate, to our joy or sorrow, that the child's affections vary from extreme love to extreme hate; and, even subculturally, we are not surprised when there *may* be deviations from the norm of the society, as among followers of distinctive sects (U.S. Amish, young adults; Wittmer, 1971). Ego may be more attracted to the Alter with whom he interacts than to someone with whom he has no contact, but (*again but;* and why not?)—as indicated by a review of the 289, yes 289 studies, emitted largely by American investigators of college students during the dozen years beginning in 1950 (Lott & Lott, 1965)—that attraction also depends upon umpty-ump other factors, including the nature of the interaction (e.g., is the group being threatened by outsiders?), the nature of the participants (e.g., their status, their background, their values), and of course Ego's own personality.

The ever-present empirical challenge, however, should not obscure the importance of the Ego-Alter relation: the voluntary relation of friends gives rise to judgment categories different from those between a soldier and his officer; the candidate for public office in a democracy is judged by the voters and, though unable to react to every person in his constituency, he must be affected by their collective opinions. It is valuable, consequently, to appreciate the possibility that Ego's view of Alter and himself *may* depend upon which of the two controls their interaction (Usual; Edney, 1973); it is even more tantalizing to observe what happens when judgments are passed by groups of four or fewer persons whom professional investigators assemble because they are small enough to fit within the comfortable, narrow, artificial confines of a university laboratory (Collins & Guetzkow, 1964), though again we are challenged to find the exact facts that emerge and to discover how such findings can be utilized in the particular Ego-Alter relation of interest to us. Likewise, provocative generalizations must be cautiously handled. "The more narrowly prescribed the relationship, the more particular are the categories likely to be" (Hastorf et al., 1958, p. 57). True enough. *Perhaps.* Yes, we might on occasion consider a waitress not only as an efficient or inefficient, friendly or unfriendly person who takes our orders, but also as a human being with an existence of her own outside her occupational role.

Pathway I, the behavior potential, refers to general tendencies influencing Ego's behavior; Pathway II, the understanding potential, suggests more specific tendencies directly affecting Ego's judgment of others. Five broad questions are being asked which in the practice of our time can be embodied in a single interrogatory sentence: (1) *Who* is judged (2) concerning *which attributes* and (3) for *what reason* by an Ego, (4) with *what skill*, and (5) with *which convictions?* One by one I shall tick off these topics, if only temporarily.

Who is judged? We have here a very, very tricky problem; hence grit your teeth, get ready. So far we have been discussing an Ego who judges an Alter or a Group Alter, or else we have looked upon an Ego-expositor who tries to account for Ego's judgments. Ego, however, does not necessarily judge Alter: he may judge himself, or he may judge Alter's judgment about himself, about Ego, or about yet another Alter or Alters. *You are now caught in an infinite regress: Ego judges one of Alter's judgments, etc.* Yes.

To understand naturalistic and advisable pathways it is not enough merely to admit the existence of an infinite regress, rather we must doggedly explore it. I shall try to make the process as painless and as rapid as possible with the help of relatively straightforward diagrams, each of which is immediately and lucidly explained and illustrated. *Modesty or sarcasm?* If you are impatient, I would ask you only to observe casually, intuitively, and aesthetically the number of diagrams and not details—for you will have a valid impression of the possibilities available to Ego and will never, I trust, simplify
II.1 Simplification them. For simplification or oversimplification,
and Multivariance whether it springs from forgivable or unforgivable ignorance, is another negative pathway to be avoided in analyzing

Ego, in judging Alter or in any endeavor purporting to be objective or scientific. At this point I would mention in passing, but not utilize until later, the reciprocal, more respectable twin of simplification, which is multivariance, the need to take many factors into account before passing judgment. An illustration of this pathway: in the field of psychotherapy "there is not one cause or one villain" responsible for Ego's and Alter's troubles, hence "not only must one search oneself and the behavior of one's associates, one must also examine the nature of social structures, communication systems, and cultural ideation" (Scheflen, 1972, p. 200).

Each situation below begins with a symbolic representation in which E stands for Ego and A for Alter, with a subscript added for more than one Alter. The direction of the arrows indicates who is judging whom. The regress, if any, is suggested first by parentheses and then by brackets. Accompanying each diagram are, mercifully, two sentences labelled *a* and *b*. In *a* the symbols are translated into straightforward English, or as straightforward as English or any language can be in depicting an infinite regress. In *b* an illustration is given with you generously playing Ego's role and a nondescript character, "him" or "he," playing Alter's. *Why not put all this into a Postscript?* It is too important, it is better for you to immerse yourself in the bare classifications.

I. Direct judgments (final referent is Alter)
   (1) $E \rightarrow A$
      a. Ego judges Alter
      b. You judge him to be a fool
   (2) $E \rightarrow (A \rightarrow A)$
      a. Ego judges Alter's own judgment concerning himself
      b. You judge that he judges himself to be a fool
   (3) $E \rightarrow [A \rightarrow (E \rightarrow A)]$
      a. Ego judges Alter's judgment concerning Ego's judgments concerning Alter
      b. You judge that he judges that you judge him to be a fool
   (4) $E \rightarrow [A \rightarrow (E \rightarrow [A \rightarrow A])]$
      a. Ego judges Alter's judgment concerning Ego's judgment concerning Alter's own judgment concerning himself
      b. You judge that he judges that you judge that he judges himself to be a fool

II. Reverse judgments (final referent is Ego)

  (5) $E \rightarrow (A \rightarrow E)$

  a. Ego judges Alter's judgment of Ego

  b. You judge that he judges you to be intelligent

  (6) $E \rightarrow [A \rightarrow (E \rightarrow E)]$

  a. Ego judges Alter's judgment of Ego's own judgment concerning himself

  b. You judge that he judges that you judge yourself to be intelligent

  (7) $E \rightarrow [A \rightarrow (E \rightarrow [A \rightarrow E])]$

  a. Ego judges Alter's judgment of Ego's judgment concerning Alter's own judgment concerning Ego

  b. You judge that he judges that you judge that he judges you to be intelligent

III. Extended judgments (final referent is another person, A_2; any environmental stimulus, S; or Ego's judgment of A_2)

  (8) $E \rightarrow (A_1 \rightarrow A_2 \text{ or } S)$

  a. Ego judges Alter's judgment of another Alter or of a stimulus

  b. You judge that he judges another Alter (or cheese) to be first-rate

  (9) $E \rightarrow [A_1 \rightarrow (E \rightarrow A_2 \text{ or } S)]$

  a. Ego judges Alter's judgment of Ego's own judgment concerning another Alter or a stimulus

  b. You judge that he judges that you judge another Alter (or cheese) to be first-rate

  (10) $E \rightarrow [A_1 \rightarrow (A_2 \rightarrow A_1)]$

  a. Ego judges Alter's judgment of another Alter's own judgment concerning himself

  b. You judge that he judges that another Alter judges him (the original Alter) to be first-rate

  (11) $E \rightarrow [A_1 \rightarrow (A_2 \rightarrow E)]$

  a. Ego judges Alter's judgment of another Alter's own judgment concerning Ego himself

  b. You judge that he judges that another Alter judges you to be first-rate

IV. Self-judgments (final referent is Ego)

  (12) $E \rightarrow E$

  a. Ego judges himself

  b. You think you are insecure

(13)

$$(A \to E_1)$$

   a. Ego compares his own judgment concerning himself with what he judges Alter's judgment to be of that same self

   b. You judge that you are insecure and that he also judges you to be insecure

(14)

$$(A \to E)$$

   a. Ego compares his own judgment of Alter with what he judges Alter's judgment to be of Ego himself

   b. You judge that he is insecure and that he also judges you to be insecure

V. Comparative judgments (final referent is Alter)

   (15)

$$(A \to A)$$

   a. Ego compares his own judgment concerning Alter with what he judges Alter's judgment to be of himself

   b. You judge that he is attractive but that he has the opposite opinion of himself

VI. Multiple judgments (final referent is a number of Alters, a number of Egos, or Ego.

(16)

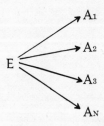

a. Ego judges more than one Alter
b. You judge that all the persons in that group are conservative; or you judge that one is a conservative, another a liberal, another a radical, etc.

(17)

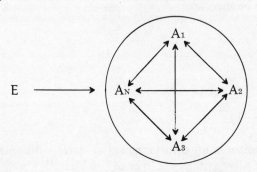

a. Ego judges the group product of a number of Alters
b. You judge that these persons have decided they are conservative

(18)

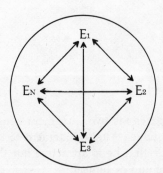

a. Two or more Egos judge each other or one another
b. You all judge one another and yourselves to be conservative

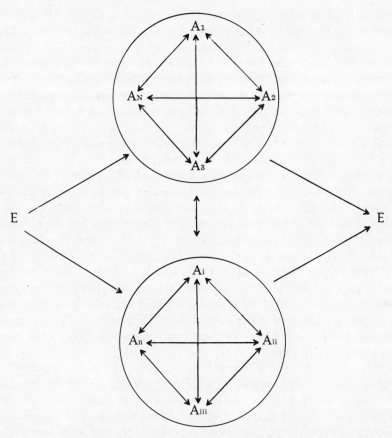

a. Ego judges Group Alters and also judges their judgments of one another and of himself

b. You judge that one group is more conservative than the other; that those in each group judge themselves but not the other group to be conservative; and that the members of one group but not the other judge you to be conservative

I shall refrain from considering other possibilities, first because I think the above 19 serve their stated purpose of pointing out the complications that ensue as we traverse the infinite regress of human relations, and secondly because I might then have to go into a third dimension and that would never do. I would stress that every possibility has been approached exclusively from Ego's standpoint: it is he who judges Alter or Alter's judgment of himself or a Group Alter. If we were to try to consider Alter's viewpoint simultaneously—if we asked, for example, just what Alter perceives rather than what Ego believes he perceives—we would indeed be driven into a fourth dimension. But even this is done sometimes by an Ego-expositor when he tries to comprehend simultaneously a number of interacting Egos who are judging one another; thus perhaps only he and not they can have a rounded view of what takes place in situation 18 above. It is not unreasonable to assume that Ego at some time utilizes all these possibilities, depending of course on who or what the ultimate referent is. In our discussions, for example, the emphasis is upon Direct Judgments (#1) as we evolve advisable pathways, only because they can be more simply expressed than the others. Surely, however, Ego often wonders what Alter thinks about himself (#2) or what Alter thinks Ego thinks about him (#3); possibly, in contrast, Ego does not often wonder what Alter thinks Ego's opinion is concerning Alter's opinion of himself (#4). I do not believe we have drifted into clouds of fantasy when we suggest that a paranoid Ego often speculates about Alter's opinion concerning him (#5); it is much less likely that Ego will concern himself with the problems of Alter's opinion concerning how Ego appraises himself (#6) or of Alter's opinion concerning how Ego thinks Alter appraises him (#7).

Have you, nevertheless, been playing with bubbles in diagramming and describing these various possibilities? I think not. Others have had such ideas which turn out to be useful. *Folie à deux?* No, really not (Postscript II.1: The Infinite Regress). What we need and do not have and may never have is knowledge concerning the circumstances under which a given Ego actually makes use of the 19 possibilities. Perhaps an introspective person judges himself more frequently than he does others. Or the extrovert worries about the judgment of others. One hunch: the shorter the regress involved in a judgment, the more likely it is that such a judgment will be passed. *Why?* Less effort, less sophistication, less information are needed when Ego judges Alter than when he tries to imagine, for example, what Alter thinks about himself, about other Alters, or about Ego. At any rate it seems reasonable to assume that Ego's understanding potential includes tendencies to utilize some of these possibilities more frequently than others. Allegedly an unreflective individual has a regress less "infinite" than an introspective one.

I turn abruptly to the second question: which attributes of Alter or of himself is Ego likely to judge? Toward what kinds of information do the pathways lead? For convenience, the phrasing of the *what* is given here exclusively in terms of Ego's judgment about Alter:

1. *Activity:* what is Alter doing?
2. *Achievement:* what is Alter accomplishing, what has he accomplished?
3. *Affection and thought:* what are Alter's feelings or emotions, what is he thinking, what are his ideas?
4. *Intention:* what does Alter wish to do, what goal or satisfaction does he seek?
5. *Personality:* what kind of person is Alter, what are his traits (viz., intelligence, sociability, style, self-responsibility, temporal orientation)?
6. *Status:* what position does Alter occupy in society or a group, how can he be described demographically?
7. *Background:* why is Alter the way he seems to be, what is his life history?
8. *Attraction:* is Alter attractive?
9. *Similarity:* is Alter similar to Ego?

The terms, I trust, are self-explanatory and not particularly jargonistic, and so perhaps their arbitrariness may be forgiven. I shall use them frequently but unobtrusively, frequently because they are a convenient point of reference, unobtrusively because I would not force them upon you or any Ego who prefers different words. *You certainly like to exhibit your philosophical anarchism, don't you?*

II.a   Judgment Motives

Next question: why does Ego pass judgment on himself or others? You do not wait for an answer because you believe I cannot provide one. *It would be easier to count from here to infinity than to identify the motives for passing judgment.* I would say meekly that I am trying only to incorporate the problem of passing judgment into a more general category, that of motivation.

We judge our fellow men and ourselves only when there is some good reason for doing so, we do not judge them for their own sake unless we are playing a game, are bored, or agree to perform as subjects in an experiment. Less frequently, I suppose, do we ask others to judge us, although young children, extreme narcissists, and the socially

insecure may be prone to seek approval by soliciting favorable judgments from persons they respect; and the severely or fashionably
disturbed consult psychiatrists to receive judgments in the form of
diagnoses. Without a motive Ego is not likely to pay attention to the
clues provided by the Alters in his milieu who ordinarily may not be
easily observed. I want to know whether you are angry because my
guilt makes me wonder whether I am responsible for the way you
feel, because my compassion urges me to try to calm you, or because
my cowardice makes me run for cover when I judge you to be somehow aggrieved. Really, I am not postulating an entity to be called
judgment motive that functions whenever a button is pushed. I am
saying only that obviously Ego must somehow be motivated to pass
judgment before he actually does so. One task of an Ego-expositor is
to try to discover what that motive is. There are, in short, judgment
motives, not *a* judgment motive.

*Linking judgment and motivation is doing nothing more than in-
voking a deterministic doctrine: are you trying to lead me into a metaphysical trap?* No, not a trap, rather an invitation
to use determinism as a potentially useful, advisable pathway. Ego's judgment, for example,
is improved, I assert in general terms, if he believes it fruitful to discover Alter's intention and background and if indeed he is further
convinced that the behavior is lawful. Note my caution: "if he believes"
and "if indeed he is further convinced" suggest the pragmatic function
of the hypothesis. I hasten, therefore, to assure you I am not asking
you to make an ultimate decision about determinism and that I am far
from deluding myself into believing that any of us can ever uncover a
final solution to this eternal problem. Postpone the problem until you
are older and less bellicose or view it privately in church or late at
night, but here and now you and I, in spite of differences and disagreements, meet and deeply appreciate the opportunistic, pragmatic utility
of seeking to link causes and effects. *I do not like the idea of determinism, I like surprises.* Of course everyone likes some surprises, but
not others. You may laugh gaily when the car's engine surprises you and
suddenly stalls; then if you are to move on, someone like a mechanic
must establish the cause of the failure. Although, like me, you have
ceased anticipating finality, you admit freely, graciously, and compulsively that we require some sequences to be more or less predictable.
Much of your thinking is devoted to seeking meaning in life, and a
deterministic hypothesis maintains that no sequence of acts is mean-

II.2   Determinism

ingless, that rather it has antecedents or serves some function. And so you find a mechanic to repair the lifeless engine because you admit he knows more about engines than you and has a deterministic faith in that knowledge. *All you wish me to do, then, is to adopt the same attitude concerning the judgment motive?* Yes, but there is more to say (Postscript II.2: Cultural Determinism).

Including the concept of judgment motive in a deterministic framework, in short, enables us to raise the same questions that arise in connection with any other motive. As I once viewed the jungle of studies and reports about time, for example, it became clear that temporal judgments, even in antiseptic laboratories where all factors other than the crucial ones are allegedly constant, depend upon whether the subjects have been instructed in advance to judge an interval's duration, while perceiving it, or afterwards (Doob, 1971, pp. 22, 108–09, 175, 181). Similarly, Ego's judgment about Alter may depend upon when the judgment motive is evoked. A tendency to place a halo around Alter—to judge him fairly consistently either favorably or unfavorably—*may* be stronger when Ego knows he must continue to appraise him than when he believes no further judgment is required (Usual; O'Neal & Mills, 1969). Some judgments may grow sweeter, others less sweet with the passing of time. Or Egos react differently to the presence or the memory of Alter. Since I have a tendency to repress the unpleasant, my judgment about most Alters is likely to be more mellow later than when they annoy me face-to-face; I suspect the reverse is true of you. Timing, consequently, must be viewed not only as a naturalistic but also as an advisable pathway:

II.3   *Timing*   Ego must appreciate the fact that his judgments are time-bound and may change with the passing of time.

As we seek pathways to Alter, you and I may occasionally forget that Ego has other problems in life than to judge Alter or himself. With a deterministic hypothesis we can now say, however, that judgments are made when some kind of motive is salient. This concept of salience has wide implications: it calls attention

II.4   *Salience*   to the fact that Ego's judgment or any other bit of his behavior depends not directly upon his total potential but on the particular processes that are actually functioning at a given moment. *But is your argument not circular, are you not saying that salience refers to ongoing processes and that ongoing processes are salient?* In a way, yes, but the challenge is to uncover the salient or ongoing processes. If we now return to the judgment motives, we must ask the direct question: under what circumstances is a motive likely to be salient? There are many answers, although all of them relate to Ego's personality, his goals at a given moment, and the demands of the situation (Postscript II.3: The Arousal of Judgment Motives). Actually I find it difficult to imagine a situation in which under some circumstances a judgment motive is not salient. Like personality traits, however, the motive may be relatively central or segmental (Pathway I.6). When you need information in a large shop or a supermarket, you search for a person who seems to be a clerk; your judgment motive is segmental, it is evoked as part of the instrumental response leading to whatever it is you want to buy. But when you would persuade someone that your viewpoint is correct. . . . *This seldom happens because in general I do not care or believe I do not care whether others agree with me or not.* Still, when you do, your judgment motive is quite central: you cannot be effective unless you appraise that person rather fully.

The judgment motive partially determines not only the judgment's referent and hence the kind of judgment selected from among the 19 possibilities so neatly diagramed a few pages ago, but also the attributes of the Alter being judged. Ego's interest in Alter may be narrow or broad, which in turn may depend upon the kind of bond between them (Pathway I.c). He may wish only to know whether Alter is reliable or self-confident, and nothing more. Or he may seek comprehensive knowledge, he would know "everything" about him. If Alter is to be hired as a night watchman, it may be sufficient to note only his conscientiousness; but if he is to lead a group, it is essential to know him much more thoroughly. An Ego comparing and judging two Alters *may* come up with quite different judgments depending upon whether the motive for his evaluation affects his own welfare or leaves that welfare unchanged. The behavioral consequences of the decision must thus be taken into account (Usual; Sewell, 1973).

One final bonus appears when judgments about Alter are considered within the framework of motivation: we are alerted to the probability that some form of reduction occurs or is sought whenever a motive is aroused or rearoused. You cannot believe that Alter is the angel or devil you have heard that he is, or observed him to be; and then you go out of your way to discover more about him until. . . . *Until what?* Until you feel satisfied; and thus, you see, you end up where you began, satisfying yourself.

II.b Sensitivity and Skill

I agree with you when you say you are more sensitive to many Alters than most of us; you take pride in this ability of yours. Well and good, and for once the professionals are on your side at least partially and agree that you are not unique. For differential sensitivity has been shown in two different ways: some Egos can gauge Alters' emotions more accurately than can others, and a positive, though often a low, correlation between judgments based on different cues also suggests the possibility of some sort of general ability. *This does not make sense, it stands to reason that for some Egos sensitivity or skill in judging others may be specific with respect to one and only one Alter, a small number of Alters, or a type of Alter, whereas for others it may be more general and therefore applicable to large numbers of persons, even including those from societies quite different from our own.* I agree, perhaps you may wish to glance at what some of the professionals claim to have established (Postscript II.4: Generality vs. Specificity of Judgmental Skill).

I might add that Ego is probably more sensitive to some moods of his friends than he is to others. Yes, and therefore sensitivity varies not only from person to person but also from time to time or from judgment to judgment within the same individual. An Ego may be sensitive to physical pain in almost every Alter, a feeling presumably easy to detect. The same or another Ego detects anxiety only in the few Alters he knows well. No facile naturalistic pathway here.

I wonder: are there not types of persons more skillful than others, are not women more sensitive than men? The research findings on the latter point, for what they are worth, are "equivocal" (Warr & Knapper, 1968, p. 190). Even if they were not, the differences would have to be attributed to the different experiences imposed upon the two sexes by our particular culture. Other comparisons on the whole tend to be negative; in fact, it is possible that clinical psychologists, psychiatrists, social workers, and a group not specializing in the study of behavior, viz., physical scientists, *may* not be significantly different from one another in judging how patients will respond to a direct or projective questionnaire, although each Ego of course has "a working hypothesis" concerning the Alter he is judging (Usual; Luft, 1950). *Yes, the professionals are supposed to be preeminently sensitive to others by virtue of their training and experience, but many of them are just a trifle, some are more than a trifle, blinded by their own theories or conceptions of human beings. If "vital" art "manifests something which the artist perceives at greater intensity, and more intimately, than his public"* (Pound, 1968, p. 67), *then the artist ought to be more sensitive to others than the rest of us or rather his heaven-sent sensibility must be greater.* Really? Your evidence?

Whether general or specific, deep or superficial, peculiar to some persons or not, sensitivity would seem to involve four different processes:

Projection: Ego ascribes to Alter, correctly or not, one or more of his own momentary or enduring attributes. "Alter is afraid the way I am."

Identification: Ego ascribes to himself what he believes, correctly or not, to be one or more of Alter's momentary or enduring attributes. "Like Alter I am afraid."

Empathy: Ego ascribes to Alter, correctly or not, one or more momentary or enduring attributes which he then experiences within himself. "Alter is afraid, his fear makes me feel afraid."

Sympathy: Ego ascribes to Alter, correctly or not, one or more momentary or enduring attributes which he himself is not experiencing but which arouse within him a positive or tender feeling regarding Alter. "I am sorry that Alter is afraid."

It is useful to have a single term covering all four of these concepts in order not only to refer to them en masse or without differentiation but also to indicate that abstractly they have much in common. Since convention does not provide such a word, I arbitrarily allocate the conceptual responsibility to "imagination." The con-

II.5   *Imagination*   cept certainly suggests the solipsistic predicament in which, I keep stressing, every Ego finds himself: he never knows what Alter is experiencing; he must imagine that experience; and his imagination functions by projecting, identifying, empathizing, or being sympathetic. What would you do if you were I? What would I do if I were you? Don't you feel the way I do? In English, moreover, the word imagination denotes the very qualities that characterize the pathways we pursue: it may be creative or banal, correct or incorrect, consciously or unconsciously motivated, expressed or unexpressed. The term, moreover, appeals to me because it is neither neologistic nor jargonistic (Postscript II.5: The Subjectivity of Imagination).

Is sensitivity, skill, or imagination correlated with other aspects of personality? *It ought to be, I should think.* Yes, I add cynically, the professional who works hard and long enough on any problem in the clinic or laboratory and then has a computer produce tons of printouts ought to be able to find some trait, impulse, or bit of behavior that is related to some other aspect of the individual of interest to us. In this instance, however, the results are largely disappointing (Postscript II.6: Sensitivity Traits: The Search). *Come, come, use your imagination and squeeze what you can from the literature.* Under such pressure I would propose a half dozen factors that seem to be promising correlates of the understanding potential. *Why promising?* Well, there is some evidence for each one, but I must add a dash of your technique. *Mine?* Yes, intuition. They are: (1) intelligence and style; (2) sociability; (3) self-knowledge; (4) ability to manipulate Alter; (5) patience and restraint; and (6) practice. My defence for including each one is a bit longwinded (Postscript II.7: Sensitivity Traits: A Proposal).

We have every good reason to anticipate that general sensitivity to others, over and beyond responsiveness to one's mother and the immediate milieu, increases with age as the world unfolds and then perhaps decreases later in life as Ego disengages himself in order to recapture the past and thus avoid the present with its overtone of lurking death. The primitive drive of the hungry infant motivates him to grow sensitive to the source of his nutriment and hence he begins to practice the kind of actions leading to the development of the skill (Postscript II.8: The Development of Sensitivity). Every society encourages its young to develop a sensitivity to some persons, perhaps not so formally as boys in our society are required to learn how to add numbers and in many African societies how to tend cattle, but informally, as good manners on the whole are acquired anywhere. Filipino children, for example, are supposed to learn the following "interpersonal skills":

1. Recognize subtle cues which reveal the unspoken feelings of others
2. Cope with angry feelings without striking out at others
3. Give and receive help; pool [one's] well-being with that of [the] nuclear and extended family
4. Ignore activities of others which, although visible, are said to be none of [one's] concern
5. Tease and be teased without losing . . . self-control
6. Recognize . . . obligations to others for favors received (Guthrie & Jacobs, 1966, p. 203).

Persons with such skills must perceive and judge persons differently from the way you and I do; and now that these socialization practices have been pointed out to us we should be in a better position forever to judge a Filipino Alter or—in the role of Ego-expositor—to understand the way in which a Filipino Ego passes judgment. Obviously such behavior must be carefully rehearsed again and again, and properly rewarded or punished, if a Filipino child is to become a good citizen.

This hymn to practice cannot go on indefinitely; when, as you always do, will you sound some sour notes? I believe that practice or experience is essential: young children are naive, contact with many persons over a period of time results in sagacity, and the value of practice is suggested by the prestige accorded old age; therefore experience is an advisable pathway (Pathway 6.a). But I am also willing to acknowledge that wise insights can burst out of the mouths of babes, that practice can produce prejudice, and that the veneration of the aged may be a tribute not to their judgmental skill but to their past accomplishments. Frequency of judgment by itself, moreover, does not necessarily produce sensitivity. Mothers, for example, may recognize that their disturbed children are in fact disturbed but fail to agree with the children themselves, concerning the symptoms of the disturbance (U.S.; Levitt, 1959). In addition, practice seldom operates in a vacuum. In the United States, for example, liberals and others in favor of change *may* be better informed concerning the opinion of their peers than conservatives (Breed & Ktsanes, 1961). Why? In general individuals may judge the opinion of their own group more accurately when they themselves agree with that opinion than when they do not. According to this view, an Ego with a liberal attitude on a particular issue *may* be a better judge of majority opinion only when most persons are also liberal and not conservative (Usual; Hendershot & Eckhardt, 1971).

Practice may entail a spiral: sensitivity feeds upon sensitivity. You know how to judge, let me say, peasants and poets, hence you continually do so, hence you improve your skill, hence you exercise it all the more. A spiral (Pathway 4.b) unfolds, I assume, since you must find it rewarding to make these judgments: you achieve better rapport with these Alters and it is gratifying to do something well. They then come to treasure you all the more when you offer them proof again and again that you comprehend them, they make themselves more accessible, and you thus have the opportunity to perfect your skill still more. The spiral never unfolds, however, or it comes to an abrupt halt, when either Ego or Alter is a boor who alienates others by his very insensitivity. Alter, therefore, may share with Ego the initial, the continuing, or the final responsibility for the spiral (Pathway 1.a). The trait Alter perceives in a sensitive Ego, however, may not be his sensitivity but some other trait, such as generosity or responsiveness.

II.c   Convictions

Do we ever meet anyone for the first time? *The question is silly, I was introduced last night to a perfect stranger about whom I had previously heard absolutely nothing beyond his nationality and occupation; and then, as I listened to him pontificate during the meal, I found him arrogant and empty.* But, I persist, were you really meeting him for the first time, had you not previously encountered similar persons whom he quickly caused you to remember not as specific individuals but as types? I am not quibbling, because quibbling wastes time we can devote to more fruitful or enjoyable pursuits during brief moments of being alive. That man last night you could not view through unclouded lenses; you had to see him in the framework of your conviction acquired from similar and dissimilar Alters in the past. You may meet a particular person for the first time, but you meet his attributes for the nth time. Who is anyone over and beyond the attributes he exposes to view?

And so it always is, it seems to me: Ego has a complicated arsenal of convictions that affect his understanding of Alter; he has not only feelings and attitudes, which will be considered in due course, but also egocentric beliefs concerning the nature of Alter, any Alter, on whom he passes judgment. Some of us judge many or most Alters sharply, they are either good or bad; others anticipate a combination of the desirable and undesirable. The same *may* be true of modal or ethnocentric tendencies within other societies: the Dobuans of New Guinea conceive of persons as being treacherous and malignant (Benedict, 1934, pp. 171–72), whereas the Navaho assume that everyone is a blend of both evil and good (Kluckhohn & Leighton, 1946, p. 230). It makes a difference, I agree, whether you meet the stranger, as you did last night, with no preconceptions concerning him other than his nationality and occupation, or with many more specific ideas about his individuality as a human being.

Undoubtedly we also have convictions concerning Group Alters. Concepts like national character, mob rule, democratic regime suggest that the attitudes and behavior of groups as well as of those belonging to them are anticipated. *Perhaps* we believe that decisions by groups are less subject to change than those by individuals in isolation (Usual; Linkskold et al., 1974). *Why?* You guess. *Groups have bureaucratic machinery that can obstruct change; and group members are under pressure to conform to previous decisions, whereas—oh, the rest should be obvious.* To whom? *You.*

Most important of all, as foreshadowed in the Prologue (Postscript 0.2), and as I shall now more fully suggest, are Ego's convictions about personality: he has a set of psychological assumptions concerning people, some of which may be "silent" or unexpressed even to himself (Ichheiser, 1970, p. 75). Fantastic as it may seem, on one occasion American high-school students were actually able to answer questions about a fictitious person after having been told only that he was named "Jim" and before being given any additional information about him. There were "expressions of puzzlement and bewilderment"; but, having been informed that "in life we often have expectations or ideas about a person before we meet him," they replied to the questions and, on the whole, tended to consider good old Jim somewhat outgoing. After receiving descriptions of him, their views changed but, after ten weeks, their judgments of Jim continued to reveal the effects of their preconceptions which, being derived only from his name and sex, must have reflected the general views of personality prevailing in their society and internalized within each of them (Luchins & Luchins, 1970). You have, I think, a strong penchant to link traits or bits of behavior. She or he is attractive in appearance, and such a person must also be honest. *This fallacy I recognize, but—I wonder.* You wonder.

Every Ego, moreover, is convinced to some extent that he can explain, perhaps also predict, behavior. Or he has convictions enabling or compelling him to evaluate what Alter does; thus we certainly believe, don't we, that the seriousness of an accident *may* indicate the extent of Alter's responsibility or that martyrs are less to be admired than innocent victims (Usual; Berscheid & Walster, 1969, pp. 12–14). Some contemporary convictions are personal and derived from introspection, knowledge about ourselves, or general experience. Others may be affected by the views of professionals, such as the proponents of conditioning, existentialists, psychoanalysts, or theologians. But what is your opinion of a person who interrupts a conversation either completely or incompletely, who directly or indirectly changes the topic being discussed, who asks a question while others are speaking, or who often assumes the initiative during periods of silence? These are the ways, *perhaps,* in which individuals try to intrude themselves into other person's talk (Ingersoll, 1972); surely you have a theory about such intruders, don't you?

It makes a great difference whether Ego's view of human nature leans him in the direction of selfishness or altruism, or whether he believes in free will or determinism. The role of lay theory is seen especially clearly in connection with the judging of foreigners or ethnic groups other than one's own. The same bit of behavior is perceived quite differently when Alter's group is considered to be inferior rather than superior, attractive rather than unattractive. Similarly any explanation of behavior—whether based upon genetics, astrology, phrenology, graphology, endocrinology, etc.—affects the kind of information Ego seeks concerning Alter and then the way in which he utilizes that information. The theoretical assumption, persisting for centuries, that parents have an overwhelming influence on children may cause some of us to overlook the reverse view that at a given moment the child's behavior, whether dependent, independent, or stubborn, *may* produce marked changes in the adult trying to help that child solve a problem (U.S., mothers; Osofsky, 1971)—and, again, the assumption may affect the other person's perception and judgment.

Behind Ego's personality theory lurks a conviction concerning the metaphysical nature of human nature which includes an assumption involving the mutability or perfectibility of mankind. Within our own society there is no agreement as to whether we are doomed to compensate eternally for the original sin bequeathed to us either genetically or traditionally or whether we can be saved through beneficent surroundings. Either view affects our way of judging and evaluating others. In contrast, the Navaho are convinced that each individual possesses some quantity of "good" and "bad," and "no amount of knowledge and no amount of 'religious' zeal can do more than alter somewhat [their] relative proportions" (Kluckhohn & Leighton, 1946, p. 230).

Ego also has a conviction concerning his own understanding potential: he feels confident or not that he can accurately judge Alters in general or particular Alters. Such confidence enables him, perhaps, to be more or less attentive to other persons and hence may affect his acumen. At a minimum he is convinced he can anticipate the moods of someone he loves like his parent, spouse, or child, if he is not to feel lost in a dreary world. Possibly he also feels insecure in front of some category of persons such as superiors or strangers. More than past practice is probably involved in this self-evaluation, for there is no exact calculus through which even the brightest or the most reckless individual can grade his own past record of understanding.

And what advice should Ego be given concerning his convictions? No new pathway is needed: as you would know yourself, know also your convictions, for some may be valid, others quite invalid. (Pathway I.1).

Postscripts

II.1   The Infinite Regress

As I contemplate the diagrams, I fortunately have a bit of evidence with which to comfort myself and remove doubts concerning my own sanity: others have followed a similar primrose path from Ego to Alter and back again. After having plotted the diagrams in an isolated Tyrolean village, I discovered in a library that three professionals refer to "whirling phantasy circles"; for example, "Peter's view of Peter and Paul's view of Peter, Peter's view of Paul and Paul's view of Paul, Peter's view of Paul's view of Paul and Paul's view of Peter's view of Paul's view of Paul, Peter's view of Paul's view of Peter and Paul's view of Peter's view of Paul" (Laing et al., 1966, p. 22). The authors of this regression have brought their analysis out of the clouds by designing an elaborate technique they call the "Interpersonal Perception Method." The method requires Ego to respond to a dozen questions following each of 60 items. Seventy minutes are needed, they say, to answer the 720 questions. All 60 have the same format. The illustration below is the first in the series and assumes here that Alter is a female. She rates each of the trio of four alternatives on a five-point scale consisting of "very true," "slightly true," "slightly untrue," "very untrue," and "?":

1. A. How true do you think the following are?
    1. She understands me.
    2. I understand her.
    3. She understands herself.
    4. I understand myself.
    B. How would SHE answer the following?
    5. "I understand him."
    6. "He understands me."
    7. "I understand myself."
    8. "He understands himself."

C. How would SHE think you have answered the following?
    9. She understands me.
  10. I understand her.
  11. She understands herself.
  12. I understand myself. (Laing et al., 1966, p. 145).

The three authors and I, moreover, are not alone in pursuing an infinite regress. *You sound defensive.* I am, let me mention two other instances. Respectable research has stemmed from the answers to two questions which contrast Ego's judgment of Alters and Alter's judgment of Ego: "With whom would you most like to associate?" and "which members of the group do you think would most like to associate with you?" (Tagiuri, 1958, p. 318). In another investigation "empathic ability" has been measured by first having the subject or patient rate himself with respect to six characteristics ranging from self-confidence to sense of humor. He then rates some other person in the same respects. Next he tries to imagine that other person's own self-ratings and the ratings he would give the rater. In the end, his ratings are compared with Alter's. The data thus obtained have correlated well with another measure of empathy derived from examining the same person's stories in response to TAT drawings (Usual; Dymond, 1949).

All right, then, you are not alone in your madness, but what good comes out of considering the infinite regress? The Interpersonal Perception Method has been used to test the hypothesis that "the schizophrenic sees the mother's point of view better than the mother sees the schizophrenic's":

> The schizophrenic realizes that the mother does not realize that he sees her point of view, and that she thinks she sees his point of view, and that she does not realize that she fails to do so. The mother, on the other hand, thinks she sees the schizophrenic's point of view, and that the schizophrenic fails to see hers, and is unaware that the schizophrenic knows that this is what she thinks, and that she is unaware he knows (Laing et al., p. 47)

Such information, I submit, is valuable since the psychiatric goal presumably is to discover the misunderstandings between persons and to improve the communication between them. To employ this particular method, however, the patient and his mother must each make the 720 ratings mentioned above. *Whew—720 × 2 = 1,440.* Of course we ordinarily cannot obtain so many ratings (Pathway I.3), but at least we have an ideal model in front of us (Pathway 0.1).

The infinite regress conceivably may have real implications for international understanding, maybe even for peace. American sterotypes concerning Russians include characterizations of them as well as beliefs concerning the ways in which they view themselves and Americans. Of course the Russians judge Americans in similar respects. The very real question arises as to whether "mutual images of conflicting groups are based on contradictory interpretations of reality and tend, at least to some degree, to mirror each other" (Kelman, 1965, p. 236).

II.2   Cultural Determinism

Within limits, culture—that potent source of behavior (Pathway I.a) —places demands upon us, a state of affairs which, I think, even further strengthens one's faith in some kind of loose determinism. You and I move about, and retain our self-respect, our sense of individuality, in fact our dignity as human beings by asserting the conviction that sufficiently often we seem to initiate or control our own actions. We are free, we think, and our decisions come from us: whether and how we judge Alters is a private matter. And yet, like the teacher who must conform to his school's standard and pass judgment on his students by grading them at the end of term, again and again we are constrained and must judge our fellow men. Of course a vast difference may exist between what we say when called upon to deliver our opinion and what we think; but both reactions are a function of social demands to which in many instances we willingly and even joyfully accede. Think, for example, of any kind of free election when the electorate decides— or tries to decide—on the capabilities of the candidates running for office. Frequently a mélange of attributes must be judged: the politician's ability to perform effectively, his record in the past, his intelligence, his attractiveness, his ability to command the respect of his subordinates and his superiors, etc. In fact, the judgments voters are required to make in national or even local elections in the United States are so numerous that usually ballots are cast along traditional lines: I vote for the best (by which the voter means the better) man, and my party always nominates the best one. Cultural demands, however, can be less formidable, though important nonetheless. Perhaps before seeking advice or assistance Czech adolescent boys and girls do not need to make subtle judgmental distinctions because they merely appraise Alter's status: they select the person in accordance with conventionally established relations in the family, the peer group, and the rest of the social milieu (Jurovsky, 1971). Finally, the arousal of the judgment in whole or in part may be taboo in some situations: judging gods or evaluating leaders of tightly authoritarian countries unfavorably is, respectively, a sacrilegious act or a criminal offense. In all these instances Ego's judgments are predetermined. *More or less.*

II.3 The Arousal of Judgment Motives

The arousal of a judgment motive must be related to some of the personality traits delineated on the previous pathway (Pathway I.b), such as sociability. The Ego who obtains joy from associating with other persons necessarily judges them: some are more attractive to him than others. Or there may be a spiral (Pathway 4.b): the motive is first aroused, and Ego seeks out those who will please him and avoids those who will not. Possibly the motive to judge accompanies frustration more frequently than it does gratification. For hatred puts us on the defensive and we then assess the power or skill of our adversary. But love offers little incentive to assess, except perhaps either when we fear that it cannot endure forever and hence that it must give way to frustration, or when we would increase its glory by heaping praise upon the beloved.

Ego's goal affects the inclusion or exclusion of the judgment motive as the instrumental means to the end. Contrast the judgment Ego makes when he walks down a crowded street, when he looks for a porter in a railway station, or when he tries to select a wife. During the walk he has no interest in other people, except perhaps to avoid bumping into them. He cares nothing about all of the porter's attributes, he would know only that he is able and willing to carry luggage. And if he is sagacious and not just in love, he judges an infinite number of the lady's attributes which you are better able to specify than I. A domineering Ego searches out the strengths of Alter in order to combat them, and his weaknesses in order to exploit them. In contrast, a security-seeking Ego may magnify the same strengths and overlook the weaknesses. You continually seek certainty for some private reason concerning which I have the delicacy not to make inquiry, you find it difficult to tolerate the ambiguity associated with a suspended judgment about most Alters; and therefore your judgment motive is constantly aroused. Now perhaps you are beginning to tolerate more amiably the advantages of a deterministic assumption: you discover more interconnections within Ego and within yourself. *I really wonder.*

The relation between Ego and Alter in a given situation affects the arousal of a judgment motive. That relation may be "focused" or "unfocused" (Goffman, 1961, p. 7), and it seems likely that the motive is more likely to be evoked when the participants wish to interact (a committee meeting) than when they just happen to be together (on a bus). We might also say that friends judge each other frequently because the goals they jointly seek are more easily attained when their judgments are valid. But then if we were to inquire into the reason for the friendship in the first place, we would be confronted with a staggering number of possibilities ranging from external factors, such as propinquity (U.S., adults; Festinger et al., 1950, pp. 33–59) and social structure (Usual; Barnlud & Harland 1963), to relevant subjective consequences or counterparts, such as the knowledge Ego and Alter have or think they have concerning each other's behavior, values, or attitudes (Usual; Byrne, 1961). *Enough, too much; yes, I agree, we simply must limit our quests (Pathway I.3).*

Obviously Alter may be the source of the arousal of a judgment motive. That man in the train compartment with you—you are travelling on a European train and I leave to you the decision as to whether you have a first- or a second-class ticket—has just bought a tray of neatly wrapped food from the dining-car attendant who has passed through. He has sprung upon the food like a beast. You find it impossible to look at your book or the passing landscape: the noise of his lips and the gestures of his whole body force themselves upon you. Will you then simply call him a pig or will you try to make other observations about him and relate his piggishness to his culture or other traits you intuit? The answer may rest with your interest in your book or the scenery, with your philosophy about mankind, perhaps even with the masochism-sadism component of your personality. You judge him first because you virtually have no alternative; then the aroused judgment motive does or does not lead you elsewhere as he voraciously pushes more chicken into his mouth before the last mouthful has reached the outer boundaries of his throat. The advisable pathway is the avoidance of goal- or personality-induced egocentrism (I.4) when and if Alter is to be more fully comprehended.

I suppose the ultimate explanation of the omnipresence of the judgment motive is the omnipotence of culture. For so great is the impact of culture upon the judgment motive that I quite unhesitatingly say to you. . . . *A minor miracle.* I say motivation to judge Alters must be universally acquired. Our journey would again be long delayed if I were to ask you to step off the pathway and listen as I would try to bring together the relevant data on this point which the professionals think we possess. I would begin with the young infant who quickly learns to respond with pleasant gratitude or longing to the person who is his source of food and to ignore the Alters who are irrelevant to that goal. Surely, I would argue, hunger, thirst, and other drives involving comfort and discomfort cause the child to make such a discrimination and then to be motivated to do so. I might continue by pointing to the political and social inequalities we find in every society, so that traditional and non-traditional peoples obviously are motivated to make significant distinctions. On a crowded street Western Egos are not set to judge the persons confronting them unless they are searching for someone; but in the old days, a Ganda man travelling with his wife would have her carry the load so that he could protect both of them after deciding whether an approaching stranger was bent on attack (Roscoe, 1911, p. 23).

II.4   Generality vs. Specificity of Judgmental Skill

Even the early skeptics who reported by and large that American college students could seldom decode facial expressions in photographs or drawings did also note vast individual differences: most of their subjects rendered inaccurate judgments, but a few of them were reasonably accurate (Hunt, 1941). More recently, as the research fashion has turned from skepticism to praise concerning non-verbal communication, the opposite conclusion has been drawn: the degree of accuracy is high, but nobody reports virtually perfect or imperfect judgments (Davitz et al., 1964; Ekman et al., 1972). Indeed, there *may* be differences between types of individuals; perhaps emotions are judged less accurately from speech by the blind (even though, perforce, they are very attentive) and by schizophrenics than they are, respectively, by the sighted and by the normal (U.S.; Davitz et al., 1974, pp. 113–27, 129–42). But, as ever, it depends; thus American female college students *may* perceive some but not all the expressions on the photographs of a gifted actress more correctly than males (Levy & Schlossberg, 1960).

More important, *perhaps* a statistically significant, though not a very impressive, relation exists between the accuracy with which emotions are judged from voices and from facial expressions, musical phrases, or abstract art (Usual; Davitz et al., 1964, pp. 31–42, 87–100, 180). A reasonable interpretation is that some Egos *may* be more skillful than others in decoding emotions on the basis of varying information. The consensus, nevertheless, seems to be that there is "no evidence of a general ability" to predict accurately the attributes of others (England, students; Mehryar, 1969); the skill is said to be neither completely general nor specific (Allport, 1937, p. 512; Taft, 1955). Indeed, persons who skillfully diagnose Alters may make very poor predictions concerning them, and vice versa, perhaps because diagnosis and prediction are really different kinds of tasks. In short, situations can be discovered in which generality or specificity is demonstrated (U.S., medical students; Crow & Hammond, 1957), especially when a sophisticated mathematical analysis is feasible (Cronbach, 1955).

In addition, the problem of specificity and generality involves not only the source but also the kind of judgment that is made. *Perhaps*, for example, the skills required to characterize other persons and to predict their behavior are negatively correlated (Usual; Fancher, 1967).

II.5 The Subjectivity of Imagination

Imagination and its components are indisputably subjective. Identification, for example, may refer not to observable behavior as such, when Ego deliberately dresses like Alter or tries to behave like him, but to Ego's effort to feel and think the way Alter appears to him to feel and act, a consequence of which may also be overt behavior (Bronfenbrenner, 1958, p. 128). Ego may try to imagine how he himself would feel if he were Alter or simply how Alter feels at a given moment or in a particular situation (Aderman & Berkowitz, 1970). Imagination occurs in human beings because, as was pointed out long ago (G. H. Mead, 1934, p. 254), each man—perhaps unlike any other animal—"has the capacity to stimulate others in ways other than those in which he is himself stimulated" (Rose, 1962, p. 7). Empathy is experienced "virtually never" with reference to objects, but undoubtedly "to some extent" whenever an Alter is perceived (Sarbin et al., 1960, pp. 14–15). It is essential in role-playing, when Ego tries deliberately to behave as he believes Alter would behave in some social context (Weinstein et al., 1972). It *may* arise when in objective fact Ego and Alter have similar personalities (Usual; Bender & Hastorf, 1953) or when similar emotions are subjectively but incorrectly assumed. An example of the latter: young children, particularly twins, *may* believe they have fears similar to those of other children who, in reality, do not ascribe those fears to themselves (U.S.; Lazar, 1969). But with equal vigor it may be argued that imagination giving rise to empathy is not only based upon similarity, but may also create the conviction of similarity.

II.6   Sensitivity Traits: The Search

Social scientists are eager to show that criminals are different from non-criminals in ways not associated with crime; energetic persons must have glands, mothers, or childhood experiences distinguishable from those of the lethargic—and, sure enough, the proposition usually turns out to be valid if the researcher collects sufficient data, particularly from large samples, and if he squeezes those data through an innocent computer. In actual fact, however, the computer-established difference between those allegedly possessing and those not possessing a given trait or aptitude stems from comparing the central tendencies of the two groups; even though that difference, according to our notions of probability in which justifiably we must have faith, could not have arisen by chance within certain well-accepted limits, the amount of overlapping between the two groups is ordinarily considerable. And so the finding turns out to be not a truth trumpeted from Mount Olympus but a tendency, often microscopic or picayune which—since it accounts for or explains very little—is not likely to be replicated in another study even derived from American college students. *This is more than cynicism, it is defeatism.*

Yes, though the defeatism springs not only from me but from others; for example, "the literature on personality correlates of the ability to judge emotions is scanty and unclear," moans one competent professional (Tagiuri, 1968, p. 406; italics omitted). "Authoritarianism" should be related, we might think, to sensitivity: those rich in the first attribute may ruthlessly disregard the nuances of others. Indeed, a survey of relevant studies, based mostly on American college students, offers what appears at first to be a hopeful generalization: "authoritarians seem to differ from nonauthoritarians in the characteristics they attribute to others." But in the very next sentence the same writers more accurately depict the true state of affairs: "Of the specific patterns about social perception derived from authoritarianism, there is little evidence supporting specific relationships" (Kirscht & Dillehay, 1967, p. 64). Even when there is a relation between the two, other factors *may* also affect the outcome, including not only Ego's but also Alter's attributes (Usual; Rabinowitz, 1956; Scodel & Freedman, 1956). A similar concept, dogmatism, which seems on the surface to be closely related to authoritarianism, *may* function quite differently (Germany,

Belgium, Italy, & Netherlands, adolescent students; Doise, 1969). Judgmental accuracy *may* likewise be related to some traits, such as the need to affiliate or dominate, but not to others, such as deference or heterosexuality for which just as strong a case could be made (Usual; Chance & Meaders, 1960). A trait—the need to affiliate just mentioned —*may* be linked to judgmental accuracy not always but when Ego believes that Alter values such accuracy (Usual; Exline, 1960). And, finally, the ability to judge the emotional content of speech from its non-verbal elements *may* be unrelated to a variety of paper-and-pencil tests (U.S., graduate students; Davitz, 1964, pp. 57–60). These chaotic findings are not unexpected if one believes that skill or sensitivity to others is not general and that the abilities to judge oneself, one's friends, and strangers are unrelated, for then how can one expect to find an invariant relation between skill and personality (Usual; Vernon, 1933)?

Conceivably, too, sensitivity may be either a cause or an effect of personality traits and behavior. Consider, if you have the patience, this finding: American children who are more sensitive to the emotion displayed on videotape *may* be more altruistic in word and deed than those less sensitive (Fry, 1976). The correlation, you agree, could be argued either way, or both ways. *What do you mean?* Sensitivity leads to altruism because it produces keener appreciation and sympathy; altruism requires sensitivity because Ego must be able to perceive those in distress; or there can be a little bit of both. *You mean a spiral?* Ah, yes.

II.7   Sensitivity Traits: A Proposal

Before offering the defense, I take courage from one view that patient digging has uncovered: "although there is no reliable evidence that the judge's personality is related to his accuracy, there are clear suggestions that several personality characteristics have some influence upon the types of judgments he makes" (Warr & Knapper, 1968, pp. 238–9). "*Some* influence," you note, does not provide a dependable pathway. But the defense:

1. *Intelligence and Style* (Pathway I.b). The significant effects of experience, the discussion of which I postpone until later (Pathway 6.a), can be achieved only if Ego is capable of selecting components from the past likely to prove useful in the present and the future. Here are some scattered wisps: intelligence-test scores *may* be linked *with* judgments concerning the intelligence of others (U.S., adults; Wiggins

et al., 1969) and positively *with* the ability to judge oneself and complete strangers, though negatively *with* the ability to judge friends and associates (Usual; Vernon, 1933). A more inclusive ability, overall competence to deal with the environment, is said to include "effective behavior in relation to other people" (White, 1960). Variability in modes of perception *may* be associated with variability in evaluating others (Usual; Gruenfeld & Arbutnot, 1969) and with a preference for one form of behavior rather than another (Usual; Crandall, 1969). Readiness to change judgments about Alter after securing additional information *may* be weakly correlated with simple rather than complex judgments (Usual; Leventhal & Singer, 1964). The ability, mentioned above, to identify emotions from the non-verbal components of speech *may* be somewhat impressively associated with verbal intelligence; and that an intellectual or cognitive process may be involved is suggested by the tendency for this ability *perhaps* also to be modestly related to the ability to differentiate auditory stimuli, skill in using abstract symbols, and a knowledge of vocal characteristics (U.S., children, college, and graduate students; Davitz, 1964, pp. 31–38, 60–86). But there are also negative findings; for example, between various perceptual measures and judgmental skill (Usual; Danielian, 1967). *Not very convincing evidence and, as you say, quite scattered.* In addition, I could add that every single one of the above relations has to be surrounded with if's, but's, and exceptions. A component of conventionally measured intelligence, viz., speed, moreover, has an unknown relation to accuracy in judging Alter. On an ancedotal level I believe that some persons are like you: they judge others rapidly and they are certain they are right, but are willing and able to revise their judgments. Others are like me: stuck in ruts; sometimes judging quickly, sometimes not; never certain of their judgments; changing very reluctantly.

2. *Sociability* (Pathway I.b). Much that can be said in behalf of this factor will be expressed when we consider the general pathway of attitudes (Pathway 4). Here I would only raise the possibility that the perceptions of a misanthrope or misogynist concerning Alter are likely to be different from those of a lover of human beings and therefore. . . . *Less skillful?* No, not necessarily. Instead let me suggest that Egos dependent either upon others for emotional reasons or upon the physical environment for bodily cues *may* be more attentive toward other persons and hence more discriminating than those who are more independent in those respects (U.S., children & adults; Witkin et al., 1962, pp. 147–49). Naturally a spiral is also possible: the more sensi-

tive may find dependence either more convenient or more desirable.

3. *Self-knowledge* (Pathway I.1). This ancient, venerable virtue, however, can no longer be uncritically accepted as a result of the revelations by the Sage of Vienna from whom we have also learned that insight into the self is not easy to come by. *Is there any reason to believe that Ego must have access to his own unconscious before judging others accurately or acutely?* At the extremes the relation between insight and sensitivity to others may be very intimate: an Ego with supreme self-knowledge and one with paranoid delusions about himself is likely to be, respectively, skillful and unskillful in judging Alters. For the vast regions in-between where most of us find ourselves, the relation zigzags back and forth. Egos who are adjusted and hence presumably, though not certainly, realistically aware of their own assets and liabilities *may* be more likely to assume a greater degree of similarity between themselves and other members of their group than those who are maladjusted (Usual & military groups; Fiedler et al., 1959). This assumption of similarity probably facilitates empathic imagination and hence, if it is in fact true, better understanding. Also if Ego's general mental attitude toward himself and the outside world is favorable, he is perhaps better able to judge others without allowing his own biases too greatly to intrude. Egos "free from excessive complaints, worries, and self-doubts," for example, *may* judge Alters more sympathetically and accurately than those without such relative freedom, but the differences have to be wrenched out of a long, long schedule containing so many items that the discovery of these particular differences is not a cosmic event (Usual; Hjelle, 1969). Our assumption concerning the relation of self-knowledge to personality and hence to judgmental skill, finally, may be too glib: a discrepancy between Ego's self-image and his ideal self *may* not be a symptom of maladjustment, as you might think, but of growth and intelligence (U.S., children; Katz & Zigler, 1969).

4. *Ability to manipulate Alter,* a special variant of the Ego-Alter relation (Pathway I.c). Just as Freud sought to facilitate a sense of relaxation and freedom from restraint by placing his patients upon a couch and himself behind them so that they would not be influenced by his facial reactions and other non-verbal modes of expression, so a skillful Ego in face-to-face situations knows how to conduct himself in order to elicit the information or behavior he desires from Alter. Obviously manipulation assumes many forms, one significant one being intervention at an appropriate moment (Pathway II.3). Psychia-

trists, particularly psychoanalysts, know that they must often wait a long while before presenting Alter with a challenge or a diagnosis: first the patient must attain sufficient insight or at least be in the proper mood to receive new information. Although there are no certain advisable pathways to follow, some may seem to have face value, such as the dictum that an anxiety-producing question is not likely to prove effective in yielding new information when Alter is suffering from anxiety. Similarly there is a time for joking and a time for seriousness, and somehow the inquiring Ego intuits or learns from experience when either interval is optimally at hand. This timing component of sensitivity is so delicate that I am at least tempted to agree with you that it must be innate. But only tempted. For I can recall that neophytes in the psychoanalytic trade discover, by subjecting themselves to the control analyses of experienced analysts, that one of the most potent and agonizing weapons to elicit repressed or semi-repressed material from an analysand is silence, silence stark and unbroken, which few of us have sufficient bravery to endure without breaking into speech. *You speak the truth.*

5. *Patience and restraint* (Pathway 6.b). Suppose Alter displays aggression against Ego or some of the persons or values Ego holds in high esteem. Ego can of course merely perceive the aggression and incorporate it into his conceptualization of Alter; he may also have a theory that the aggression results from some prior or continuing frustrations he himself has imposed upon Alter or that it originated elsewhere and is being displaced upon him. A calm analysis of this sort requires skill in manipulating the Ego-Alter relation: instead of yielding to an impulse to be counter-aggressive toward Alter—for hostility is usually frustrating—Ego utilizes the behavior as a source of information. Here is an advisable pathway: the skillful Ego regulates or curbs his own impulses in a way most likely to elicit maximum information from Alter. *And that is no easy task.* Even for a professional. An impatient Ego, moreover, may reach a decision before he has adequate information concerning Alter; or, if it be true that "human beings prefer an amount of cognitive uncertainty which matches their processing ability" (Usual; Munsinger & Kessen, 1964), then an Ego tolerating uncertainty concerning Alter at a given moment is more likely to acquire additional data about Alter than one less tolerant. *How much information does Ego require before he is willing to pass judgment, whether rapidly or slowly, with certainty or uncertainty?* Individual differences loom large, and they *may* reflect other personal-

ity attributes, such as a tendency to think abstractly or concretely (Usual; Ware & Harvey, 1967) or to be more greatly influenced by facts received initially rather than subsequently (Usual; Asch, 1952, pp. 212–13). Possibly, however, the critical factor here is not patience but intelligence. For sensitivity *may* rest upon the ability to utilize information at one's disposal or to remember and then profit from these data (presumably Usual; Atzet, 1969).

6. *Practice* (Pathway 6.a). Sensitivity and skill in judging others are propensities which, as the Samoans say (M. Mead, 1930, p. 81), are like swimming and must be learned. I admire your sensitivity to works of art which is far greater than mine, especially when—not always patiently—you try to help me see through your eyes what I have failed to see through my own. Your skill is greater because your milieu has been different, and in that milieu you have always been encouraged and taught to make such observations, whereas I grew up in an impoverished atmosphere in comparison with yours. I can never be as sensitive as you in these respects, although we may reduce the distance between us. Very simple interactions between two persons *may* enable them gradually to acquire sufficient information to make more accurate predictions concerning each other's behavior (Usual; Hammond et al., 1966).

II.8   The Development of Sensitivity

Piaget (e.g., 1969) has repeatedly confirmed common sense by offering evidence indicating that younger children are egocentric, which must mean they need not at the outset be sensitive to the Alters who feed and protect them. In comparison with younger children, for example, older ones *may* employ a greater number of more highly organized concepts to describe peers of the same or opposite sex and those who are liked or disliked, but they *may* also tend to use fewer concrete and egocentric concepts and more abstract and non-egocentric ones (U.S.; Scarlett et al., 1971); hence their reports may be longer and are likely to cover a wider range of activities, to evaluate Alter's perceived attributes somewhat differently, and to stress Alter's attitude toward himself and other persons to a greater degree (Soviet Union, children, adolescents, & young adults; Bodelev, 1968, 1970–1). Very young children *may* pay closer attention to "accessories," such as a hat, than to facial expressions in judging photographs, but by the age of eight or so their attention may shift from the former to the latter (France; Lévy-Schoen, 1964, pp. 68, 77). *Perhaps* sensitivity to happiness in others may develop sooner than sensitivity to fear (U.S., children; Borke, 1971). Learning the descriptive categories of a society (e.g., kindness: U.S., kindergarten to college; Baldwin & Baldwin, 1970), utilizing explanatory concepts (e.g., causality: U.S. & India, 3rd & 6th grade children; Walker et al., 1971), organizing impressions of others (e.g., while helping or cheating: U.S., children & adolescents; Rosenback, 1968), or evaluating Group Alters (e.g., nations: U.S., children & adolescents; Signell, 1966) develops slowly in children, often with great difficulty, and perhaps at rates that vary from society to society. As they grow older, children *may* be better able to identify photographs of their classmates when parts of their faces are concealed (U.S.; Goldstein & Mackenberg, 1966). Between the ages of 20 and 40 men *may* use different categories to judge women's faces (Usual; Secord & Muthard, 1955), doubtless as a result of their changing interests and intervening experiences. And of course practice.

Ego, with all the psychological equipment in his behavior and understanding potentials, proceeds, it may be assumed, to judge Alter, several Alters, a Group Alter, or himself. From some standpoints that person or persons is just another stimulus in the external world to which he responds as he does to sticks and stones, gazelles and zebras, musical chords and ambulance sirens, caresses and itches, poetry and comic strips. When his verbal ratings of them are analyzed statistically, they all seem to fall into the same three categories concisely labelled evaluation, potency and activity—and, mirabile dictu, essentially the same trio emerges in 20 different cultures (Osgood et al., 1957, pp. 180–86; Osgood, 1969).

Do you not think that calling Alter a stimulus, just another stimulus, robs him of his dignity by placing him in the same category as animals and machines? Not at all, for many, many reasons. Stimuli differ in complexity: an inspired painting and a hideous modern town, a rondo played by talented musicians and the cacaphony of strident quarreling voices, a rose with an appealing name and one with the label of "Squashed Skunk" (Ogden & Richards, 1936, p. 45), each pair, it is worth noting, reaches us through the same modality, before we react and evaluate them differently. The fact that Alter is infinitely more complicated than many other stimuli and that he often stimulates not a single modality but many modalities ought to be a tribute sufficiently sweeping to impress you. Of course human beings differ from objects —two professionals once suggested that they are more mobile, more capricious, and more unpredictable (Krech & Crutchfield, 1948), a common sense observation if ever there was one—and therefore complete or incomplete photographs of persons *may* be recognized more quickly than those of objects perceived during brief exposures of the stimuli (U.S.S.R., children & university students; Bodelev et al., 1972). In addition, human reactions to human or non-human stimuli are not completely mechanical. A machine has no alternative except to respond to the stimulus or the series of stimuli activating its operation. A person may often be like a machine—he responds to the irritant on his nasal membranes and willy-nilly sneezes—but more often than not he is active and seeks out stimuli. Look, we cannot get bogged down in metaphysics; when I call Alter a stimulus I merely restate the deterministic hypothesis (Pathway II.2) concerning which I have already rung from you a measure of assent for pragmatic reasons. I repeat again, you are not in a trap, you are moving down an ancient pathway to try to discover, as I am, where this kind of thinking leads and whether it is fruitful and useful. Alter, then, is a stimulus behaving in a particular context: these are the three variables to be dissected.

1.a   Alter

What can Ego know about Alter as a single individual? He may examine him as an abstraction: he catches a glimpse of him at a distance, sees a photograph of his face, hears his voice over a telephone, glances at a sample of his handwriting. These are expressions of him which can be directly perceived and interpreted. Many, maybe most, Egos may be willing and able to rate a hypothetical stranger when they only know, as previously suggested, that his name is Jim; or they may judge him with apparent discrimination on the basis of a single attribute such as occupation and, of course, sex (Usual; Rosenkrantz et al., 1968; Friedland et al., 1973).

A truism afflicting us all is that, just as Egos differ in skill and sensitivity or in imagination, so Alters can be judged with varying degrees of dispatch. Some persons are more "transparent" than others: they *may* more readily express or betray their emotions, thoughts, or intentions (Israel, workers & foremen; Foa, 1958), or in some way, either through words or deeds, they *may* provide more information about themselves (Usual; Pyron, 1965). Some of these differences are to be attributed to cultural influences (Pathway I.a). The norm of the society may be to gesticulate loudly or to appear passive and immobile, and consequently the meaning of bodily expressions can be correctly apprehended by those living in, or acquainted with that society. Others must be traced to Alter's own life history; unconsciously or unwittingly he has learned that giving vent or not giving vent to the outward expression of what is within him proves to be rewarding or punishing (Pathway I.b). Perhaps very young children, being without guile, can be judged more easily than sophisticated adults, though again this may not always be so: their scattered impulses, which may be expressed less guardedly than those of adults, are also less well organized and hence more elusive to comprehend as a total package. Whether or not Alter can be readily judged depends not only on his personality but also on the particular attributes being judged (Postscript 1.1: Easy vs. Difficult Judgments). Both must be taken into account, and their relative importance—the weight to be assigned to each—varies from Ego to Ego, from Alter to Alter, and from situation to situation.

Why do people reveal information about themselves? Obviously some information is involuntarily communicated: height, hair color, nose and ear shape, language, etc. Many non-verbal symbols which function as stimuli for Ego are likewise produced unintentionally. A sudden shift in illumination or a very loud sound may cause Alter to blink; no matter how hard he tries, he cannot prevent himself from stuttering, blushing, or quivering; or of course he—or she—blushes, much to his or her own embarrasment. On the other hand, he can control numerous symbols that convey information about himself. He points to the swatch he likes best; he keeps his eyes riveted on Ego to prove he is attentive; he—or perhaps she—pouts his or her lips to suggest unwillingness or inability to be cooperative. Such non-verbal communication, furthermore, may be deliberately learned like language, as when an adolescent girl in the West is taught to "sit like a lady" or when a Japanese host conveys harmony and tranquility through the ceremony attached to tea-drinking.

Usually, moreover, Alter's motives play a role in the information he conveys to Ego. To conceal oncoming advancing age, he may dye his hair, she may use cosmetics. Why did Alter originally write the diary fame-seeking scholars are trying to analyze, why has he gone to a psychiatrist, why is she carrying on a conversation with you? Obviously what Alter wrote, does, or says must reflect in part his own reasons for selecting the data to be communicated. When Alter knows he is being observed or assessed, what kind of impression does he try to create upon Ego? We have here a problem appearing on most pathways: the validity vs. the objectivity of the sample of Alter's behavior that Ego views (Pathway 8.a).

To achieve objectivity, the clinical professional is inclined to test persons in standardized situations and in a standardized manner which includes giving them uniform instructions. Under these conditions objectivity is likely to be achieved in the sense that any competently trained investigator can probably obtain similar results. But Alters may react quite differently to the testing situation: for some, a fair behavioral sample may be obtained, for others, a very atypical one (Pathway 1.2).

Then there is deception: Alter can or may deliberately conceal information about himself or play a role at variance

1.1   Deception   with his "true" self or actual intention. Deception can be considered a naturalistic pathway when an Ego-expositor thus explains how Ego has been duped; it is an advisable pathway for an Ego who assumes the probability of its occurrence in some form and hence is on his guard. In many situations Alter would "fake good" in order to create a favorable impression or "fake bad" in order to conceal desirable traits whose revelation at the moment would work to his disadvantage (Usual; Edwards, 1957, pp. 53–58). Some persons *may* even know the kinds of responses they should make on a standardized questionnaire in order to appear in a favorable light and thus achieve a goal, such as obtaining a job (Germany, students; Hoeth & Gregor, 1964). Deception can be ably accomplished by gifted actors on the stage; practice and talent enable them to mask their internal feelings and convey an external facade befitting the action of the play, or else they succeed in evoking within themselves the appropriate feelings which then mediate their external posture. Few nonactors in real life, it appears, possess this gift; somehow a bit of their behavior may betray, especially on a non-verbal level (Cozby, 1973), whatever it is they are trying, consciously or unconsciously, to conceal. Freud again has taught us well when he analyzed the slips of tongue committed by his patients and acquaintances, so well that those of us educated in the West have been forever stripped of our innocence and hence perceive dark and devious impulses behind Alter's every lapse. Alter's success at deception or role-playing depends not only upon his own gifts but also upon Ego's skill and prejudgments. In addition, we must not overlook a special form of deception, ingratiation, in which Alter's desire to please or influence Ego may sometimes be matched by Ego's own wish to be flattered (Postscript 1.2: Ingratiation). Are you horrified by the spiral of Ego-Alter-Ego and then of Alter-Ego-Alter?

What kinds of persons are likely to deceive? This is a fair question: I am not like you, I judge real persons, not abstractions. Perhaps the very ambitious, those whose need for achievement is so strong that they can overlook their own and their society's ethical principles; perhaps the insecure who are seeking to make favorable impressions upon almost everyone in their milieux; perhaps the aggressive who thus sadistically punish those with whom they come in contact. Self-disclosure *may* be related to traits such as cooperativeness, emotional stability, being happy-go-lucky, and reflectiveness (Usual; Pedersen & Higbee, 1969); but in a given situation (Pathway I.5) it *may* also depend upon whether Alter likes Ego and whether Ego in turn has provided information about himself which then may affect Alter's liking of him (Usual; Worthy et al., 1969). And of course Ego may deceive himself: he fails to disclose himself to himself. *I have a theory about self-deception: only the exceptionally weak or the exceptionally strong deceive themselves.* Possibly.

Can you conceive of situations in which Alter must be free from deception? Third-degree methods in all countries—including the democratic as well as the fascist and the communist—are based on the assumption that violence or the threat of violence is an efficient pathway to the kind of truth the inquisitor seeks. Even this technique, however, cannot avoid error: the confession obtained by the Ego with a whip may be false and motivated only by Alter's desire to avoid the misery of the moment. So-called brain-washing provides little or no insight into the personalities or the deceiving capacities of the victims since what they say or do after being subjected to alternating punishments and rewards results from what they have learned during the indoctrination and is far removed from what they originally believed or did. It is noteworthy, however, that some persons are more susceptible to this kind of forced learning than others.

I act naturally when I am alone, when I am with friends or persons I trust, when I do not have to pose for anybody's benefit or for some objective of my own. Under these ideal, pleasant circumstances I am free from the normal pressures that might cause me to deceive. All right, you are an authority on yourself, but must I accept what you have just said? Surely you cannot deny that on occasion you act unnaturally—though feeling furious or faint, you press a button that releases your sparkling charm in front of guests or strangers—and you deliberately seek to ingratiate yourself with persons you would impress or feel you must impress. Would you unmask everyone who in the face of adversity behaves bravely in order to spare his immediate associates the misery he himself is experiencing? I am saying, you must understand, that there are many you's and that the one on stage at a given moment may be the one called for by the setting: no one is completely consistent, the choice of one role demands some deception if the behavior linked to the other roles is to be suppressed (Postscript 1.3: Decreasing Deception).

What of self-deception? If Alter seldom knows himself, how can he possibly deceive Ego? Yes, Alter may wish to be honest and then unwittingly he may deceive Ego: he may wish to deceive and then unconsciously vent his true self or motive. Freud, again more than anyone in our time, summarized and added to human wisdom when he indicated explicitly and convincingly the long catalogue of devices each of us uses to achieve self-deception: rationalization, repression, denial, displacement, symbolism—the terms are legend, redundant, impressive. And we know from the same source and from our own introspections how important these processes are in the service of bolstering self-esteem and hence in preventing unhappiness, madness, and suicide. *When you say that I do not know myself, you are admittedly becoming metaphysical; or at least I would make that charge until you produce some kind of objective criterion.* Do I know you better than you know yourself if I can predict more accurately what you will do or think or feel in some future situation? The psychiatrist who says that therapy must continue, even when the patient himself believes he is cured, is making such an assertion. Professionals are of the opinion that self-disclosure depends not only upon interpersonal relations and interpersonal trust but also upon a long series of prior events which they summarize under the heading of personal growth. I am sorry I have had to tangle with you on this point, and I immediately express that sorrow by piercing myself with the same stiletto: in some ways I think you know me better than I know myself. Still. . . . *Are you removing the blade?* If I know that this is so, do I then not have more insight into myself than into you?

Ego's advisable pathway, I conclude, is slippery: some deception by Alter, some self-deception is inevitable; try to detect as much as you can.

1.b Behavior

Behavior refers to any of Alter's actions that can be perceived by Ego, and includes language, bodily movements, and even affection and thoughts which somehow can be monitored. Whether that behavior is perceived directly through Ego's own sense organs or indirectly as a result of a mechanical device or projective test or as a result of a report by someone else, the problem of sampling arises. Sampling is a pathway which, though containing a ghastly, unavoidable collection of thickets, also serves the function of being a convenient though hazardous shortcut. Different modes of assessment

1.2 *Sampling*   sample different kinds of behavior and hence have varying degrees of utility and validity. In general, Ego must obtain a representative sample of Alter's behavior before passing profound judgment upon him.

But what is meant by "profound"? If Alter performs one heroic act during his entire existence, is that not more significant than a representative sampling of his behavior that enables us to decide whether he typically puts on his left shoe before the right, or prefers raisins to prunes? You are right either because "significance" means for you some external criterion or because you do not happen to care whether that heroic act is characteristic of Alter as a person. Otherwise you and any Ego must constantly reach some conclusion concerning whether the glimpse you catch of Alter really represents a fair sample of him. Or again and again, for example, Alter provides both verbal and nonverbal information about himself; which is more typical of him? Do actions speak louder than words? *I adopt your manner, it all depends.*

Since the Ego-Alter relation (Pathway I.c) so often affects the sample of behavior Alter offers, professionals sometimes use one-way vision rooms to observe their subjects: behind the innocent mirrors one or more Alters are viewed, and through concealed microphones their spoken words can be heard and recorded. The Alters thus spied upon are not self-conscious and therefore, it is hoped, reveal a truer sample of themselves than they do in the presence of Ego. Still, it may be contended, Alter's behavior in front of Ego is also part of his behavioral repertoire and for many purposes is more important than the way he appears when he believes he is not being watched. Which sample should Ego note? An Alter with a tendency to react impulsively cannot be appraised validly, it might be contended, if Ego observes him only on one occasion. Intelligence tests often suffer from such a deficiency. But the very impulsive behavior which prevents Ego from obtaining a reliable sample is in itself significant; for how else can impulsiveness be gauged except by determining whether or not Alter impulsively replies to questions or impulsively behaves on a test or in a real-life situation? Likewise if Alter delays his responses, he may perform poorly according to the norms of a standardized intelligence test which emphasizes speed; or in a given period of testing or of behaving in a real-life situation he may exhibit very little of his repertoire. In either instance, however, he is again displaying significant behavior with reference to the trait in question. Ego is thus really caught between the devil and the deep, deep sea; and only under utopian conditions—a large sample of Alter's potentiality and behavior over an extended period of time (Pathway 0.1)—can he extricate himself, poor chap.

With increasing age, less and less information about affection and thoughts is externalized through the body and through words. The very young child, when disturbed or happy, squirms all over; whereas a poker-faced adult may conceal his chagrin or joy except, for example, for a scarcely noticeable movement of his lower lip. In our society, perhaps in most or in all societies, we also learn to be less outspoken as we mature. A child may indicate directly and dramatically that he would go to a toilet, an adult in the West usually uses all sorts of subterfuges and euphemisms before departing discretely (Pathway I.7). To the thesis, already stated, that some Alters can be judged more easily than others, I would add what is almost a corollary, viz., that each Alter reveals himself more directly in some way than in others (Allport, 1961, p. 469). We both believe that one person says more with a scowl than with words, another reveals less in his mode of hand-shaking than in his position on a chair, etc. Such knowledge has been hard to come by and represents not only Alter's propensities but also our own experience in ascribing them to him and others. Alter's revelation about himself, consequently, is a function not only of him but of us.

In the last section it was suggested that deception is easier or more likely to occur on the conscious than on the unconscious level. A complementary proposition must be that Alter may unintentionally reveal, at least to some sensitive Egos, unconscious impulses, whereas he may deliberately prevent outsiders from becoming acquainted with those of which he is aware. You are able to a certain extent to conceal your disparaging reactions to rudeness or, for that matter, your opinion about me at a given moment, but your blush after a compliment is not completely under control. Ego, however, must be especially sensitive if he is to relate involuntary tics or frowns to unconscious compulsions or impulses.

Neither the professionals nor we can settle the question as to whether it is more or less difficult to judge Group Alters than a single Alter. *You have been talking so long about a single Alter that I am surprised to find you suddenly referring again to Group Alters.* I am guilty, let me rectify this a bit (Postscript 1.4: Perceiving Group Alters).

Ego is affected by Alter's effect upon himself. *Perhaps* only a super-human Ego or a real masochist, for example, is likely to have a favorable impression of an Alter from whom punishments and not rewards in a liberal or figurative sense are generally received (Usual; Griffitt, 1969b). When Ego knows or thinks he knows Alter's opinion of him, his own judgment of Alter may be affected (called a Reverse Judgment on Pathway II); an Ego believing Alter to be friendly, for example, *may* then feel friendly towards him (Usual; Murstein, 1958). Subtleties appear. The precise ways in which Alter asks Ego for assistance *may* lead Ego to pass favorable or unfavorable judgments (Usual; Lerner & Lichtman, 1968). *Of course, of course.* How will Ego judge an Alter who intrudes when Ego is engaged with someone else? If Ego is *en rapport* with that other person and has certain personality traits, and if the intruder chooses to participate in the ungoing activity, Ego may not judge him too harshly (Usual; Heiss, 1963).

As a consequence of the Ego-Alter relation (Pathway I.c) and of the previously mentioned tendency for many Alters to ingratiate themselves with Ego, one advisable pathway in particular becomes relevant (Pathway 6.b): the kind of detachment Ego must usually strive to achieve in judging Alter should include, if possible, the minimizing of Alter's effect upon himself as he renders judgment. To find this pathway, however, often demands godlike qualities even I do not possess. With feedback, detachment is particularly difficult to attain (Postscript 1.5: Feedback Complexities).

1.c   Context

The meaning of a word varies with the sentence in which it is embedded, a medium gray looks whitish against a dark background and darkish against a white one, a man is known by the company he keeps —illustrations of the supreme effect of context are almost as numerous as—and you could supply a brilliant, original metaphor, but I shall say only that they are exactly as numerous as the total array of stimuli in the external world. Unquestionably and similarly Alter as stimulus is embedded in a context in which Ego may also be embedded and to which he certainly reacts. Nothing very metaphysical is involved. I am only saying in effect, both literally and figuratively, that the punishment does not always fit the crime, rather its severity *may* also be dependent upon the identity of both the defendant and his victim

(Usual; Landy & Aronson, 1969), for the accused is appraised in the context of events.

Beneath the banner of context, a trio of German psychologists in the twenties pleased themselves and stimulated many of us by maintaining ingeniously and breathlessly that the whole is more than the sum of its parts since those parts—or, rather, I suggest, their functioning—may be determined by the whole (Wertheimer, 1938, p. 2). Change, add, or subtract a single note from a melody and the entire melody may change, just as the tilt of a nose can make one person look handsome, another ridiculous. The organization of stimuli or of a stimulus's components thus can be affected with ease or difficulty, and the interaction of the parts may be so intricate that we never know what will happen until we tinker with them. Even the amount of energy and the state of well-being attributed to human faces appearing vaguely in the negatives of photographs *may* be affected by the room in which they are rated; the rating may be higher in a "beautiful" room and lower in an "ugly" one than they are in a room considered "average" (Usual; Maslow & Mintz, 1956). *Whoever judges faces from negatives?* Sometimes, however, the context may be changed without affecting judgment. When hypothetical persons are appraised, the addition of a single trait name *may* have an appreciable *or a non-appreciable* effect, depending upon whether the description consists of a simple list of trait names, whether the names are embedded in a vignette, and whether the vignette is long or short (England, undergraduates; Warr & Knapper, 1968, pp. 126–32).

Similarly there is no way of knowing whether Ego's skill improves or declines when he observes and passes judgment in the presence of other persons who thus are contextual factors for him. On the one hand, he may become more alert in order not to make a fool of himself or to increase his prestige in their eyes. On the other hand, he may grow nervous and under many but not all circumstances may accept their suggestions either because he believes they are right or because he has good reasons to conform. *What effect, then, does the presence of others have upon Ego's judgment?* Jurors must feel differently when they are hearing a case from the way they do when they are discussing it among themselves at the end of the trial and before reaching a decision. *Surely the professionals have a thing or two to say about this.* Indeed they do, scores and scores of investigations are available (Postscript 1.6: The Effects of Groups).

For many purposes it is often sufficient to perceive the context and to know nothing more about Alter before passing judgment. If you see someone hurrying into a restaurant, you assume he is hungry; if you notice that he drinks one glass of water after another, you conclude that he is thirsty; and if he is young and has his arm around a girl, you have the privilege of projecting onto him whatever you yourself experience under the circumstances. *But these are very crude inferences, no matter how important they are from a practical standpoint; they stem from Ego's knowledge not only of basic drives that approach the physiological but also of the situations in which those drives are likely to be expressed.*

What I have said, however, remains true even when the behavior is less physiological. That Alter is boasting about his accomplishments: is he, therefore, a boastful person? Ego's reply probably has to take into account the context of the boasting: is Alter trying to impress someone, is he desperate? An admittedly sentimental illustration: outside my window, in Germanic South Tyrol, where I am typing these thoughts, I see a boy of about six and his father. The father is scything a field; the boy is trying to rake the clover together so that it can more easily be heaped into a basket which the man will carry into the barn, hopefully before the rain begins again; both of them are wearing blue aprons, a symbol of Tyrolean patriotism to be displayed aggressively before the Italians since the region is part of Italy. What can I say about the boy without speaking to him? From the expression on his face, from the eagerness with which he works, I believe he must have deep affection for his father; and from the context at hand I might also add that he must identify with his father, he must want to be like him, an ambition he can achieve by wearing similar clothes and by learning to be a good peasant.

Of course in all these instances you or I may be quite wrong: the man hurrying to the restaurant may have just eaten but wants to have a cup of coffee there with a business associate; the drinker may have no ordinary thirst but is suffering from diabetes; the young lover may be trying to display heterosexual impulses in public because he is afraid his peers will discover his homosexual bent; the boasting Alter may be under the influence of an hallucinogenic drug; and the Tyrolean lad may really hate his father for good psychoanalytic reasons and be working hard only to achieve the reward of being taken to see a carnival. *Far-fetched.* I am not so sure. These other possibilities exist, however unlikely they may seem—and few inferences are ever perfect (Pathway I.3). Inferences from context may be as valid or even more valid than those based upon ascriptions involving psychological or physiological assumptions, provided Ego knows what kinds of responses the situation is likely to facilitate or demand (Wallace, 1967). And so two persons may agree that Alter is behaving in a particular context but disagree concerning its effect upon him. Yes, for example, that man is filling out his income tax return, but you have less confidence in the validity of his replies than I. These differences must reflect differences in style within the Ego passing judgment. Quite possibly Ego's appraisal of the context depends upon the correspondence between his evaluation of its effect upon Alter and the effect it has or would have upon himself; thus he may think Alter must be afraid or embarrassed to speak up in front of an audience because he knows or imagines he himself would have those feelings (Pathway II.5). Ego's problem is always that of finding an advisable pathway on which he can judge whether an immediate judgment will suffice (Pathway 5) or whether after reflection (Pathway 6) a secondary judgment is needed (Pathway 7).

In previous sections, especially those in connection with culture and personality (Pathway I.a & b), reference has been made to the roles individuals learn and are then more or less forced to play in particular contexts. Certainly the concept of role provides an advisable pathway for Ego as he seeks to understand Alter's behavior. The discussion of this concept can progress with dispatch, I think, by referring to the clever, brilliant, stimulating tour de force by a sociologist who suggests that Alter's behavior is a function of the role he is compelled to play as a result of the particular context or setting in which he finds himself (Goffman, 1959). His theses I believe are relatively straightforward. Alter behaves according to the rules of the group in which he happens to be at the moment. In so doing he may be engaging in deception. Also, since he is a unique person, he discharges the role at least somewhat uniquely. Upon closer examination of these theses (Postscript 1.7: Role Theory), I think it fair to conclude that Alter's role is just one of the constraints affecting his behavior, however important it is (cf. Pathway 2.c). It would be stretching the concept too far to say that all constraints compel him to play one and only one role. *For example?* Some but not all tasks performed under time pressure *may* yield different or lower scores than those performed at a pace set by Alter (Usual; Siipola & Taylor, 1952; also Germany, children; Bartmann, 1963). It would be equally silly to maintain that the expectations of any reward

1.3 Role

or punishment that influences behavior is a function of the induced role, although a role may simultaneously be involved.

Some professional psychologists and psychiatrists have been caught up in a version of the role-theory boom and have produced their own iconoclastic inversion: the analysis of situations and roles, they say, provides more insight into verbal or non-verbal behavior than postulating the existence of personality traits (Hunt, 1965). What we do, therefore, depends much, much less upon what we are than upon what is demanded of us; look not at Alter's traits but at the rewards and punishments offered somewhat uniquely in each situation. Even intelligence and aptitudes may be specific and not general tendencies. In the jargon of the trade: "Behavior tends to be extremely variable and unstable except when stimulus conditions and response-reinforcement relations are highly similar and consistent" (Mischel, 1968, p. 178). It is, therefore, both unnecessary and defeating, according to this view, to believe that traits intervene between the situations confronting Alter and the responses he makes; it is more fruitful and economic to seek a direct link between the situations and the responses. *Are these academic sophisticates suggesting that we respond only to external pressures and have no guiding principles of our own; what about the soul?* Soul aside, in a sense they are suggesting just that, and they have somewhat impressive supporting evidence that cannot easily be gainsaid. They concede, however, that there are also good reasons why the doctrine of traits has not been abolished; therefore I agree with you and retain the view that postulating traits is both useful and justified (Postscript 1.8: The Attack on Personality Traits).

One special reason for not abandoning the concept of trait is too compelling to be relegated to the postscript. Even the most ardent defender of the situational approach cannot deny the existence of uniformities in a society that may persist sometimes for generations. Culture in the form of traditions, folkways, mores, etc. is embodied in individuals who therefore exhibit the uniformities, sometimes, I agree, in single contexts, but more often in many contexts. These uniformities are the very advisable pathways to be sought when lasting Group Alters (associations, social classes, regions, nations) are judged.

Virtually all the studies suggesting that personality traits are of minor importance or that they are a fiction within the tool kit of the amateur or professional Ego simultaneously indicate significant interaction or spiral effects between those traits on the one hand and the situations, the persons in the situations, or the kinds of responses being measured therein on the other (U.S., boys; Raush et al., 1959). Here is just the kind of evidence needed for an advisable pathway that would improve Ego's judgment concerning Alter. Postulating a trait in Alter by itself may furnish no certain clue to his behavior, just as a knowledge of the situational or role requirements of the context in which the behavior occurs may prove misleading or downright incorrect. What is usually essential is insight into both the trait and the context, viz., the situation with its accompanying role-demands (Pathway I.5). Of course there are extreme instances in which one of the factors rather than their interaction proves crucial. A conscientious religious zealot may follow his principles no matter what he is doing, even in the privacy of his own reveries, and not merely in front of his parishioners. And every sane or sober adult living in a Western society conducts himself in a subdued rather than a boisterous manner when entering a church. Both factors, consequently, must be taken into account and weighed differently as a function of the particular person and the particular situation.

Surely you cannot leave the topic of context without saying something about the fact that there is one question human beings always or eventually raise, no matter who they are, no matter where they live, no matter what the context? Yes? A feeling about the human condition. . . . Trite, you surprise me. *I mean the inevitability of death and hence some preoccupation with that idea.* Ah yes, the idea that death must occur to all men everywhere in any context because the evidence of mortality surrounds them on all sides: they need only reach a slight age to comprehend that they too eventually will perish. Their wish to be immortal must often seem unrealistic. If they are to survive during their own life span, therefore, they must somehow come to accept the fact of pending death. This can be accomplished by repressing the thought of death; by believing in the continued existence of the soul or the reappearance of the body in another form after death; or by providing themselves or by being provided with faith or a set of beliefs concerning the ultimate rationale of existence, whatever their religion or philosophy or that of the society in which they have been reared. To think is to remember, to experience, and to anticipate—and dying must be part of the content. As we grow older, death comes closer and closer, and only a totally repressed fool—yes, I think, in any society, or in any religious order— fails to appreciate this unequivocal fact. It is reasonable, therefore, for Ego to assume, on the basis of his knowledge concerning Alter's age and health, that he contemplates death in some manner ranging from an obsession to indifference and from indifference to longing.

Postscripts

1.1   Easy vs. Difficult Judgments

Undoubtedly an attribute considered abnormal within Ego's society
or by Ego himself is more likely to be perceived than one within the
normal range (Pathway I.7). This would certainly be true of an organic
defect or an epileptic seizure. At the same time a bizarre symptom,
though observed, might not be correctly interpreted if it is outside Ego's
own experience or frame of reference. It is difficult to suppress a sophisticated or supercilious smile when a writer on "esoteric psychology"
contends that persons subscribing to the tenets and self-discipline he
advocates "have a degree of inner development which is immediately
felt by those with whom they come into contact who have the ability
to sense it" (Benjamin, n.d., p. 83), unless we patiently and generously
transcend his doctrines and try to imagine—more generally—what he
conceivably means. He might be saying that Egos are more likely to
comprehend those holding similar beliefs or behaving more or less similarly: ethnocentricity and egocentricity are less hazardous (Pathways
I.2 & 4), when imagination is solidly grounded. A homosexual or saint
may be able to recognize, respectively, another homosexual or saint by
virtue of the fact that both have similar characteristics externally and
internally. From some standpoints this is like looking into a peculiar
kind of mirror and seeing there an image not exactly like oneself but
sufficiently similar. On the other hand, I dare say, each of us is convinced that we are able easily to detect certain undesirable or characteristics just because we do not possess them. Again homosexuality might
be the illustration, but unperversely I prefer one of the popular concepts
of our time, charisma. It matters not whether Ego uses or is even acquainted with the Greek word because he probably knows that certain
persons, especially prominent leaders in public life, are especially attractive to their followers and command their respect and obedience; even
some of their non-followers may recognize this quality. So many Egos
of the same society are likely to agree that a given individual has or
does not have charisma that I am almost willing to assert that this attribute is not distributed normally along a continuum: a woman or man
either has or hasn't it and almost everyone in her or his group concurs.
A characteristic similar to charisma has an old-fashion designation,
probably is employed in the same way, and is never, never out-of-date:
sex appeal.

Let us suppose, however, that, although Alter has charisma according to the considered views of persons competent to judge his magnetism, we do manage to discover someone who disagrees. Perhaps Alter has failed to exhibit in this Ego's presence those traits or bits of behavior associated with charisma in general or at least in Ego's estimation. Or Ego may not have observed Alter's charisma, although it had been certainly on display, either through inattention or lack of knowledge concerning the concept or its equivalent. Possibly, too, Alter expresses charismatic traits or behavior too infrequently for Ego to assign that label to him. For this particular Ego, the charismatic judgment is not easy, but difficult or impossible to pass; hence facility in judging an attribute varies with the capability of the judge and the opportunities available to him.

But which attributes in general can be easily judged? The professionals are not very helpful. One straw: *perhaps* negative attitudes can be communicated more effectively than positive ones (Usual; Zaidel & Mehrabian, 1969), though undoubtedly only under very specialized conditions that cannot be definitely specified. I know you well, yet I am not certain which of your moods I am able most readily to detect when you are silent or, for that matter, when you speak. Somehow I grasp you in your entirety and I do that unsystematically and only after years of experience. Also my knowledge of how to interpret you I think is not transferable to other human beings, or at least it does not seem to be to the best of my intuition. *Don't be too sure.*

1.2   Ingratiation

Ingratiation has been formally defined as "a class of strategic behaviors illicitly designed to influence a particular other person concerning the attractiveness of one's personal characteristics." The propounder of that definition has published a monograph packed with laboratory experiments by himself, his colleagues, his students, and others, most of whom—alas—have been the usual American college students. He has run the gamut from the motives of the ingratiator (acquisition or self-benefit, self-protection under conditions of dependence, receiving indications of "basic lovableness or respectability") to the reactions of the Ego who is the target (ranging from "affection, affiliation, attraction" to "feelings of disgust, moral indignation"). Included, too, are the tactics of the ingratiator which are grouped under three headings: communicating "directly enhancing, evaluative statements" about himself; conforming "in various ways" to Ego's values or behavior;

behaving or describing his own attributes so that they will appear attractive to Ego. Obviously, it seems, the deceptively innocent topic of deception calls into play all the variables displayed in our master chart. In my view, and to a large extent the author's, his experiments reveal three significant trends. First, ingratiation may promote conformity at least on a "public" level. Secondly, the modes of ingratiation may be dramatically affected by the status relation between the ingratiator and Ego (Pathway I.c). In one study, for example, low-status Alters tended to de-emphasize their strengths in important areas and conceal their weaknesses in less important areas, whereas high-status Alters tried to appear approachable and friendly by being modest with respect to unimportant self-attributes and by giving the impression that they agreed on issues irrelevant to their superior status. And, thirdly and most important of all, "there seems to be little room for doubt that the average undergraduate subject [in the U.S.A.] behaves differently in a setting in which he wants to be liked than in a setting in which he is striving to be an accurate informant about himself" (Jones, 1964, pp. 11, 24–25, 34–35, 40, 47–48, 159, 164–66, 192, 194). Do you grasp the impact of that last academically expressed statement? It suggests, to me at least, that normal, respectable students have so well practiced the art of making themselves agreeable to others that at a moment's notice— which means here, after verbal instructions by the investigator whose credibility for the time being they do not doubt (Pathway 2.b)—they adopt that ingratiating role and hence, to some extent, deceive poor Ego. *Why "poor Ego," doesn't he also deceive?* Oh, just a *façon de parler.*

1.3 Decreasing Deception

At first blush it might seem as though Alter's deception is likely to decrease as rapport between Ego and himself increases—and rapport means a favorable Ego-Alter relation (Pathway I.c.). Alter presumably feels free to reveal his "true" self to someone he likes and trusts. *The complete truth?* Much depends, I would think, on the exact nature of the relation. Two lovers may be *en rapport* concerning their immediate feelings of a sexual or friendly affective nature, but they may also try to conceal from each other deeper, more serious motives. Most psychoanalysts and non-psychoanalytic psychiatrists note how difficult or impossible it is for their patients at the outset and often later to follow the basic rule that they must express all that comes into their mind, even though as patients they realize that the rule exists in order to help them uncover and alleviate their neuroses or other difficulties. The psychoanalyst who does achieve transference of a positive sort—the analysand comes to love and respect him—is more likely to obtain more intimate information from his patient. When there is negative transference or when rapport is bad, however, Alter may be so disturbed that he bursts forth with very revealing words or deeds. By and large Alter is relaxed or uninhibited in front of an Ego who is not a threat to him in any way: the two of them are not competing for the same status, and what Alter says or does, he believes, will be revealed to no one. In our society familiarity is asserted to breed understanding and peace, not just contempt, and hence Egos who have been friends for a long time are supposed to be well acquainted with each other. But there are contrary situations in which threats produce anxiety, leading in turn to self-revelations. The amount of information disclosed by persons reluctant to disclose information about themselves *may* depend upon the information disclosed by those with whom they are in contact (U.S. college females; Jourard & Resnick, 1970). And so it all depends, it depends on that Ego-Alter relation (Pathway I.c.). The feeling exists among professional clinicians that often, though not always, the efficient way to decrease deception and to elicit valid information is to tap Alter when he is partially or completely unaware that one or more of his personality traits is being assessed. For when he is interrogated directly about his desires and ambitions, his fears and anxieties, or his orientation toward the past or future, he may erect defenses and provide the replies he believes to be respectable or a credit to himself. But when he is told, in contrast, only to report what he perceives in a series of blots as well as the place in each blot in which he sees what he reports and his reasons therefor; when he is shown a number of drawings and asked in effect to exercise his imagination by telling a story about each; or when he agrees to say quickly the first word or idea that comes into his mind after being confronted with a word or idea or a series of them, he is caught off guard and does not and cannot know what the "right" response should be, or he has no time to fabricate. His responses to the blots, drawings, words, or ideas come from him rather than from the visual or auditory stimuli; in fact, Rorschach plates and Thematic Apperception drawings are deliberately vague and ambiguous. Alter's projective statements are used to make inferences concerning the same or similar processes as those ascertained through a direct approach. If both direct and projective data are obtained from the same Egos, the two assessments are likely to be somewhat, perhaps markedly, different. Are clinicians justified in having greater confidence in the projective than in the direct data? Their argument, I think, is fairly impressive: the reaction to blots or pictures, being spontaneous, may reflect unconscious tendencies and hence reveal how Ego "really" is, whereas that to direct questions must be conscious and defensive.

The methodological problem, however, is not so simple. Projective data by themselves reveal nothing of any significance until the professional makes inferences concerning their significance. It is said, for example, that reporting movement in stationary Rorschach blots is a sign of intelligence. Such as inference stems not only from considering how Ego is reacting to the whole series of blots and to the testing situation but also from actuarial reasoning: in the past movement has been reported more frequently by intelligent Egos than by stupid ones. Of course the inference may be in error for a particular Ego. Data directly obtained, however, may not be free from uncertainties. If I ask you whether you are afraid of the dark and you say no, I must believe that you have understood my question and that with a single word you are both able and willing to summarize all the emotional experiences you have ever had in the dark, which may or may not be so. And so the issue becomes one of evaluating differences not in data but in inferences about data; and inferences, though necessary or useful, are always risky (Pathway 3.c). In addition, while it may be true that the projective situation allows Ego's unconscious greater freedom than the frontal attack, for some purpose his reply to a direct question may provide a more reliable clue not perhaps to a bundle of traits but to specific actions. Taking at face value your assertion that you have *no* fear of meeting strangers allows me to infer correctly that you will in fact not avoid strangers, no matter how much you tremble inside. Although you are afraid, you may wish to prove by deeds the truth of what you assert. In contrast, your response to the Rorschach plates or the Thematic Apperception Test drawings may only suggest some kind of general instability from which a second inference concerning your behavior in front of strangers would be perilously drawn.

Other objective and subjective data also require dangerous interpretations if deception is to be circumvented. Data concerning bodily processes that are objectively measured—brain waves, sweating, heart and respiratory rate—are meaningless until they are interpreted, and then they may be correlated only with crude changes in the organism, such as the intensity but not the type of emotion. The body does not easily reveal its secrets, otherwise data from lie-detectors would be infallible or easily interpretable. Through some mediating mechanism like images or thoughts, all of us can influence even our autonomic nervous systems which ordinarily are not subject to so-called voluntary control; one cannot directly or immediately cloud one's eyes with tears but one can often do just that by imagining oneself in a sorrowful situation. The case for dreams as phenomena providing clues both to the unconscious and neurotic tendencies has been argued convincingly by Freud and his followers. Most Alters on this planet as a whole have not heard of Freud or, if they have, they cannot or will not grasp thought, and hence are willing, often eager, to report their dreams without distortion, especially since they do not comprehend the meaning of what they have dreamt. More often than not, according to the usual Freudian interpretation, however, the Ego in search of a pathway to Alter via his dreams cannot by himself interpret them without Alter's help, which he obtains by having him give his free associations to what he is reporting. Similarly available, and less subject to deception, but requiring some decoding, are other manifestations of the unconscious that Freud stressed: children's play, slips of the tongue, wit, fantasy, day-dreaming.

Professionals who use interviews and questionnaires face another kind of unwitting deception. Many Alters have a tendency to agree or disagree with statements almost regardless of their context when an objective test calls upon them to indicate whether they agree or disagree or whether they consider each item to be true or false; these are, respectively, yea-sayers and nay-sayers, as they have been somewhat flamboyantly but appropriately called (Usual; Couch & Kenniston, 1960). The solution here is the simple one of mixing the items in such a way that agreement and disagreement do not always have the same meaning in terms of what is being measured. There is no easy way, except perhaps through subtle wording, to combat another response tendency of many Alters, viz., to provide what they consider to be the socially desirable response. A purely linguistic example: a hypothetical person *may* be given a more extreme rating when the information is positive rather than negative, and this inclination *may* appear regardless of whether the information is favorable or unfavorable (Usual; Izzett & Leginski, 1971). "You are intelligent" and "you are not unintelligent" are denotatively equivalent but may be, apparently, differentially provocative.

One way to avoid deception is so simple that I am almost embarrassed to mention it: ask Alter only sensible questions, avoid those you know he is either unwilling or unable to answer. Pollsters, for example, realize that Americans are reluctant to disclose details about their incomes or their sexual behavior and hence they usually refrain from seeking such information either blatantly or at all. Adults *may* be able to give reliable demographic information about themselves but what they report about the education and occupation of their fathers *may* be quite unreliable (U.S., Navy enlisted men; Erickson et al., 1971). But then of course Ego may need from Alter the very kind of information he is reluctant to reveal.

We have been speaking as if only Alter could be guilty of deception. But Ego may be deceiving Alter, or he may be deceived by another Alter or by himself. Projective devices are actually forms of deception by Ego to obtain information about Alter or, when devised by professionals for purposes of research, to increase human knowledge. They involve ethical issues of informed consent that I mention here only in passing, knowing full well that someone with your conscience will immediately dwell upon them at length—as I, too, shall later (Pathway 8.c). Then Ego may misinterpret, without being aware of the fact, his own reasons for wanting to understand Alter, or he may mistakenly believe he understands Alter when the reverse is true. Ego, through no fault of his own, may also receive misleading information about Alter from another person or source.

1.4 Perceiving Group Alters

Surely behavior viewed from on high would seem to become proportionately more complicated as the number of persons to be judged increases. Ego may be interested in each of them individually, as professionals are when they bring together small groups of students in a laboratory and there attempt to observe how each one behaves, for example, in the presence or absence of leaders or while being frustrated or otherwise depressed. Under such circumstances more than one observer may be necessary, or else the equivalent of a video-tape is employed so that the separate reactions can be studied leisurely and reliably. In a sports stadium a spectator may focus his attention upon one particular player and ignore the rest of the spectacle.

Come, come, groups cannot be reduced to specific persons. Although obviously they are composed of individuals, it is possible and necessary very often to disregard individual actions and to observe the interaction as a whole—look again, if you would, at the diagram called Multiple Judgments, No. 17, on Pathway II. There is nothing strange about this observation, there is no need to resort to a concept like group mind which was used by some professionals, especially in France, earlier in this century (LeBon, 1921) and which eventually provoked howls of derision among other professionals, particularly in America (F. H. Allport, 1933). We note that one team is playing more skillfully than the other; in saying this, we may single out individual players, yet it is the coordination among them that seems to be leading to victory. And it is the crowd that cheers; yes, some cheer more loudly than others, and some may be silent, yet it is the cumulative shouts of encouragement we hear. Obviously, however, an Ego judging a Group Alter has a host of stimuli he may or may not perceive (Pathway II.4); and he can never hope to perceive them all (Pathway I.3). He may raise questions pertaining only to the group as a whole or at least to modal tendencies: will the crowd become a mob, does the audience seem to be enjoying the play, are Germans more aggressive than Italians, do Catholics more closely adhere to the principles of their church than Protestants? In these instances it is necessary for Ego to have only a general impression of everybody or else focus upon selected aspects of their actions or beliefs, a task that may well be performed with greater dispatch than securing a clinical profile of a single individual. I conclude: in dealing with Group Alters it is both foolish and futile to concentrate totally upon either the group or individual Alters; both may yield valuable information.

There are also uncountable situations in which a kind of Group Alter is observed only piecemeal or in purely symbolic form. A very large group such as a nation or a society is never viewed in its entirety, instead Ego is more likely to come in contact with only a few of its members (Pathway 1.2). More often than not, he receives second-hand information from his peers or one of the mass media, even before he ever has first-hand contact with these groups—if, in fact, he ever does. We have entered again the dark realm of prejudice or attitude (Pathway 4). But we are not alone, for sociologists, anthropologists, and psychologists are faced with the same difficulty when they seek through informants or documents to characterize an entire people in terms of culture or of modal or basic personality.

1.5 Feedback Complexities

The usual infinite regress in the form of feedback appears when Ego judges himself: he experiences, observes, and judges his own behavior in the present, that judgment affects his future behavior, which then may strengthen or change his self-judgment, and so on—on and on.

Generally Ego is the most frequent observer of his own behavior. He is not always the most perfect observer, for—I shall suggest later—the explanatory concepts he uses for himself may differ from those he uses for others. The self-concept, moreover, is often so fragile that it can be affected simultaneously by numerous factors. Outsiders may intervene in the chain. Patients with damaged self-concepts, psychiatric material suggests again and again, have acquired unfavorable information and evaluations concerning themselves at an early age from their parents and peers. When they follow the suggestions of therapists and change their physical appearance (make-up, clothes, weight), American adolescents *may* also modify the conception they have of themselves to either a minor (Cole et al., 1969) or a major degree (Collins, 1972). The self-esteem of American children *may* be greater when their teacher rewards them and generally expresses approval of their behavior during the school than when the reverse is true; but interacting with this one factor *may* be others, such as their sex and mental age, their attitude toward the teacher, and the teacher's method of exercising control (Sears & Sherman, 1964, pp. 4–5).

Ego and Ego-expositors may become embroiled in another infinite regress when they simultaneously seek to comprehend the group to which Ego himself belongs. For Ego-expositors, Ego is an Alter, the context is the group; for himself, he is the Ego influencing the group he is seeking to judge. His judgment affects not only his own behavior but also that of the group and perhaps that of Ego-expositor whose judgment in turn may also affect him and them. *This sounds unreal.* No, you are a spectator at a game, Ego is captain of one team, you as another Ego are watching him as Alter and the two teams as Group Alters; he is frequently judging his team and their opponents (both as individuals and as Group Alters) in order to plan the next play. Your cheers or jeers, based upon your judgment of him and all the others, may affect him, his teammates, the opposing side; his judgments affect the way both teams play and your reactions to what you see.

1.6   The Effects of Groups

Much of the research is concerned not with here-and-now groups but with so-called reference groups, groups to which Ego refers his behavior and from which he secures the values and standards determining his judgment. American college males *may* have a more favorable opinion of a peer when they observe him in the presence of an attractive rather than an unattractive girl who is, they think, his "girl friend" rather than a stranger; and they *may* be convinced that they too will appear more attractive when linked with a beautiful girl, presumably because they assume that she, being beautiful and hence having her choice of males, would select only an attractive companion (Sigall & Landy, 1973). Ego himself makes different judgments as his mental context shifts; thus American police *may* claim to notice personal attributes when they size up a dangerous suspect but they refer more frequently to the situation itself when they recall how they have actually detected danger (Rozelle & Baxter, 1975).

Face-to-face groups are also popular objects of professional research. Decades ago it used to be thought that the mere sight and sound of others or even just the knowledge that others are performing laboratory-type tasks *may* have an incremental effect on quantity and a decremental effect on quality (mostly Usual; May & Doob, 1937). Very recently some professionals have become addicted to what they dramatically call the "risky shift" phenomenon, viz., a tendency for their subjects to agree to a riskier decision (especially regarding hypothetical situations) after discussing the alternatives with their peers than when they make a selection alone in the quiet of their own minds (mostly Usual; Pruitt, 1971). Presumably riskier judgments concerning Alter would emerge under similar circumstances. The rub, though, is that not all persons in a laboratory behave in this manner (some never do, some are inconsistent); indeed even American students *may* not reveal the tendency when they are confronted with a real and not a hypothetical situation (Clement & Sullivan, 1970). Here is but a variant of the hoary problem of individual vs. group decision. When hypothetical Alters are judged under controlled conditions, the evidence points in both directions: sometimes the group decision *may* be superior to that of the individual members (Usual; Cline & Richards, 1961), and sometimes the reverse *may* be so (Usual; Fancher, 1969). Obviously—and I fear that is all we can say—the superiority or inferiority of group decision must be affected by the cultural background of the individuals and their own relevant experience; and, even more obviously, some persons are better judges when alone than when pushed together with others.

If forced at a dagger's point to name the most crucial factor emerging from the investigations of groups as context, I would hesitatingly mention Ego's own judgment concerning how his own peers judge Alter. Is he aware of their impression of Alter and, if so, does he have confidence in that impression (Usual; Luchins & Luchins, 1961)? Does he know or does he think he knows that he himself is in the minority during a group discussion of Alter (U.S., high school; Altman & Mc-Ginnies, 1960)? Do those peers give him slight or distinct signs of approval or disapprovel if he repeatedly expresses his own judgments (Usual; Levy, 1961)? *Aren't you simply saying that he always tries to please or conform?* Not quite, for I offer you another thicket: an Ego who is aware of others' opinion—not only their judgments concerning Alter but their opinions in general—*may* not change his private opinion but may merely conform outwardly in order to win social approval or not to appear different; he may deliberately abandon all semblance of independence and conform more or less mechanically; or he may not pass judgment at all and only agree with the others in order to conform and impress them; he may conform without realizing that his judgment has been affected; or of course he may retain his independence and ignore the others (Usual; Asch, 1952, pp. 465–73).

1.7 Role Theory

The discussion here is confined to Goffman (1959) because he has presented role theory most cogently and convincingly. Behavior is viewed as a "performance" with Alter on stage either alone or in conjunction with other players such as his family or peers. The actors may be in the rear of the stage or downstage: workers conduct themselves differently when they are together on a bus from the way they do on the floor of the factory. The audience has certain expectations the players try to fulfill, as when children exhibit the respect their parents demand. The audience may be deliberately deceived: salesmen communicate with each other in coded expressions in order to swindle helpless customers. The actor may seek to influence the audience by creating a favorable impression, or he may unwittingly display the conduct he has been taught in his society. Any channel of communication can be utilized, from a lifted eyebrow to a perfunctory bread-and-butter letter. This provocative approach to Alter via the concept of role emphasizes at least three major theses that are useful in any analysis of Ego and Alter.

First, we see again that Alter, according to our sociological friend, cannot be perceived in the abstract; the context of his behavior must be appreciated. From that context an Ego who knows the rules of his culture may be able to infer whether the behavior is culturally or idiosyncratically determined (Pathways I.a & b). If Alter is simply conforming, little may be revealed about his behavior other than the fact that, for either an obvious or a subtle reason, he is doing just that. He becomes, perhaps, a more interesting person when he does not conform; and then the challenging question arises as to whether his non-conformity is really anti-social, creative, psychopathic, or some combination thereof (Holt, 1969, p. 581).

Next the role of role playing sends us lunging back into the problem of deception in another form (Pathway 1.1). The obsequiousness of an essentially aggressive waiter in an expensive restaurant must be attributed to the role that the occupation forces upon him and that he wishes to perform to increase his tips. Only by observing him in other contexts, if the opportunity were to arise—as it usually does not—can Ego determine whether that behavior also reflects a personality trait (Pathway 1.2). From Ego's standpoint the neat, conventional appearance of Alter in his law office is a deception if in fact Alter prefers to dress informally and sloppily—and if he does exactly that after working hours. But Alter is not trying to deceive, he is only wearing, as it were, a standard civilian uniform, and Ego ought to know that before he is tempted to call Alter's appearance deceptive. All situations, therefore, require Alter to behave in a particular way and hence neither role playing nor deception in this limited sense can ever be completely avoided. In addition, Ego himself inevitably plays a role vis-à-vis Alter when they are face-to-face. Each may function as a stimulus for the other, each may to some extent affect the role the other plays. Both, therefore, may be playing roles determined by the ways in which they perceive each other (Pathway 1.b). Thus if either feels threatened, he may try to adopt the role that will cause least damage to himself. You must judge her, you think, because she is judging you; you don a mask and become the perfect lady; and she seeks a mask for herself because, wanting to impress you, she finds a role most suited to her judgment of what she thinks you expect of her. Similarly, whether or not Ego seeks to save face in front of Alter. . . . *A form of deception.* This *may* depend upon Ego's sex and of course upon Alter's prestige (U.S., high school; Garland & Brown, 1972).

Our sociological troll, thirdly, recognizes the existence of individual differences when he writes of "discrepant roles" and of variations in "the art of impression management" that may involve "disruption . . . . through unmeant gestures, faux pas, and scenes, thus discrediting or contradicting the definition of the situation that is being maintained" (Goffman, 1959, p. 239). Every role, therefore, is discharged in a somewhat unique way, just as Hamlet or Tartuffe is played differently by each actor assaying the part. Some persons conform more readily and fully than others to the role requirements of the context (Pathway I.7).

The way Alter discharges his role at a given moment may fluctuate for reasons not to be found totally in the role requirements of the situation. He is probably subject to moods; like you, for example, he may change as his energy level fluctuates, bouncing after a good night's sleep or feeling discouraged and even contemplating suicide when weary and discouraged. He is likely to be affected by the presence of Ego or—in a formal assessment situation—by Ego's surrogate, such as a paper-and-pencil test. Investigators of operant conditioning have demonstrated quite rigorously a fact we have all known. . . . *Who is the "we" of whom you speak?* We have known since the time of Adam or ever since we acquired a dog or cat that the emission of gentle praise in the form of an "ah" or a not polite reproof in the form of an "ugh" or a groan can serve as a source of reinforcement and hence can markedly influence role performance. *Yes, yes.*

1.8   The Attack on Personality Traits

The evidence for the provocative inversion that would abolish personality traits as a professional concept comes from numerous experimental, clinical, and observational studies revealing non-significant or pathetically low correlations among the actions of subjects in varied situations. Decades ago American school children were found to be not consistently honest or dishonest when given the opportunity to cheat, to steal, to lie, etc. (Hartshorne & May, 1928). Nursery school children, especially boys, have revealed little or no relation between bits of behavior presumably involving the trait of dependency, such as gaining attention (a) by being naughty or seeking praise; (b) by touching, holding, following, or standing near one or more persons; or (c) by seeking reassurance (Sears, 1963, pp. 35–36). Slight changes in situations, furthermore, can produce marked alterations in behavior, sometimes because different roles must then be performed. When high correlations actually appear that might justify the assumption of a trait, they usually involve not overt behavior in different situations but verbal responses to a battery of questions, or else the situations in which they emerge are very similar.

Two deadly opponents of traits have raised a very relevant question: if the evidence is against them or at least against their utility, "what sustains the belief in traits" especially among the professionals (Jones & Nisbett, 1971, pp. 11–13)? *A very good question.* First, Alter's behavior may be inadequately sampled: he is observed only in a limited number of related roles (Pathway 1.2). He may be affected by Ego's conception of him and behave according to that conception. Ego may wish, since the idea of a trait can be more easily stored and recalled than a bill of particulars listing specific actions in many situations, to see consistency in Alter; or he may prematurely judge Alter to be consistent, assign a trait name to him, and then not alter his judgment. As a stimulus Alter's appearance changes only slowly; hence it is too easily assumed his disposition must also remain more or less fixed. Our language provides us with convenient labels, and the labels persist unchanged (Pathway 3.a). Ego may not wish to have his trait assumption disproven, and so he interprets Alter's behavior to make it appear consistent and hence subsumable under the trait category. Actually, in spite of the fact that some Egos may prefer the challenge of inconsistent data, especially from different informants (Usual; Hendrick, 1969), others come to expect the consistency suggested by a trait hypothesis as a result, for example, of the consistency that *may* exist in non-verbal behavior (Usual and adults; Allport & Vernon, 1933). *Perhaps* those Egos who conceptualize Alter via traits make more accurate judgments than those who do not (Usual; Fancher, 1966). Finally, the trait explanation may simply be very useful. Information about Alter can be more easily processed. The two writers cited at the start of this paragraph suggest that, even if the professional can show that inferring traits is "erroneous," the Ego who is "habitually insulted" by a particular Alter must indeed feel that it makes "little difference" whether the reason for this consistent behavior is Alter's "hostility," his "dislike" of Ego, or the fact that Ego sees him "only in the early morning" when he is "always grouchy." *It could make a difference if the Ego subscribing to the explanation for the last reason were to decide to see Alter later in the day—then he might find him to be as overtly friendly as St. Nicholas.*

Thus the facts revealed by investigations debunking traits cannot be denied, but the interpretation they merit is another matter. As ever, most of the subjects have been Americans, and all of them have resided within the Western orbit. It is possible that these societies do not encourage or succeed in developing character traits that function in a variety of situations. American children may have been warned about cheating in school, but they may not have been told what to do with a dime they imagined had been carelessly left in a puzzle box. They may have been inconsistent vis-à-vis the situations in which the investigators chose to test them, but consistent within themselves in terms of some principle not relevant to the study (Allport, 1937, p. 250). Some persons always turn out to be less consistent than others, but that is no reason to abandon the assumption of centrality for everybody. Women and therapists, for example, *may* be more situation-bound, respectively, than men and patients, and some traits—or should I say so-called traits?—may be relatively general, others relatively specific (Usual; Endler & Hunt, 1968) (U.S., patients & staff; Moos, 1968). Even the staunchest opponent of traits, moreover, eventually confesses that situations or roles seldom if ever induce completely uniform reactions. The variations must be attributed to differences among individuals, which means again that determining tendencies, traits, or whatnot must be postulated as an explanation. In fact, as one deliberately impudent professional suggests, consistency or non-consistency may itself be a personality trait (Alker, 1972).

So far our story has been told with detachment because attention has been paid only to pathways involving Ego's total potential and Alter's attributes as a stimulus. Now exciting complications arise as Ego approaches Alter more closely. Yes, there have already been references to Alter's own reaction, especially his interaction with Ego, for all pathways are so closely connected that they can never be completely separated even on behalf of lofty analysis.

It is scarcely necessary to belabor the fact that Ego learns about Alter through a channel of communication. The channel may be so obvious that it is neglected because it is assumed to be functioning, as when Ego hears, sees, smells, or touches Alter in a face-to-face situation. Or it may be as remote as the trace of a paleolithic cave drawing which conveys limited information about the artist, his society, and his times. A number of interrelated distinctions can be drawn: between the immediate perception of Alter through Ego's senses and indirect evidence of him obtained through his writings or the report of someone else; between one- and two-way communication (radio vs. telephone); between the number of sense modalities being stimulated (radio vs. television). Ego's advisable pathway is to recognize that the kind of information he receives about Alter and the opportunity to interact with him—and hence to affect and be affected by him—in all probability are influenced by the channel or channels being utilized.

2.a   Attributes

So many effects or pseudo-effects of channels have been noted by professionals and reformers that attention need be focused only on some of the broader issues. As ever, doubts and generalizations arise whenever we are tempted to be specific or dogmatic. At first glance, it might seem as if an increase in the number of sense modalities being stimulated ought in turn to improve the accuracy of judgment. I am, however, not at all sure you can more easily or efficiently understand a televised Alter than you can one whose voice alone reaches you by radio. The addition of vision to audition provides more information, to be sure, but the sight of a body *may* be distracting rather than helpful and may lead the audience to be less active in trying to comprehend the communication (Usual, hospital personnel & graduate students; Shah, 1960). Individuals, therefore, *may* agree with one another to a slightly greater extent when they rate only the speakers' voices than when they simultaneously hear them on videotape or its equivalent (U.S. & American-Japanese college students; Uno et al., 1972), but agreement is not the same as validity. At the same time judgments concerning Alter may be more comprehensive or more accurate when one medium rather than another is employed, regardless of whether the reward for passing accurate judgment is high or low (Canada, college & nursing students; Boyd & Perry, 1972; Perry & Boyd, 1972). If I tell you something about the scholar we both dislike, you may not comprehend all I have to say, or your thoughts may wander as I speak; but you may read carefully the same words in a letter I send you. This does not mean, however, that the medium is the message, as was once so sensationally proclaimed (Postscript 2.1).

As channels of communication, the sense modalities convey varying degrees of intimacy. According to one suggestion I think you will readily accept, the most distant and the most frequently employed medium both physically and emotionally is likely to be vision, followed by audition, olfaction, touch or pressure, temperature, and taste (Melbin, 1972, pp. 17–21). *Yes, this makes sense.* He looks longingly at his love, he tells her that he loves her, and so on, until he comes so close figuratively. . . . *You mean literally, I would hope.* So close that he kisses her. Since touch is likely to receive perceptual priority and hence to be salient (Pathway II.4), I believe it merits a postscript (Postscript 2.2: Touch). *A high honor.*

The discussion of channels need not be only from Ego's standpoint, for it is also true that Alter may be affected by the channel through which information about himself is communicated, provided he appreciates in fact that the information is being transmitted. Most persons who are not politicians become self-conscious in front of a camera, and hence the skilled photographer tries to open the shutter at a moment when the individual's face seems to have a "natural" expression. Similarly the concealed camera, the concealed microphone, the tapped wire of a telephone serve the same function as the projective tests and one-way vision screens that have been mentioned, it must now seem ages ago, on the last pathway.

You who have through necessity been so preoccupied with letters, diaries, and other written documents must certainly wonder whether any Alter is ever oblivious of the channel through which an impression of himself is being, or potentially might be, communicated. Alter, as the trite metaphor would have it, pours out his heart in a letter to his love and therefore honestly believes that he has probed the depths of his feelings and encoded them faithfully. But, as a cynical guide, I am very, very skeptical. The Alter in love is hemmed in by a mass of conventions, concerning many of which he, poor fellow, is not totally unaware. His knowledge of the language in which he writes, even when it is his native tongue, compels him to express himself in ways that would be quite different if he were writing in Chinese or Turkish. He and the person receiving the letter have undoubtedly established intimate or distinctive ways of expressing affection and reporting facts, and he almost automatically conforms to those practices—why should he do otherwise? On some occasions words actually fail him because they reflect only palely the emotions within him. He remains conscious of the respondent, and perhaps of other Egos who might conceivably see his words and pass judgment upon him. Do you really expect no one but you ever to see your diary? In short, one is never alone except in a physical sense; some Ego is always lurking nearby, a fact that Alter, you, and I can never forget (Pathway I.c.).

As a concrete illustration of the channel's effect, do consider one feature of many communications, viz., the fact that the communication's content reaches the audience not all at once, but sequentially. Ego, for example, learns about Alter as an account, story, or play unfolds; the bits of information about him are not tightly organized and could in fact be interpreted as being mildly contradictory. Under these not unreal circumstances, which bits will make the deeper impression upon Ego, which ones will he have a tendency to remember or forget, those coming first, last, or in the middle of the communication? I would like to hear your answer to this non-academic question because you often think and sometimes say that most research in social science demonstrates either the obvious or what poets and artists already intuitively know beforehand. *First impressions have a lasting effect, they force*

subsequent bits into their mold. But you might also advance the opposite argument: the bits coming last can change all that has come before,
and they have the additional advantage of being most recently perceived
and learned. With an ingenuity we should not waste, I am confident
that you or I could make a strong case for the middle of the communication. Well, then, where do common sense and intuition leave you as
you consider this momentous problem? What research has done, I say
quickly to spare you further misery, is to say at least, "Well, it depends," and what it depends upon are identifiable variables. *Such as?*
Ego's interest in the communication and his commitment to it as well
as the content of the parts being communicated and the timing (Postscript 2.3: Primacy vs. Recency). A faint trace of lawfulness has thus
been delineated. *I wonder.* Quite right, but this is just our first skirmish
with what Ego does when he attempts to put together successive bits of
information; see Pathway 7.a., if you are impatient. And I do think
an advisable pathway becomes visible: Ego must know that he may be
affected not only by the data concerning Alter he perceives or receives
but also by the channel and the sequence in which information reaches
him.

2.b   Credibility

The credibility of a channel, like that of individuals, may markedly
affect Ego's judgment of Alter. You trust some persons as informants
more than others, I hold some newspapers in higher esteem than others.
Alter's status in terms of age, education, or professional status *may*
influence not only his credibility but also his attractiveness and the
intentions attributed to him (U.S., unspecified; Pepitone, 1958, p. 266).
The arbitrary or subjective character of a painting is probably more
obvious to most Egos than that of a photograph. The painter, it is
assumed, has carefully selected the pose before setting to work, and
then has tried to portray his conceptualization of the person. Each of
us is likely to feel, if we think about the matter, that some painters are
more trustworthy than others. *What do you mean by trustworthy?* The
ability to offer a faithful likeness. *What do you mean by faithful likeness?* In contrast, a photograph appears to present Alter more faithfully
than a painting. *But you know that this is not so, the photographer also
controls many factors, perhaps almost as many as the painter: the pose,
the parts of the body to be included, light and shadow, the sharpness*

of focus, etc. Yes, and credibility interacts with other factors. The untrained observer may not detect the subtleties of a non-realistic painting or an off-beat photograph, and may therefore fail to accord it the credibility it merits according to those sensitive to its nuances. Similarly, the effectiveness of a single adjective employed to describe Alter *may* be twice as great when it comes from a source with high than from one with low credibility (Usual; Rosenbaum & Levin, 1968 b); Ego's response to a stressful communication *may* depend not only upon the communication as such but also upon whatever information he has previously been given concerning that communication (Usual; Lazarus & Alfert, 1964) and hence the communicator.

There are some persons—and I think you are one of them—who accord highest credibility to information received through no channel or medium in the usual, conventional sense. Information, they say, is obtained intuitively. I must accept what they have said because they have said it: information so obtained they are likely to acclaim and perhaps never question. At the same time I am skeptical; it is more parsimonious and ultimately fruitful at least to try to determine exactly how the information has reached them. Perhaps a combination of modalities is stimulated, perhaps they simply value one particular cue in a face-to-face situation, such as the wrinkling of the brow, of which they remain unaware. Similarly, extrasensory perception (ESP) has high prestige among certain individuals: in a flash they think they know what Alter is thinking and therefore they can accurately determine his beliefs about himself or Ego. The scientific status of ESP is uncertain, hence I prefer to search for conventional channels through which the information may have been transmitted, a procedure unobjectionable to the professionals believing in ESP since they also first try to eliminate or control the normal channels before ascribing communication to extra-sensory cues.

Many beliefs prevalent in society have to be challenged if various dangers are to be avoided (Pathway I.2). There is, for example, the view that direct observation is more reliable and hence affords greater credibility than hearsay information. *Of course I trust my own observation more than I do a second-hand or fourteenth-hand report.* Perhaps you are right because generally you are an acute observer, you reach conclusions about Alters very rapidly, you tend to distrust intermediaries. Nevertheless, you must concede, an astute sentence about Alter may be more compelling and even more accurate than your

own direct perception, provided—and here is the rub, resulting from a
host of other factors, including the effect you or the intermediary have
had upon Alter, the confidence you have in that intermediary, the relative sensitivity of the two of you, and so on, as suggested by the many
factors in our guiding chart. It has been, it must be oft repeated, that
nobody lies like an eye-witness or a gossip, and
2.1   Informants   I would not try to choose between the two. And
yet we are so continually dependent upon in-
formants or their surrogates for reports or documents providing information about others that we dare not ignore this advisable pathway in
spite of its pitfall. But beware: even parents in our society *may* offer
data concerning their own children (such as age of weaning, onset of
toilet-training, and thumb-sucking) that contradict what they themselves have reported three years earlier and that may be distorted in the
direction so-called experts have recommended to them (U.S.; Robbins,
1963). Gossip and rumor, often reaching us through channels of low
credibility, may turn out to be effective in the long rather than the
short run: the source of information, which means the channel, *may*
be forgotten more rapidly than the content and hence, when the source
is no longer remembered, the content that had been discounted at first
may later be approved (Pathway II.3)—the so-called sleeper effect
(Usual & U.S. soldiers; Hovland et al., 1953, pp. 243–59) whose existence may, however, be questioned on technical grounds (Capon &
Hulbert, 1973). Partially bilingual school children in Africa *may* remember correctly sentences they have seen without being able to recall
whether the communication has been transmitted in their own or in
the European language they know well (Togo & Ghana; Doob, 1961,
pp. 205–07).

The variety of available channels makes the problem of credibility
arise again and again. Suppose I wish to indicate that I am in agreement with you about either a simple or a profound matter. The
agreement I can communicate to you: by telling you I agree, by smiling,
by shaking your hand or even patting you on the shoulder, by writing
you a note to that effect. Which sense modality, which mode of communication are you most likely to believe? You must answer the question, and you can do so in one or two ways. You can say that one
mode is more convincing to you than another; or you can say again
that the channel is unimportant, it is the message that is conveyed as
well as the relation between you and me that leads you to trust my
assent no matter which channel I employ to express it to you. *Fine.*

2.c Restrictions

The man-made restrictions placed upon channels and persons are so widespread and hence considered so obvious that they are often overlooked. The professionals who use experimental methods take care that their communications reach an audience without obstruction, for only then can they make fancy statements about the different sense modalities to which the channels cater and about the extensity or quality of the information being transmitted. But even in a simple conversation Alter may restrict the information he conveys about himself (Pathway 1.2). In fact, written and unwritten rules surround every channel reaching Ego. Within the mass media, obscenity is somewhat curbed legally and conventionally—even now. Media in the West are subject and subject themselves to numerous forms of voluntary censorship; and laws against libel and the invasion of privacy are variously enforced. Less obvious and perhaps more important are the inevitable selection and omission of information in every channel as a result not of cussedness, evil intentions, or legal statutes but of the realistic fact that space or time or both are limited: nobody can afford to say all there is to say about anything (Pathway I.3), simplification is inevitable (Pathway II.1).

When suspicious professionals, reformers, you, and I carefully consider the problem of simplification, we immediately note that each channel transmits information about Alter with varying degrees of fidelity. The problem does not arise in this form—though it does arise in other forms, as the next two pathways suggest—when there is but one Ego and one Alter and when they are confronting each other face-to-face, but it is dramatically present when Alter is absent and information about him reaches Ego over some channel, especially in symbolic form. Alter's voice heard through electronic devices can be transmitted faithfully or it can be distorted; and Ego's judgment may be correspondingly affected. The usual ethical-political assumption concerning the mass media in democratic countries is that they have the responsibility to be accurate and that the criterion of accuracy is the face-to-face situation: would Ego gain the same impression of Alter in real life that he obtains when he sees him on television? Ego obviously is dependent upon what the communicator deliberately or unwittingly communicates, and the communicator's judgment may or may not be superior to, or more valid than, his own. A simple Ego might gaze upon an Alter in the flesh for hours upon end without detecting in his face qualities a gifted painter could see there and then convey in a portrait. Here the better, the truer vision belongs to the communicator and is communicated to Ego through the channel of the art. But of course it may not be communicated even when Ego views the portrait, for he may be impatient or untutored.

Reasons for the restrictions, it seems clear, are found in the society as well as in Alter and Ego. An Alter occupying a very superior position —as leader of a country or an institution—may permit himself to be perceived rarely and then, for most persons, only in a mass medium. Ego, for his part, may selectively expose himself to certain channels and the somewhat biased communications they transmit concerning Alter. In America, for example, there *may* be a tendency—which some professionals rightly indicate has not been thoroughly documented (Weiss, 1969, pp. 89, 158)—for many persons to pay attention largely to communications with which they are in agreement and to avoid those with which they disagree and which, consequently, might prove disturbing. If this is so, Ego might judge Alter differently if he were to give himself the opportunity to do so, and not isolate himself in order to retain the opinion he already possesses. Obviously a spiral.

It is not through direct observation that most of us learn about many persons but through the restricted channels of word-of-mouth or the mass media. We are thus dependent upon intermediaries, upon what they say to us directly or upon what they have written or transmit. Propaganda, advertising, public relations, agitation, publicity—you need only note these words to agree that you have definite views concerning human beings or associations you have not had the opportunity to observe. We are, in a real sense, children who must inevitably acquire the views of our dictatorial, if benign, parents.

With patience, considerable patience, it is possible to discern modal processes even in connection with very informal channels. *I note your tendency to protect yourself from me and from less friendly critics by using the word "modal."* Metaphorically and literally you must not object to the procedure: you do not forever shun a beautiful road in Africa because it is impassable during the short rainy season in contrast with its modally satisfactory condition during the rest of the year. Enough rumors and gossip may have been more or less systematically observed for us to appreciate the kinds of distortion that creep in as the communication passes from mouth to mouth. There *may* be levelling: details, especially qualifications, tend to be omitted. There *may* be sharpening: one feature, no doubt a juicy or inviting one, tends to be exaggerated. And there *may* be assimilation: the characterization or the tale tends to grow simple and coherent (Allport & Postman, 1947, pp. 75–116). These tendencies. . . . *Not certainties, you have been saying.* They are the negative pathways Ego can still avoid in evaluating hearsay evidence concerning Alter.

Since there is no ultimate escape from man-made or natural restrictions, we compel ourselves to be realistic and ask whether there are channels through which Ego obtains intimate, relatively unrestricted information about Alter. I leave it to you to define "intimate." My immediate impulse is to agree with your belief which I express in my manner and obviously not in yours: intimacy of information varies inversely with the number of Egos and Alters reached by the channel. *That certainly is not my manner—I suppose all you are trying to say is that two's company but three's a crowd.* Ego and Alter may be indistinguishable as they interact in the privacy of their own home, there and only there do they communicate both the trivial and the profound to each other. In contrast, a mass medium such as a meeting or a newspaper usually transmits more discreet information. But, having made these banal observations, I must immediately deny what I have said. *Of course.* Two persons may share the same dwelling and remain hostile strangers; and scandal-mongering need not be confined to the back door, but can be promoted by a public orator or a yellow press.

Likewise in the absence of external restrictions people ought to be able to communicate with one another, but they may be blocked by restrictions that are seemingly self-imposed but are in fact the result of external ones they have had to face in the past. Day after day an employer greets an employee and has an opportunity to exchange cosmic verities with him. He does not do so because of self-imposed restrictions, of his criteria concerning the proper topics for discussion between persons of different status, of his conviction that his subordinate is not interested in and cannot understand the subtleties, and of his belief that one learns about character not through words but through actions. Here, as in many other situations, the roles being played block the pathway to intimacy. *It stands to reason. . . . And what does that mean? It stands to reason that persons well acquainted with one another communicate more efficiently and reveal greater understanding than superficial acquaintances.* Perhaps you *may* be right (Usual & graduate students; Goodman et al., 1968). Then friends, or persons calling each other that, might be expected to communicate more effectively in a word game than relative strangers, but in fact religious affiliation rather than friendship in such a controlled, artificial situation *may* be more helpful (Usual; Weinstein et al., 1972), perhaps because the connotations of words arise from institutional affiliations to a greater extent than they do from personal associations established later in life.

Let us temporarily end this discussion of channels by lifting ourselves skywards for a paragraph. We are, it is clear, sealed in our private beings (Pathway 3.1). We reach out to try to grasp Alters, those who are close at hand as well as those who are more distant. We are often pushed away from what we want to know, or would want to know if we but had the opportunity or imagination to realize it is there, by restraints either inherent in or imposed upon the channels being used to transmit and receive information. Insight into the imperfections of these channels, however, should enable us to judge and evaluate more fully whatever they do communicate to us, and perhaps should incline us more vigorously to combat some of the imposed restrictions. *The sky is not too bright.* But neither is it hopelessly bleak.

Postscripts

2.1   The Medium Is Not the Message

In the sixties there was a good deal of lively, well-publicized chatter about the medium being the message (McLuhan of course; e.g., 1964) which means, I imagine, that Ego's judgment must depend less or not at all upon his total potential or the content of the communication about Alter but upon the channel through which he perceives Alter. *I do not understand this take-and-give, I focus upon the content of a communication: what you tell me is important, not whether you say it to me in conversation, in a telegram, or over that devil's instrument you claim to hate so much, the telephone.* You must, however, take cognizance of the McLuhan tempest now past because we obviously receive some impressions about many Alters as a result of the media through which information concerning them reaches us. It is easy to agree that the presence or absence of channels in a society affects the ways in which people have contact with one another and hence the impressions they receive. The invention of movable type certainly expanded the amount of information easily accessible to both the literate and the illiterate, and television conveys information in a manner that does not and often cannot reach us in any other way. Talking drums have the capability of transmitting fewer subtleties than telephones. We thus agree with the self-evident proposition that each channel or medium has more or less distinctive capabilities. What Ego perceives, therefore, is not the medium but the message affected by its medium.

I do not deny, moreover, the overall effect of media upon people in a particular era. Ego within a traditional society lacking writing and the electronic media learns about Alter only by direct contact or through hearsay; he knows about a limited number of Alters in perhaps a penetrating manner. In contrast, although we also have intimate ties with a small number of other persons, we have or think we have some knowledge about thousands of others, the dead as well as the living, whom we have never met. Thoroughly intriguing is the suggestion that a society as a whole and each of its members have a quota of energy and time to be devoted to Alters: Ego may know a small number of Alters very well or a large number relatively superficially (Wilson & Wilson, 1945, pp. 28, 40). In slightly different words: if we concentrate on those we love well or too well, we have less energy or time for a wider circle of friends or acquaintances—and we may never wish to look at television.

The good Canadian provocateur has called attention to another attribute of channels, viz., the demands they make upon audiences to participate and, as it were, to fill in the details (McLuhan, 1964, pp. 22–32). If it is true that television reveals more about a public Alter than radio and that therefore Ego is less active when his eyes and ears are simultaneously stimulated than when only his ears can respond, then McLuhan is justified in calling television "hot" and radio "cool." Yet, I must immediately suggest, these designations refer at the most only to modal tendencies and hence may not embrace many Egos under some circumstances or some Egos under all circumstances. For sophisticated you, a bit of obscure poetry is cool because it makes you work hard to uncover its meaning which therefore becomes very precious to you, and you reject the libelous term "obscure." *And you?* For unsophisticated me, its flavor is quickly if superficially conveyed, I do not tarry long because I get on to other matters. I call the verse hot and the flavor I am able to detect I consider sufficient, not superficial. *And which of us is right, must we count noses?* The medium itself may indeed be used differently in different eras. It has been asserted that writers in the Middle Ages, who knew that their printed words would be read aloud, composed in a style quite different from that of some modern authors who, anticipating that their words will be only seen, deliberately manipulate the language in a way they think will appeal to the eye. *Like E. E. Cummings?* Yes, but he is an extreme case; thanks also for sparing me the conventional affectation of coyly printing his name in lower case.

Our conclusion must be, I think, that media affect individuals differently not because of the intrinsic nature of the media but because of the different kinds of information they may convey. Seeing and hearing a leader on television provides more data about him while he is speaking than hearing him on radio, and hence an *attentive* television audience may be more or less deeply swayed than an *attentive* radio audience. The message, however, comes from him, and obviously is transmitted differently by the two channels. *Perhaps* judgments concerning fictional persons are more severe when they are passed on the basis of printed narratives than when they are made by seeing and hearing actors on videotape (Usual; Sheehan, 1975).

2.2 Touch

Touch may signal intimacy or affection under some circumstances, and hostility under others, for "no organism," a comprehensive survey of the literature on both animals and human beings concludes, "can survive very long without externally originating cutaneous stimulation" (Montagu, 1971, p. 250). Little wonder that the use of body contact has been developed into a philosophy of therapeutic change (Pesso, 1969). "Does he love me?" she asks. He may say he does in her presence or he may send her a sonnet in the best romantic tradition; are these modalities to be trusted less than what happens when he shakes her hand or kisses or caresses her? Actually the words or the sonnet may be less ambiguous than the body contact, so that the critical point is not the modality but the meaning that is conveyed. An Alter of superior status or power may assume the privilege of initiating body contact and he thus invades the other person's private space: the policeman handcuffs the criminal, the dominating male in our society embraces the female, a pat on the shoulder comes not from the clerk but from his chief. It is usually more difficult to ignore tactual stimulation than sensations mediated by other modalities, particularly if touching has a sexual meaning which generally, of course, but not always involves deep emotions. In Western societies, except for handshaking, fondling of children by parents, and the perfunctory kissing of the cheek or cheeks by good acquaintances or friends of the same or opposite sex, body contact usually has more or less exactly that meaning. In many parts of Africa, however, two males may hold hands while strolling without evoking the trace of a suspicion that they are homosexually inclined; they are good friends, and that is all. In fact, the frequency with which this mode of expressing affection occurs *may* be related to the stresses in the African society which in turn may be associated with population density (East Africa, secondary school students; Munroe & Munroe, 1972). But this last bit of information concerns an Ego-expositor of Africans and not African Egos who undoubtedly are unaware of the ecological association.

2.3 Primacy vs. Recency

Since "it all depends" on a number of factors as to whether the first or the last part of a communication has the greater effect upon Ego, let me simply mention illustrative studies concerned with each of the variables.

Interest and Commitment: a disinterested Ego *may* be affected more by the last part of the communication than by the first (Usual; A. R. Cohen, 1957); and an Ego who comes to a decision after hearing the first part of a communication containing contradictory information *may* be influenced to a greater degree by that part than by the second (U.S., high school students; Hovland et al., 1957). In addition, Ego's interest, or perhaps his attention, may be affected by whether he passively reads or actively pronounces the tidbits of information about Alter, and then he *may* be differentially influenced by what comes first or last (Usual; Hendrick & Costantini, 1970).

Content: Ego's impression of a hypothetical Alter *may* be less affected by a paragraph describing him favorably which follows one offering an unfavorable description than it is when the order is reversed. *Why? Perhaps* in our society we optimistically expect Alters to be decent and therefore we think a favorable account reveals only the superficial that can be changed by subsequent information. In contrast, an unfavorable portrayal, we imagine, must reveal something deep-seated and hence we are not prone to have our impression altered by subsequent information (Usual; Briscoe et al., 1967). *Are you not saying that unfavorable information affects us more than favorable information, regardless of which comes first?* I continue because I do not know the answer. The internal relation of the items of information concerning Alter plays a role; *perhaps*, for example, you are affected more by what you perceive at the outset than later when the bits are inconsistent rather than consistent (Usual; Anderson, 1968). *Why?*

For a reason similar to one mentioned in the last paragraph: maybe it is easier not to pull out the copy after going to press when later information is contradictory than when it is confirmatory.

Timing: Ego's impression *may* depend on whether the bits of information are received in one gulp or over a period of time: primacy *may* be more important during a gulp than seriatim. With the passing of time Ego *may* come to have such a clear impression of Alter that he cannot fail to notice discrepant information he subsequently receives; he may be tempted to revise his first impression (Usual; Luchins & Luchins, 1968). Thus a sharply formulated first impression, for whatever reason, *may* under some circumstances be less rigid than a less clearly formulated one (Canada, high school; Luchins, 1958). You must not, however, think that a bright halo around Alter is more likely to affect subsequent judgments less than a weak one under all circumstances; otherwise how could we retain our preferences for and prejudices about people?

Perception as a pathway suggests a spiral relation between Ego's outer and inner world, an interaction between himself and Alter, including the context in which Alter is embedded. The professionals who consider Alter another stimulus also try to demonstrate that the perception of objects involves similar if not identical processes: what we perceive we seek to structure into a meaningful whole (Hastorf et al., 1970). Just as we achieve constancy by always calling the top of a glass circular even when the light rays reach us at an angle and hence are "really" elliptical in shape, so we try to perceive Alters as well as ourselves as more or less constant regardless of circumstances (Cantril, 1957). Familiarity or any preexisting affect or emotion *may* affect the ways in which either persons or objects are perceived, especially when they are viewed through special stereoscopic lenses that distort their appearance (U.S., various; Ittelson & Slack, 1958). Once again, however, such similarity, however striking, does not help us unravel the infinitely greater complications usually characterizing human perception. Alter may be viewed as both a person and an object. *My advice to Ego: view him as a person, for that is what he is.*

But surely perception does not always spiral; Alter's skin color is a fact in the outer world which must be perceived by Ego. Perhaps the salience of that fact at a given moment, however, must also be ascribed to Ego's interest in ethnicity, sunburn, dermatology, or whatever it is that skin color signifies for him and not merely to the color as such. In some multi-racial societies, it is alleged, skin color is seldom noticed, or at least little or no significance is attached to it. And so it is with other acts of perception: the proportion contributed to the percept by Alter and by Ego himself varies, but neither contribution ever quite reaches zero.

Ordinarily, moreover, Ego is confronted with a multitude of stimuli originating in Alter and the context in which he is perceived. Which ones become salient and affect his judgment (Pathway II.4)? Even if he sees only Alter's face in a photograph, which feature or features induce him to infer the emotion being portrayed on that face? Again the choice is affected not only by the nature of the stimuli and their interaction but also by Ego's own beliefs or predispositions. And this is triply so when Group Alters are being judged because they usually emit many different stimuli and are likely to arouse many different responses.

3.a   Speech and Language

The first point to note about Alter's language is its presence or absence. Obviously many of the visual channels conveying information about Alter, such as paintings and photographs, are devoid of language in spoken or written form; and his speech whispered at a distance or conveyed through a defective public address system may be useless because it cannot be heard or is unintelligible. Language is so important that we reach out to perceive whatever we can, and often we are bravely tempted to ascribe words or sentences to mute Alters. I suspect that all of us, in our society at any rate, feel uncomfortable when we must judge Alter without hearing or seeing a sample of his language and that in the face-to-face situation, when we can perceive much more than Alter's speech, we are likely to give priority to what he says. *Why is this so?* For one thing, in spite of its imperfections language is likely to be much less ambiguous than many, not most, non-verbal communications. A policeman's uniform does convey information about the wearer's occupation, yes, but is not the meaning of the word *cat* a bit clearer than that of a human smile which most of us perceive more frequently than the animal or its name and yet which we cannot easily interpret? In society children are deliberately taught their mother tongue; even those very, very modern writers who argue that linguistic ability must also have a significant innate basis (Chomsky, 1972, pp. ix–x) do not fail to note that some components are learned. In contrast, children receive little or no formal instruction in the use of non-verbal media. *You mean syntax receives more attention during socialization than correct posture?* No, parents function as models for both syntax and posture, but the model for syntax has more learnable, more specific components than that for posture.

In addition, everyone at some time—and some of us more often than others—experiences discomfort as he contemplates the discrepancy between his private thoughts and feelings on the one hand and his public language on the other. Although Ego realizes that what he says or writes never quite conveys what he knows to be within himself, nevertheless words are usually all he has while making the attempt. He seldom makes that attempt with another part of his body, except perhaps when he expresses a strong emotion: love, by fondling a child or caressing his beloved; anger, by attacking another person physically. A male Alter in our time and society may let his hair grow long to show that he feels alienated from what he calls the "establishment," but he thereby conveys few of the nuances characterizing his rebellious feelings. All that we can often do to try to communicate what we feel is to use some kind of simile or metaphor—"I feel washed out"— which either we have been taught by our peers or we more or less create outside our normal "verbal community" (Skinner, 1957, pp. 92–93). Somehow, you agree, words come closer to communicating what is inside me or—if I may make the first of many fruitless at-

3.1 Solipsism

tempts to escape the solipsism I truly feel—
inside you. *Why call solipsism a pathway?* I
cannot halt right now to give an adequate reply, but I would say that on occasion, when we reflect or deeply contemplate ourselves, we feel solipsistically encased and believe, whether as Ego or Alter, that it is either impossible *or* undesirable to convey the subjective reality that is consciously within us. "No man is an island," quotes a character in the novel and another character in it replies: "Pah. Rubbish. Everyone of us is an island. If it were not so, we should go mad at once. . ." (Fowles, 1965, p. 129). To the extent that solipsism is valid, to that extent there is no convincing pathway to people; the sooner we appreciate this inevitable, impassable barrier, the better and, furthermore, the greater the confidence we can have in the necessarily finite character of our imagination (Pathway II.5) and our judgment. *Cheers, cheers.*

But isn't there anything more, anything more comforting that can be said about solipsism? I do not think so. To be certain, however, we must turn to the philosophers. "I can witness what your body does," one of them says, "but I cannot witness what your mind does, and my pretensions to infer from what your body does to what your mind does all collapse since the premises for such inferences are either inadequate or unknowable"; we must be resigned, therefore, to the fact that we understand others only through what they "say and do" (Ryle, 1949, pp. 60–61). Perhaps Ego is faced with the same problems when he ascribes experiences to himself as he is when he ascribes them to any Alter (Ayer, 1963, pp. 104–06), since all ascription requires verbalization. Dicta like these only increase our hopeless despair; comfort must come from the fact that as sentient beings we recognize our own human predicament and try, as in our conversations and our search for pathways, to break out of our shells through communication.

This urge to communicate is so great that normally under many circumstances, perhaps in all societies, it is to be expected that two persons immediately or eventually will carry on some kind of conversation when they are face-to-face or otherwise not engaged. Acquaintances utter at least a perfunctory greeting or nod as they pass if they are not to be considered ill-bred or hostile. An individual who suddenly, as it is phrased, goes dead in the midst of a conversation is considered strange, and his enemies and semi-friends wonder what kind of person he really is. To induce his patient to reveal unconscious tendencies, the psychoanalyst keeps quiet; the strain of silence often goads the analysand into saying something significant. *I know someone who can make an obnoxious or impolite person absolutely furious by remaining mute or by ostentatiously changing the subject when he is asked a question to which he chooses to give no reply.* You mean me? "Much silence has a mighty noise," a Swahili proverb states. When Ego anticipates speech and when he hears none, he is disturbed; he is left alone inside himself; his judgment of the other person and usually, too, his own actions are affected.

Most of us may happily assume that Alter's language is the same as our own. There are, however, regions in which Ego's first problem is to identify Alter's speech because more than one language is used in everyday speech: in most parts of sub-Saharan Africa, as well as in India, Pakistan, Switzerland, the South Tyrol, Yugoslavia, and Cyprus. Or individuals in the same area speak on occasion one language, on another a dialect, as in Germany and in France. An Ego familiar with several languages or with a dialect must quickly discover which linguistic channel within himself he must open before he can comprehend what he hears. On the basis of the language or dialect, moreover, he may make one or more judgments concerning Alter's ethnic, social, or educational background (Pathway 3.c).

Do the vocabulary and structure of the language spoken by Alter influence his perception and behavior and therefore provide a clue Ego can readily utilize in judging him? The view of some professionals is that they do in fact markedly affect or—a more conservative version—may affect the user's view of the external world, his mode of expressing himself, and ultimately his behavior (Sapir, 1921; Whorf, 1956). Again and again it has been written that the Eskimo, whose language provides him with a rich vocabulary for the various kinds of snow, and the Arab, whose language has a plentiful supply of words for camels of differing ages and conditions are likely to perceive more details, respectively, in snow and camels because knowledge of the specialized terms directs their attention to those details. *A far-fetched example.* Well, then, consider our word *uncle* which refers to four kinds of relatives, mother's or father's brother as well as the husband of mother's or father's sister; surely, speakers of Bantu languages having separate names for two or more of these relatives must constantly judge them, as far as kinship is concerned, with greater precision than do we, who lump them all together under a single symbol.

To the extent, then, that the broad thesis of psycholinguistics is true, Ego may be able to gain some insight into Alter merely from knowing the language he employs. But now we are leaping along much too rapidly, we again must assume that Ego is acquainted with the peculiarities of Alter's language and its effects upon him. The hypothetical Eskimo who knows Arabic or the imaginary Arab who knows Eskimo is likely to be aware of these elaborate vocabularies in Alter's language, but the monolingual must accept his own language's vocabulary as a matter of course and hence does not and cannot employ a naturalistic or an advisable linguistic pathway. Variations between languages, moreover, do not always mean that their speakers are thereby forced to be correspondingly different in a psychological sense. Frenchmen may have modal personalities different from those of Englishmen and Americans, but I find it impossible to think that any trace of those differences springs from the fact that the French language usually demands a monosyllable both before and after a verb to make it negative and English an auxiliary verb and a single monosyllable ("je *ne* comprends *pas*" vs. "I do *not* understand") or that the English word *know* must be translated into French in one of two different ways determined by the context if the French word is to be correct (*savoir, connaître*). Even when colors are poorly represented among the concepts of their language and when size is well represented, some Africans *may* give responses involving color rather than size (Ghana, Ewe children & adults; Doob, 1960b), for reasons to be found perhaps in the qualities of the stimulus and not in the language. In short, the vocabulary and structure of a language may provide a clue to Alter's perception, but it is a probable and not a certain clue (Postscript 3.1: Misunderstanding).

Professionals make elaborate analyses of Alter's speech. Statistical attention can be concentrated upon the context of psychotherapeutic interviews, and thus some insight *may* be gained into the patient's progress (U.S., various; Dollard & Auld, 1959). Variations in grammatical structure, such as the ratio of nouns to adjectives or the variety of the vocabulary (the type-token ratio), *may* be related to intelligence and some varieties of mental disorder (U.S., various; Johnson, 1946, p. 258). Efforts have also been made to judge the comprehensibility of prose by measuring some of its attributes, such as word and sentence length (U.S., children; Flesch, 1948); thus Ego *may* be able to anticipate whether Alter will be or has been understood by an audience with specified educational qualifications. There are, however, three shortcomings to these techniques when they are considered as advisable pathways and not simply as tools for analyzing speech or prose as such. First, their use requires care, precision, and patience after Alter has expressed or is about to express himself. Ego can almost never use them during the give-and-take of a conversation or while Alter is speaking (Pathway 0.1). He may employ them impressionistically, but his impression may turn out to be wrong as determined by the computer's printout. Then, secondly, the relation between quantitative measures of speech and Alter's personality or behavior is not invariant, so that Ego at best can be assured of a probable but not a certain association between the formal properties he perceives in Alter's language and such-and-such traits. Many of Alter's speech attributes—such as his use of ego pronouns, noun-qualifiers, negatives, verbs, etc.—*may* be unrelated to his mode of behaving under clinical and laboratory conditions (Usual; Doob, 1958). Thirdly, clearly perceived content may be difficult or impossible to interpret; or little agreement may exist among divergent Egos concerning the psychological significance of a communication device. What shall we say about an Alter who bubbles over with humor in contrast with one who does not, on the assumption of course that everything else about the two of them is more or less equal? Humor or wit *may* affect one's judgment of Alter's character but not of one of his traits, such as authoritativeness (Usual; Gruner, 1967).

I think that this time you are being too subtle when you keep insist-

ing that Ego runs a risk in trying to make inferences about Alter from his chatter or his written words; aren't you forgetting the straight-forward possibility that Ego can learn about Alter simply from what he says? No, I am not—one problem at a time. Of course Alter may provide an identifying label about himself ("I really am an atheist"), a description of his internal state ("Last night I had a dream about an elephant"), a statement of intention ("I am going to a bullfight"), a sociological fact ("I thought I would study law but never did"). Ego can perceive statements like these if he is attentive and understands the language, and he may use them as the bases for primary or second-ary judgments. When a Group Alter is being judged, a banner or a leader's speech may serve a similar function. Identical information can be conveyed by an informant (Pathway 2.1) concerning Alter ("I tell you, he really is an atheist") or a Group Alter ("They are do-gooders, they claim to believe in non-violence"). In fact, in our society it is rare for Ego to escape from perceiving such verbal labelling: people talk about themselves and others; the caption under a picture tells us what to perceive. Need I say that these labels, whether utilized by Ego him-self or by others concerning him, whether applied to one Alter or to a group, are a pathway fraught with dangers already mentioned in con-nection with the general problem of deception (Pathway 1.1)? As I turn to the next pathway, I would remind you and myself that Freud, seek-ing clues to his patients' troubles, again and again disregarded part of the content of their speech and instead observed the non-verbal attrib-utes of what they said as well as their so-called body language (Mahl, 1968, pp. 286–7).

3.b   Non-Verbal Symbols

Quite obviously in the face-to-face situation Ego perceives not only the words of Alter but also the other stimuli just mentioned. Surely there are no certain pathways to follow. We are faced with the fact of multivariance: Alter bombards Ego with a multitude of stimuli (Path-way II.1). Most professional investigators have sought to simplify this problem by adopting the strategy of focusing upon one aspect of non-verbal communication at a time. Frequently the interest has been very microscopic and has included only one part of a total configuration, such as mouth curvature as a component of facial expression. It is true, though too facile to assert, that such research can be helpful if and when Ego concentrates upon a single component as he may in a photograph, but that in real life he is likely to respond to the diverse information Alter usually provides (Pathway 1.a). True—but, since multivariance is always present, the best advice to give Ego is to induce him to try to profit freely from his knowledge of the pieces and then to see them in the context of the other stimuli (Pathway I.7). Do not oversimplify the constellation. *Yes, but then why direct research to one component at a time?*

Alter offers Ego stimuli extending literally from his head to his toes, from the non-verbal aspects of his speech to the kind of shoes, if any, upon his feet. The first question that occurs to an Ego-expositor is: which of all these many stimuli are likely to be salient? Again we immediately note the interaction between what Alter offers and Ego's own predispositions or reactions. Finger-wiggling by Alter, unless conspicuously displayed, can easily be ignored. In contrast, since touching you enables me to "know that you *exist* in a way that hearing you or seeing you cannot confirm," the part of his body Ego permits or wishes Alter to touch, and vice versa, *may* vary with the formal or informal relation between the two of them (Usual; Jourard & Rubin, 1968; italics theirs); hence this form of non-verbal communication is almost always deeply impressive (Pathway II.4). Otherwise the efforts to take a census, as it were, of Alter's features that are actually observed provide only very insubstantial naturalistic pathways. In photographs, for example, the most carefully noted physiognomic features *may* be "age, skin texture, fullness of lips, and facial tension" (Usual; Secord et al., 1954). Would this be true, I ask, when a repressed person views a pornographic picture? After very brief exposures, complete or incomplete photographs of the human face *may* be recognized as persons rather than objects on the basis of the following cues listed in order of the frequency with which they are utilized: hair style, shape of face, hair, overall proportion of the face, eyes, and facial expression (U.S.S.R., children & university students; Bodelev et al., 1972). *No, I do not think these studies even begin to solve the problem of salience.* Nor do I: they just state the problem, and that is all we can ever ask. . . . *Forever?*

The next question is the really crucial one: when Ego in fact pays attention to one or more of Alter's non-verbal features, can he understand them? First, I would observe that within recent years the professionals have been striving to compile the equivalent of a dictionary for decoding these symbols. Some of their efforts to decipher what has been happily termed the "silent language" (Hall, 1959) and to validate their systematic approach are reviewed in a postscript (3.2: Decoding the Silent Language). In our society, children generally are neither taught nor made aware of these non-verbal languages. *As you have already said.* And by and large they and we are also encouraged to ignore, or at least to minimize, the importance of non-verbal communications under most circumstances and instead to concentrate upon Alter's words or his overt behavior (Dittmann, 1971). If Alter exhibits non-fluencies in his speech or if his face is blanched, we may infer in passing that he is nervous but, unless we are his parents or friends, or function as his psychiatrist, we pay much closer attention to what he tells us in words or to what he does. Human beings are not like the other higher animals who, in the absence of verbal communication or with only its rudiments, must react to body language and sounds within and outside their own species if they are to survive or mate. Monkeys, for example, *may* have an inborn ability not only to respond but also to interpret correctly some of their peers' facial expressions and gestures (Sackett, 1966).

As Ego-expositors we note, as we did in connection with statistical analyses of language, that ordinarily Ego is unable to use the coding devices of professionals, even if he knew them, either to encode or decode information he receives. So much of his non-verbal behavior is spontaneous and immediate, it is not deliberate as is much of his spoken and almost all of his written language (Pathway 1.b). Often he must respond instantly, too, and therefore the audio- or videotape as well as the computer, which usually is required to implement a professionally devised analytic schema, is not at his disposal (Pathway 0.1). It is as if in the give-and-take of a conversation you were compelled to stop and consult a dictionary and a grammar in order to speak and understand a foreign language with which you were not acquainted. In another sense, the situation is like ascribing a startle to an apparently totally composed Alter on the basis of a very uniform bodily pattern that follows in men and beasts a sudden, loud noise but that is in fact observable only on film in very slow motion since it appears during the first milliseconds after stimulation (Landis & Hunt, 1939).

At the same time probably all of us know that, wittingly or unwittingly, we transmit and receive non-verbal information. The professionals, no matter with whom, where, or with what stimuli they are carrying on their research, are always able to find subjects who are willing to convey emotions non-verbally or to try to decode non-verbal communications (Ekman et al., 1972). In this respect the situation is

analogous to speaking: we can pronounce and understand words correctly without knowing the position of our or Alter's tongue or lips
or the difference between an aspirated or an unaspirated sound. Decades
of research, moreover, have quite conclusively demonstrated that non-
verbal symbols can be judged correctly in some but not in other
respects and that some but not all Egos are reasonably skillful in decoding these symbols (Postscripts 3.3: The Validity and Variability of
Non-Verbal Judgments).

*Before I look at the Postscripts and read further, I would like to say
a thing or two. Surely we are again only inching along a very superficial level when we pay attention to Alter's "uh's," "ah's," grunts, and
incomplete words or sentences or when we take too seriously the frown
on his face or the agitation of his leg. You are brushing aside noble
samples of human language, the sublime poetry and prose of Shakespeare, Goethe, Dante, and all the rest.* That is true, but again one
topic at a time. The undisputed fact is that the most noble examples
of speech, if I may refer again to spoken language, display these im-
pediments, these dull, prosaic characteristics. Nevertheless, they are
trivial; as you yourself have implied, they go unnoticed; they are pathways discovered by patient professionals; they are not advisable pathways to be recommended to Ego. You must admit, however, that you
intuitively know that a shrill voice signifies something about Alter,
though sometimes you may be perplexed when you would comprehend
its precise meaning and at other times you may be wrong. Actually
some of the judgments concerning personality traits that are made on
the basis of the non-verbal content of an Alter's speech (e.g., the rate
and intensity with which he speaks, the pitch of his voice) may be
fairly consistent from Ego to Ego within a culturally homogeneous
group and yet may vary as male or female voices are judged—which
means that for valid and invalid reasons we *may* have definite stereotypes concerning the relation between voice and personality attributes
(Kramer, 1964). Alter's squeaks and er's, moreover, may affect your
judgment even when you deliberately decide to concentrate upon the
meaning of the verbal components of his communication or when you
are unaware of their presence or intrusion. Shakespeare and other
dramatists on occasion reach you not through their written words but
from the stage; there the delivery of the actors (aside from all the rest
of their acting) undeniably facilitates or inhibits nuances of meaning.

*On the other hand, I think you have exaggerated the unconscious or
unwitting nature of non-verbal communication.* Perhaps I have, for I

have been thinking of squints and nail-biting, so-called autistic actions (Mahl, 1968) that may serve a function within Alter but are themselves not intended to be communicative. In contrast, language, more often than not, is used deliberately to communicate. *But there are exceptions.* Yes, Alter may most deliberately wish to say or write one thing, but then his tongue or pen slips. Or consciously or unconsciously even an American Alter whose gestures ordinarily are not so pronounced as those of an Italian or a French Alter *may* gesture more profusely in a face-to-face conversation than over the telephone (Usual; Cohen & Harrison, 1973). Non-verbal communication is admittedly useful when information is to be conveyed to one person and not to another. We may slyly wink to a bystander when we want him to know that we have no confidence in what someone else is saying. An Azande prince in Africa would convey to his retainers his decision to have someone killed by half-closing his eyes. The victim would thus receive no warning of sentence, and later the prince could deny responsibility for the execution since he had not given verbal orders (Evans-Pritchard, 1962, pp. 220–21). Just as deliberately some persons in the West don the latest fashion to proclaim their status or influence. *All right, then, verbal and non-verbal symbols cannot be sharply differentiated on the basis of Alter's intentions.*

In appraising the evidence concerning the validity of non-verbal communication, I would remind you of our omnipresent solipsistic dilemma (Pathway 3.1). Validity means in most instances congruence between what Alter says he is experiencing and Ego's judgment on the basis of his observation of Alter's voice or his face. Alter says he is "anxious" and Ego judges that he is "anxious." But the words, the vocal vibrations, must have different meanings to the two of them, and therefore the correspondence is to some extent superficial (Pathway 8.a). *You have said this well.*

Enough general issues, at least for the moment. Let me now turn to some of the features of Alter's body and quickly examine a few of the non-verbal symbols they provide. I start with the face. The creasing of the forehead into a scowl is not a sign of happiness within Alter, it is—it is what, and are you sure? Similarly what do you say is communicated when the brows are arched, the nose wrinkled, the lips pursed, the chin wiggled from side to side? The versatility of the eyes is almost boundless, ranging from the squint to the glint—sorry, it was involuntary—and from mobility to fixation; their gaze can be directed into Ego's own eyes or turned askance at what seems subjectively to be hundreds of miles away; and, as you already know, we are likely to be aware, with a high degree of accuracy, when someone else is looking at us (U.S., adults; Gibson & Pick, 1963). *But what does Ego learn about Alter by observing whether his gaze is toward or away from himself?* In fact, the professionals have been hard at work on this question, and some of their gems are enshrined in the previously mentioned Postscript 3.3.

Reference need only be made to the arms, hands, fingers, or overall posture or gait to suggest that these have symbolic significance but the quantity and meaning of such movements or gestures probably fluctuates markedly from culture to culture (Pathway I.a). *Is it not true that the farther north we go in Europe, the fewer the gestures people customarily employ in normal conversation?* Skillful actors convey subtle information with their bodies as well as with their voices, and pantomimists dispense with words completely.

Sorry, what you have just said compels me to return to a general issue: can gestures and both facial and bodily expressions be explained completely by culture? A very characteristic question, one I would expect from you, and what you imply may be right. Probably they do have a biological basis, but their cultural components prevent them from becoming totally dependable cross-cultural, advisable pathways to significant behavior. Certainly, it has been argued, cultural factors determine the kinds of public situations in which people display facial expressions; certainly, too, the face appears to be "the best 'non-verbal liar' capable not only of withholding information but of simulating the facial behavior associated with a feeling which the person in no way feels"; but the actual expressions themselves, nevertheless, may be genetically determined and hence may be judged quite accurately if they are perceived before those cultural factors affect their display (Ekman, et al., 1972, pp. 23–24, 153–167, 179). *Interesting, really most interesting* (Postscript 3.4: The Innate Character of Non-Verbal Behavior).

Back to Alter's body which we may look at not as he speaks, moves, grimaces, or gesticulates but as we catch him in a moment of rest or in a photograph or painting—or as he is described by a journalist, novelist, poet, physician, social scientist, or undertaker. We observe or can be made to observe another cornucopia of symbols that may be split into two large groups: those inevitably appearing on any body and those deliberately created by Alter himself (Doob, 1961, pp. 64–68, 82–91). The inevitable clues include genetically determined attributes:

skin color, bodily proportions or somatotype, color and type of hair, shape and size of nose and ears, length of fingers, and so on—in short, any aspect of the human body to which significance can be attached as a result of its distinctive features. Some of these attributes are affected by experience or actions after birth: weight, muscular development, facial wrinkles, etc. Many are likely to be subsumed under a single category by Ego as he views Alter, that of attractiveness. A judgment concerning attractiveness, more often than not culture-bound, is likely not only to be passed very frequently but also to affect other judgments (Pathway 5.a). Usually, too, a relation between physical and personality attractiveness is assumed. *With few exceptions I believe that attractive bodies belong to attractive persons and that attractive persons are likely to have attractive bodies.* You might add that women in our society who are considered attractive *may* be more assertive than those believed to be unattractive (Usual; Jackson & Huston, 1975).

Unquestionably some bodies receive higher acclaim than others. Regardless of their own weight or shape, for example, both American college males (Dibiase & Hjelle, 1968) and females (Lerner, 1969) *may* prefer males who are mesomorphs rather than those who are ecto- or endomorphs. Male preferences for particular female attributes (breasts, buttocks, legs) *may* be associated with their own personality and demographic attributes (Usual; Wiggins & Wiggins, 1969). Ego, moreover, judges his own body as well as Alter's; and there may be a marked relation between his overall evaluation of that body and especially particular parts of it (such as his or her facial complexion, nose, thighs, etc.) and the feelings he has about himself as a person (Usual; Lerner et al., 1973).

Since antiquity, the body's appearance, it has been assumed, reflects Alter's traits or temperament and justifies some kind of evaluation. *The person with the lean and hungry look is not to be trusted and fat persons are jolly?* I am not so sure; the fact that individuals from the same society *may* make similar deductions concerning personality from physiognomic impressions (Norway, secondary school students; Secord & Bevan, 1956) may mean only that they hold similar stereotypes in this respect. More important, even when it is assumed that the genetic structure or the endocrine glands affect both physique and personality and even when body types are objectively determined in modern undress (somatotyping), the association between behavior and these types *may* turn out to be significant but far, far from perfect (Sheldon, 1949, pp. 721–50). Body type, therefore, is not a shortcut; at best it is a very risky advisable pathway.

Since there is often a close relation between ethnic affiliation and appearance, the latter can be used as a clue to the former which then provokes various judgments concerning the Alter so identified (Pathway 5.b). His skin is black, therefore he is a black, therefore he . . . . He is short, his skin is brown, his eyes are almond-shaped, therefore he is Japanese (or maybe Chinese), therefore he . . . . The sentences can be concluded by anyone with ethnic stereotypes or prejudices. Certainly ethnicity can be crudely determined from appearance, but it is usually precarious to make subtle judgments about Alter on this basis alone. Even you admit enormous variability among blacks, Japanese, and Chinese, though each group in fact has modal—if not easily ascertainable—characteristics.

Let us return to the other kinds of body attributes that can be perceived, those that are not inevitable but produced deliberately by Alter or his contemporaries. The body itself can be permanently changed: the skin scarred or tatooed, the ear lobes pierced or elongated, a finger or one or more teeth removed, the penis or clitoris circumcised. And almost any member of the body can be disfigured or deformed through disease, accident, or war. Again it must be monotonously intoned that the meaning of this body vocabulary is likely to be clear only to those who belong to the group employing it or who know of its practices. In Africa, for example, a foreign Ego can note that Alter's face has symmetrical scars on either cheek, but only a member of the same or neighboring tribe knows instantly the tribal affiliation thus signified.

Less drastic or violent and certainly less permanent are the changes not of but upon the human body. Only passing reference is needed to gain assent, especially from you, to the fact that information about Alter can be conveyed by his clothes, his coiffure, the cosmetics on his face or any other exposed part of his body, and the insignia or ornaments he wears. *Yes, but now add the usual qualifications.* The variation is almost infinite, but the information conveyed by these symbols may well be unequivocal to those acquainted with the code. The soldier on the battlefield knows whether the man approaching him is a friend or foe by his uniform and appraises his intentions accordingly. Stereotypes concerning the status of persons wearing particular kinds of clothes, however, seldom operate in isolation, but may interact with other characteristics of Ego and Alter (Postscript 3.5: Clothes and Eye Glasses).

One physical characteristic of Alter is almost inevitably perceived as a result of his body and clothing and is so obvious that I have left it to the very end of this section: his sex. In any society the two sexes perform different roles and have correspondingly differing interests. A knowledge of Alter's sex, therefore, is surely an advisable pathway to seek, for it provides preliminary insight into those interests as well as into his values and behavior. Statements such as these slip effortlessly out of our experience and immediately receive your assent. But they are vague, they merely suggest possibilities, they do not specify the exact differences likely to appear. It is, for example, interesting to know that, when asked to judge the degree of friendliness revealed in photographs, male students *may* judge females within a more restricted range than females judge females, and that female students *perhaps* also judge males within a similarly restricted range but only with respect to friendliness and not unfriendliness (King, 1970). But then I add, as you anticipate, these tendencies were revealed by Australians who were judging not live persons but photographs, who were asked to think only of friendliness and not of other human attributes, etc. Also could we have anticipated these trivial sex differences? We can be certain, however, that a difference between the two sexes will often, sometimes, infrequently appear. It is fascinating to note that you are always eager to point out differences between the sexes, and I look for similarities. I wonder what *that* difference signifies.

3.c Indices

In the discussion of speech, language, and non-verbal symbols we have been stepping back and forth across an invisible line separating fairly direct and fairly indirect perceptions of Alter. His words and the color of his clothes can be noted without hesitation, but his educational status, when it has to be inferred from his grammar and pronunciation or from his clothing, cannot be so instantly apprehended. The line between the two is admittedly invisible since any aspect of Alter may produce a delayed response, and in fact is one reason why we shall eventually consider primary and secondary judgments at such length (Pathways 5 & 7). There is, however, a difference in the perceptual processes: inferences stemming from direct perception are closely associated with Alter as an individual, but those stemming from indirect perception can be made very generally even without reference to a specific Alter. The word *ain't* in a sentence, heavy cosmetics, backslapping mean that Alter, any Alter, is . . . you finish it.

Any extension of Alter can be used as an index to his status within a social group or society, and then the assumed status may be employed by Ego to make further inferences concerning him. The car in front fails to move after the traffic light turns from red to green: will an Ego in the car behind honk or not? His decision *may* be affected by the status he attributes to the slowly responding driver on the basis of the age and condition of the car: he is inclined to honk if the car looks old and rickety, to endure the delay silently if the car is obviously new and shiny (U.S., adults; A.N. Doob & Gross, 1968). Certainly you feel you know something in advance about a person when you observe the neighborhood and the kind of house in which he lives, the church and other organizations to which he belongs, his occupation—and so on through a long list of demographic attributes.

But why bother about Alter's status, why not judge him as an individual? Come, come, you constantly worry about your own status, though you phrase this concern in terms of dignity, tradition, and style. More often than not, Ego must know Alter's status if he is to adopt the appropriate role (Pathway 1.3) and hence his judgment motive is aroused to determine, literally or figuratively, whether he is confronted with sage or a fool: "I look for signs that tell me *who* you are" (Sarbin et al., 1960, p. 149; italics theirs). This is not to maintain that a high-status person is necessarily evaluated more favorably than one of lower status, but that what he says or does obviously *may* be taken into account (Usual; Iverson, 1964).

Surely the most frequently used indices are not Alter's words or non-verbal symbols but his overt behavior, his activities. Yes, obviously, especially when we remind ourselves that the individual Alter is constantly doing something (Pathway 1.b). *Constantly doing something, what about the person who says he has wasted an entire day by doing nothing?* Obviously the description is careless; he may have accomplished nothing in terms of some goal he seeks, but surely he has been doing something during the wasted day. He has fidgeted, he has made fruitless attempts to accomplish whatever it is he seeks to accomplish, he has eaten. These activities of his become the indices for Ego to perceive and judge.

The assumption of omnipresent activity and indices has metaphysical overtones, to be sure, and unabashedly so: it is activity that distinguishes life from death in all living matter. But the difference between plants or animals on the one hand and human beings on the other is that we and presumably not they are conscious of both the activity and the assumption concerning it. Freud and the neurophysiologists have shown that even sleep is not a passive state but one in which the body is constantly active in a variety of ways, only some of which ever reach consciousness through remembered dreams. In theory, at any rate, Ego has an infinite number of indices to use as pathways to Alter if and when he has access to them and if and when he can use them shrewdly.

In a real sense any action, even the simplest one, provides only an index to Alter. You are picking flowers in your garden and suddenly you go into the house. Unquestionably I observe these two separate acts because you have engaged in them; thus a portion of my perception depends upon what you do. But I do not know why you are picking flowers, whether the act brings sorrow or joy, why you suddenly move away, etc. You offer perhaps additional clues; I may note whether you pick the flowers carefully or quickly and whether at the moment you are smiling or frowning. My knowledge remains inexact until you supply some direct information about yourself in verbal form or until I know more about your life history. But of course the situation is not quite so hopeless. Either because you and I know each other well or because we come from approximately the same culture, I doubtless have had enough experience with your actions to be able to use them as an index to your feelings and intentions (cf. Gottman, 1973).

Frequently the only kind of information about Group Alters is derived from indices. Ego cannot observe or measure everyone, he can note merely the behavior of the group as a whole or a consequence of such behavior. A riot has taken place, he decides, because he sees the broken store windows, the overturned cars, the burnt-out buildings. He then uses the physical facts to infer not only the occurrence of certain actions—a very obvious point—but also the participants' motives. The inferences are likely to be more valid when they are guided by theory. Do people at church, for example, lock their cars? Americans adhering to a strict religious creed may be more likely than those subscribing to a liberal one to feel that strangers are unrestrained and not law-abiding; hence they *may* feel more inclined to worry about theft and to lock their cars (U.S.; TeVault et al., 1971). Were this finding generalizable and were locking cars more closely associated with rigidity, religious or otherwise, such behavior could be more confidently employed as an index of the group's traits, that is, of the modal tendency within the group's members. *But surely there must be some liberals who lock their cars and some conservatives who do not.* Yes, and that was certainly true in the monumental study just mentioned.

Ego, I have already indicated, is often confronted with a variety of non-verbal symbols; he may also be forced to choose between conflicting verbal and non-verbal indices. At this point I can only suggest and illustrate the conflict since Ego's decision arrives in the form of a secondary judgment (Pathway 7.a). He may validly comprehend, for example, the non-verbal aspect of Alter's stimulus configuration but be unable to evaluate or weight it when other information, especially a verbal communication, is also available. *Perhaps* each Ego selects the one better or best source of information that he believes can guide his judgment and *perhaps* his judgment is likely to be improved when he himself is given an opportunity to make the choice (Usual; Rodin, 1975). Even so, Ego may be puzzled: "the lips may say no, no, but there's yes, yes in her eyes"—the song writer, presumably, meant that the eye-language was unambiguous. Actually non-verbal communication *may* be congruent with, contradict, or anticipate the expression of personality traits or verbal utterances (U.S., adult; Mahl, 1968). Thus Alter's non-verbal gesture of abruptly moving away from the place where Ego is seated *may* have a greater negative influence on Ego's desire to work with him than a verbal indication of disagreement (Usual; Mettee, Taylor, & Fisher, 1971), but it takes little imagination to conceive of another situation in which an unkind word can be more devastating than the behavioral gesture.

Non-verbal symbols may also supplement speech and thus emphasize more strongly or convincingly what has been spoken. Alter says he is disgusted and the frown on his face and the gesture of despair supplement his statement. A combination of communications may convey information that one of them alone may not suggest. In front of her immediate leader an Azande woman might have suggested that she had committed adultery without explicitly saying so—but an accompanying gesture of hanging her head and picking at the ground with her fingers was an explicit admission of the offense and also an expression that she was ashamed to say so (Evans-Pritchard, 1962, p. 220). The no-no of speech, however, is likely to prove more credible in a Western court than the yes-yes of the eyes; the maiden, for example, can claim that her visual and not her oral communication was misunderstood. Sometimes, however, Ego should ignore Alter's words and watch, experience, or touch her or his body.

In our ignorance concerning the ways in which one person comprehends the emotions and motives of another (Gibson, 1951), we have naturalistic or advisable pathways concerning ways of dealing with or reconciling conflicting information (Pathway 7.a). On the one hand, it may be argued that the expressive movements of the body, such as a twitch or a frown, result from "deep-lying determinants, functioning, as a result, unconsciously and without effort" and hence have the potentiality of revealing significant information about the twitcher or the frowner (Allport, 1937, p. 466); but on the other hand, we know these indices are difficult to decode, that sometimes Alter does speak the truth as he sees it, and that—as I have argued earlier in this chapter (Pathway 3.a)—there are usually good reasons to accord priority to speech and language. Or, more specifically, variations in photographs and in the skills of Egos prevent us from emerging with convincing generalizations about whether photographs or verbal data convey more about Alter (England, undergraduates; Warr & Knapper, 1966. Usual; Lampel & Anderson, 1968. Usual; Zaidel & Mehrabian, 1969. Shapiro, 1961). Small wonder, as we shall see, that the pieces of Humpty-Dumpty are not easy to assemble.

Amid this multitude of often confusing, conflicting indices, it is not surprising that human beings everywhere try on occasion to experience and not to reflect. This urge to comprehend sense impressions effort-lessly accounts in part for the appeal of alcohol and drugs. In addition —no, I shall stop before I discourage us both, for we have agreed to search for pathways to people. We cannot progress unless we assume that the perception of Alter results in some sort of impression that can be fitted into one of Ego's categories applicable to relations between human beings. Classifying the categories is difficult because they include all the varied types of interactions of which people are capable. They range from the category of non-person to that of close relative; from simple age- or sex-typing to assigning Alter to a very special social class or group; from a conviction of strangeness and unfamiliar-ity to that of knowledge and familiarity; from non-involvement to involvement in Ego's own welfare or strivings. These are the bases for the arousal of attitudes and the primary judgments, the weighty sub-jects to which we turn on the next two pathways.

Postscripts

3.1   Misunderstanding

Misunderstanding is especially likely when Ego is dependent upon a translation of what Alter has expressed or even when Ego himself makes the translation. Whoever does the translating must first comprehend the communication's meaning in the original language and next find an equivalent word or expression or proposition in Ego's language. Poetry or poetic prose poses acute problems not because a longer or shorter, though equivalent, expression cannot be found but because the change may destroy some or all of the beauty or brevity of the original. Even the existence of ostensibly exact equivalents in two languages may lead to a faulty translation. It appears simple to employ the English word "justice" as a translation of *la justice* from French, *giustizia* from Italian, *Gerechtigkeit* from German, etc., but each word undoubtedly evokes its own somewhat distinctive, culturally determined connotations. For that matter, however, Ego may run into the same difficulty when he and Alter both speak English and Alter says "justice," for the meaning of this lofty abstraction in any language also fluctuates from person to person.

Speakers of the same language and of identical or similar status within the society, however, are less likely to misunderstand one another. When an American guest says some time after dinner that "It is rather late," his American host knows his intention just as clearly as if he had said, "I want to go now" (From, 1971, p. 58). The Alter who uses the circumlocution, however, is conveying to Ego not only his intention to leave but also his desire to be polite and friendly. Similarly some sentences can be constructed in any language to communicate —and to communicate along a continuum from almost complete ambiguity to almost complete clarity—any one of Alter's attributes. *Including his affection and thought?* Neither of us knows, for here again is the challenge of solipsism.

3.2   Decoding the Silent Language

Considerable progress has been made in decoding an aspect of non-verbal communication that is not silent, viz., the non-verbal attributes of speech or paralanguage (Duncan, 1969). The units of measurement have been borrowed from physics and phonology, and range from the timbre of the voice to the kinds of phonemes accounting in large measure for accent. They include the tempo and speed of speaking, the loudness or softness of expression, variations in pitch, etc. There are also the sounds resulting from yawning, laughing, grunting, belching, etc. When college students are asked to identify the emotions conveyed by voices that have recited the same sentence with varying pitch, loudness, and timbre, and at different rates, they *may* succeed sometimes above, sometimes even far above, chance expectancy (Davitz et al.,

1964, pp. 23–26, 32–36), even when the words are whispered or when the speech samples are extremely brief (Usual; Pollack et al., 1960). A non-fluency index based upon the number of changes in sentences as they are spoken, of words or phrases that are repeated, of stutterings, of parts of words that are omitted, of incomplete sentences, of tongue slips, and of incoherent, intruding sounds (but not including the sounds "ah," "eh," "uh," and "uhm") *may* be related to the experience of anxiety (Usual; Kasl & Mahl, 1965). Also the quantity of words— regardless of their meaning—employed by individuals to explain prov- erbs, for example, *may* distinguish deluded schizophrenics from non- deluded ones or both types of schizophrenics from normal persons (Canada; Payne et al., 1964).

For non-verbal communication as such there are no universally accepted units corresponding in speech to phonemes, morphemes, words, sentences, etc.; and likewise there are ordinarily no rules for combining the units corresponding to syntax in spoken or written lan- guage. Manuals or pseudo-manuals which portray "body language" always supply captions or explanations of the illustrative photographs (e.g., Scheflen, 1972), so that in most instances the "language" appears clear only because the accompanying words decode it.

To establish a grammar and a system of semantics for non-verbal communication, a few professionals have attempted to follow the pat- terns of musical notation which preserve a composer's composition and instructions in a reproducible form. One technique of coding enables a choreographer more or less to comprehend the body movements and interactions involved in the original dance (Laban, 1950, pp. 25–90). An anthropologist proposed two decades ago an intelligible way of re- cording facial expressions and other body movements and has called his system "kinesics" (Birdwhistell, 1970); but, it has been since sug- gested (Dittmann, 1971), little progress has been made in evolving the principles or rules of this language. Concealed cameras, microphones, and one-way vision screens enable investigators to obtain an accurate record of Alter's body movements at a specially equipped site, usually an indoor room.

The naturalistic pathways people actually use as they communicate non-verbally, whether deliberately or not, have been observed in real- life settings. Americans, it has been stated, *may* establish eight different kinds of space between each other. The distances vary from "very close" (3 to 6 inches) to "stretching the limits of distance" (20 to 40 feet indoors and up to 100 feet outdoors). Corresponding to these distances may be appropriate ways of speaking and suitable subject matter: "soft whisper" and "top secret" to "hailing distance" and "departures" (Hall, 1959, pp. 208–09). *But do these so-called norms correspond to reality, do people in fact use such a coding system?* Yes, norms have been shown to exist (U.S., Greek, South Italian, & Scottish students; Little, 1968), but the actual distance Ego and Alter maintain between themselves *may* depend upon a variety of factors that have been isolated experimentally or empirically: degree of intimacy between the two and their style of speaking (Usual; Leginski & Izzett, 1973); similarity in attitudes and beliefs ascribed to Ego by Alter, which in turn may be associated with the latter's judgment concerning the former's attractiveness (Usual; Byrne et al., 1971); the age and sex of the two persons who are inter-acting (Usual; Allgeier & Byrne, 1973); exhibitionistic and impulsive personality traits (Usual; Sewell & Heisler, 1973); ascribed political beliefs (U.S., adults in Little Italy & Greenwich Village; Thayer & Alban, 1972); economic status and the site of the interaction (U.S., Negroes, Puerto Ricans, Italians, & Chinese; S. E. Jones, 1971); stig-mata, the number of persons present (U.S., various; Pederson & Shears, 1973), etc., etc.

3.3   The Validity and Variability of Non-Verbal Judgments

Virtually every available investigation substantiates the two points made in the text: only some non-verbal symbols can be judged accu-rately, and individual differences among Egos is almost inevitable. Let us begin again with the non-verbal aspects of speech. The traits Ego identifies correctly from only hearing Alter's voice *may* vary with the linguistic family to which they both belong (Germany & U.S., young adults; Scherer, 1972); they *may* involve, in the harmless jargon of the measuring instrument (the semantic differential), emotions concerned with activity but not with valence or strength (U.S., presumably college; Davitz et al., 1964, pp. 101–12). Similarly, on the basis of facial muscles some Egos accurately judge at a minimum Alter's emotions along the dimensions of pleasantness-unpleasantness, intensity, and activity while employing categories as diverse as happiness, surprise, fear, anger, sadness, disgust or contempt, and interest (largely usual: Ekman et al., 1972, pp. 57–108, 176); and the features in photographs giving rise to valid judgments *may* be "mouth curvature" and "facial tensions" (Usual; Secord et al., 1954), although not only the accuracy with which inferences are made concerning attributes like occupation or age but also the bases for the judgments themselves *may* vary greatly from person to person (Usual; Gahagan, 1933), especially when the Egos come from different cultures (U.S. & Sarawak, children; Looft et al., 1972). Intriguing, in view of the attack on personality traits (Postscript 1.8), is the possibility that photographs and motion pictures, when judged quickly and without reflection, *may* lead Ego to describe the situation rather than to judge the emotions of the persons being portrayed (Netherlands, young adults; Frijda, 1953).

We must pause and remind ourselves as devout Ego-expositors that our hero, Ego, in the absence of a systematic way to decode non-verbal communications, may often depend on his own stereotypes concerning the relation between those communications and behavior. In the West, for example, he *may* judge persons with widely open eyes to be more intelligent than those with squinting eyes, yet be oblivious of the cue that has guided his prejudice (Germany, children & adults; Kiener & Ahrens, 1973). The stereotyped judgment may spring from a facile generalization: a carelessly clothed Alter is considered careless in general. Or a person with heavy eyebrows may be categorized as "rough" and hence unkind or boorish (Secord et al., 1958, p. 309). Still, in spite of stereotypes, age and the presence of mental illness *may* fairly well be inferred from photographs (U.S., nurses; Gottheil & Joseph, 1968). Accuracy in judging the emotions displayed in photographs, moreover, *may* be improved as a result of practice (Pathway 6.a) and by seeing the context in which the pictures had been taken (Pathway 1.c), but improvement also depends upon the expressions of the persons being judged—and sometimes a decrease in accuracy is associated with practice (Usual; Ekman, 1965). Stereotypes offer no certain naturalistic pathway as a trivial example suggests: male college students *may* have greater difficulty correctly distinguishing a beauty queen from an honor student from photographs (Terry & Snider, 1972).

Alter's eyes of course may either be turned toward or away from Ego. Eye-avoidance, it is said, *may* occur not only in human beings but also in animals when a strong drive has been aroused (Hutt & Ounsted, 1966). *Intuitively this makes sense, for an Alter who does not look me straight in the eyes must be afraid of me.* But he may also be showing disrespect; or during an unpleasant conversation he *may* look away from you in order to gain time to think, to reduce the number of distracting stimuli reaching him, or to try to inhibit you (England, students; Kendon, 1967). *But are not strong drives involved in these instances?* Yes, though I rather suspect that an anthropologist could find some society, as anthropologists almost always manage to do, in which exactly the opposite eye behavior occurs under such circumstances. Unquestionably, moreover, eye-gazing reflects diverse tendencies within Alter. A speaker *may* unconsciously signal the end of what he has to say by looking into the eyes of the listener who then tacitly acknowledges his readiness to accept the offer to begin speaking by averting his eyes (Kendon, 1967). Unlike some animals who avert their eyes to appease an attacker, autistic children *may* look at others to inhibit their aggression (England; Hutt & Ounsted, 1966); and American college students *may* use the same communication device to reduce the punishment they feel or know they are going to receive, a form of communication that in fact may produce the desired result only when the Ego at hand is aggressive and when they consistently look at him (Ellsworth & Carlsmith, 1973). On the other hand, Alter conceivably looks at Ego for more positive reasons; possibly he wishes to discover how he is reacting or to express interest or respect. Eye-gazing or aversion, to be sure, fluctuates from individual to individual. Some persons more readily than others *may* meet the eyes of those with whom they are interacting, for the quantity of eye contact can roughly serve some need, such as, for example, the general urge to comprehend events in order to control them (Canada, college; Lefcourt & Wine, 1969). The need is "roughly" served because the relation between needs and eye contact is never perfect *and* may be affected not only by personality traits but also by the subtle reinforcement offered by Ego in the form of an "uh" or an "ah" as contact occurs (Usual; Exline & Messick, 1967). Other things being equal—never the case—you will look in my eyes more often if somehow I praise you for doing so, provided, of course, I keep your negativistic streak dormant by not telling you I am doing that.

Not only may Ego try to use Alter's eyes as a pathway, but he himself may also be affected by those eyes. He *may* draw closer to Alter—and still feel comfortable—when Alter gazes at him than when he does not (Germany, students; Cranach et al., 1968). His evaluation of an Alter who looks him straight in the eye may become more favorable if what that Alter says pleases him, and more unfavorable if Alter's words displease him (Usual; Ellsworth & Carlsmith, 1968). In our own society, self-disclosures by Alter in general *may* not be affected by eye contact with Ego because a personality trait, authoritarianism, interacts with contact: those markedly authoritarian may be more greatly influenced by the disclosure when there is contact than when there is not, whereas the reverse may be true of those low in the trait (U.S., female students;

Worthy et al., 1969). Once more individual differences intrude, don't they?

3.4   The Innate Character of Non-Verbal Behavior

Darwin suggested that body movement may be innately associated with basic emotional patterns and that they serve, in animals and in man, not only an autistic function but also as signals or forms of communication to members of the same or different species (Darwin, 1872). A frown is likely to be an involuntary accompaniment of an unpleasant rather than a pleasant state of affairs: for Alter it is unintended, but it may convey his feeling to Ego. Women in childbirth *may* display regular and interpretable changes in facial expressions as their pain increases (U.S.; Leventhal & Sharp, 1965). Animals, as indicated in the text, use non-verbal modes of communication, presumably without being dependent upon what they have learned in their milieux. Aside from the voluminous, brilliantly intuitive collections of human and non-human symbols offered by Jung as proof of the universality of a racial unconscious (e.g., Jung, 1959), some cross-cultural research also supports Darwin's theory. American students and others in the United States coming from different cultural backgrounds *may* do equally well in judging the emotions conveyed by samples of the non-verbal aspects of speech obtained from speakers belonging to the same or different backgrounds (U.S., American, Israeli, and Japanese students; Davitz et al., 1964, pp. 148–150). Facial expressions of Caucasians may be interpreted correctly even by non-Caucasians and by persons who have only casual contact with the West (Brazil, Japan, & U.S., students; Borneo & New Guinea, adults; Ekman et al., 1969), particularly when and if relatively culture-free samples of such expressions are being judged.

Darwin, however, also recognized cultural components in nonverbal behavior among human beings (Pathway I.a). The same movement, such as a smile or the shaking of a finger, may occur modally under quite different circumstances in different societies. A frown may be so primitive that its counterpart can be found among chimpanzees everywhere, and it may involuntarily appear when Alter is angry or disturbed whether or not he himself is consciously aware of this state of affairs. But he may also regulate its appearance: he deliberately creases his brow to impress his audience or through long practice (dictated either by his culture, or, idiosyncratically, by his profession or manner of life) he inhibits the neural impulses and achieves what we glibly call a poker face; or he creates a frown through mediation, that is, he thinks of an unpleasant situation in the past and the thought or image functions as the stimulus to produce the effect. It is true that persons within a given culture, consequently, *may* more or less agree into which of three categories their judgments concerning a given body movement should be placed: (a) hate, rage, anger, etc.; (b) pleasure, satisfaction, joy, etc.; or (c) contempt, superciliousness, scorn, etc. (Finland, education students; Kauranne, 1964). But it must be obvious to you that these are very broad categories and involve only the tone rather than the real content of the emotion behind the non-verbal expression. Or finally let me invoke the old standby, the photographic stimulus. Alter's pose in a photograph, whether full-face or profile, *may* affect Ego's judgment but in ways that are difficult, if not impossible, to specify in advance and that *may* be less important when additional information is supplied by an accompanying text (England, presumably students; Warr & Knapper, 1968, pp. 305–10)—and the text is clearly a cultural component.

3.5   Clothes and Eye Glasses

As you can well imagine, psychoanalysts (e.g. Flugel, 1930) have seized upon clothing as a key to the wearer's personality, but I shall not dwell upon their arresting, speculative comments. Instead I shall mention a few tidbits suggesting the kind of research demonstrating or illustrating the effect of Alter's clothes upon Ego and the reverse. Those clothes, for example, *may* produce extreme judgments in Ego only when he is of the opposite sex (Usual; Hamid, 1969), and their influence upon him *may* be affected by his own tendency to project, which in turn perhaps depends upon his self-esteem and sense of security (Usual & nurses; Dickey, 1968). Both Alter's clothes and his coiffure *may* determine whether Ego will help him when he asks for two nickels in exchange for a dime (U.S., adults; Raymond & Unger, 1972), a ride to the nearest station to get gasoline for his apparently stalled car (U.S., adults; Graf & Riddell, 1972), or a lift while hitchhiking (U.S., adults; Crassweller et al., 1972). *Pretty obvious*. More than Alter's clothing can influence Ego's decision regarding the momentous requests just mentioned: Alter's sex and skin color as well as Ego's age and social class. Ego's own clothes *may* determine whether Alter will be honest (U.S., adults; Bickman, 1971) or whether he will be polite (U.S., adults; Franklin, 1973). Oh, yes, eye glasses. Although young Alters wearing glasses *may* be rated more intelligent, industrious, dependable, and honest (if not more friendly) than those without glasses by their peers in Germany (Manz & Lueck, 1968) and the United States (Thornton, 1944), the accuracy with which a woman is judged *may* be affected—at least among New Zealand students—not only by whatever stereotypes her glasses evoke but also by her makeup and the sex of the Ego passing judgment (Hamid, 1972). In short, nothing simple about judgments based on clothes or eye glasses even in these restricted samples; more multivariance (Pathway II.1).

Ego is never indifferent. Although this happy, sad fact has already been mentioned, especially in connection with his convictions (Pathway II.c), it is so important that it must be considered a major pathway. Before or after Ego has perceived Alter's language, his non-verbal symbols, and his activity, or while he passes initial judgment, he has feelings of various kinds: attitudes toward Alter or himself as a stimulus are evoked. *Is indifference impossible?*

The case for assigning to attitude a positive or a negative but not a completely neutral tone is relatively straightforward. If you have known a person previously, you very probably have an opinion about him and consequently certain expectations; his presence or a symbolic reminder thereof is sufficient to evoke that opinion. If he is a stranger, he or one of his perceived attributes may remind you of someone else, you generalize from past experience and draw on your general understanding of persons. *But can you be indifferent toward him?*

Let us assume you are again seated in the compartment of a European train with five other persons. If you were to give thought to the question, you would conclude that you would never see these individuals again; you would be indifferent toward them. Such indifference, however, persists only as long as you do not perceive them as persons. The moment one of them appears attractive in appearance or speaks too loudly or lights a cigarette, a judgment motive is likely to be evoked (Pathway II.a). In the process of passing judgment, some kind of attitude plays a role: you like him, you dislike him, you are not quite indifferent no matter how mild you feel.

Attitudes exist and are evoked, therefore, because it is inefficient, painful, or impossible to approach each situation or each person *de novo*. Just as Ego tries to make sense of each stimulus configuration—

seldom is anything just a blur, rather it is made to represent something commonplace or at least intelligible—or just as he categorizes the actions of Alter, so he tends to assume an approaching or withdrawing stance, literally or figuratively, toward whoever confronts him. Why risk being friendly to a stranger when persons looking or acting like him have previously brought only grief? Why waste time asking more questions when her manners indicate she is unfit for the position at hand? Why not trust them implicitly since their uniforms prove them honest and reliable? The unbiased person is an unattainable ideal; the most we can expect is an Ego who pushes aside his immediately evoked attitudes and seeks to gather additional evidence which conceivably might induce him to alter a preconceived judgment. When you are depressed—because you have not had enough sleep, because others have angered you, or because, so you think, the moon is on the wane— only divine assistance can protect those crossing your path, and your judgment of them is a wee bit negative. Most of us are sinners, not saints, a fact that ought to keep us contrite as we walk the torturous pathway of attitude (Postscript 4.1: The Importance of Attitude).

The non-indifference of Ego, however, does not mean that he is always misled or dominated by attitudes. What Alter says or does at a given moment may be so striking that, regardless of his own attitude, Ego cannot usually disregard him, just as a mailbox painted in garish colors and placed in the center of a sidewalk is likely to be noticed by passersby who have no letter to post (Pathways 1.a & b). Although many attitudes are prejudices, those stemming from direct experience may induce valid, or at least useful, judgments. An employer interviewing an applicant may repress his convictions or attitudes for a considerable time until he has the information he needs or makes the decision to employ or not to employ the aspirant. Attitudes may sometimes be inconsequential; even the zealots who would show that many psychological investigations are affected markedly by the investigator's bias have evidence suggesting that in the laboratory the perception of persons "seems less susceptible to the effects of experimenter expectancy than most of the other areas investigated" (Rosenthal & Rosnow, 1969, p. 228). Ego may be affected by actual information and his final judgment may turn out not to be in accord with his initial prejudice. Or the attitude may function inconsistently, that is, be efficacious under some conditions and not under others; thus the feelings toward an ethnic group *may* influence the rating given photographs of one sex but not of the other (Usual; Hicks, 1972). And then, as ever, there is multivariance: attitudes interact with stimuli or with one another (Pathway II.1). Ego's reaction to the stimulus of Alter's humor is affected not only by the humor's content but also by his attitude toward Alter: if Ego considers Alter aloof, the humor *may* have greater impact than if Ego believes him to be a clown (Usual; Mettee, Hrelec, & Wilkens, 1971). *Aren't you exaggerating, is not humor humorous per se?* Consider how your judgments about almost any Alter may be influenced by your attitudes toward the beauty, intelligence, honesty— or any trait—that you consider of crashing importance and that you attribute to him. Perhaps the stronger the attitudes or values, moreover, the greater the perceptual distortion of the external world (Tajfel, 1959).

4.a   Groups

As one of the principal channels through which culture is transmitted and reinforced, groups significantly affect the genesis and functioning of attitudes. The basic assumption is almost Darwinian in its simplicity-complexity: attitudes are learned as a result of meaningful experience in the past and are, therefore, as previously suggested, ways of storing feelings of attractiveness and repulsion toward persons and objects in the milieu. That experience may be of various kinds (Allport, 1954, pp. 285–339). Consider a prejudice against extroverts. One incident after another takes place from which gradually an Ego generalizes and acquires a distinctive feeling about whatever he believes the incidents seem to have in common. As a very young child, he might have been disturbed by various kinds of persons who, he slowly learned, had the attribute of extroversion in common. Then, secondly, a single traumatic experience may be sufficient to produce and perpetuate an attitude. Ego may never forget the outgoing manner of the man he thought was going to attack him, and so forever after be uncomfortable in the presence of persons with similar extroverted characteristics, no matter how friendly they appear to be. Attitudes, thirdly, may also stem from the opposite of generalization, which is differentiation: in place of a feeling toward an entire class, Ego focuses upon a subcategory. He once tended to be anxious in front of all strangers, but became convinced that one type of person was more anxiety-arousing from his standpoint than the rest; he acquired a bias against extroverts. In all three instances, Ego himself has had the relevant experiences in acquiring an attitude, whether the method has been that of accumulation, generalization, or differentiation.

The fourth method skips over personal experience and depends upon symbolism learned in the group: Ego adopts the ready-made attitudes of persons in his milieu whom he respects or loves. They tell him that extroverts are back-slappers who are to be avoided. All parents, wittingly or unwittingly, exert some pressure toward conformity. Children in effect wish to know whom they are supposed to love and hate: they are eager to comply since they are rewarded for doing so and since they cling to those who indoctrinate them. They thus acquire more or less distinctive attitudes toward groups to which they belong as well as toward the out-groups concerning which their own in-groups have developed friendly, neutral, or unfriendly relations.

A number of pathways emerge from the fact that attitudes so frequently can be traced to groups. An Ego-expositor or an Ego can assume that Ego or Alter, respectively, shares the modal attitudes of his group (Pathway I.7). Then neither can expect these heavily reinforced tendencies to change very readily. *But surely* . . . . Wait, I shall contradict this view in a moment or two. Here also is a danger and hence a negative pathway for Ego to recognize as he passes judgment: his own rosy or darkened glasses distort his perception of Alter. In addition, his self-insight can be improved when he appreciates other attributes or attitudes. Again because they have been so strongly reinforced, attitudes are usually related to other significant tendencies within the individual. A very simple illustration: in contrast with educators and schizophrenics for whom art normally is relatively unimportant, American students of art *may* have a tendency to prefer character sketches of "conventional, cautious, reliable" individuals (Wild, 1965). If attitudes are unconventional or reflect divisions of opinion within a society—such as hostile feelings about ethnic groups in the United States—they may be associated with deeper layers of the personality than when they spring from tradition and only an inclination to conform.

Attitudes arise or are evoked by the groups in which Ego finds himself at a given moment or to which he refers his behavior (Pathway 1.c). It may be difficult for him to be objective about Alter when he knows his judgment will be communicated to his own peers or, for that matter, to Alter's. The other persons, it must be stressed, need not be physically present to affect Ego's attitudes: Ego's relevant attitudes are likely to become salient when he reflects upon a group's norms and values while passing judgment (Pathway II.4). If you think of yourself as an American, you may judge me differently from the way you do when you try to employ, let us say, Italian standards. Or,

if agreement with Alter's self-judgment serves as the criterion of accuracy and if black Alters are being judged, black children's judgment
may be more accurate than those of white children; but if white Alters
are judged, neither group may be more accurate than the other (Usual;
Christensen, 1970). *What does that prove?* The children must have
had differing experiences with and resulting attitudes toward the two
groups that have given rise to the different judgments.

But there are difficulties when we would use group membership as a
pathway to attitudes and hence to Alter. We must first determine which
group or groups are salient for a particular Alter (Pathway II.4). If he
is functioning actively within a group—he is playing a game or attend-
ing a church service—the inference may be relatively easy to make.
When he is alone or reflective, we cannot immediately or easily state
which of many groups is influencing him. After all, each of us in a
sense belongs to a large number of groups based upon age, sex, occupation, family, social class, recreation, etc. Also we cannot assume
automatic consequences of group membership. Thus when Egos are
asked to estimate the views of their own peer group, they *may* be less
accurate and express themselves with less certainty concerning those
issues on which they themselves deviate from majority sentiment; and
they *may* be more accurate concerning items on which their peers feel
more rather than less strongly (Canada, college students; Lay &
Thompson, 1968). Members of a group or a society considered as a
group may have their own distinctive methods of judging Alters as
well as an explanation for those methods. According to a folk hypothesis, attitudes of a child or adult are to be ascribed to the values
of one parent rather than another, they are often thought to be "inherited" from that parent. We know of course that children resemble
parents for many different reasons, including perhaps inherited inclination and most certainly environmental pressures in the home. But
there is no hard-and-fast rule that the traits of one parent will prove
dominant.

Ego may or may not be aware that many of his judgmental standards
spring out of groups or a zeitgeist (Pathway I.a). Are human beings
basically rational or irrational? The question in this form cannot be
answered because the terms are undefined and the dichotomy too glib.
But most non-professionals and some professionals attempt a reply
whose nature fluctuates from generation to generation; thus rationality
may have been stressed in the eighteenth century but irrationality has
been the common assumption during the first half or so of this century.

The answer to the question that Ego gives, moreover, affects the way in which he judges Alter and evaluates his behavior, as, for example, when he assigns responsibility for Alter's conduct or utterances. At this point Ego draws upon the general convictions comprising his understanding potential (Pathway II.c). In addition, Ego's judgment may be affected by the groups to which Alter belongs (Pathway 1.c); in fact, it is even possible that a more favorable view of Alter *may* be obtained by observing not his personality but the way in which he interacts with members of a group (Usual; Brickman, 1969).

Ego also has more or less distinctive attitudes toward Group Alters. A critical factor must be his own relation to the group: is it for him an in-group or an out-group? By and large, attitudes toward in-groups are likely to be friendly, though there are exceptions. Certainly, too, the converse need not be true; for example, you do not feel favorably disposed toward all the groups to which you belong (your local community), and you admire others with which you have had no connection (the ancient Greeks). *Does this mean that I can have negative as well as positive attitudes toward the very groups originally responsible for many of my attitudes?* Yes, there are such intricate spirals, and spirals must be, consequently, our next pathway.

4.b   Spirals

The reader, even one as conscientious as you, may have failed to notice that the only double arrow connecting the outside circles on our beloved chart lies between perception and attitude. *Is this very tragic?* The function of the arrow, may I say, is to indicate the interaction between the two. Attitudes, it has been suggested above, may be evoked either before or after perceiving Alter. Either way, they exert an influence upon continuing perception. In a relaxed mood, if you ever are relaxed, you begin reading the poem a bit carelessly, a line or two makes you feel you like what you see and hence you become favorably disposed toward the poet; as a result you read on in a less relaxed mood and with greater care. You cannot pay attention to what you wish to pay attention to until you wish to do so; and you may wish to do so only after you have paid attention. Imagine, as you can, some persons in a South Tyrolean inn who are speaking Italian. If Ego is an Italian, he may never notice them or, if he does, he considers their behavior normal and perhaps pleasant. But if he is a Tyrolean—a German-speaker of that region—he undoubtedly perceives their conversation and he disapprovingly calls them "noisy like all Italians."

A specific variant of the spiral has been encountered in the Ego-Alter effect (Pathway I.c), the ramifications of which can now be more fully explored. But first a danger inherent in the relation of Ego and Alter: Ego's vision may be distorted when he possesses or acquires a strongly favorable or unfavorable attitude toward Alter or a Group Alter. He *may* find a group attractive when he is convinced its members receive him cordially (Usual; Dittes, 1959). He may be unable or unwilling to conceal his attitudes from those whose behavior is in turn affected, perhaps correspondingly affected. Such a self-fulfilling prophecy, as it has been named, obviously is a spiralling relation between the two who are interacting. The medicine man in a traditional society, if we may make the not necessarily true assumption that his prescription has no real biochemical effect or at least no known one, believes in the efficacy of his medicine; he is able to convey his confidence to clients who may therefore be affected. Similarly if I anticipate that, when I see you again, you are going to treat me pleasantly, you may well do just that as a result of my expectation: upon meeting you, I behave in a manner that induces you to be pleasant and thus, consciously or not, I validate my own prediction. Doubtful as well as convincing evidence has been breathlessly accumulated in recent years which shows that even the so-called objective investigators of behavior may thus transmit their theoretical expectations to both rats and college students who are their subjects (Rosenthal, 1966).

Many professionals recognize the danger of bias and try to introduce safeguards into their research. Whoever has contact with the subjects does not know in what way the critical variable is being manipulated, or he is not even acquainted with the hypothesis being tested; thus his influence is kept at a minimum or at least cannot be intentionally exerted. Subjects in drug experimentation as a matter of course are not told whether they are being given a placebo or a drug; and the observers, too, may not know which subjects have had placebos and which subjects drugs. In real life, however, Ego may consciously or unconsciously avoid a valid procedure: wishing Alter to conform to his expectation, he is only too pleased if his own behavior or intervention facilitates the realization of that expectation. An Ego who believes that he has brought misery to Alter may feel guilty, and try to compensate for that feeling by judging Alter favorably. Or he may seek to justify his own misdeed by devaluing Alter who, consequently, Ego convinces himself, truly merits what has happened to him. Or, again in his own behalf, Ego *may* tend to reject an Alter who suffers when Ego feels powerless to assist him in the present or to alleviate the suffering in the future: it may be easier to believe that people get what they deserve or deserve what they get than to sympathize with them (Usual; Lerner & Simmons, 1966).

No simple pathway exists enabling you, me, or a professional Ego-expositor to predict Ego's judgment concerning Alter or his actions from a knowledge of Ego's probable attitude toward Alter. Ego, therefore, has the same difficulty when he would forecast Alter's attitude or action toward another Alter on a similar basis. It might seem reasonable to suppose, for example, that generally we are not likely either to harm those who help us or to help those who harm us, but a moment or two of reflection suggests circumstances or persons demonstrating, in the non-immortal words of those investigating the reactions of American college women in a laboratory setting (Nacci et al., 1973), that *perhaps* "we often hurt those we love and sometimes like those who hurt us." The advisable pathway for Ego who would appreciate these varied spiral effects has already been uncovered: it is self-knowledge (Pathway I.1). He must learn to stand off from himself, in order to appreciate the feelings that are welling up within him, coming perhaps from unconscious impulses that are not completely verbalized or verbalizable. In conversing with Alter, for example, does he find himself saying "You and I both like prunes" or "We both like prunes"? The subjects of the two sentences have the same referents, but the single pronoun "we" *may* suggest greater intimacy or interaction than "you and I" (Wiener & Mehrabian, 1968, p. 4). This distinction is not just grammatical and it may not be trivial if Ego catches himself expressing an attitude toward Alter through one of these verbal formulas (Pathway 3.a). Of course he may note Alter's attitude toward himself in exactly the same way, and noting that may in turn arouse a similar or dissimilar attitude within him. *I wonder: when "we" rather than "you and I" is employed, is Ego or Alter—whoever the speaker is— really expressing a feeling of intimacy and trying, consciously or unconsciously, to indicate "immediacy" between the two?*

Perhaps the most significant spiral of all involves objective or attributed similarity between Ego and Alter on the one hand and favorable attitudes (or attractiveness) on the other; Ego likes Alters similar to himself, and the Alters he likes he perceives as similar. This spiral involves so many complications that it intrudes at least twice in the judgmental process (Pathway 5 & 7: Primary and Secondary Judgments). And of course, we shall discover, the relation between similarity and attractiveness is not straightforward; thus the popularity of the traits considered similar *may* also affect Ego's feeling of attraction toward Alter (Usual; Posavac & Pasko, 1974). In more general terms, we also know or intuit a relation between the evoked attitude and the nature of the judgment that is passed (Postscript 4.2: The Effects of Attitude).

The challenge to the professional Ego-expositor who seeks a naturalistic pathway to Ego and to the Ego who would find an advisable one to Alter is to assign weights to Ego's attitude and to the reality, which is the Alter being judged as well as the context in which he is perceived. Common sense, trainloads of studies concerning human perception, and the really vast experience of clinicians who use projective methods (whether free association or the Rorschach) suggest a pathway: the attitude or any predisposition is likely to exert a stronger influence when the information from Alter and the context is scanty or vague. Think of the difference between judging Alter from a photograph and from a lifetime of conversations with him: other things being equal, as they never are, Ego's attitudes stand more of a chance of being both salient and efficacious in front of Alter's photograph, which can convey only a limited number of details, than they do when they must compete with the facts conveyed by frequent contacts with him. But frequent contacts simply produce different kinds of attitudes. Consider an Alter with glasses or with a particularly long or short nose; certainly the glasses or the nose is more likely not only to be perceived but also to evoke a dominating attitude when Ego is viewing only a photograph than it is when he is facing or conversing with Alter. On this pathway, then, the professional may know when to anticipate the facilitating effect of attitude, and Ego when to beware of its biasing effect.

I end the catalogue of spirals, at least for the time being, by a reference to the Ego-Ego situation: Ego passes judgment upon himself. "What a fool I am," Ego thinks and thus reveals, as existentialists would have it (Brandt, 1967), a distinction between the self as subject and the self as object, with the former expressing an attitude toward the latter. The split between the selves may be so great that the objective self, as it were, is depersonalized, a condition that *may* "often" occur when the individual would commit suicide (Usual; Waltzer, 1968). Without additional evidence, except that gained through introspection and hence favored by you, I suspect that the self-judgment motive, like the motive to judge Alter, is more likely to be evoked under conditions of distress than of contentment, for then something is amiss and Ego may wonder whether he himself is to blame. And perhaps he judges himself to be happy when he is happy only because he feels that the joyous state will fade. *You are projecting your cynicism and pessimism upon the rest of us.* Perhaps. I would also guess that psychiatrists, if not laymen, agree that self-insight is no more easily gained than insight into Alters, maybe in fact we can be more objective about others than we can be about ourselves; we *may* not even agree with one another concerning apparently simple self-judgments involving, for example, the question as to where in the body "the self" is to be located (U.S., children & college; Horowitz, 1935). An Ego believing that what happens to himself is externally determined by events in his milieu or by sheer chance, moreover, is less likely to look within himself than one who conceives that he alone is responsible for his own destiny. Ego's own ego usually, I imagine, blocks a consistent attitude of self-deprecation from coming into existence. Without such a block, the consequences could be disastrous: besides suicide, neuroses or psychoses might arise. Otherwise the momentary, unfavorable attitude leads to action or rationalization enabling Ego, he hopes, to feel more favorably disposed toward himself.

Spirals, spirals, spirals—enough of this nihilism. Surely our opinion of Alter does not always depend upon spirals or upon the role we happen to be playing, whether we are a member of this or that group, whether we are thinking of this or that person whose opinion we revere or despise. You would know what Alter "really" is, regardless of Ego's attitudes, prejudices, or other preoccupations? *Yes, for Alter exists as solidly and objectively as a cake of soap or the stone once kicked by Dr. Johnson.* In an absolute sense I believe you pursue a will-o'-the-wisp, even though I have already rejected the more general view that Ego is what others think him to be (Postscript 1.8). How can you expect Ego to function objectively like a camera? Perhaps I am exaggerating the idea that Alter can never be objectively photographed or perceived. Unlike the sinner, the saint I suppose is much less likely to be blinded by his attitudes, his opinion is not always altered when he performs a different role or refers his behavior to another group. *You do seem fixated upon saints and sinners, I wonder why. Or are you trying to prevent me from pointing out the metaphysical position into which you have pushed yourself?* I do not think I am stretching a good point or merely repeating a banal one when I insist on this obvious, though neglected, pathway: objectivity is difficult to achieve. *But you are not saying "difficult" but "impossible" to achieve.* Yes, I guess I am.

4.c   Change

The obstinate character of attitude is well documented (again, Postscript 4.1). We have known each other for years, we have endured miseries and joys together, we have discussed every conceivable subject from birth to death and from Aristotle to Zanzibar; yet I do not think I have influenced you in any significant manner, and I believe I have not been appreciably affected by you. Our state of affairs results not from a mysterious tendency for the fruits of behavior to grow independent of the roots but from a whole series of petty and important rewards which reinforce, as it were, the status quo within each of us. In spite of all the evidence testifying to the conservative nature of men and their societies, however, people do not stand completely still, their attitudes can and do change. Attraction, one professional has stated, is a "positive linear function of the proportion of weighted positive reinforcement" associated with Alter (Byrne, 1971, p. 279). Translated, this means that the persistence of attraction depends upon the rewards being offered—few rewards, less attraction; no rewards, no attraction. You and I know there can be sudden, even violent changes that are not necessarily superficial and may long endure. If we sit back for a moment and try to forget the weight of childhood and of history hanging heavily upon us, we can see that a large component of attitude consists of sentences directing or expressing our feelings one way or another: I love him, I hate him, I respect him, I ignore him. What can be changed are these sentences—changed sentences mean changed attitudes, and changed attitudes may mean changed actions.

As a result of historical experience and the codification engineered by practical communication experts and other professionals, moreover, we are able at least to mention some of the important factors associated with change. To do this, we must consider Ego's or Alter's attitude separately as the dependent variable and exclude from consideration the relation between the two, which of course is another source of change but which, being the theme of this book, must be analyzed step-by-step. The question thus becomes: under what circumstances does the attitude of Ego, which is part of his total potential and may affect his judgment of Alter, undergo change; or, similarly, when and why are there changes in Alter's attitude that can influence his behavior and hence Ego's judgment of him?

Change requires the same kind of laborious, step-by-step analysis being assayed here in examining Ego's judgment of Alter. We should begin with the agent of change, the communicator, and end with Ego's or Alter's reaction to the environmental stimuli, pressures, or the communication. We know, as we observed in connection with channels, that the prestige and credibility of the communicator can exert a significant influence. Ego's attitude toward Alter is more likely to change when he acquires new information from a source he respects rather than from one he holds in contempt or low esteem; but we also know —or think we know (Pathway 2.b)—that with the passing of time the direction of the change may be altered or even reversed.

Why do you say "think we know,"; do we not know, as you said two pathways ago, that sources of communications tend to be forgotten more readily than content and that therefore. . . We know this, I repeat, only from samples of American soldiers and adolescents who were the subjects of the investigation; we simply cannot say whether it is true for all mankind, whether it is universally applicable. *But, when is any generalization universally applicable?* You are repeating yourself, your taunt to the professionals and me continues. You are willing to say that *all* human beings grow hungry, are pained when their skin is pierced, sneeze when pollen or dust irritates their mucous membranes, become sexually excited under X conditions. *These bits of behavior are so unsubtle. What about the generalization concerning source and content, what good is it unless you can say whether it is applicable elsewhere?* I have an even more damaging fact to reveal: the fascinating tendency was not even apparent among *some* of the American subjects—they did not forget the source more quickly than the content. No, we can never be sure that we are not dealing with a cultural artifact until we empirically ascertain whether a generalization obtained under one set of social conditions reappears under another; and obviously by having continually to test the validity of a generalization we deprive ourselves of one of its assets, viz., being saved the trouble of investigating a new situation. But at least, I say somewhat lamely, we arrive in the new situation with a hypothesis to be tested, and that is an advantage you cannot completely gainsay (Pathway I.5).

Back to our topic of change. In Postscript 4.3 (Variables Affecting Attitude Change) I mention a few of the variables. On a very broad, abstract level it appears that attitudes or behavior change when congruence exists between the individual's needs and the satisfactions or rewards the proposed, pending change seems to demand or provide. Many of us, professionals and laymen, Marxists and non-Marxists, have toiled and struggled to arrive at some kind of general formulation to specify the changes of which men seem capable, whether involving their toothpaste or religion, their convictions or anticipations, their ancestors or descendants. I cannot halt, even in a postscript, to review this encyclopedia of hypotheses and guesses or the evidence and the intuition supporting or refuting them. As a personal aside only, I quickly append my own, my latest formulation not because I would proselyte in its behalf, but because not surprisingly it seems to me at least to raise the salient issues. A change is likely to be accepted by one or more persons:

1. When it is not in conflict with their traditional beliefs and values which are proving satisfactory

2. When it appears to them to have advantages which can be intelligibly demonstrated in the present or which are anticipated in the future

3. When it is introduced by persons whom they consider important and competent and who have adequately consulted them or their respected leaders

4. When it is in accord with the modal personality traits of their society or group or with a goal they are seeking

5. When it makes demands whose components they have already learned or feel confident they can learn (Doob, 1968a, p. 342).

In my view, three circumstances, having a close relation to one another, induce one or more of these conditions and hence facilitate rapid change: transplantation out of the normal milieu, transformation of the way the milieu or a portion of it is perceived, and conversion in a broad sense (Postscript 4.4). It is, I admit, much easier to suggest the various ways in which attitudes change than to devise really practical stratagems that induce desired changes. How, for example, can the prejudice many Egos have with reference to other people be reduced so that more valid judgments can be rendered? There is no infallible advisable pathway; many factors must be taken into account; each situation, each individual must be examined uniquely (Pathway I.5). Travelling abroad, like any contact between different groups, can be broadening but it can also reinforce previous judgments. Legal regulations, such as those pertaining to the busing of American school children to achieve integration of ethnic or social groups, may bring members of the groups together in a common setting without necessarily or markedly influencing their attitudes or behavior. In spite of important exceptions here and there in individual instances, the conclusion must be drawn that only by altering modes of socialization and education can prejudices be appreciably affected; and this is a long-run strategy. But the individual should not feel secure in his prejudices or hopeless about them: they can be modified, mitigated, even changed by forces in his society and within himself.

Are you not being overly optimistic about the possibility of swift change? Yes, perhaps. Certainly Ego's own body image, the ways in which he appraises that body, is especially stable (U.S., patients in hypoanalysis; Klemperer, 1968), and hence his view of himself in this respect is not likely to shift. Some professionals, therefore, especially psychoanalysts, think that effective psychotherapy must be slow: the therapist must delve deeply into the patient's past in order to uncover the source of his trouble, and delving is almost always a very painstaking process. In contrast, the adherents of behavior and nondirective therapy are able to point to cases in which changes have been dramatically rapid, provided of course the patient can be quietly or effectively rewarded for altering his behavior or for revealing his problems in front of a sympathetic listener. The experience of the best known proponent of nondirective therapy indicates that "as changes occur in the perception of self and in the perception of reality, changes occur in behavior" (Rogers, 1947).

To make you feel a trifle less restless, let me shoot again into the gay, gray mist of our philosophical differences. In spite of your aesthetic distaste and your preference for the unparsimonious, the unexpected, and the mysterious, I continue to try to have you see the virtues of a deterministic approach to Ego and Alter. Part of your displeasure arises from your assumption that determinism means passivity: poor Ego is powerless to judge Alter otherwise than the way he does and that judgment stems from Alter's words and activities. But now, I hope, you appreciate the fact that determinism definitely does not exclude Ego's substantial and active contribution while judging Alter: his attitudes affect his judgment and they can change. *Yet do you not also claim that those attitudes are also predetermined, are you not caught in your own infinite regress?* Perhaps you have the last word.

Postscripts

4.1   The Importance of Attitude

Attitudes are important because they affect Ego's initial perception of Alter and his subsequent reactions. When an Ego with a strong prejudice against Alter is unable to avoid him but is forced into his presence, for example, he *may* be consciously or unconsciously vigilant, so that he fails to perceive some or many of Alter's attributes, or may try to keep him at a psychic or physical distance (England, students; Beloff & Coupar, 1968). He may even have an attitude toward the timing Alter employs to reveal information about himself: he *may* find an Alter unattractive who too readily discloses his own good fortune; he *may* consider an Alter more attractive when he discloses his own misfortune readily rather than reluctantly but then only when he considers Alter responsible for the bad luck (U.S., female college students; Jones & Gordon, 1972). I do not expect to provide you with a sudden burst of insight when I mention that the connotations of words can evoke strong attitudes. *You don't say.* I am thinking not only of political epithets, obscenities, and other value-saturated words but also of simple ones like "warm" and "cold" when applied to an Alter. In the last instance the addition of these attitude-arousing words to a character sketch of a hypothetical or a real individual *may* have an overwhelming effect upon Ego's judgment and, in the latter case, to a certain extent upon the way he interacts with that person (Usual; Kelley, 1950). But of course not all words evoke such attitudes and not all words have such a dramatic effect.

Attitudes, moreover, probably affect the order in which Ego perceives the attributes of Alter in a manner previously outlined (Pathway II). Perhaps, as phenomenological analyses seem to suggest (From, 1971, p. 5), activity is likely to be perceived first and then intention. But I think a strong case can be argued for affection and thought, intentions, status, and background under circumstances when Ego is set to judge one of them rather than some other aspect of Alter. Thus a portrait painter may immediately note affection; a policeman, intentions; a census-taker, status—but I rather suspect that background seldom appears salient in the first few seconds of perception. Phenomenologists who accord priority to one attribute rather than another may therefore be ego- or ethnocentric.

The stability of attitudes is another reason why they are important. After Ego has evaluated an Alter (which is a way of saying that he has an attitude toward him for good or for superficial reasons), the evaluation *may* remain more stable than his actual behavior vis-à-vis Alter, in fact the attitude *may* subsequently affect the behavior more than the behavior affects attitude (U.S., children; Campbell & Yarrow, 1961). Ego's attitude toward an Alter who displeases him *may* remain unchanged, provided the displeasure is in accord with what he expects Alter to do (Usual; Stapleton et al., 1975).

4.2 The Effects of Attitude

Among professionals a mild debate has ranged as to whether a greater number of judgments or more discriminating ones are passed when the attitude is positive or negative. Finer or more complicated judgments *may* be directed toward individual or Group Alters evoking unfavorable rather than favorable attitudes either because Ego may be more careful to avoid or anticipate threats or punishments from a hostile than from a friendly source (Usual; Irwin, et al., 1967) or because he *may* feel compelled to find reasons for justifying his hostility (Usual; Soucar & DuCette, 1972); perhaps under these circumstances some Egos may be vigilant, others resort to rationalization (Usual; Koenig & Seaman, 1974). Perception *may* be more discriminating and attention more concentrated when Alter unexpectedly evokes an attitude as, for example, he does by departing from the role Ego has expected him to play (Touhey, 1972). For then the deviation requires an explanation, one that possibly can be provided by additional information. You note only the skill of the man at the wheel of the taxi since driving is what he is supposed to be doing; when he is garrulous and offers a political opinion, you may then begin to observe attributes heretofore overlooked, such as his ethnicity, age, manner of speaking, etc.

In the text, reference has been made to two of the nine attributes of Alter which Ego may judge (Pathway II), viz., attraction and similarity. To trumpet the effects of attitude, let us consider here two additional attributes, sense of responsibility and temporal orientation. Sense of responsibility, you recall, refers to the feeling or attitude the individual has about his own destiny: is it controlled by forces that are within or outside himself? If he feels that external powers affect him markedly, he may be less active and more fatalistic; he may not seek out copious information in the external world, and he may discount much of what he finds there. But if he feels that control is largely internal, he is likely to plan his life, to believe that he is master of his destiny to a greater degree, and to perceive and utilize information that will push him forward. As ever the sharp distinction is too glib, most of us are mixtures. *I belong to the external camp.* And I to the internal. *As a result, I often speak of a person's karma or destiny.* And I almost always think I must struggle even when defeat seems unavoidable. You agree, nevertheless, that education also formeth the man, and I that we are often at the mercy of externalities. Actually when the two tendencies are measured crudely by means of a paper-and-pencil questionnaire, internal Egos *may* wish more information about an Alter before passing judgment than do external Egos, provided they believe that the problem at hand involves skill or at least ambiguity rather than chance (Usual; Davis & Phares, 1967). On the other hand, Ego advisedly should know that internal Alters, to a greater degree than external Alters, *may* seek more vigorously to influence the evaluations they receive from him, again when they feel their ability is being challenged (Usual; Jones & Shrauger, 1968).

Ego's temporal orientation affects the kind of information he gathers concerning Alter and the way in which he evaluates that information; and the information he is given may arouse one orientation rather than another. If he is convinced, for example, that Alter has had an unhappy childhood or that he has suffered later on so traumatically that he has required psychiatric attention, his judgment and also the way in which he deals with Alter *may* be affected (Usual; Farina et al., 1966). If he knows or is told that Alter is mentally ill, his judgment is influenced in ways difficult to anticipate; thus he *may* judge him on the basis not only of his behavior but also of the future consequences of that behavior for himself, provided he is convinced that he can simultaneously affect the behavior (U.S., adults; Gergen & Jones, 1963).

4.3   Variables Affecting Attitude Change

First, the order of presentation: will the first or earlier part of a communication be more effective in producing change than the last or later part? The answer is another "well-it-all-depends" (Postscript 2.3). Should Ego be told explicitly what his attitude toward Alter ought to be or, instead, should he be offered the evidence which enables, perhaps compels, him to draw the same conclusion? If the communicator wishes for some evil reason to besmirch Alter's character, should he communicate to Ego only damaging evidence or should he also present Alter's attractive features and then immediately explode them? If he would shield Ego from an opposing viewpoint about Alter, should he or should he not see to it that Alter is exposed to a very mildly hostile viewpoint in order to accustom him to contrary evidence and hence to render him less vulnerable to a full-scale attack? These questions involve the drawing of conclusions by Ego, the presentation of one rather than both sides of an argument, and the acquiring of immunity through exposure (U.S., high school & college; Hovland et al., 1953). They point to practical and pressing problems in eliciting change, but again no simple set of principles seems to function as an advisable pathway: we can only identify the issues but we cannot resolve them in an absolute sense. For any resolution depends upon an interaction between the communication per se and the capability and personality of the responding Ego or Alter. Thus susceptibility to the appeal of a communication *may* be affected by the intelligence or education of the audience, though not in a simple manner. On the one hand, the more intelligent or better educated *may* be able more readily to learn content or to fathom meaning and hence be perhaps more vulnerable; but on the other hand, their superior wisdom *may* also make them more skeptical and so less prone to change (U.S., soldiers; Hovland et al., 1949, pp. 147–75).

Similarly, under some circumstances any personality trait may conceivably be related to persuasibility. Why don't you choose a trait and with the assistance of a spiral I shall spin a theory out of nothing—what shall it be? *Altruism or generosity*. Nothing could be simpler. The altruistic or generous Ego is more likely to expose himself to the influence of others, but he may be less likely to accept or at least not discredit unflattering reports about Alter. Try again. *Consider a total person like me.* That is more difficult. You live in such comfortable, exclusive surroundings that you have drawn the blinds and have erected barriers to many pathways; you cling to your views because they are yours, and for better or worse you are proud of your opinions which you often consider precious or even esoteric. Your character, your personality, have become so well formed, so stable, so rigid that heaven and earth are not likely to change any of your well-formed or long enduring attitudes toward most of the Alters in your midst. If you think I have been praising you, then fine; otherwise my apologies, for as ever I may be quite wrong.

4.4   Facilitating Rapid Change

1. *Transplantation.* The individual is removed from his usual milieu. Ego changes his job, he goes on a holiday, he is thrown into an army or jail, he joins a new organization. Or, to give the economic deter-

minist his due, his milieu is changed by forces he himself does not control. Altered conditions require changed attitudes—as well as other kinds of behavior—and Ego modifies what has sustained him in the past, though not always enthusiastically. In the new or changed environment he may become more or less anxious or insecure and so more or less misanthropic in general with the result that he feels more or less kindly disposed toward a specific Alter.

2. *Transformation.* The individual obtains a new or sudden insight, and this may occur in an old or new milieu. Do you remember those puzzle pictures you used to have in your childhood: hidden among the scrawls depicting a barnyard scene was the figure of a human face which at first could not be seen but which, after you had discovered it yourself or after some unkind person spoiled the fun by pointing it out to you, forever after forced itself upon your consciousness? Similarly, Ego may not observe one of Alter's traits until someone else suggests the significance of a bit of behavior; then all his other traits may be transformed and the attitude toward him correspondingly changes. Ego may also provide himself with the pivotal impulse inducing the transformation. At least on a paper-and-pencil basis, for example, he *may* alter his attitude toward aged persons in general by imagining a fictitious scene in which he is generously helped by an elderly man (Usual; Cautela & Wisocki, 1969).

3. *Conversion.* The individual undergoes a more radical version of transformation involving central parts of his personality (Pathway I.6); and again the milieu may remain unchanged or be changed. Not a single attitude of Ego but a significant component of his central philosophy is transformed, as a result of which a large number of attitudes and much of his behavior are affected. The convert views or tries to view members of the sect and all mankind as his brothers. Conversion may not be sudden, but may appear so only after a series of prior transformations and transplantations.

Since I have tried elsewhere to describe the psychological—not the sociological—precipitating circumstances responsible for each of these three conditions (Doob, 1971, pp. 401–03), I shall not repeat myself here. *Applause, though of course I am not going to look up the reference, at least not right now.*

Pathway 5: Primary Judgment

A distinction, not sharp but important, must be drawn between Ego's primary and secondary judgments, between first- and second-order abstractions concerning Alter. Enlightened or blinded by his attitudes, Ego usually does not merely perceive Alter, he transforms his immediate perception into judgments. These primary judgments spring from his behavior and understanding potentials, they may occur without reflection, they are strong and basic. He receives, perhaps, an impression of Alter and passes judgment without necessarily clearly formulating that judgment and likewise without expressing or acting upon it (McCollough, 1961). In a precise branch of psychology, psychophysics, the method of absolute judgment—also called the method of single stimuli—functions either analogously or identically. A subject is given no standard to serve as a basis for comparing two stimuli, instead he is simply asked to judge, for example, whether a sound is loud or soft. At first he finds the task difficult or impossible—what is loud, what is soft? He cooperates, nevertheless, and he guesses. Eventually, after being bombarded with a series of sounds and judging each one, he establishes a scale of his own; thereafter his judgments tend to be both relatively consistent and accurate. Similarly, after perceiving Alter, Ego knows, or thinks he knows, at a glance whether Alter is good or bad, attractive or unattractive; he does not consciously compare him with other persons he has previously judged, although past judgments have given rise to his standard.

Ordinarily the primary judgment is evoked by and hence refers to externalities—Alter's appearance and his perceivable behavior—and is likely to include only crude inferences concerning Alter's feelings, thoughts, or intentions. It is like glancing at a picture and observing the broad outlines and receiving a general impression without noting or concentrating upon the subtleties. No attempt is made to find or identify the cues that have produced a primary judgment, which is a way of saying that intuition is the guide (Hathaway, 1956). Frequently, however, Ego passes secondary judgment: he goes beyond the stimulus having immediate impact upon his senses and attitudes; he challenges or hears someone else challenge his initial judgment; or for some reason he would diagnose or evaluate deeper trends within Alter. On the primary level Ego may have little if anything to say in order to justify or explain his judgment; it comes to him informally, he is not able immediately to find appropriate words. In contrast, on the secondary level he can offer a bill of particulars, for he has had the opportunity to reflect; and reflection among human beings is likely to produce words and sentences. That woman is frail and brittle, the primary judgment of an Omaha Indian may be as he observes her grief-stricken face; then, he adds secondarily, such weakness is an attribute of all women who, he believes, have less power than men to resist misfortune (M. Mead, 1952, pp. 140–42). In general, praising or condemning an Alter by almost automatically invoking the moral standards of a society is different from carefully attempting to decide on the basis of various criteria whether his behavior should be considered good or bad. A child can easily announce that his playmate is naughty by applying his parents' standards or those of his play group, but a juvenile or adult philosopher must hesitate and ponder before approving or disapproving conduct from some ethical standpoint.

I am not disparaging primary judgments, for they need not be inaccurate. Ego may judge both validly and confidently a trait or bit of behavior that he has experienced again and again either in himself or in others and that he knows he has satisfactorily judged in the past (Pathway 6.a). Dentists may usually anticipate and also perceive correctly when the drill will pain their patients, and they may often also judge, on the basis of the tooth they are treating as well as from a knowledge of the patient's sensitivity, the degree of the pain. If there are mysterious forces either within Ego's unconscious or within the universe—such as ESP or some cosmic power we ordinarily can neither accept nor gainsay—the perception and judgment are likely to be immediate. The deliberate judgment we call secondary may well cause such forces to be obscured or distorted by mundane reasoning or verbalization. An Ego who would perceive not the present but the potential or ideal may eventually be blinded by his biases, but at first, fresh glance he may possibly catch a glimpse of an elusive, utopian Alter he will seldom be able to capture through reflection.

Ego's primary judgment, nevertheless, may be false or slanted and spring not from what he perceives in Alter but from his own conception of Alter. At this level, all the speedy processes ascribed by professionals to their subjects and patients—projection, identification, empathy, pity, compassion, etc. (Pathway II.5)—operate full force, and Ego quickly arrives at a judgment. First impressions may be rich and varied, but they—oh, let us postpone evaluating them until later (e.g., Pathway 6.a), though I would quickly note here only that they may be derived from an atypical sample of Alter's behavior or from an unassorted conglomeration of segmental and central traits. Many times, perhaps more often than not, no other pathway is pursued and the story ends with the primary judgment: it is final and leads to actions, the fruits of which are probably stored within Ego (Pathways I & II).

This contrast between two kinds of judgment sounds vaguely familiar. Yes, it should be; indeed the concepts of primary and secondary judgments have in effect been employed by others, I have not received them atop Mt. Sinai for purposes of the present analysis (Postscript 5.1: Primary vs. Secondary Judgments).

5.a   Description

Primary judgment may involve, one, two, or all three of the following: Ego describes Alter; Ego ascribes motives or goals to him which Alter himself may not recognize; or Ego imputes to Alter beliefs concerning those motives and goals as he thinks Alter himself formulates them. Before analyzing each process in its own right, it is essential to do battle with a problem applicable in large part to all three: the concepts or categories Ego employs when imputing, ascribing, and particularly describing. *Do you imply that Ego constantly, perhaps always, categorizes Alter's action and that therefore he inevitably goes beyond what he perceives?* I think so, and on this score I anticipate no objection from you, who quickly and often surely are able to report the nature of human activities. We are generally uncomfortable when Alter's behavior is unclear or obscure, and therefore we find meaning in what he does by categorizing what we perceive.

Any lay Ego has his own set of categories to be invoked quickly when he would or must judge Alter. Some professionals have devised techniques not to impose their own concepts upon Ego but to try to determine the actual concepts he employs in passing judgment. According to one investigator, Ego can be asked to consider three persons, such as his mother, father, and spouse, and then to say *in his own words* how two are similar and how two differ from the third one in important ways (Kelly, 1955, chapt. 3 & as elaborated by Bannister & Mair, 1968, pp. 6, 45–47)—and usually he is able to comply quite readily. The ability to resort to categories in this manner means that Ego has a repertoire of concepts within himself and that he uses them as naturalistic pathways (Pathway II.c).

In discussing the ways in which personality can be conceptualized (Pathway I.b), it was noted that professionals and laymen alike somewhat capriciously but inevitably select concepts referring to traits they ascribe to Alters. The traits so postulated may not be helpful in understanding or predicting behavior in the broadest sense unless their interaction with situational requirements (especially the role the Alters are more or less required to perform) is also taken into account (Pathway 1.3). In addition, professionals frequently conduct their investigations by offering Ego their own list of categories on the basis of which they then have him judge Alter. This procedure achieves methodological elegance and simplicity and may be considered both unrealistic and realistic. More often than not, in everyday life Ego is not given ready-made categories ("Tell me what you think of him"), but sometimes he is ("Tell me whether you consider him selfish").

Any categorization, regardless of origin, is hazardous. For, regardless of its predictive power, a concept applied to Alter can easily become a word-sentence or proposition concerning him, and then immediately give rise to other sentences that are in effect an evaluation. You describe that old friend of yours as an "alcoholic" and that word implies for you. . . . *You mean for you, not for me.* It implies the probability that in your opinion he drinks excessively, he drinks by himself, he suffers from amnesia concerning what transpired during his bouts, and he cannot assume some or many of his normal responsibilities. In addition, you have definite notions suggesting why he or anyone has become an alcoholic; and you may also have various beliefs related to his prognosis and to that of all persons called alcoholic. The question here, you see, is not just whether he is in fact an alcoholic but whether your characterization of him affects, rightly or wrongly, your judgment about him. The concept becomes a label and hence may function virtually as a judgment. Similarly, sophisticated Egos in the West are often tempted to pass judgment which *may* persist and prevent Ego from ever changing his judgment (Usual; Kanouse, 1972). Too many sophisticates in the West are often tempted to plaster psychoanalytic labels upon Alters, for it sounds profound to be able to say that he suffers from castration anxiety and that she once experienced penis envy. Professional clinicians may also display this malady: the lady holds onto her words not because of a linguistic tendency within her mother tongue but because of a reluctance to part with anything she possesses. In their sober moments, however, extreme psychoanalysts, especially Freud, do not utilize dramatic labels until they have collected scores and scores of facts concerning analysands in tedious, painful hours devoted to diagnosis and therapy.

A label may have connotations of its own and thus be associated with other traits. Calling Alter intelligent, for example, *may* mean that he is then considered active, clever, enterprising, conscientious, independent, reliable, responsible, etc., and calling him both intelligent and considerate *may* imply that he is also judged to be even-tempered, honest, modest, warm, etc. (Usual; Bruner et al., 1958). The advisable pathway is an awareness that descriptive epithets may have profound implications.

Their implications, moreover, become, like attitudes, even more profound with the passage of time. At the outset the categories Ego uses to describe Alter necessarily omit some of the details he has perceived, but later more or all of the details—the possible qualifications, the images—are gradually forgotten and perhaps only the verbal formulation remains. "She was self-centered and conceited," he recalls and neglects completely the nuances of the relationship when it was alive. Such unavoidable simplification is especially pronounced when Group Alters are judged. You cannot possibly perceive every individual in Italy, Germany, Austria, Tanzania, Ghana, Israel, Burma, or the Sandwich Islands, some of which places you have visited, others learned about through informants, television, and written reports. Your many first- or second-hand impressions you do not or cannot recall whenever you hear the name of a country. You summarize your catalogue of impressions, facts, and judgments in a few words or sentences, and the residue may become farther and farther removed from reality or from what you initially experienced. Again the advisable path is caution, however unattainable: what you or Ego says about Alter or a country is bound to be incomplete and to become more so later on; every word, every sentence that is stored should be qualified, tentative, subject to change, and should never, never be sanctified. *But I haven't the time to qualify or to be forever concerned with the passing of time.*

As Ego-expositors we must raise a puzzling, straightforward question: why does Ego select some concepts to describe Alter and not others? Happily or unhappily we already have a naturalistic pathway available on which the reply in abstract form is to be found: concept selection is a part of behavior and therefore selection depends upon the components of the behavior potential (Pathway I) which, you vividly recall, are culture, personality, and the Ego-Alter relation.

And so you will now examine these three factors, one by one. Yes. This makes me feel quietly furious again: is there no "correct" way to describe Alter? Are you not leading yourself and me astray with this determinism of yours? Let me offer a simple reply this time. I look at the beauty of the scene in front of me, as I write here in the South Tyrol. *You certainly like to talk about the South Tyrol, don't you?* Yes—and I designate the objects I see as church, houses, trees, mountains, grass, snow, men in blue aprons. Someone else, however, could describe the same scene differently: he might overlook the aprons and concentrate his attention upon the various species of trees or the kinds of clouds in the sky. No concept, in brief, is simple, and it seems perfectly legitimate to try to account for the variability—as I shall now try to do.

The pervasive influence of culture determines in no small part the categories in general use within a society (Pathway I.a). In fact, after a moment's hesitation I would suggest that through trial and error, over generations, people in a society acquire a conception of behavior, accompanied by a relevant set of categories, that is based upon more varied and real experiences than professionals have had when they investigate particular subjects and emerge with their own pet concepts (Postscript 5.2: Cultural Determination of Concepts). *Again your favorite point about relativity, but is it not also true that some categories are virtually universal and so transcend culture, such as a tendency for human beings everywhere to resort to animism, personification, and anthropomorphism and thus to apply to animals and inanimate objects categories derived from persons?* Yes, and the reverse may be true: persons are described in terms usually reserved for objects: warm-cold, straight-crooked, sweet-sour—and metaphors of this sort exist in a variety of languages, such as Burmese, Chinese, Hausa, and Thai (Asch, 1958). I suppose the reason for the transcultural uniformity must be traced to the obvious fact that peoples in all societies are human and therefore, just as they blink their eyes when an object approaches their face, so they arrive at somewhat similar conclusions concerning the universe (animism), and find it easy to generalize their concepts from persons to objects (personification) or animals (anthropomorphism).

You might also suggest another way to transcend relativity: subsume the variety of judgments employed by all Egos who have ever lived under a very abstract set of categories. I would agree, largely because higher levels of abstraction are always possible. This procedure has occurred to many writers (e.g., Warr & Knapper, 1968, pp. 7–16), and I am of the opinion that the classical and well-used trio of cognition, affection, and conation are especially useful. Cognition suggests Ego's conception of what Alter is responding to in the external world; affection, his subjective reactions, feelings, and emotions; and conation, his motives and goals, and also his expectations. These terms, however, are very broad; they leave untouched the nuances encountered on Alter's naturalistic pathway. For precise knowledge not of universals but of the distinctive categories within a society, especially those embodying central values, provides Ego-expositors with insight into the categories Ego is likely to employ. He is a pious Christian and therefore—is it not more important to know this fact (and hence to assume that he frequently employs some variant of an ethical or religious category to express his primary judgment) than to classify his categories as affective or conative?

Ego's personality plays a role in his selection of concepts (Pathway I.b), for at a given moment he seldom if ever describes Alter without having the description serve some function; otherwise a judgment motive would not be evoked (Pathway II.a). He may wish merely to identify Alter in some respect (he is a vegetarian), to warn himself or others concerning Alter's potentialities (he is carrying a stiletto), to arouse sympathy or disgust (he has his arm in a sling or he picks his teeth in public after cupping the toothpick with his free hand). To a minor or a major degree, then, Alter is what Ego needs him to be.

Our deterministic bias would suggest that Ego uses those concepts somehow compatible with his own personality or needs (Pathway II.2). The connection, however, is not easy to establish. Do very aggressive Egos judge Alters more frequently in terms of aggression than non-aggressive Egos do? You or I could argue either way, couldn't we? Or if there is a tendency for some Egos to note similarities rather than dissimilarities between themselves and most Alters and for others to do the reverse (Usual; Leventhal, 1957), then in what respects can we anticipate that the personalities of the two groups differ? *I am sure I don't know.* What we do know beyond skepticism is that within our society—and presumably therefore in other societies—the concepts individuals employ differ markedly with respect both to type and to content (Postscript 5.3: Individual Differences in the Use of Concepts), from which fact it is legitimate to deduce that the differences must originate within Ego's culture and sub-culture, more particularly within him as a person.

One more attempt to puncture your nihilism: cannot we make a decision not about the ultimate descriptive categories Ego uses but about the ones he is likely, we guess, to use; does he not give priority to some? I have already mentioned culture as the source, but there is more to say: more often than not, I suspect, the primary judgment begins with a feeling which indicates, quickly and intuitively, whether Alter is attractive or unattractive, harmless or harmful, likable or not, for so much of social life depends upon the affective bonds existing between persons (Pathway I.c). These categories slip effortlessly through Ego as he responds, although their eventual effect upon his secondary judgment may be most varied. In appraising photographs of persons of the opposite sex, American undergraduates *may* react more positively to faces considered attractive by comparable peers than to ones thought to be unattractive, and also more favorably to faces of persons allegedly having attitudes similar rather than dissimilar to their own. Their reactions, however, *may* also be affected by their sex, by their judgments concerning their own attractiveness, and by the kind of contact anticipated with Alter (whether working together, dating or marrying) (Stroebe et al., 1971). Another guess: among the attributes proposed in connection with Pathway II, I would suggest an order of priority, which might be activity, similarity, attraction, affection and thought, intention, achievement, personality, status, background. *I wonder.* And quite rightly.

At first glance category choice as a function of the Ego-Alter relation seems straightforward. *At least it does, until you introduce the complications.* Thus spectators judge tennis players with a set of categories different from the ones they would employ if the same persons were performing a duet or quartet at a chamber music concert. Originally Ego may or may not have selected the context in which to perceive Alter, but at the moment of judgment the situation is likely to be salient (Pathway II.4). Equally commonplace is the phenomenon of generalization: Alter A reminds Ego of Alter B and therefore the categories employed to describe A and otherwise to judge him at first blush are the same as those previously applied to B. Such an association functions like any attitude toward Alter based upon his group affiliation (Pathway 4). We may ascribe certain attributes to Alter because he is Japanese, in which case Alter B is the ethnic group. But why is Ego reminded of B when he perceives A (Hays, 1958, pp. 295–99)? Ego may value B highly, or the thought of B may simply be salient; thus he is predisposed to perceive B or to find B's attributes in other persons, and he happens to chance upon A. *Come, come, you who believe in parsimony: A in fact may resemble B in some obvious respect.* Now, then, the complication you have anticipated and one I have previously referred to as a spiral is the relation between the objective similarity of Ego and Alter or the similarity Ego assumes to exist on the one hand and Alter's attractiveness on the other. Cause and effect, consequently, cannot easily be distinguished as the spiral swirls, and the relation may well function in both directions more or less simultaneously. The painful details I relegate to a postscript (5.4: Similarity and Attractiveness). There you will discover that similarity affects attractiveness, may not affect attractiveness, or may lead to other judgments; and attractiveness affects similarity, may not affect similarity, or may lead to other judgments. *Very helpful.*

Otherwise Alter may affect Ego's choice of categories in ways about as numerous as the possible relations between them. *Perhaps*, for example, more complex categories are employed as Alter or his relation with Ego increases in importance (largely Usual; Crockett, 1965). Alter can be Ego's reference group, for the categories Ego selects may depend on whether his judgment will be private or eventually expressed in front of someone else.

When Ego is judging not a single Alter but a Group Alter, he may or may not invoke a different set of categories (France, students; Doise & Zavalloni, 1970). The interaction between only two Alters usually involves a new phenomenon not easily derived from the terms applied to each of them. One might be called generally either competitive or cooperative, for example, but to decide whether together Alters are competing or cooperating requires different observations and descriptions. Similarly, judging the affective bonds between two persons is different from judging the warmth of their individual personalities.

Now perhaps it is even easier to understand why the promising categories of professionals—such as the previously mentioned elaborate analyses of concepts which have reduced Ego's verbal reactions to the categories of evaluation, potency, and activity (Osgood, 1969), or the investigation of formal scales which has resulted in a very similar trio (England, adults; Warr & Haycock, 1970)—have had little impact upon other professionals and almost none upon laymen. There just are too many different ways to describe Alter; he is too versatile. *Maybe this is as it should be.*

I shall try very hard to end this section on an optimistic note: there need not be a lack of correspondence between Alter's action and Ego's description of what he perceives. Alter's ear-scratching can be described as ear-scratching. A discrepancy arises when the behavior is more significant. *You call this optimism? Behavior is almost always more significant, and when description leads to ascription. . . .*

5.b   Ascription

Ego is seldom content with judging what he perceives in Alter but almost instantly ascribes Alter's behavior to some informally intuited cause. Explanations take two broad forms: some combination of circumstances in the past or a trait or disposition within Alter is held responsible. The alert or non-alert reader must immediately note that this dichotomy is the same one dividing the professionals, some of whom stress situations, others traits. Ego's impulse to ascribe goes beyond what he perceives in either case, and he resorts to indices (Pathway 3.c).

Ascription regarding traits or types arises from a conviction of both Ego and the professionals that personality is "visible and invisible" (Ichheiser, 1970, pp. 23 ff.), and hence that Alter's words or actions must result from some central tendency within him (Eysenck, 1954, p. 171), a style of behavior (Allport, 1937, pp. 323–24), or a motive. Let me again use a concrete illustration from the same small village in the South Tyrol. Yesterday I watched a wedding there. The church bells began ringing at 9:45 in the morning; before 10 a small crowd assembled on the road in front of the church. Promptly at 10 the village band, in traditional dress and playing loudly and unsteadily, marched two-by-two in that direction. Behind them were the bride and groom and their relatives. As soon as the band had entered the churchyard, two small girls, overflowing with smiles, closed the metal gates and thus blocked the entrance of the bridal pair and the rest of the party. For a split second I was shocked; but then I assumed—correctly—that the girls were not setting up a barrier but must have been carrying out a traditional ritual with which I was not acquainted. The smiling bridegroom took some coins out of his pocket, gave them to the girls who laughed and opened the gates. My judgment stopped at that point when I realized that the girls' behavior was culturally determined (Pathway I.a). I had provided myself with an explanation motivated, I am sure, not by mundane gain or a desire to increase my rapport with the villagers but by curiosity. I did not raise additional questions concerning the incident; I did not go on to formulate a secondary judgment.

Ego often believes that Alter's behavior springs from the momentary situation and may therefore quickly change. But such episodic behavior, as it has been called in contrast with dispositional tendencies (Warr & Knapper, 1968, pp. 8–9), may be a function not only of external factors but of internal ones that include a momentary mood as well as more enduring traits. Your cheerfulness right now may result from your desire to bring joy to someone else, from good news you have just heard, from your physical state, or from a sunny temperament, if you have such a temperament. Ego, therefore, will ascribe traits to Alter when he assumes that what he has done, is doing, will do—no matter how long the duration—results at least in part from more or less enduring tendencies within him. His ascription is based upon inferences from what he assumes to be antecedent or consequent data. He wonders why Alter is rushing down a street; could he be hungry? He may ascribe that motive to him if he knows that Alter usually goes out to eat at a particular hour or if he observes him entering a restaurant. Similarly he assumes that Alter has an ethical code stressing honesty on the basis either of an antecedent factor such as his strict family background, or of a consequent one, such as an action apparently demonstrating this virtue. To be sure, these inferences, being based on indices, are not necessarily correct and require validation (Melbin, 1972, pp. 4–5).

For reasons associated directly or indirectly with Alter but ultimately with himself, Ego may try to explain Alter's behavior in terms of both situational and personality forces. Alter slips on an icy walk, and Ego immediately ascribes the fall both to the ice and to some trait within Alter such as carelessness, haste, or accident-proneness. He will also ascribe an intention to him, viz., to get up, unless he has been knocked unconscious or is unable to do so. "When we experience such actions," a phenomenologist maintains, "we normally observe a part of the material sequence only; but often the whole of the action can be present nevertheless in our experience" (From, 1971, p. 17)—whether the entire action is thus consciously salient or whether its backward and forward parts are added by inference I leave for you to decide.

A non-professional Ego may be able to appreciate the presence of abnormality without being able to ascribe it to the technically "correct" category other than to say that it is abnormal (Pathway I.7). Someone with a facial tic, a person foaming at the mouth and sprawled unconscious on a city street, a wealthy woman who shoplifts, a man who constantly invents falsehoods unnecessarily—such behavior can be quickly perceived to fall outside the normal range, but is not likely to be "correctly" interpreted by an Ego who is not a psychiatrist or who has not had comparable psychiatric experience. The problem is compounded when cultural differences play a role, for then Ego's categorization of abnormal may apply only to the norms of his own society, whereas the behavior may be quite normal within Alter's group (Pathway I.2).

Ego does not necessarily function in the manner suggested by the logical connotation of the word "inference." He seldom formulates a major premise ("People who don't look you straight in the eyes cannot be trusted") and a minor premise ("Alter is not looking me straight in the eyes"), from which a formal conclusion is derived ("Alter, therefore, cannot be trusted"). In fact, the premises, though present in the sense that an outsider may postulate them or drag them out of Ego by persistent, impertinent questioning, may not be verbalized or even conscious, and the cues giving rise to the minor premise may only be dimly perceived, so that Ego is convinced his judgment stems not from logical or semi-logical inference but from intuition (Sarbin et al., 1960, pp. 184–85). For Ego, in short, the judgment possesses the attribute of "immediacy and objectivity in perception" (Allport, 1937, p. 527).

Why does Ego undergo the risks of ascription? The question is very misleading; first because Ego himself may infrequently recognize the risks, he feels he is dealing with certainties, subjective certainties; and secondly because, being human, he is as powerless to resist ascription as he is to prevent himself from scratching an itch or swallowing the liquid in his mouth. "You are wearing a green dress," I observe, a descriptive judgment that is phenomenologically immediate from my standpoint. "You are wearing a green dress that compliments your complexion" is less immediate, involves more of a judgment. "You are wearing a green dress because you think it shows you off to best advantage" clearly involves a far more daring inference. Even the simplest of my three judgments implies that I must have some interest in judging the color of your dress: judgments are made only when there is some motive to do so (Pathway II.a).

Ego and most of us believe it is not sufficient merely to describe Alter's achievement or non-achievement: we seek to infer his intention or motive, we speculate as to whether he is driven by impulse or conscience. Why is that man so friendly when you scarcely know him? Is he a humane person or has he some ulterior aim? From the very outset we learn and are taught to react either with favor or disfavor to types of Alters in our milieu, and forever after it is useful to do just that. Human beings may not be precisely divisible into friends and enemies, although these end points of the continuum are the ones along which they are invariably placed. If Alter suddenly raises his hand over his head, the action can be described in physical terms (though the units and direction must be specified by concepts that are arbitrary or at least culturally saturated), but its significance—its goal or relation to Alter's traits or personality—is supplied by Ego himself. Alter is like the philosopher's tree falling in the forest: it makes no sound unless a living organism hears it. *Halt—Alter is not a tree or at least he is a very special kind of tree that hears itself fall.* But, then, what about a Group Alter, can people hear themselves? All I am saying is that it is reasonable to suppose that Alter has some goal—to relieve an itch, to rob a bank, to compose a sonnet, to move a boulder, to win a love—and his conduct is governed accordingly. When Ego may not have an immediate answer, he is puzzled.

Now you are pulling out your doctrine of determinism again, this time ascribing it to Ego. Surely you are projecting upon him your own way of viewing Alter, surely Ego is not always that sophisticated. No, I am not maintaining that Ego considers all the metaphysical niceties of determinism (Pathway II.2). He is uncomfortable, I repeat, when he cannot offer some kind of explanation of the behavior he perceives, and that explanation is likely to involve motivation. *But what about the passenger who falls down when the train comes to a sudden and unexpected halt, do you invoke motivation then?* Of course not, Newton's conception of momentum suffices in this instance, although here I do not think I stretch my thesis too far when I wonder why Alter was not holding onto something that might have prevented him from falling. I do agree, however, that Ego himself may not think in deterministic ways when he would explain Alter. He may believe that Alter possesses a full or partial measure of free will: what he does, Alter himself decides at the spur of the moment, perhaps out of sheer cussed-

ness, perhaps after seriously considering the scores of choices open
to him. Voluntarism, however, is also an explanation: it is a form of
indeterminism almost as compelling as determinism. I do not appraise
either its validity or utility, I note only that it serves that function.
Normally, though, hairs need not be split: Ego looks for motives and
his search is likely to involve not a snap but a reflective judgment
(Pathway 7.c.).

When a central tendency is ascribed to Alter (Pathway I.6) and
symbolized by a trait, Ego gains two advantages (Holt, 1962). *I see
you cannot move away from the trait-situation controversy (Pathway
I.b)*. It is so relevant in this context. Ego's first gain from the trait
assumption enables him to anticipate Alter's future behavior in a variety of situations and to compare Alter with other persons. Regarding
anticipation: since the "general intentions" of an individual are less
situationally determined than his "behavioral intentions," Ego *may*
have keener insight into Alter by knowing that he seeks usually to be
helpful than that he wishes to wash dishes (Triandis et al., 1968, p.
39). But this does not mean that Ego can anticipate the precise form
of Alter's future behavior. For example, did American undergraduates
react a few moments later in a friendly or unfriendly manner to a
fellow student (actually the investigator's confederate) who had treated
them "in a dastardly manner" by failing to adhere to an agreement
in a game and thus ostensibly depriving them of their prize money?
Being frustrated, you might think, they would be aggressive or at least
sulky—and some of them in fact were. But others interacted with the
frustrator in a friendly, admiring manner; *perhaps* the aggressive ones
had a low need for social approval, the non-aggressive ones a high
need (Conn & Crowne, 1964). Expression in this situation *may* have
depended not only upon the frustration but also upon personality
traits; and numerous other factors, such as the degree to which Alter
viewed the frustration as willful or arbitrary, *may* likewise have been
involved (Usual; Pastore, 1952). The latter study, moreover, poses
another problem for Ego: it would have been difficult if not impossible
for him, I surmise, to have inferred the existence of a suppressed
aggressive tendency among the students with a high need for social
approval merely by observing their friendly behavior.

Then the behavior to which a trait gives rise fluctuates from person
to person and therefore Alter is being compared, implicitly or explicitly, with other individuals, perhaps his peers, no matter how he is
characterized. Conceivably, since Alter is unique, he could possess a

trait that should not be ascribed to anyone else on the planet; conceivably, yes, but highly unlikely, since there are enough people in existence for us to be confident that any strange or exotic behavior usually appears more than once. This does not exclude the possibility that Alter, though his individual traits are not unique, may have a personality that is quite distinctive; thus the most ardent humanist, including even you, ought to be satisfied. Any trait must vary in degree, beginning with the limiting case of zero—the trait is absent— and ending with a virtual overflow into the entire personality (Pathway I.6). Even if trait names are invented to fit a unique Alter, the invention can perhaps be employed later in passing judgment on others.

You consider this complicated? Come, come, think about me for a moment. I always try to be punctual, I keep my promises, I worry about missing planes, etc.—you could draw up quite an inventory, couldn't you? You summarize all these bits of behavior by calling me compulsive. Having named that trait, you have suggested—other things being equal—that I shall behave similarly in diverse situations, such as those involving routine and perhaps conscientiousness; and also that I possess this tendency to a greater degree than most persons, particularly more so than you. I may be quite unique, I fear, but there is nothing, absolutely nothing unique about any of my traits.

One view makes yet another use of both the situation and the trait approaches, but applies them to different persons. Ego, it has been cogently and somewhat convincingly argued, *may* have a strong tendency to believe that his own behavior, whether successful or not, results from situational requirements or restraints and Alter's from the traits or dispositions he, Ego, ascribes to him. The professional proponents of this view have offered a series of really ingenious laboratory experiments supporting their contention (Usual; Jones & Nisbett, 1971; Ruble, 1973). A mishap to himself, they think, Ego blames on circumstances, but one to Alter, on Alter's character. *Why, then?* More or less the same information can be processed differently. Ego does not perceive himself in the situation, what he notices are the cues there to which he is responding. The reverse is true when he judges Alter; then he perceives him as the outstanding stimulus in the context of the situation and hence is tempted to consider him the cause of his own action rather than the surrounding milieu. Ego, having necessarily incomplete knowledge concerning Alter, easily and unwittingly can ignore circumstances in Alter's past or present and hence ascribe his actions to a trait; in contrast, he knows the circumstances within himself—or thinks he does—and so can blame or credit them with responsibility rather than any aspect of his own character. Also Ego, as I have previously argued, may feel more comfortable when he believes that Alter is consistent rather than inconsistent—and consistency assumes the existence of a trait. An Ego who uses the category of trait may consider any trait within himself unique, but a trait of Alter to be common to a class of persons.

Again, of course, only tendencies have just been indicated. There are always some Egos in the laboratory and in real life who explain their own behavior or that of Alter quite similarly, whether they invoke traits or situations. The individual, for example, who tends to ascribe behavior to external forces—the locus-of-control variable already discussed—may not invoke the situational explanation either for others or himself.

A special kind of judgment may be ascribed by Ego to himself that involves, as those acquainted and unacquainted with Freud often say, an Ego ideal. Each of us has a set of favored traits with which we judge ourselves. We note with pleasure the extent to which we think we possess them and with pain the extent to which we do not. Domesticated undergraduates in America are able to fill out with dispatch and amusement questionnaires asking them to rate almost any conceivable array of traits with respect to (1) their attitude toward the traits as such, (2) the extent to which they themselves possess them, and (3) the gap (if any) existing between their alleged possession and their admitted desire to possess them. *Is there any reason to believe that such ascription is more or less facile or valid than that concerning the traits of Alters?* I do not think so, because a great deal depends on the traits being judged as well as on the Ego or the Ego and the Alter who are involved. On the one hand, Ego has access to himself as he does not have to other persons. Up to some unknown point he knows what his own motives are and he is in a good position, the very best position, to determine, if he is so inclined, the traits or values around which his behavior or even his life is organized (Pathway II.4). But on the other hand he may lack the will to probe himself, he may be devoid of insight, he may be able to judge other persons with greater objectivity.

Ascribing Alter's behavior to the situation at hand requires two kinds of knowledge: of the situation and of the situation's effect upon persons in general or upon Alter in particular. Knowledge of the situation refers to the context in which Ego's judgment is made (Pathway 1.c): is Alter alone or with other persons; is the weather at that moment hot or cold; is Alter rich or poor? Such facts may or may not be easy to ascertain, and their determination is simple in comparison with the problem of evaluating them. For Ego must resort to a host of theoretical assumptions concerning the effects other persons, the weather, and income have upon behavior. When you and I view the possibilities, we are torn between two extreme interpretations, that of Marx who attributed so many aspects of behavior to what he unprecisely defined as economic conditions and that of Freud who of course attributed even more actions to the family situation. But neither Marx nor Freud helps us, I think, when we would decide whether Alter's ill humor at this moment *may* be due to the weather (Kenya, adults; Doob, 1968c). Similarly there are innumerable other environmental conditions whose behavioral consequences are impossible to specify precisely: unemployment, bombing, the four-day week, pollution, divorce, etc. Ego, nevertheless, has some sort of theory about these consequences when he ascribes a role to them in determining Alter's behavior.

Why have you been so silent for so many pages? *I am silent when I have nothing to say or when I am thinking. Your talk about ascription terrifies me somewhat, you have not convinced me that ascription is real.* All I can add, if that is your view, is that the ascriptions of Ego, though obviously complicated, are likely to be relatively simple in comparison with those arising out of secondary judgments. For the level of sophistication required to infer that various bits of behavior are interrelated and spring from central tendencies requires more prolonged reflection. In fact, growth in judging others which occurs during socialization may be viewed as a gradual shift from reliance upon primary judgments to greater confidence in secondary judgments. An advisable pathway is visible: since ascriptions come from incomplete descriptions and contain elements of risk, they must be considered tentative and subject to later revision.

5.c Imputation

Ego's very general beliefs or convictions have already been discussed; now attention is focused upon one aspect of this problem, his beliefs about Alter's beliefs, or at least the conscious components imputed by him to Alter. What are Alter's private ideas, precious values, and—the fashionable, unnecessarily fancy phrase intrudes—cognitive structure?

Alter decides whether to go forward or backward, to vote for a radical or conservative candidate, to love or to hate, to please or to frustrate, and the decision springs, he thinks, from what he believes to be right or wrong or, in more general terms, to be conducive to his own welfare. The extent to which the rationale for action is really a "conscious," accurate, or indeed critical determinant of behavior may be challenged, but what cannot be challenged is Alter's belief that he knows why he behaves as he does and hence that he can usually justify his own actions and thought. For worthy or unworthy reasons, consequently, Ego would become acquainted with these beliefs, which, obviously, cannot be discussed directly but must be imputed to Alter.

The beliefs Ego believes Alter holds about himself and particular persons, including Ego, may determine his own secondary judgment concerning Alter. I am devoted to you because I know, I think, I infer that you are likewise devoted to me; if I thought otherwise, my attitude toward you would be quite different. The beliefs can be infinitely complicated, inasmuch as they may involve, as we have seen in connection with the understanding potential, the infinite regress of reverse and multiple judgments. How, for example, does Ego judge Alter's belief concerning what Ego thinks either about himself or about Alter? This regress should not terrify you who are interested in subtleties because you know that human thinking often coils back upon itself. If Ego judges himself and his comrades in similar terms or if he feels closer to those whom he chooses as friends or who, he thinks, will choose him (Italy, students; Loprieno, Emili, & Esposito, 1967), Ego's own beliefs should be deducible from a knowledge of those held by his associates.

Ego's judgment motive may lead him to have an interest in a belief of Alter considered either per se or as a basis for further judgments. Thus he may wish to appraise Alter's competency to perform a particular task, and the making of that judgment is important in its own right. But as a means toward another end the primary judgment may be only part of the judgmental process. Will Alter be grateful for the help Ego proposes to give him? The knowledge of at least two beliefs *may* be essential before the prediction can be hazarded: does Alter believe he is going to receive assistance and how significant does he believe the assistance will be in his scale of values (Italy, students; Morse, 1972)? As ever, there are of course surprises as Ego tries to slide from one belief of Alter to another. Alter's desire to believe in a just world, for example, may cause him to judge an apparently in-

nocent victim or even a martyr quite unfavorably, for then he can feel
that such a person deserves to suffer (Usual; Lerner & Simmons, 1966).
Sometimes a knowledge of Alter's very general system of beliefs makes
imputations concerning related beliefs less hazardous. If Alter is a
devout Christian whose particular type of Christianity can be ascertained, we might fairly well predict his opinions on a number of subjects ranging from the function of prayer to the use of contraceptives.
This is not a redundant statement seeming to assert only that people
hold the views of the groups to which they belong; rather it suggests
that the same criteria for establishing one set of beliefs can be further
utilized to anticipate additional beliefs. According to one political
theorist, people do or should evaluate political systems—governments,
institutions, or small groups—by considering whether they believe that
the decision makers reflect their own wishes and are competent and
whether they themselves are able to expend the time or energy demanded of them by the decision-making process (Dahl, 1970, p. 8). If
this analysis is correct, Ego's problem might be to determine which
of the criteria Alter customarily employs in passing judgment upon
groups that affect him; then, I think, he could predict, within some
margin of error, Alter's beliefs regarding relevant political issues that
have not yet arisen.

It would seem self-evident that—barring ESP—the principal source
of information about Alter's beliefs ought to be his own statements.
For salient beliefs usually can be expressed in some form and, if they
are not verbalized voluntarily, Alter may be asked to do so. Do you
trust me? *Yes*. I have thus ascertained your belief regarding my trustworthiness. But obviously the transaction is not that simple. I may be
too shy to ask the question in the first place, you may not be directly
available to hear me, you may not care to reply—and why should you?
—or you may reply evasively or untruthfully (Pathway 1.1). Or it may
be necessary or desirable for me to probe more deeply into your words
for reasons not directly connected with your motivation. You and I, for
example, may agree that your viewpoints on many matters are truly
your own, while in fact—at least according to my analysis of the facts
—they stem from your surrounding milieu and hence, though personal,
they are also consensual (Scheflen, 1972, p. 156). Language, which
provides or ought to provide an efficient, valid way of conveying information about beliefs, in short, confronts Ego with the same kinds
of problems that puzzle him as he passes judgment on conduct or traits.

When a belief system is very sophisticated, it may be doubly or

tenfold more difficult to infer the belief—the psychology or the
philosophy—behind the action. Suppose Alter subscribes in effect to a
view of the later Freud that "an instinct is an urge inherent in organic
life to restore an earlier state of things" and hence "the aim of all life
is death" (1959, pp. 67, 70). Even if that instinct is represented in
consciousness, an individual in our society might be loath to admit so
much pessimism; and only a virtually omniscient Ego could discern a
link between it and, for example, some self-defeating decision by Alter
or, for that matter, a suicidal inclination. Beliefs may function at different levels: you may assume "in principle" that all men are good or bad,
but then "in fact" you treat each person as an individual in his own
right (Ichheiser, 1970, pp. 43–44). And of course we all allegedly subscribe to the Christian ideal but in reality. . . .

The cue or basis for making an inference concerning Alter's beliefs
may often be one of his easily observable attributes, such as his sex,
ethnic group, or occupation. Or the imputation of the belief may involve a sociological or psychological assumption. In our society, for
example, it may be presumed that married couples are similar or dissimilar and that therefore when Ego knows the beliefs of one it is
safe for him to assume that the other is likely to subscribe to the same
or to opposite beliefs. This pathway is very dangerous because the
relation between the attributes and the beliefs is never perfect and
hence inferences concerning a particular Alter may turn out to be
erroneous. Thus young couples in the United States in general *may*
hold similar views regarding erotic materials which in turn *may* be
related to their authoritarian proclivities (Byrne et al., 1973): but the
tendency, being only a statistically significant one, is valid, as ever,
only in a very general sense.

Fruitful inferences concerning Alter's beliefs can be made by assuming that he carries within him the values of his society, whether those
values are more or less universal or specific (Pathway I.a). In any
society there are broad ethical principles that may not be totally
conscious but that must be deliberately obeyed at least in part if
efficient learning is to occur. When is murder justified; is it per-
missible to marry my father's brother's daughter or son; under what
conditions may land be sold; what courtesies are to be extended to a
guest? Men have answers to these questions everywhere, though of
course their answers differ from society to society; and therefore they
have corresponding beliefs. Likewise I should think that individuals
have varying degrees of confidence concerning the future: they are

optimistic or pessimistic, certain or uncertain about their own ability to achieve their goals or about the ability of their group to do so.

The content and strength of beliefs can be as varied as the colors of the spectrum or, for that matter, as the behavior of which Alter is capable and the personality traits which he wittingly or unwittingly displays. No classification seems possible when we consider, if only in an academic sense, the sweep of human knowledge, the propositions and the viewpoints it includes, but the apparent impossibility is—and I see your pleasant smile—an irresistible challenge. I do think, nevertheless, that a useful division would be the usual one between beliefs that must be inferred from the individual and those that can be inferred from the society (Pathways I.a & I.b).

Now I would turn about and suggest that one of Alter's beliefs that Ego would often ascertain concerns his view of determinism, the very doctrine Ego uses in ascribing tendencies to Alter (Pathway II.2). *Determinism to investigate determinism?* Yes, and only three pathways lie open. First, there is heredity or the germ plasm: most or all of what we do results from inborn tendencies, the way spiders must spin webs and not fly or compose epic poetry. Second, there is the environmental explanation, expressed in more sophisticated terms within anthropology and sociology in so-called cultural terms: through the socialization process the individual learns to conform, which means that he behaves in a socially approved manner, performs the various tasks assigned to him. In the third place, however, a completely either-or explanation is likely to be rejected by laymen and professionals alike; instead the determining tendencies within an individual during most moments of his existence are attributed to a combination of both heredity and environment. Ego's problem, therefore, is twofold: to try to ascertain whether Alter emphasizes heredity or environment and how he weights the combination in different situations. Alter may believe, for example, that the environment is generally more important than heredity but does not affect the limits within which a person's intelligence may fluctuate; or, like you, he may almost always search for an innate factor in most behavior.

I can ill conceal my humanistic glee when I see you ascribe the three explanations both to laymen and professionals. Here is proof of my well rehearsed thesis that poets and artists are as well acquainted with promising pathways to people as are experts. This thesis I do not deny, in fact my more general proposition is that we are all experts of sorts because, as I keep repeating, only thereby can we survive among our friends and enemies. Without doubt some persons, whether laymen, poets, or scientists, are better able than others to understand specific Alters or Alters in general (Pathway II.b). The professional, whether biologist, psychiatrist, psychologist, anthropologist, or sociologist, however, is different in two respects. He tries not only to understand Alter or to understand how Ego judges Alter, but also to discover and lay bare the principles through which his understanding is achieved. In addition, if he remains true to the tradition of his craft, he is likely to use not a single factor or variable as the basis for his principle but a set of factors. *But did not Freud reduce all behavior to sex and therefore by implication categorize thus the relation between Ego and Alter?* No, the answer must be, this is a vulgar, inaccurate interpretation of Freud, and Freud needs no defense because in all his writings he concentrated not upon sex as such but upon the elaboration of basic motives (whether sexual or not) giving rise to infinite complexities. These complexities he never brushed away but sought, within his own frame of reference and of course in spite of blind spots we all possess, to comprehend fully, maybe sometimes too fully. At any rate, the professional, more so than the layman or the humanist, is likely to employ a multivariant approach to the problems of human behavior, or at least to be aware of the undoubted fact that such an approach is needed. (Pathway II.1).

Almost any Ego is likely to be interested in Alter's genesis because from our own experience we tend to think of human beings as "more extended in time" than objects (Heider, 1958a, p. 23). Since you are not a geologist or a botanist, you can look at a mountain or tree without necessarily speculating about its geological or botanical past; you are likely to rest content with judging it at the moment in terms of its grandeur or its condition. In contrast, especially if personality traits are involved, you quickly wonder why Alter is as he is, what forces in his milieu produced such desirable or undesirable traits. Perhaps we are very ethnocentric, you and I, when we display this interest in origins: we have contact with diverse peoples and we feel more comfortable in the face of diversity by venturing to explain it. Conceivably, isolated tribesmen in other cultures are confronted with fewer individual differences and hence are no more puzzled by their peers than they are by the mountains or trees in their midst. A negative, advisable pathway is the following dictum: the existence of a trait, type, style or motive, inferred whether by professionals or laymen concerning Alter or by Ego concerning himself, provides no direct insight into its genesis. Similar fruits can come from quite different roots (Postscript I.3). Stinginess in some persons may have arisen, as the classical Freudians think it must, through an extension of anal eroti- cism. But in others it may represent frugality acquired as a result of reality-based deprivation. Or its modal presence or absence among many persons in a society may be due to a natural environment pro- viding little or much of what is needed to survive.

I conclude this discussion of primary judgment by reverting—again —to the unfinished, unfinishable topic of inference. I agree that I have been stressing, perhaps overstressing, its perils. Quite probably I leave the impression, more or less as a negative pathway, that communica- tion between persons is more likely to break down or at least be im- perfect than it is to be efficient and reliable. And that, I admit, is precisely the impression I would convey. *Are you not overcautious: would you deny that, if two persons commune with each other, like lovers, real lovers, that each easily comprehends the subtleties of the other?* Of course you are right, you often are. Yet alongside the idyllic pair I must place most of us, most of the time: we fail to understand each other, we do not have the vaguest idea concerning the motives, traits, or beliefs of the human being right next to us. I retract nothing, this bitter dose of solipsistic negativism (Pathway 3.1) seems absolutely essential.

Postscripts

5.1 Primary vs. Secondary Judgments

The distinction between primary and secondary judgment has been variously expressed. In fact, after writing a draft of this book I dis- covered that a Norwegian investigator has been "tempted" to use identical terms to make what appears to me the same distinction (Rommetveit, 1960, p. 26). Freud of course referred to primary and secondary processes, a distinction that can be used in analyzing an- other judgmental process, that of time (Doob, 1971, pp. 34–37). Jung contended that the "affects" of Alter "are revealed" at once to Ego and hence are "unproblematical" and are unconsciously perceived, whereas his subtler attributes are grasped only when Alter grapples with them "consciously" (Jung, 1928, p. 296). Theories accounting for the way in which Ego perceives Alter's emotions or moods have been divided into two kinds: those that are "non-inferential" in character and stem from "instinctive biological reactions," empathy, or some sort of "direct and primitive process," and some "special faculty of insight"; and those that are inferential and are derived from past experience, projection, analogy, and Ego's own feelings, induced by Alter (Vernon, 1964, pp. 47–49). Non-inferences are thus classified as immediate and hence primary, whereas inferences are seen as requiring deliberation and as secondary.

5.2   Cultural Determination of Concepts

Psychologists and particularly anthropologists provide copious illustrations to demonstrate the cultural relativity of concepts. It is not astonishing to learn that peoples in different societies may apply quite differently exotic metaphorical categories (e.g., ripe fruit, flowing water, straight street) to Alters for the simple reason that their observation and evaluation of human attributes vary (Germany & Thailand, students; Ertel, 1964). When passing judgment, Samoans follow "a set and objective pattern: sex, age, rank, relationship, defects, activities." Other judgments, which they seldom make spontaneously, rest on the assumption that human beings are beautiful, wise, and kind; they classify Alter's attitudes and behavior in terms of good or bad, easy or difficult. Particularly important is the primary judgment concerning Alter's age group since different categories are employed to evaluate boys and adults (M. Mead, 1928, pp. 126–30), but age categorization I presume exists in any society.

The effect of a society's mode of categorization must be inferred. Among Omaha Indians "the idea of personality is dominant in the language and in the religious beliefs and practices" and its force is "recognised as that of the will, that power which directs one's actions, so as to bring about desired results" (Fletcher & LaFlesche, 1911, p. 609). Postulating this force may make behavior seem generally intelligible in innumerable situations and hence ensuing actions may not be ascribed solely to situational requirements. Locating abilities and traits in various parts of the body—for example, among the Thonga the seat of genius and intellectual gifts is thought to be the heart, of eloquence the chest, of conscience the diaphragm (Junod, 1927, p. 361) —may give Ego confidence in his judgmental concepts.

5.3   Individual Differences in the Use of Concepts

Headings have been selected to illustrate the variety of individual differences:

Age: with increasing maturity there *may* be a tendency to describe peers Ego knows well with concepts that refer not to particular contexts but to his individuality more or less independent of context; younger children, for example, *may* be more likely to mention Alter's "qualities of will" as manifested in "discipline" or school "studies" than are older ones, who in turn *may* refer more frequently to Alter's "intellect" or his "attitude toward collectives" (Soviet Union, children, adolescents, & young adults; Bodelev, 1970–71). Only gradually and with great difficulty *may* children be able to attribute the "mechanisms of adjustment" (such as displacement, wishful dreaming, projection, regression, repressions, rationalization, and denial, as one catalogue would have it) to the discrete actions of those they judge (U.S.; Whiteman, 1967).

Breadth and depth: while judging creativity in solving simple problems, some Egos, more than others, *may* have the inclination to emphasize Alter's talkativeness, in fact they *may* value more highly the quantity and not the quality of speech (Usual; Regula & Julian, 1973); some *may* have a tendency to use a relatively larger and others a smaller number of judgmental categories (Usual; Leventhal, 1957); some *may* use categories that subsume a great deal of Alter or his behavior, others relatively less (Usual; Gifford, 1973).

Personality theory: whether or not Ego uses similar categories to judge friends and strangers may depend upon his own personality theory (Usual; Passini & Norman, 1966)—and this possibility suggests a need to account for that theory in terms of Ego's own personality. *Personality to explain personality theory?* Exactly.

Assumed utility: some concepts (e.g., being skillful, trusting, dominating) *may* be considered to be more revealing and hence to be more useful in categorizing Alter than others (e.g., being restless, discreet, alert); similarly the knowledge or belief that Alter is financially secure, has many friends, or has lived in the same community for many years *may* appear more informative than knowing or believing that he has a new job, lives near a park, or enjoys a great deal of leisure time (Usual; Gifford, 1973). I cannot restrain my customary cynicism: when we are told, for example, that extroversion, agreeableness, conscientiousness, emotional stability and culture in the artistic, intellectual, refined, or imaginative sense *may* be the favored concepts of American college students while judging their fellows (Norman, 1963), how can we be sure that the same clusters of traits would emerge in other groups of students or in the same group ten years later?

5.4 Similarity and Attractiveness

The relation between these two factors is truly a spiral (Pathway 4.b). On the one hand it *may* be argued that traits meeting with Ego's approval or that he believes characterize himself may be attributed by him to an attractive Alter (Usual; Child & Doob, 1943); yet on the other hand, Ego *may* be attracted to an Alter who has such traits or who in his opinion shares similar attitudes (Usual; Posavac & Pasco, 1971) or a similar world view, including the way in which the attitudes in question are structured or organized (Usual; Tesser, 1971; Johnston & Centers, 1973), regardless of how important the relevant issues are considered (Usual; Byrne & Nelson, 1964). There *may* thus be a "linear relationship between similarity and liking" (U.S., large variety, including children, clerks, Job Corps personnel, and schizophrenics; Byrne et al., 1969), but it is not one devoid of possible qualifications. When called upon to estimate the opinion of an Alter he likes, Ego *may* minimize what he thinks to be the difference between that opinion and his own (Usual; Berkowitz & Goranson, 1964). He *may* also project onto someone he likes and not onto someone he dislikes undesirable traits he thinks he himself possesses (Usual; Secord et al., 1964). Such projection may stem not from his desire to diminish Alter's attractiveness but from a need to feel more comfortable with his own self-image: I cannot judge myself harshly for being thus-and-thus if someone I admire shares my blemish. Possibly real or projected similarity is unimportant as such but may only mediate, consciously or unconsciously the conviction that gratification rather than frustration is to be anticipated from a similar Alter—and so gratification is likely to be associated with similarity, though not always.

Attitude similarity, moreover, *may* be more powerful in determining attractiveness than personality similarity (Usual; Singh, 1973). Whether or not similarity affects Ego's feelings concerning Alter's attractiveness must also depend upon the attributes with respect to which the similarity exists or is thought to exist: similarity on a concrete level, such as agreement on the naming of a color, *may* perhaps be less important than similarity on an abstract level involving a basic value, at least when Ego and Alter belong to the same ethnic group (Usual, & adults; Triandis et al., 1975). Ego's conviction concerning whether or not he is liked or understood by Alter *may* be more influential in determining Alter's attractiveness from his standpoint than the extent to which he believes Alter to be similar to himself (Usual;

Aronson & Worchel, 1966; and U.S., high school; Lewis & Wigel, 1964), although the factor of similarity may still play a role (Usual; Byrne & Griffitt, 1966).

The way in which cause-and-effect are hopelessly entwined is also suggested by the fact that friends or married pairs, persons who presumably find each other attractive, *may* have been initially attracted by their similarity, or the similarity may have resulted from the contact originally facilitated or created by the feeling of attractiveness (Usual; Byrne, 1971, p. 31). Two persons liking each other *may* not only believe they have similar needs but they *may* also be aware of each other's needs (Usual; Poe & Mills, 1972); yet again more accurate knowledge may lead to greater attraction, and greater attractiveness may promote contacts that render the knowledge of Alter more accurate. The spiral as an advisable pathway, therefore, is slippery.

The spiraled relation is even more complicated when Ego receives a series of apparently contradictory communications, some of which may reveal that he is similar to Alter, and others that he is dissimilar. He *may* be more attracted to an Alter concerning whom he first receives information suggesting dissimilarity and then similarity rather than information indicating first similarity and then dissimilarity, provided he is somewhat affectively involved in making the judgments (Usual; Worchell & Shuster, 1966; Jones & Wein, 1972). The same tendency *may* appear when Ego is called upon to judge different Alters: one who is similar to himself may meet with greater approval after he has judged others who are dissimilar (Usual; Stapert & Clove, 1969). Order of judgment thus appears to play a role, but this effect *may* prove less powerful than many bits of information suggesting similarity rather than dissimilarity (Usual; Byrne & London, 1966).

And of course similarity may play no role or a minor role in determining attractiveness. Young persons of the opposite sex *may* be attracted to each other not because of actual similarity but because of perceived attractiveness (Usual; Walster et al., 1966). Some persons in our society select mates with attributes complementing their own. Similarity as such *may* not facilitate attractiveness unless Ego believes Alter likes him and unless he also values highly the attributes he believes he and Alter have in common (Usual; S. C. Jones et al., 1973); or actual similarity may affect the judgment of attractiveness only when Ego is unable to predict Alter's behavior (Usual; Touhey, 1973). The connection between similarity and attractiveness *may* even be weakened when judgments are made under uncomfortable conditions, such as high temperature or overcrowding (Usual; Griffitt & Veitch, 1971), but not under others, such as the presence of a loud noise (Usual; Bull et al., 1972). The reverse may also be true: obnoxious Alters *may* be disliked more when they are considered similar rather than dissimilar (Usual; Taylor & Mettee, 1971). And then of course a personality factor, such as self-esteem, *may* also affect the spiral (U.S., children; Simon & Bernstein, 1971).

Similarity, moreover, may lead to judgments other than attractiveness. When he considers Alter similar to himself rather than dissimilar, for example, Ego *may* be less impressed with Alter's status or prestige (Usual; Byrne & London, 1966); his opinion of Alter *may* be less affected in a joint venture when both of them or only he himself succeeds than when both or he alone fails (Usual; Harvey & Kelley, 1973); he *may* even judge him more accurately (U.S., graduate students; Exline, 1957). Similarity may also be important in some relations and not in others. Only a small degree of similarity may be needed for Ego to enter into relatively non-intimate relations, such as having Alter as a friend or eating together with him, but a greater degree of similarity resulting from religion and ethnicity *may* be required in more intimate relations, such as accepting Alter in one's neighborhood or in marriage (Usual; Triandis & Davis, 1965). And yet the significance of the attitude Ego believes he shares or does not share with Alter *may* not affect his judgment (Usual; Byrne & Nelson, 1964); or what is assumed to be a shared attitude may not alter his judgment but may affect the attention he pays to Alter (U.S., college females; Murray & McGinley, 1972). There is also a time factor (Pathway II.3): for longer rather than shorter friendships a high degree of agreement between Ego's view of Alter's view of Ego and Ego's view of himself *may* be more important than perceived or actual similarity (Usual; Bailey et al., 1975).

On a primary level, other factors besides attractiveness may induce a judgment of similarity. Many of the demographic facts Ego knows about himself—his sex, age, nationality, etc.—he can perceive more or less easily in Alter. When he is surrounded by persons from different ethnic groups, his assumption *may* be that those speaking the same language or coming from the same areas as he are at least similar in those and probably also in other respects (Brislin, 1971). Obviously projection may also function (Pathway II.5).

Cutting across the factors of similarity and attractiveness are undoubtedly personality traits that may account for some of the complications and inconsistencies in the spiralled relation. Highly anxious Egos, for example, *may* find a dissimilar Alter less attractive than less anxious ones; or those with a high need for approval *may* even be more attracted to Alters with whom they seem to disagree than those with a low need (Usual; Johnson & Gormly, 1975). Even this variable of paper-and-pencil personality traits may conceivably be related to the judgment of attractiveness under conditions only of assumed similarity and not dissimilarity between Ego and Alter.

Another way to seize upon the multivariant nature of the relation between attraction and similarity is to refer at some length to a "short book" published by two professionals, both psychologists, in 1969 which is "directed toward the student with no prior background in social psychology" and which would cover the topic of "interpersonal attraction." The authors valiantly attempt to extract from the literature the factors associated with attraction. *What literature?* Occasionally they quote the ancients (e.g., Tacitus and Aristotle) and some of their semi-professional successors (e.g., George C. Homans, Carl R. Rogers, Groucho Marx, J. Edgar Hoover, Dale Carnegie, Alexander Graham Bell, Theodore Reich), but by and large they concentrate upon the results of experimental studies. Of course they are really describing, almost without exception, the loves and hates of American college students. In order to suggest how attraction is embroiled with other factors, I think it useful to list some of the factors yielded by their approach. I follow them chronologically and place in italics their chapter headings. By and large I have omitted some of the qualifications they conscientiously supply. You will quickly note that "similarity" as a "reward" is only one of many headings they have chosen to use.

The effect of accidental consequences on liking

1. A tendency to blame someone, especially the victim, as the seriousness of an accident increases

2. A tendency to justify oneself when the harm done to others increases

3. The degree of public commitment concerning a judgment
Rewards others provide: reduction of anxiety, stress, loneliness, or insecurity

4. A tendency to like those providing rewards and those present when rewards are given

5. A tendency to like the group that accepts Ego especially when his self-esteem is low

Rewards others provide: propinquity

6. A tendency to like those who are close in a physical sense, though hostility may also result

Rewards others provide: the reciprocity-of-liking rule

7. A tendency to reciprocate degrees of liking, provided the reciprocity is "congruent with one's self-esteem"

8. A tendency for liking to increase with a gain in esteem rather than invariant esteem, and vice versa

Rewards others provide: similarity

9. A tendency to perceive similar attitudes among those who are liked and/or to like those with similar attitudes, especially when the issues are important

10. A slight tendency for similar personalities to associate with one another and/or for those associating with one another to develop similar personalities

Rewards others provide: cooperation vs. competition

11. A tendency to like cooperators and dislike competitors

12. A tendency to be aggressive toward frustrators (Berscheid & Walster, 1969).

Finally just in passing—because this Postscript is already long enough—I would note that similar spirals and complications are evident when the attractiveness or similarity of a Group Alter is being judged. A single example: Ego *may* be attracted to some extent to groups whose leaders' personalities, attitudes, or values he believes are similar to his own, but only when he values highly human relations in the group rather than its tasks or goals (Usual & soldiers; Hansson & Fiedler, 1973).

On a truly primitive level, a primary judgment is likely to suffice. The animal, the infant, or the adult who believes beyond question that he is threatened by an enemy takes appropriate action immediately, without reflection or hesitation. He does not stop to wonder whether he "really" is in danger, whether his judgment may be in error, or whether by retreating he is acting like a coward or a Christian. Some of the time, however, mature organisms hesitate and, if they are human, they reflect and sooner or later pass a secondary judgment, which is either a reaffirmation or revision of the original primary judgment. Pathway 6 is concerned with the mediating responses that, when aroused, intervene between the two levels of judgment. They might be considered detours because they move Ego off the main pathway for a moment, slow him down, and then enable him to attempt a more valid, or at least a more considered, secondary judgment. Assembled are many of the suggestions that writers on clinical and lay assessment have made to improve the practices of their craft (Vernon, 1964, pp. 36–43).

6.a Experience

In order to understand Alters or to predict their behavior, professionals administer tests whose scores may be referred to actuarial tables representing past experience. That experience has been codified by means of variables weighted on the basis of laboriously gathered and analyzed information. The tables *may* give rise to more valid forecasts than the immediate, intuitive judgments of clinicians, at least in the areas of school performance, recidivism, and recovery from a major psychosis, though not perhaps in connection with the minute-by-

minute, hour-by-hour, day-by-day series of events and verbal expressions that appear in the therapeutic sessions with a particular patient
(largely U.S., Meehl, 1954, especially pp. 119–28). On the other hand,
a clinical approach has the advantage of proudly recognizing the uniqueness of each individual who in effect is judged less formally, without
mathematical aids, by somehow considering what other more or less
similar Alters have done or revealed in the past. Professionals, I suppose, are unable to say whether one approach is always preferable to
the other; my only point is that both acknowledge the significance of
experience while utilizing it differently.

The chicken, we were once taught, makes the mistake of pecking a
caterpillar, dislikes the taste, and forever after does not confuse a
caterpillar with a grain of corn. By analogy, perhaps by the same process of learning, Ego learns not to trust his first or primary impression.
Past experience contributes to his overall skill in judging Alter, any
Alter (Pathway II.b).

*But should Ego learn from experience that primary judgments based
upon first impressions cannot be trusted?* There are many reasons why
distrust is the advisable pathway and they reach from here to heaven
and run the gamut from Ego himself to Alter. When confronted with
Alter for the first time, Ego may be in an unresponsive mood or he
may be dominated by wishes that make him perceive selectively and
inaccurately. Some of what is perceived may be most salient but misleading: you cannot fail to note that Alter is speaking softly, but this
perception should not induce you to conclude that he must be a tender
person. Every Ego, though blissfully unaware of the trait-versus-role
problem that disturbs the professionals (Postscript 1.7), knows vividly
or dimly that behavior often depends in part upon the role the person
is called upon to play at a given moment, and that this role is elicited
in turn by the situation at hand (Pathway 1.c), including the presence
of Ego himself, and may provide an atypical sample of Alter (Pathway
1.2). Your first impression of a nomad in Somalia would depend upon
whether you observed him leading his camels and goats to pasture,
hunting a gazelle, or listening to traditional poetry. In our own society
the impression a person creates depends in part upon whether his role
at the moment is a dominant or a subservient one. Investigators of
so-called operant conditioning have rigorously demonstrated a fact we
have all known since the time of Adam or from our pet dog or cat:
the emotion of gentle praise in the form of an "ah" or a nod, or a
polite reproof in the form of an "ugh" or a groan can serve as a source

of reinforcement and hence may markedly influence conduct. Alter may be posing or deliberately trying to deceive (Pathway 1.1), he may not be given the opportunity to reveal or display his propensities by others who are present, or he may simply be bored or overwhelmed so that he keeps quiet and hence affords no one the opportunity to gain insight into the subtlety and originality of his thinking.

First as well as later impressions may require revision, and *may* in fact improve as more information is accumulated (Usual; Leventhal, 1957). Ego *may* be reluctant or unable, however, to alter his initial impression even when information about Alter is supplied to him continuously during a single encounter (England, adult males; Lovie & Davies, 1970) and particularly when his primary judgment prevents him from assimilating contradictory information (U.S., children; Feldman & Allen, 1975). Alter is disagreeable, Ego says, or the judgment is mediated by the thought that he is like Jake Smith and hence must be disagreeable. It is tempting to avoid expanding one's original judgments and instead to fall back upon limited chunks of experience. Often we do not have the time to pay attention to details, either to collect them or to organize or to evaluate them; rather we prefer to have the bits effortlessly snap into place and to emerge both immediately and in the long run with a synthesized impression. "Generally we expect other people to be consistent; we assume that people will do what they usually do in a particular situation" (From, 1971, p. 152)— and our experience turns out to be most valuable, provided the assumption of consistency is correct, provided Alter does not change.

You are not completely convincing: is it really true that all first impressions should be suspect? No, remember I did pay homage to primary judgments when I began discussing them. *Perchance I did not memorize what you said.* All right, then, let us reconsider the problem (Postscript 6.1: The Validity of First Impressions). In a word, though, what I fear most in first impressions is the alluring, dangerous pathway of simplification (Pathway II.1). *And what I fear most from reflection is the loss of spontaneity and fresh insights.*

I do not have to remind you about the arguments in favor of simplification or oversimplification because you use them. *Yes, let us be realistic; most persons, the good, simple, grass-roots persons who claim your devotion, do not care about nuances.* Quite a value judgment, but not unexpected. If Ego happens to sell hats and Alter is a prospective customer, then Alter will not be interested in the merchant's divine personality or his beliefs or tastes; all Ego wishes to know is the size of Alter's head, the style of hat and materials he wants, and what he can afford to pay (Pathway II.a). *Many pages back you advanced a similar thesis about a pathetic waitress and a night watchman.* A problem we all face is that we inherit what appears to be the experience of the ages in the form of proverbs, maxims, parables, and aphorisms. You cannot trust a person who does not look you straight in the face; you cannot teach an old dog new tricks; once a liar, always a liar; old friends wear well—the banalities jump out at us at every turn, and sometimes we believe them and at other times they may affect us even though we are not completely aware of them. *I have confidence in these sources of wisdom, otherwise they would not be part of our tradition.* And I am skeptical: the experience of our ancestors does not always provide dependable pathways in this or any other frame of reference; nothing is that simple.

But any judgment is a simplification. You are persistent, but really Alter can never be grasped as God sees him, or for that matter as he is seen by his best friend, his beloved, or himself. *This time I agree.* Any Ego appreciates his own complexity and therefore assumes that others are also complicated (Pathway II.5), perhaps not as complicated or as sensitive or as worthy as he knows himself to be, but still complicated.

The beneficial effects of practice—experience in the past—seem self-evident at least on the surface. Not unexpectedly, for example, Ego's ability to judge Alter's emotions from the non-verbal aspects of his speech, with verbal content held constant, improves with Ego's age and training, although the improvement *may* be slightly greater for expressions allegedly depicting sadness and anger than for those involving happiness and love (Usual & U.S. children; Davitz et al., 1964, pp. 69–86, 152–53). And we know that the art of interviewing can be improved through training and practice; indeed even in simple situations the ability to judge Alter's mode of behaving *may* follow a learning curve resembling other types of learning that do not involve other persons (presumably Usual; Hammond et al., 1966). *Practice makes perfect?* By no means; let me explain.

First, Ego somehow must learn the significance of cues that can be utilized in future situations. You may see a person again and again, like the driver of a bus, without improving your insight into him as a person. Improvement can occur only if Ego acquires subsequent information concerning the accuracy or inaccuracy of previous judgments and only if he is able, upon receiving such information, to assume that

Alter will be consistent; if Alter is not consistent, for example, in filling out a questionnaire about himself, then feedback concerning past
replies *may* not be helpful (Usual; Squier, 1971). Similarly, *perhaps*
Ego himself must not be dogmatic if he is to take advantage of repeated
exposure to Alter and then judge that Alter's dogmatism with a relatively high degree of accuracy (U.S., graduate students; Jacoby, 1971).
Experience may be more valuable with members of the same culture
than with outgroupers; not only *may* they believe that they have similar
feelings toward one another but they *may* also actually have such
feelings (U.S., delinquent & non-delinquent boys; Baker & Sarbin,
1956; also U.S., various children & adult males; Tagiuri, 1958). If it
is true, for example, that women in our society are better judges of
other persons than men, the explanation would have to be sought in
the differing experiences of the two sexes: as mothers, women must
learn to interpret the nuances of the child's behavior; being subordi-
nated (or at least they used to be), they must play a more passive role
while being courted and hence must acquire the knack of being sensitive to the male's whims; perhaps they are able to practice their skill
by gossiping; etc. In addition, some Alters may remain inscrutable, no
matter how often they are observed (Pathway 1.a).

False judgments also result from utilizing generalizations that have
been only partially validated through experience in the past and that
may not be applicable to the Alter being judged. In order to maintain
that Alter is X and that therefore he must also be Y, Ego must be convinced that various attributes cling together, that they constitute a
syndrome (Pathway I.b). A halo is conferred upon Alter because he
possesses one favorable trait Ego has found to be associated with a
host of other favorable traits, or that he believes is. *He is intelligent
and therefore I approve of almost anything he does, for intelligent
persons, I have found, usually behave themselves.* The link between
X and Y may be more specific, so that Ego *may* or *may not* attribute
one or more traits to Alter after knowing only that he possesses one
particular trait (Usual; Wishner, 1960). *He is intelligent and therefore
he must also be sensible.* A variant of this potential error operates less
directly and has been given the fancy name of *parataxis* (Sullivan,
1953, pp. 92, 235–36): Ego observes that Alter has some traits in
common with one or more Alters whom he may or may not consciously
recall at the moment of passing judgment, and he attributes to Alter
all or almost all the most salient traits associated with the other person
or persons. *He is intelligent and all intelligent persons I have known*

always turn out to be shy; hence he must be shy. The difficulty in thus generalizing this way is that Alter may be unique and hence his personality or behavior may not fit the postulated syndrome; it is not necessarily true that an Alter who appears to have a particular trait will also have the additional traits found previously to have been associated with it in other persons (Sarbin et al., 1960, pp. 61–68). Syndromes, like trait categories, vary not only from person to person but also from culture to culture, so that they are not easily transferable. And experience may give rise to a premise that appears to Ego to be, in the language of classical logic, universal but is in fact particular. Not all intelligent persons are sensible or shy, though some may be. In your case, experience with the English suggests that they have certain assets and liabilities; if Alter is English, you assume he has the same assets and liabilities. Your error consists not in disregarding Alter's uniqueness and attributing to him attributes he may not have, but in your initial characterization of the English.

Professionals, especially clinicians, charge themselves with the responsibility of improving their judgmental skill as a result of the experience they constantly have with patients or subjects, and undoubtedly they sometimes succeed. Still they may be no better able, for example, to infer the presence of the verifiable attribute of brain damage from one of their standardized instruments than less experienced semi-professionals or inexperienced laymen, although one very, very experienced and skillful professional *may* outdo all the rest (U.S., staff, trainees, and nonpsychologists; Goldberg, 1959). Experience gained through systematic instruction concerning the ways in which Alters can be more accurately appraised *may* not necessarily increase judgmental accuracy; in fact accuracy *may* decrease, perhaps because the trainees become more sensitive to individual differences and thereby less able to fit their judgments into standard categories (U.S., medical students; Crow, 1957).

Experience may often be stored within Ego as a set of formal or informal principles he carries about to apply in the present and future. If he is a professional, he secures them from experimental or empirical data, or he deduces them from already established principles (Pathway II.c). At least that is his ideal, though in all honesty he can often be compelled to admit that extraneous elements based on wishful thinking or straight bias can enter into his formulations. If Ego is a layman, he may approximate these procedures simply through the experience he has acquired in his milieu. Both the layman and the clinical professional, however, often experience sudden illumination as a result of a single experience with another person, with a poem, or with a sagacious friend (Pathway 4.c). And such insights, justifiably or not, may be elevated to the level of new principles and there serve functions as valuable and as valid as if they had been more formally derived. Principles, however, may be too simple when they neglect the possibility of multivariance (Pathway II.1). Nothing succeeds like success, the naive Ego may believe, and hence he thinks that a successful Alter is likely to repeat his behavior and to seek additional successes. But Egos who are convinced they themselves are chronically low in self-esteem and who feel responsible for a success just achieved, *may* avoid further success presumably because such success is inconsistent with their self-appraisal (Usual, females; Maracek & Mettee, 1972).

An important pathway Ego must usually follow to evaluate his experience with Alter is that of sampling (Pathway 1.2): has his primary judgment been based upon an adequate or a representative sample of Alter's actions? The professionals, particularly the clinicians, are most conscious of this problem and hence have devised a host of sampling safeguards, such as trying to be certain that Alter is behaving "naturally," which the lay Ego might well heed (Pathway 0.1). *When practical.* Yes, when practical. In addition, Alter may have some attributes that need be noticed only once or twice for the problem of sampling to be quickly resolved. Can he wiggle his ears, does he have a bass voice, does he know how to recite patter songs from Gilbert and Sullivan, does he go to mass every day, does he ever lose his temper? If Ego is content to receive a yes-no or present-absent answer, then certainly no further investigation is needed; a first impression is valid in these instances. But only crude information may be thus obtained. From a single observation Ego cannot report why Alter learned to wiggle his ears, when he does so, what satisfaction he now receives from exercising this talent, etc. Possibly, too, a false conclusion may be drawn from negative information: however adequate the sample, the fact that the feat has never been demonstrated does not mean that Alter is inept in this respect, he may just be shy.

One of Ego's many difficulties may be his inability to utilize past experience in revising or improving his primary judgment even when he is fully aware of its lessons. Let me cite a few illustrations from professional research and then imagine that the findings are part of Alter's own experience, and therefore taken seriously by him. He knows that in the past his judgments concerning the demographic attributes of his friends (such as age, occupation, and even religion or ethnic origin) *may* have turned out to be considerably more valid than his assessment of their political attitudes and that therefore his demographic judgments tend to be more objective than his attitudinal ones (U.S., adults; Laumann, 1969). He *may* have more confidence in making inferences concerning Alter's attitudes on the basis of Alter's behavior than vice versa, regardless of how salient the issues are (Usual; Allen, 1973). But then, alas, Ego may simply not have access to the relevant information for reasons utterly beyond his control. An even more aggravating problem arises when he cannot observe Alter directly but must depend upon an intermediary or informant (Pathway 2.1). He may realize that the information he obtains from that person about Alter *may* enable him to appraise Alter more accurately when it refers to a bit of Alter's behavior than when it describes him metaphorically or concentrates upon one of his traits (U.S., psychologists; Rodin, 1972), yet he must accept the information as it is given him.

Well, what about informants? You said a while back that no one lies like an eye-witness or a gossip—what should Ego do under these circumstances? It is a long story, but let us not tarry here (Postscript 6.2: The Dependability of Informants).

Experiences culminating in, as it were, anthropological or sociological knowledge of the situation at hand must be drawn upon when Ego would decide whether Alter's behavior reflects an idiosyncrasy or a trait rather than the role his society expects him to play in that situation (Pathways I.a. & b). Is Alter cheerful because he is a cheerful person or because his profession requires him to be? To reply, you must be acquainted with the rules or customs of the profession; you realize that contrived cheer is part of the bedside manner of a physician, the disarming approach of a salesman, etc. Some demographic facts, moreover, may be easy to collect, whose psychological significance is not immediately apparent. Alter, some Ego notes—not I, because this sort of thing has zero interest for me—is not a member of a so-called service club in America or elsewhere (Rotary, Lions, and all the rest). Why? He might not be able to afford the dues, he might not be eligible, he might not be sociable, he may disapprove of commercialized friendships.

Once again I have been really referring to the situation-versus-trait problem (Pathway 5.b) which must bore you by now, but this time I am recommending an advisable pathway: on the basis of his past experience, Ego must decide whether a trait, role, or situation approach is going to provide him with the basis for passing a sound judgment about Alter or for validly predicting his behavior. A critic of the trait approach believes that the evidence collected by professionals—largely from the Usual—suggests to him that ascription of traits has not proven fruitful. "Responses," he thinks, "have not served very usefully as indirect signs of internal predispositions;" instead "actuarial methods of data combination are generally better than clinical-theoretical inferences," which suggests that "the best as well as the cheapest predictions" stem from "direct self-reports, self-predictions, and especially indices of relevant past behavior" (Mischel, 1968, p. 145). You or any Ego in this wide, wide world, however, should not feel tempted to accept this dictum if your own experience suggests otherwise; use whatever procedure has been useful, but with two warnings. First, it is sensible to remember that misunderstandings and false judgments may arise when Ego fails to recognize either the contribution Alter's uniqueness makes to his behavior in a situation or the situational requirements imposed upon him (Ichheiser, 1970, pp. 48–49). Then, Ego *may* find it difficult or impossible to use a trait or some other personality approach to Alter when external constraints or Alter's own strong drive virtually exclude any alternative (Usual; Jones & Harris, 1967; Crawford & Williams, 1974). *I do not understand.* You do not say that a person is neurotically anxious when he tries to escape from a burning building or that he is compulsively oral when he quickly eats a large meal after a day's fast prescribed for religious reasons. Clear? *Yes, thanks.*

A somewhat similar problem confronts Ego, or should confront him, when he wonders whether a judgment of his depends upon Alter as a stimulus configuration or upon a tendency within himself (Pathway I.c). That woman disturbs you: why? Is it your mood or your prejudices that cause you to feel the way you do about her, or is it her behavior? You would perhaps like to blame her. Before you do, utilize an advisable pathway (Kelley, 1967, pp. 194–97); you must adhere to certain criteria to distinguish the two modes of attribution. Is it only she or all persons with her attributes who annoy you? Do you always feel that way about her? Are you disturbed only in her presence or is the same reaction evoked when you hear about her? Do others have a similar opinion about her? I suppose most Egos prefer to blame Alter rather than themselves, just as they tend to attribute their own behavior in general to external situations rather than to their own traits (Pathway 5.b). Can self-knowledge (Pathway I.1), which means a summary of what Ego believes to be his own virtues and defects on the basis of past experience, possibly prevent him from confusing himself with reality? *You sound a trifle pompous.* Only a trifle?

Pathway 6.b   Detachment

As Ego, motivated as we now assume him to be, approaches the task of transmuting his primary judgment into a secondary one, he must usually express to himself and sometimes to others his judgment in words that are either fleeting or formal and that are likely to dominate that judgment more and more with the passing of time (Pathway 5.c). Because of all the initial and subsequent perils that are involved in categorization (e.g., Pathway I.2 & 3), Ego must achieve some sense of detachment from himself and from his own imagination (Pathway II.5). Need I remind you, for example, of the hazards of empathy? *You may, but do be brief.* Ego's tendency to attribute "warm" or "cold" traits to others *may* depend upon whether he thinks he himself leans toward one of these temperature poles rather than the other (presumably Usual: Sager & Ferguson, 1970); and his tendency to project positive or negative judgments may originate within his own feelings of adequacy or inadequacy.

The errors of non-detachment are so commonplace that some have been given special labels in our society (Holt, 1969, pp. 592–98)—remember the halo effect, parataxis, and others I mentioned earlier on in this pathway? *I only remember "halo" and I think of Giotto and Duccio. I could add to the list of judgmental sins. Do; I like sins especially if they have classical names.* Well, there is "premature generalization": a single observation is used to infer a general trait (Pathway 1.2). Ego may perceive Alter's smile, which in fact reflects momentary friendliness, as a symptom of general friendliness or of a benign character (Secord et al., 1958, p. 307). The "leniency effect" is the tendency of some persons—certainly not I, and probably not you—to judge Alter in the best possible light. The Alter may be all persons, persons in a specific group (like one nation or club), or one particular individual —a generous halo, in short. I see no reason for not inventing a term referring to the opposite tendency: the "rough-and-tough" effect. Then each of us is supposed to have a "blind spot": for reasons peculiar to ourselves we are unable to perceive or to perceive correctly certain attributes in other persons, or we feel uncomfortable when confronted with such attributes. The saint presumably cannot imagine that people can be vicious, or he immediately condones behavior others consider to be anti-social. A more general disability has been called an "intolerance of ambiguity" or simply "rigidity": black-or-white judgments that disregard nuances, individual differences, or the possibility of variation. I would be remiss, and you might be angered, if I did not mention again that the economy and comfort achieved through these forms of simplification and the easy utilization of indices are economical and produce the same feeling of smug comfort as evil prejudices and sloppy samples. I am not cruel, however, and so I would not deny that an occasional person merits, for example, the halo you see around his head. *You don't mean to say you think you have one?*

On a number of previous occasions reference has been made to an insuperable difficulty that faces us all, the solipsistic dungeon in which all of us find ourselves (Pathway 3.1). If Ego is to understand someone else, how can he detach himself from himself? This is the crucial question requiring more reflection than any other we shall have the opportunity to discuss on Pathway 6. First, I think we must fully and not obliquely consider the phenomenological grounds for solipsism. The Spanish philosopher Ortega y Gasset points to "man's power of virtually and provisionally withdrawing himself from the world and taking his stand inside himself—or, to use a magnificent word which exists only in Spanish, that man can *ensimismarse*" which his translator says might be rendered by "be inside himself." I offer you the privilege of seeing his statement at some length:

Among all the characteristics of radical reality or life which I have mentioned, and which are a very small part of those that would have to be described to give any adequate idea of it, the one that I now want to emphasize is the one expressed in a great platitude: namely, that life is untransferable and that each man has to live his own; that no one can take over his task of living for him; that the toothache he suffers from has to hurt him and he cannot transfer even a fraction of the pain from it to anyone else; that he can delegate no one to choose and decide for him what he will do, what he will be; that no one can replace him or surrogate for him in feeling and wanting; that, finally, he cannot make his neighbor think for him the thoughts that he has to think in order to orient himself in the world (in the world of things and in the world of men) and thus find his right line of conduct—hence, that he must be convinced or not convinced, must see truths and see through nonsense, on his own account, without any possible substitute, deputy, or proxy.

I can repeat mechanically that two and two make four, without knowing what I am saying, simply because I have heard it countless times; but really to think it on my own account—that is, to acquire the clear certainty that "two and two veritably make four and not three or five"—*that* I have to do for myself, I alone—or, what is the same thing, I in my solitude. And as the same is true of my decisions, volitions, feelings, it follows that since human life in the strict sense is untransferable, it is essentially *solitude, radical solitude.* (Ortega y Gasset, 1957, pp. 18, 46; italics his).

Every human being, in short, has undoubtedly faced a cosmic choice ever since it became possible to engage in self-reflection. On the one hand, we are aware, however, dimly, of Ortega's observations concerning solipsism: the pain—or the pleasure—is ours and we can never know, we can only imagine how it is experienced by someone else. For this reason I have not been overly disturbed by your repeated charge that my relativism and solipsism make me avoid the problem of deciding what Alter "really" is; instead, I keep giving good reasons why Alter cannot be grasped. Your accusation is correct, but perhaps not for the reason you suggest. I hurl one Germanic-length sentence at you: when an Ego who lives behind a solipsistic barrier tries to judge an Alter who, in turn, is always a bundle of multivariant attributes which can be conceptualized in many different ways, immediately or eventually he will find it futile to adopt a God's-eye-view of that Alter and to seek to etch him for all eternity in a manner that can conceivably meet the approval of everyone, whether they be Americans or bush Africans, psychiatrists or persons of common sense. No one, I reiterate, ever understands another person completely or can break through the solipsistic wall of fire to reach Brünnehilde; we do the best we can with the categories available to us and the insight we have into ourselves. And what we do, consequently, is to exercise our imagination in various ways (Pathway II.5).

On the other hand, imagination, though necessary, is not a very secure pathway. We know there are so many other persons about and we also realize simultaneously that they differ from us: our pain may be painful to us and theirs to them, yet in a somewhat different manner. They are like us, they differ from us. Another distinguished philosopher has pushed the argument in favor of imagination as far as it can be pushed. After writing that he believes "in God as I believe in my friends, because I feel the breath of His affection, feel His invisible and intangible hand, drawing me, leading me, grasping me," he then issues the ultimate challenge from the standpoint of finite persons in this world:

> How do you know that the man you see before you possesses a consciousness like you, and that an animal also possesses such a consciousness, more or less dimly, but not a stone? Because the man acts towards you like a man, like a being made in your likeness, and because the stone does not act towards you at all, but suffers you to act upon it. And in the same way I believe that the Universe possesses a certain consciousness like myself, because its action towards me is a human action, and I feel that it is a personality that environs me (Unamuno, 1954, pp. 195–96).

On this literary, metaphysical level, then, the issue is joined. What can one say from the standpoint of social science? Let us agree that Ego simply cannot experience Alter's private experience directly, he must make inferences about it by combining his own experience with his interpretation of a symptom he snatches from Alter or with a postulate he finds useful. Your visual imagery may be very strong, for example, but I have little or no such imagery. How do I know that you have an image? You say that you have, and I presume that the words you use have the same meaning for you as they have for me. But I cannot be sure, no more than I can be certain that your perception of that gown's redness is like mine, for I happen to have a slight touch of red-green color blindness (which suggests another methodological problem I would here avoid). I do experience, however, negative after-images, that is, I see black spots in front of my eyes after I have looked at the sun too long; and so I have a basis for inferring that your visual images are like those spots except that they have colors like the original (and are not complementary the way the bright sun appears dark) and contain details the way a photograph does. To some extent I can disregard my own experiences when I point out that persons who are instructed to use visual images or who claim to have them learn or behave differently, sometimes, from the way they do when not given such instructions or when not making the claim (Paivio, 1972). Such data, however, I find only pragmatically useful and I am left where I started: inside myself.

The evidence supporting imagination as the mechanism for understanding Alter I do not think as simple as Unamuno contends. For his argument would contradict Plato's view that, in effect, Ego himself must possess the trait or syndrome if he is to understand it in Alter. Surely common sense—that invaluable excuse for expressing prejudice —suggests that it must be easier for Ego to judge persons no more complicated than himself than it is to judge those who are more complicated. And so when a so-called normal Ego attempts to pass judgment on a severely disturbed Alter, all he can do is to use categories he normally employs with reference to himself or other normal individuals and then assert, as the professionals do too, that the differences he perceives in the deranged person are not qualitatively different from those characterizing the allegedly normal.

I have been silent for a long while; now I must speak up: the Platonic doctrine need not be true. There are individuals who seem to belie what you have been saying. Male novelists can write about females and female novelists about males. Yes, they do, but as successfully as they probe members of their own sex? *An amusing question to ask, but not one which can be conclusively settled. Consider Shakespeare.* Concerning whom we know nothing. *If we assume he was a male, how could he have created a convincing Lady Macbeth or Rosalind or, for that matter, Portia? If we also assume that he was a busy playwright and producer, how could he have known how it felt to be a king like Henry IV or Richard II; how could he have imagined characters as complex as Lear and Hamlet or as funny and tragic as Falstaff and an army of other clowns?* His rich, rich genius enabled him to transcend his solipsism more compellingly than the rest of us ever can; of course, of course Shakespeare was unusual. *A single instance like him, however, is sufficient to make us pause and reconsider Plato.*

We understand each other because all of us love and hate, feel secure and anxious, believe ourselves satisfied and dissatisfied, succeed and fail at some time in our lives, and therefore we experience and share the same or at least similar emotions. But surely you are not paranoid, and hence have never really felt like a genuine paranoid; therefore you cannot empathize with paranoids. *I may not be paranoid, yet you know full well that I am no saint and consequently I have had paranoid symptoms: at some time in my up-and-down life I have felt persecuted by almost everybody, I have believed that I was the victim of circumstances, I have grown suspicious; also on occasion I have had feelings of grandeur, I have recognized that I am a magnificent person, I have almost been convinced that I could conquer the world. That "almost"* is the rub: it is sufficient to have some symptoms of a paranoid, to be almost like one, in order to comprehend a paranoid Alter? Again I can only pose the question without being able to reply adequately. I suppose we experience analogues of most but not of all human traits, though in a somewhat uniquely meaningful manner, so that the symptomatic significance of any one trait must vary from individual to individual (Foulds, 1961). A non-epileptic may exhibit symptoms remotely resembling those accompanying a real seizure, though perhaps only metaphorically, and . . . . *Basta, enough.* No, not quite.

In the final, final analysis I suspect that the only convincing case against solipsism is a phenomenological one: just as I have the conviction I possess free will, in spite of all the arguments I advance favoring determinism, so I assert to you, to myself, and to anyone who will listen that I do not always feel encased within myself, I am not always unaware of what you have been doing or of what you are. Indeed I admit that elsewhere I have written much too much in attempting to show how people communicate with one another: they *are* able to improve or impair the messages they transmit and receive. Ultimately we may be separated from each other, but in the present we are convinced that our imagination enables us to attain some degree of understanding (Pathway II.5). Two lovers believe, or at least have the feeling, that they are one. *An illusion?* We can cast aside the inevitable solitude described by Ortega or the depression/elation of solitude, at least temporarily. But we do well to remind ourselves of solitude in an era of superficiality when the mass media and our cliques and associations strive to give the facile impression that we are all of one piece and therefore willy nilly understand one another.

Similarly, it may be true that there are various selves within each of us struggling for domination (James, 1890, vol. 1, p. 292) and that the self active at the moment is best fitted for the role required by the situation. But unless we are split or multiple personalities (Prince, 1906), one of these selves—one of these roles, as some would insist— is the significant or dominant one to which the others must momentarily conform to some extent. That dominant self might well be called the truer or truest self which understands or communicates with the other selves, and thus Ego may rebuke himself for some decision or action of his own in the past or he may claim he is carried away by one of his own ideas. Phenomenologically, however, we have some sense of continuity from the past into the present and from there into the future. You may view that person who was once you as someone different from you as you are now, as if he were in another incarnation; but you simultaneously claim possession of the body you had then and still have, and you know that in some ways it was, it has been, you, or at least the same person out of whom you have developed. In fact, unless we can maintain this sense of self-identity through the conviction that our experiences and memories in the past and present possess "continuity," we are likely to feel terrified and to slip into some form of serious abnormality (Hilgard, 1949). Somehow, then, we break through ourselves in rare moments, or we have the cosmic feeling that we do. And such a feeling is more likely to emerge and to result in a valid judgment when we are to some extent detached from the egocentricity of solipsism and the hazards of imagination, that alluring, irresistible witch. *Witch?* Yes. *Why?*

On what advisable pathway, then, can detachment be achieved? The crudest reply of all: shut off the supply of irrelevant information in order to prevent the arousal of a disturbing or biasing attitude. The teacher does not look at the name of the student whose paper he is grading in order to judge the replies "on their merits." Do not tell me what you think of her, let me first make my own independent judgment. More often than not, however, we know who Alter is and we cannot block out the poison or the praise that others pour into our eyes and ears.

More compelling, even more difficult, is another advisable pathway: Ego increases the accuracy of what he ascribes to Alter by improving the accuracy of what he ascribes to himself (Pathway I.1). For if he has a false conception of his own self and the causes of his own behavior and if he projects that conception upon others, he will judge them falsely. This time I invoke not a Spanish philosopher but an Anglo-American poet, one of whose characters asserts:

> Most of the time we take ourselves for granted,
> As we have to, and live on a little knowledge
> About ourselves as we were. Who are you now?
> You don't know any more than I do,
> But rather less. . . . (Eliot, 1958, p. 31)

In more prosaic language: accurate self-knowledge is elusive and seldom attainable. Thus a few professionals have been expressing serious concern over the problem of identity: when, under what circumstances, does an individual comprehend himself, associate himself with some kind of model, direct his energies in a manner he himself understands (Erikson, 1959)? Or if we believe, as suggested a moment ago, that Ego consists of many different selves which appear and disappear as he, the person, discharges different roles in different situations, he may not be able to designate the self from which at a given moment he allegedly is projecting his own evaluations. What we think of our shifting selves and their accompanying traits *may* be easily influenced by praise or punishment from persons in our milieu who have prestige and who indeed may be the very Alters we are trying to judge; and the effects may extend not only to those aspects of us directly criticized but also to other related, though not too distant, phases of our existence (U.S., high school; Maehr et al., 1962).

In my view, it is especially important for Ego to locate, through reflection, his own central prejudices so that he can detach himself from them as he judges Alter (Pathway I.b). *Since this is your view, could you use yourself as an illustration?* Let me try. Correctly or not, I think I am tolerant of most behavior whether exhibited where I live or in countries I visit, especially in Africa. To my amused surprise, I have come to realize, however, that I cannot abide what I consider to be table manners differing from my own. Among my peers I am aghast when I am confronted with an adolescent or adult who brings food to his mouth on a knife, who makes gurgling sounds while having soup or drinking a liquid, who wipes his plate with bread, who turns his head upside down to dip a drooping asparagus into his mouth, who uses a toothpick in public, or who springs upon food and rapidly devours it, especially before others are served. In Africa I find it difficult to watch persons eating from a common pot, using their hands instead of utensils to bring food from a vessel to their mouths, or rolling doughy substances in the palms of their hands before eating them. I do not know why I have these feelings, whether they are derived from my parents or the society in which I have been forced to live, but I am certain that whoever violates them I judge harshly within the privacy of primary judgment. Obviously I recognize this complex within myself and hence, though I may never excuse the transgressor completely, I manage to throw his bad manners into perspective and therefore, on a secondary level, judge him not as a vulgar boor but as an individual with such-and-such characteristics who happens also to have from my standpoint bad manners in this one respect. Knowledge of my own ethnocentrism enables me to devalue one bit of information or at least to judge it in perspective.

Ego, however, may not wish to know more about himself since he can intuit some of the horror he has repressed. He *may* be more likely to credit greater accuracy to platitudinous, general descriptions of himself than to those based upon the scores he has actually achieved on a paper-pencil schedule (Usual; Merrens & Richards, 1970). Perhaps, this last observation suggests, he unwittingly misleads himself in order to retain a high if inaccurate opinion of his self, or else the score from the so-called scientific instrument is not valid. *All right, let's not argue the point; I agree that we often try to avoid ourselves, we lack insight.* If so, then what we project upon Alter is this false conception and therefore . . . . *Does that mean that our judgment of him is also false?* I do not think we can reply in general terms, for the answer can go either way. Ego may judge himself falsely but be more objective toward Alter even when employing the same categories; his incorrect self-judgment, however, may lead him to misuse similar criteria in judging Alter.

"It is impossible for me to maintain a false picture of myself," a psychiatrist states, "unless I falsify your picture of yourself and of me" (Laing, 1969, p. 124). The assertion calls attention again to the reciprocal nature of social life. Perhaps Ego can be helped by others to obtain greater self-insight, provided his self-deception is not so solidly entrenched that he resists all opportunities to acquire new information and to change. Ego is not doomed to remain himself: his view of that self can be transformed, he can be converted to a new view (Pathway 4.c).

Since it may be true, furthermore, that Ego cannot think of himself "apart from society" (Cooley, 1902, pp. 149–50)—when I call something mine, I am also saying that it does not belong to others—he *may* obtain an optimal degree of detachment only by somehow making peace within himself concerning what he thinks of his peers (Usual; Kipnis, 1961) and, especially if he lacks self-insight, what he believes they think of him (Usual; Kreines & Bogart, 1974). Such peace is not easy to come by; for example, adolescents *may* believe their peers view them more favorably than their parents do, even though they also think their parents ascribe to them a self-image that is closer to their own image than that ascribed to them by anyone else (France; Tomé, 1967).

Equanimity, I quickly add, must mean that the ego of Ego plays a relatively small role in passing judgment. The ego-detached states can be identified at least negatively: Ego is neither weary nor frustrated or, if he is, he waits until the moment has passed before judging Alter.

Critical, too, can be the relation between Ego and Alter (Pathway I.c). Ego cannot unmask ingratiation unless he can sit back long enough to perceive the role Alter is performing, consciously or unconsciously, for his benefit. The flattery of one Alter may in fact affect Ego's self-image and hence his judgment of other Alters; and so *perhaps* Ego can more accurately gauge peers who reject rather than accept him as a co-worker or companion in imaginary situations (France, secondary-school students; Maucorps & Bassoul, 1958). It *may* be difficult not to like those who like us: reciprocation in interpersonal relations is often demanded "to gain social or other forms of external approval" (Usual; Jones, 1966), unless some other goal accompanies the judgment motive (Pathway II.a). Ego *may* feel favorably disposed toward Alters who appraise him accurately (Canada, college; Hewitt, 1969) or agree with his own self-evaluation (Usual; Potter, 1973); yet, since he *may* prefer Alters who describe him positively but inaccurately to those who describe him negatively but accurately (presumably England, unspecified; Eiser & Smith, 1972), he must have enough fortitude and detachment to value accuracy above mutual affection or praise. He must also guard against his tendency to assume that persons he likes are similar to himself (Postscript 5.4); and *perhaps* particularly those with high self-esteem have greater faith in such a view than those with lower self-esteem (U.S., children; Simon & Bernstein, 1971). It is difficult, furthermore, to avoid the belief that individuals who seem "factually" similar are in fact similar. When both Ego and Alter, for example, are males or females, are roughly the same age, or come from the same social class, the temptation to ascribe similar experiences and predispositions or traits to them is great; but of course these apparently objective criteria may cause Ego to overlook the possibility of deviation (Pathway I.7).

Without detachment, Ego may pass judgments whose aim is really to bring comfort to himself. He *may* have cause to dislike Alter, but he may find more peace and experience less dissonance by modifying his opinion in the opposite direction: he persuades himself or is persuaded to dislike Alter less, so that he then perhaps feels happier (Usual; Berscheid et al., 1968). If his self-esteem is low, he *may* feel less attracted to an Alter who judges him favorably in order—again *perhaps*—to reduce the discrepancy between his own harsh self-judgment and that of the other person (Usual; Koech & Guthrie, 1975).

Detachment sometimes can be very simply attained by reviewing carefully and in detail a case history presented by a competent psychiatrist or biographer. Let Ego first open the history at some arbitrary point which discloses a bit of Alter's behavior and let him then try to infer the significance of that bit for the individual's personality. The exercise inevitably engenders a sense of humility: we usually lack the kind of information a whole history reveals (Pathway I.3) but we recklessly make the great inductive leap and judge Alter anyhow.

Finally, I would mention, without embarrassment, what may seem to be a very odd and old-fashioned catalyst of detachment; viz., straight thinking. It matters not whether Ego uses Aristotelian logic in a formal sense, symbolic logic, or some admonition from modern semantics (including General Semantics), but it is important for him to recognize the implication of his propositions and the legitimacy of his reasoning (Sarbin et al., pp. 65–68). You consider this individual scattered, and you believe that scattered persons seldom achieve important objectives. Before drawing such a drastic conclusion, I suggest you halt, count to more than 10, let time pass, ponder, and ask yourself innumerable questions. What do you mean by "scattered," what evidence do you have for placing Alter in such a category? Here are problems of definition and of induction or evidence. Do you believe that all, many, some, or a few scattered persons fail in the indicated respect, how do you define "seldom" and "important"? Your major premise must thus be appraised, operational definitions must be required, precision must be sought. If you settle all these matters satisfactorily and clearly, and if your generalization applies not to all but to many persons, then the final conclusion to be drawn concerning Alter does not slip carelessly from your premises. And so it goes, on and on, as the numerous pathways involved in primary judgments would indicate. We may agree that Alter is scattered but perforce we thus neglect other aspects of his personality—and you must decide whether to take these additional attributes into account when judging him. *You want me always to be cold-blooded, critical, and logical?* No, I do not expect you or anyone, including myself, forever to think logically and straight, and I know we are often dependent upon non-logical, almost irrational intuition for our judgments, but do remember: cogito, ergo sum. *Don't you really mean the reverse: sum, ergo cogito?*

6.c.   Variation

To move onto an advisable pathway from a primary to a secondary judgment and to prevent subsequent judgments from being false, Ego must recognize the possibility that his postulation concerning Alter's consistency, which he has found so necessary and convenient (Pathway 6.a), may be a simplification (Pathway II.1) and may be partially or totally false. Actually he ought to have no difficulty in anticipating that Alter will change, for he knows that with the passing of time he himself and others have matured and have undergone varying experiences. He observes Alter in a new situation or in a different role. Has that bureaucrat's disposition improved after he has been away on a holiday; are children's imaginations affected adversely when they view too many television programs; have I been able to convince him that he is supporting the wrong candidates for public office; after losing (or winning) a war, have those people become less belligerent?

Reflection would be of greater assistance to Ego if he has available a theory specifying either the kinds of Alters or the traits in Alters likely to change. In our previous discussion of change (Pathway 4.c), I have stressed three points: usually people change most reluctantly; they are willing to accept changes when, in effect, the anticipated gains from doing so seem to exceed the anticipated losses; and under some circumstances the changes may even be rapid rather than slow. This triad, however, is too abstract from Ego's standpoint (Pathway 0.1). It is not enough for him merely to know that frustration facilitates changes, for then he cannot anticipate the form the ensuing changes will take. After transplantation there may be abrupt changes, but when and for what reasons will Alter be transplanted? Ego may emerge only with the strong conviction that some persons, for example, are more susceptible to conversions or to transformations than others (Postscript 4.4), even as some persons *may* be more field-dependent, more suggestible, and less self-reliant than others (Witkin et al., 1962, pp. 134–56). At first glance, a strong argument might be advanced that segmental traits ought to be more easily modifiable than central ones: they have been less strongly reinforced in the past, they involve less drastic change in the individual's outlook. A conscientious physician who likes beer can be persuaded more easily to change brands of beer than to abandon his profession. On the other hand, the frustration of a central tendency may be more keenly experienced than that of a segmental tendency and hence be more amenable to change. The physician may cling to his favorite brew even after an unpleasant association with it, but he may retire from medicine or shift his practice if he finds his existence too demanding or unrewarding. The advisable pathway for Ego may be a good dose of situational empiricism (Pathway I.5) for each Alter.

Hardly anyone, I imagine, fails to expect primary judgments to be reviewed when a Group Alter is being judged, particularly when the group is observed simultaneously. For when people are together, they are likely to stimulate one another so that, as a consequence, their behavior changes. We know beforehand that the team is going to win, lose, or draw—and we do not pass judgment, perhaps, on their ability or esprit until the game is over. We are aware of sudden shifts that can take place—as when a well-behaved group becomes a mob and riots—so that we are ready to abandon our first impression and to pass a series of revised secondary judgments. Many groups deliberately assemble in order to change, such as committees charged with coming to decisions for larger groups.

Primary judgments are, or should often be, replaced by secondary ones principally because it is desirable or necessary to qualify the initial impression. In the cool light of afternoon—or of reason—we know that any statement merely indicates a probability and hence we are perfectly willing to admit that the original judgment must be modified especially after additional information is received. Even the professionals can never be sure they have enough facts about Alter, though they may be measuring him for a particular purpose: have they used the right number of scales or questionnaires, or has a schedule included all the items that may be relevant to understanding or predicting his behavior? You need only say to me, "Are you sure?"—and then I ought to have enough sense to know how unsure I am. When challenged, we agree without a murmur that there are scores and scores of reasons why a particular judgment must be incorrect at the moment it is made and many more why it will turn out to be incorrect in the future; can we forever issue the challenge to ourselves? The reply must depend on the particular Ego, since the degree of certainty he attaches to his judgment reflects his personality or the amount of information at his disposal—or both. Some of us are never certain, we always prefer qualifications: all that ought to be known, we believe, can never be known (Pathway I.3). Others are almost always certain, they know when they have enough information, and they would avoid redundancy.

Additional information concerning Alter's demographic attributes is almost always advantageous: the more of them Ego knows, the more accurately he comes to understand him and predict his behavior. Alter is a man and hence. . . . He is a middle-aged man and hence. . . . He is a middle-aged man who is married and hence. . . . He is a middle-aged

man who is married, lives in a large city in the Far West, and hence. . . .
He is a middle-aged man who is married, lives in a large city in the
Far West, is a factory worker, and hence. . . . Each bit of information
ostensibly is helpful, is it not? Not necessarily—and I spoke up ahead
of you. For Alter may deviate from one or more of the various categories to which he may be validly assigned. As I have said so often
and not merely for your benefit, Ego, you, or I may not be able to
capture Alter's elusive individuality with a hundred categories; it is
nevertheless potentially useful to have these probabilities in front of us.

An Ego-expositor or you or I must ask whether in fact Ego will
seek new information about Alter. Reality, of course, may intrude:
new information is thrust upon Ego. Or if the information giving rise
to the primary judgment is itself inconsistent or contains contradictions, he *may* feel less certain, and hence reach out for additional facts
(Usual; Levy & Richter, 1963). *Another spiral (Pathway 4.b)?* Possibly
yes: the less information, the less certainty; the less certainty, the more
information that may be gathered. But only possibly: an Ego with
little information may grow impatient and plunge recklessly. *Suppose
Ego is perfectly happy with his primary judgment and suppose reality
leaves him in peace, will he then ever become restless?* The answer here
must be: it all depends upon his personality and various values. *Perhaps*, for example, more information may be sought by a female rather
than by a male Ego (particularly when the lady's so-called "cognitive
structure" is complex rather than simple), or about a male rather than
about a female Alter (Usual; Nidorf & Crockett, 1964; Nidorf, 1968).
Do not take the last finding seriously; I have cited it only for illustrative purposes and to keep faith with my deterministic hypothesis
concerning the lawfulness of behavior—in this instance the generalizability of the results beyond the two studies may be close to nil.
Actually Ego, more often than not, may have to force himself to seek
additional information or somehow, if his impressions of Alter are
contradictory or dissonant, he must feel or be made to feel the need
to organize what he knows (Usual; McGuire, 1961, pp. 9–10).

Ego may be aware that his primary judgment springs from inadequate information, but he may be powerless to remedy his plight. It
may not be practical to obtain additional information (Pathway I.3).
Alter may be dead, with no new facts about him available from documents or other persons. He may be a fictitious character whose author
has provided only a brief sketch. He may be a public personage or he
may live faraway, so that he is not available. Alter is not like a patient

entering a psychological clinic who is both able and willing to submit himself to a battery of tests. Under these circumstances, Ego may be unable to change his primary judgment, he may conclude that he should hold it more tentatively.

Ego must adopt some sort of strategy or utilize some method to obtain whatever additional information he decides to seek. He exercises his skill in judging other persons (Pathway II.b) and in finding sound ways to do so. He carefully notes whatever information is available concerning Alter, such as demographic data, expressions of feelings or attitudes, and actual behavior. Or he may be able deliberately to elicit information by questioning Alter or by enticing him into situations in which he reveals significant segments of himself, etc. And the *etc.* covers a long, long list known to professionals and amateurs alike. We may, for example, obtain a preliminary idea of Alter by observing the kinds of friends he has. We may compare our judgments with those of others, for it is possible that group judgments that are pooled after discussion or even those that are just lumped together in a statistical sense *may* be more valid than Ego's own uncontaminated judgment (Usual; Cline & Richards, 1961). Clearly, however, interactions in group situations—with or without techniques like role playing, simulation, observation, and all the other devices so ingeniously concocted and immodestly proclaimed by those now connected with the current practices of encounter groups—seem promising as a source of data if only because most lives are lived in groups and hence groups are likely to arouse profound emotions that may otherwise be repressed.

And now what advice can you give Ego or me? Seek the least possible information on the basis of which a valid judgment can be passed (Jones & Thibault, 1958, p. 152). Too much information is wasteful and may be confusing; too little means the sample of Alter is incomplete. The pathway, alas, is so much easier to imagine than to locate. *Amen.*

The additional information Ego acquires about Alter, deliberately or not, may or may not be congruent with the information he already possesses. Conflicting bits of information may reach him through different modalities (when the scowl, as we have noted, belies the cheery verbal declaration) or different channels (when Alter's reputation differs from his perceived behavior). This Humpty-Dumpty problem—putting the pieces together—is part of the secondary judgment and hence is considered on the next pathway. *Obviously, here and elsewhere, you mean chapter when you say pathway; aren't you being a bit too cute?* Perhaps, but 'tis a harmless conceit. As I was saying: at this point I would only note the potentially explosive effect of a new item of information especially when it belongs, from Ego's standpoint, to a syndrome of traits (Usual; Wishner, 1960); the injection of a single adjective like "intelligent" into a set of words describing a hypothetical character with whom that adjective is not ordinarily associated *may* lead to reactions ranging from the incorporation of the attribute into the stereotype to a denial that the person could be so characterized (Usual; Haire & Grunes, 1950).

New information, therefore, may be taken into account or, because first impressions of Alter *may* be valued more highly than those coming later (Usual; Jones et al., 1968—but see also Postscript 2.3), it may be ignored. Ego *may* be especially prone to ignore that information after his judgment has become stabilized (Usual; Davis et al., 1966); then it is troublesome to seek or utilize more facts, it is more comfortable to retain a first impression, and it may be difficult to process the new. Disregarding additional information, you will not be surprised to hear, *may* be connected with personality traits, such as authoritarianism (Usual; Steiner & Johnson, 1963). Similarly, other responses to increased information *may* also be linked to personality: evaluating Alter more favorably upon receipt of additional information *may* be related to a negative attitude toward risk taking (Usual; Posavac & Pasko, 1973). American undergraduates *may* in fact hold variability in high esteem because they prefer the simple to the complex (Levy, 1964). *I doubt whether* that *is a universal tendency.*

Redundant or non-redundant information about Alter may be used as a basis for passing judgment upon him. The very redundant, for example, *may* have less effect upon Ego's evaluation of Alter than the less redundant (Usual; Wyer, 1968). Ego may conclude that repeated actions or verbal expressions are significant because otherwise they would not be repeated; or he may grow bored or impatient. Non-variability, moreover, may suggest that Alter's personality remains stable in some respects, in fact here is one of the reasons for emphasizing the utility of postulating traits. The observed changes may be superficial, Ego may conclude, the core remains. Advisedly, therefore, Ego must learn to accept a degree of variability as an additional clue to the person he would judge.

"Dogmatic" Egos receiving discrepant information about Alter *may* be more likely than those who are "undogmatic" to avoid compromise:

either they change their original judgment greatly or they adhere to it (Usual; Foulkes & Foulkes, 1965). This relation suggests another advisable pathway regarding detachment: the need to appreciate the fact that conviction is not equivalent to validity. We may believe that what we feel deeply is likely to be true just because of the depth of our feelings: we trust profound emotions. Sometimes we may be right: the judgment approaches absolute conviction because in a manner we cannot consciously specify we may have taken into account all available evidence concerning Alter and have utilized to a maximum our skill in judging others. But we can also be wrong, very wrong. We can think of extreme cases—Hitler, in fact any tyrant—whose complete faith in their convictions leads to abysmally faulty judgments from a factual or ethical standpoint. Another way, a glib but pointed way, to phrase this advisable pathway involves qualification: be uncertain about certainty.

Up to this point, attention has been focused upon variations within Alter, but another possibility looms which may produce a change in Ego's judgment: he himself varies. As he matures, his viewpoint may be altered, with the result that the same bit of Alter's behavior, whether reviewed from the past or perceived in the present, he evaluates with new criteria and with greater or less accuracy. A shift in his values at adolescence, for example, *may* be accompanied by changes in the aspects of Alter's behavior he perceives and in the categories he employs to judge Alter (England, adolescents; Coleman, 1969). Ego's judgment may be affected by other changes within himself. He may come to feel a gap between himself and the generation to which a younger Alter belongs; he may grow more or less generous in his evaluations as he contemplates more frequently his own mortality; he may or may not be able to adjust to changing standards of morality which ostensibly occur with greater rapidity in Western than in traditional societies. Being human, moreover, Ego may simply forget either his previous judgment of Alter or its basis, so that an unchanged Alter may appear different to him. With the passing of time, spectators who have viewed motion pictures *may* remember more about characters with whom they have identified than about those of less interest to them, and the identification in turn *may* be related to the characters' sex and social class (U.S., grade-school children; Maccoby & Wilson, 1957).

Having sung a hymn to the pathway of change, I must add a sour note: there is no guarantee that revising a primary judgment as a result of new information necessarily produces more accurate judgments; in fact, some persons *may* pass less accurate judgments as information increases (presumably Usual; Obitz & Oziel, 1972). Or Ego *may* be more attracted to his peers when he discovers that the group to which they all belong is no longer threatened with a loss of prestige after failing to perform an activity efficiently (Usual; Kleiner, 1960), but this does not mean that his judgment is more valid or sensible. Not the quantity of information but its quality and the way it is evaluated are crucial. *And I suppose you mean this to be a final reason why reflection may improve primary judgments?*

Postscripts

6.1 The Validity of First Impressions

Quite obviously there are persons, including, I think, you, who have the strong tendency to trust first impressions for a number of reasons. In the past, they believe, those judgments have been more successful than subsequent ones. Somehow the initial glance was more penetrating and, in addition, unaffected by qualifications and excuses which came later and were more distorted than the original insight. On occasion Ego feels convinced he has all the evidence he needs or would need as bases for judgment; why reconsider when there is little or nothing more to be learned? He may presume that there are situations in which Alters immediately reveal themselves unequivocally, and that there- fore additional data cannot be more revealing. Or he may have such a conviction only for certain types of Alters whom he considers easy to grasp, whereas he first reflects and then passes secondary judgment on other types. He may possess great self-confidence and hence trust judg- ments made more or less intuitively.

Circumstances, moreover, compel all of us to decide on the spur of the moment: is the stranger to be feared or to be trusted? No addi- tional data are going to be available; you just have to force yourself to make a decision, you cannot inquire into his life history, you cannot force him to take a paper-and-pencil test, you cannot ask him whether he has a psychiatrist or a priest who knows him well and then, if he says yes, consult that expert (Pathway I.3). Your primary judgment must suffice, but you may learn from it that, until additional informa- tion is procurable, you should suspend judgment.

Sometimes first impressions may be validated later because of recip- rocal feedback between Ego and Alter (Pathway I.c): Ego's judgment

affects Alter who then may, more or less, conform to the original judgment. Counselors *may* have vivid impressions of their clients at the
outset, and the outcome of the therapy, dependent as it is upon the
relationship between therapist and patient, *may* be partially a function
of the initial judgment (Usual & student counselors; Brown, 1970).
Thus first impressions create secondary judgments. Obviously, however, there can be no such spiral when Ego's judgment has no effect
upon Alter. *But even then, what about a self-fulfilling prophecy?*

First impressions may be as valid or invalid as reflective secondary
judgments when similar information affects both. Appearance, manners, or mannerisms as criteria for judgment *may* be employed as stimuli for first and later impressions in the same or different Egos (U.S.,
rating of cadets by officers; Vielhaber & Gottheil, 1965). You looked
like an eager person the first time I saw you, and forever after you
have produced the same judgment within me. In this instance I was
right then as I am now, as other evidence happens to prove. *But you
know very well I am not always eager.*

I advance the unoriginal opinion that there is not, perhaps never can
be, an infallible pathway along which we can determine the circumstances under which first impressions are likely to be more (or less)
valid than later ones based upon a larger sample of Alter's behavior. If
you insist, I would express skepticism concerning the initial impact
and have greater faith in later impressions. The professionals and the
rest of us know only that some Egos jump to conclusions more readily
than others; those trusting their first impressions *may* mention traits
in Alters different from those reported by less trusting Egos; and those
with sharp initial reactions *may* utilize less information to arrive at a
judgment and retain their judgments longer than those who hesitate
(Usual; Ehrlich & Lipsey, 1969). I reluctantly conclude that on this
question each of us must work out his own advisable pathway, a tepid
conclusion not likely to be universally acclaimed by mankind.

6.2   The Dependability of Informants

First I shall mention the basic, skeletal details of the problem and
then fly off into clouds of speculation. *Mixed metaphor.* When Ego
learns about Alter from an informant, he is in effect judging two Alters,
the major one about whom he seeks information and the minor one
who provides it. There is no reason to believe that one of these judgments is easier or more difficult to make than the other. The minor
Alter, for example, cannot be judged credible without knowing his

motives for acting as an informant; and those motives may not be ascertainable with dispatch. As common sense suggests, Ego is more likely to believe statements from a valued than from a non-valued informant; and extreme judgments concerning the major Alter *may* be more likely when Ego considers the minor Alter to be a reliable source of information than when he judges him to be attractive (Usual; Rosenbaum, 1967). *The more information about the major Alter that is received from a minor Alter on whom Ego is dependent, the better?* No, for eventually additional information concerning some types of persons *may* be confusing and lead to erroneous judgments (Canada, college students; Perry & Boyd, 1974). *Any more complications?* Of course: Ego, for example, *may* have a more favorable impression of Alter when someone else rather than Alter provides favorable information about Alter, but his judgment *may* be *less* unfavorable when Alter and not another person is the source of unfavorable information (Usual; Izzett & Leginski, 1972). Then *perhaps* information about Alter's personality may produce less polarized judgments than information about his occupation (Usual; Rosenbaum, 1967). Uncomplicated, however, is the following possibility: Ego *may* be more likely to receive or comprehend information about Alter when both he and the informant come from the same sub-culture or occupy a similar status within the society (Germany, students & firemen; Willich et al., 1972).

What happens when Ego receives one impression from a direct observation of the major Alter and another from the minor Alter's report? *You ought to know by now—I expressed my view when you were discussing communication channels—that I prefer my own judgment, even when I have confidence in the informant: what I observe I can be sure of.* But certainly there are times when you are willing to admit the inadequacy of your own information. Then you listen to others, especially when your experience suggests that they are likely to be helpful (Pathway 2.1). Experience again; and perhaps a more valid secondary judgment (Pathway 8.a).

Informants, therefore, may be important because all of us to some degree are dependent upon other persons for information which can be of crucial significance as we pass judgment. If someone tells you that the man you are about to meet is an Albanian poet, you may be thrown into a strange or intriguing conflict. You hold some poets in high esteem and hence you anticipate that he may possibly be one of the select mortals on this planet; but on the other hand you have no stereotype of Albanians other than a vague memory of a king's daughters long, long ago and hence you have virtually no expectations based upon knowledge of his nationality. In this instance the information has served to evoke responses hardly enabling you to prejudge the man (Pathway II.c) or to have various feelings toward him (Pathway 4); the role these prior responses play in the secondary judgment depends not only on the previous experiences but also on the man—and his poetry. Do you have the inner fortitude to resist your prejudices? *No, what you call my prejudices are well-grounded in experience.*

Special informants in any society are considered expert judges of others and hence on the basis of past experience their opinions on occasion are eagerly sought or received as guides to secondary judgments. In nonliterate societies, my impression is, those officially having such prestige are likely to be chiefs and elders; and medicine men ("native doctors," as some in Ghana call themselves on their own English-language shingles) are thought to have supernatural ways of providing information about Alters of immediate concern to their clients. *And in our own society?* Undoubtedly parents correct their children's primary judgments, but eventually they lose some or much of their authority. It would take more courage and patience than I possess to try to summarize the reputation of psychologists and especially of psychiatrists who are supposed to be the professional experts. Except when the patients are young children or psychotics, their diagnoses are confidential and are not ordinarily divulged to anyone other than those who have sought help from them. The same is true of psychometricians who administer standardized tests or conduct standardized interviews, except that here the person who hires them or who seeks their advice—psychiatrists wishing data that will facilitate their own appraisal, employers and school officials who are interested in aptitudes—have access to the findings. Many, maybe most laymen do not understand or at least might not interpret correctly the views of these professionals. Think, for example, of the smiles the word "couch" still evokes among those acquainted with its specialized usage, even though Freudianism has been with us for more than half a century. Most individuals are dependent upon friends, persons who are informally influential in their own communities, and the mass media for information concerning individual and group Alters; and so experiences establishing the prestige and credibility of the channel purveying the information (Pathway 2.b) become highly relevant. Jurymen are elevated temporarily to the status of experts who traditionally in Anglo-Saxon society were supposed to collect relevant facts and in modern times are expected to pass judgment on defendants. Before the verdict, Alter is the defendant or the accused; immediately after, if found guilty, he becomes a criminal. Whether or not an Ego, not a member of the jury, accepts the information indicated by the changed label depends upon his attitudes toward courts and the particular trial. He matches his own competency and judgment with those of the jury whose duty it has been to review all the evidence as well as to observe the defendant in the courtroom and, usually, on the witness stand.

Ego secures information from other persons about himself, too. Psychiatric patients are again a very special case: middle-class neurotics in the West pay large fees to hear about themselves, psychotics and others may be forced to do so. The rest of us obtain such information only informally if repeatedly. *You mean I keep telling you what I think about you.* To some extent what others think of us determines what we think of ourselves (Pathway I.b), a banality we can accept without exaggerating, as indicated previously, the social bases of personality. Once more the problem arises as to whether Ego, on the basis of experience, trusts a minor Alter to provide the kind of information that increases significantly insight into a very major Alter, himself; and his own view may conflict with what he is told. One relative of yours, you say, keeps insisting you are not a very sensible person and she has said this to you so often that you almost agree with her; therefore, abhorrent as the thought is, I might find out about you by interviewing her. *Ugh.*

Ego, being alive and human, is never completely at rest. He is continually faced or refaced with problems involving his fellow men whom he must judge and rejudge again and again. He passes secondary judgment after an encounter or series of encounters with Alters through one or more channels that have led to perception, attitude arousal, and primary judgment. There are many reasons why a primary, intuitive judgment should be transformed into a secondary one. Ego may wish to justify his first impression and explain it either to himself or to others. He may appraise that impression to determine whether a correction is necessary or not, particularly after reflecting upon his experience, after becoming somewhat detached, and after appreciating the changes within Alter or himself. If sophisticated, for example, he *may* realize the possibility that he attributes more prejudice to others than he does to himself (U.S., high school; Terry & Evans, 1972). He may be uncomfortable because he has conflicting conceptions of Alter derived from a favorable bit of information coupled with a less favorable or unfavorable bit; how, then, can the pieces be combined, no matter whether he reflects or not? Or he may vaguely feel the need to improve his primary judgment without seeking or finding additional information, which is a way of saying that from his standpoint he continues to rely upon intuition (Hathaway, 1956).

If the psychophysical prototype of primary judgment is the method of absolute judgment, as previously suggested at the outset of Pathway 5, can it be said that secondary judgment relies upon some variation of the method of comparison? In some instances two Alters are placed, as it were, alongside each other—they are together in the same room or group—and are compared. But there is no method in psychophysics, other than absolute judgment itself, that precisely corresponds to the frequent situation in which Ego, after passing primary judgment, carefully compares Alter with other persons whom he has known and who at the moment of comparison are absent. The revision or reaffirmation achieved by a secondary judgment requires Ego to characterize, evaluate, and understand Alter.

7.a   Characterization

Ego's characterization of Alter depends principally upon three processes: his choice of concepts or categories, his own imagination, and the role he ascribes to Alter. Concepts and categories receive major attention here, although they have been previously discussed in two other contexts (Pathways I.b & 5.a): it is they that can be refined and sharpened by secondary judgment. Instead of simply utilizing the first label springing out of his repertoire, Ego has an opportunity to describe Alter more accurately. There are two, possibly three, attributes such categories should have (Signell, 1966). First, to capture some of Alter's nuances, a diverse set is usually necessary. A paranoid may view all persons in terms of the threat he imagines they pose to himself; in contrast, a healthy individual employs a large number of concepts to describe each Alter because he is convinced that Alters cannot be thrown into a limited number of pigeonholes. Then the category should suggest a range of behavior, not merely a dichotomy. Most individuals are not either ascendant or submissive, but somewhere in between. At one extreme is the conviction that you-either-have-it-or-you-don't, at the other the mellow view that you-have-it-in-varying degrees. Or Ego places Alter in a category and then locates him there more precisely: he is a Christian, yes, and devout, not superficial. Finally, if the judgment is to be communicated to one's peers, the concepts should be the kind whose meaning or significance they can readily grasp. You have emerged from your parental culture and consequently you judge most Alters, including me, in terms of their originality, innovativeness, intelligence, sensitivity, etc., whereas your childhood friends prefer categories such as reliability, stability, industriousness, etc. I would not take sides, I would merely suggest that all of us blind men may be touching different parts of the beast with our words.

In spite of what you have just said, I am not sure I understand the difference between description (Pathway 5.a) and characterization (the present pathway). Let me try again, this is important, for I am once more distinguishing primary from secondary judgments. Your difficulty may stem from the fact that the same word or concept may be employed to describe and to characterize. I judge that landscape to be beautiful. I thus describe the landscape when that is my immediate reaction to what I see there, when without reflection I ascribe the attribute exclusively to the stimulus and its context, when I feel passively absorbed in my sense impressions and hence do not consider the interaction between those impressions and my own tastes and attitudes. I characterize the same landscape with the same term when my judgment is more deliberate, when I have reflected, when I have evaluated what I am seeing, when I compare my sense impressions with other experiences in the past or with my verbalizable or unverbalizable notions of beauty in general, when I appreciate the interaction between myself and the stimulus in its context. *The line is fuzzy.* Yes, it is, but you see, don't you, that there is a line? *Yes, but why do you use the words "description" and "characterization" in the analysis?* I can find no better ones, and I think they may have the connotations I would communicate: the former suggests more passivity on Ego's part than the latter.

I freely, gladly, willingly admit that it is easier to formulate the ideal attributes of concepts than to realize them. Even though we use diverse categories when describing chefs or sculptors, politicians or priests, workers or bankers, we try to generalize some categories and use them in as many situations as possible. Is he intelligent? Is she generous? Are they honest? And then: just how intelligent is he? Is she more or less generous than her sister? Are they as honest as the rest of their generation? An Ego-expositor must note that the choice of concepts as well as their elaboration depends, in large or small part, upon Ego's own personality traits; even his self-concept and his self-esteem *may* be related to the way he expresses himself verbally (U.S., children; Nash & Thomas, 1973). In this connection the professionals suggest an advisable pathway: they seldom are content to note whether a given trait is either present or absent, rather they try to indicate the degree to which it is present by means of ratings, scaling, rankings, etc. Our normal thinking, however, tends to have a black-and-white character because we are lazy and it is usually easier to say that something is hot or cold than to ascertain its precise temperature on a thermometer (Pathway II.1).

For many respectable reasons, furthermore, we are addicted to primary black-and-white thinking. Social norms are seldom based on fine discriminations: you conform or you do not, you are law-abiding or you are not, you are allowed to vote or you may not. On an individual level, we must often make either-or decisions: that individual is considered qualified to be a spouse, a partner, a friend, or an employee, or he is not qualified. He does not half-qualify. If he only half-qualifies, then it is difficult to decide whether to marry, trust, or work with the person. *Are you sanctifying scales and other forms of quantifications?* No, I am merely saying they are useful, though I must immediately note again that scores on most personality tests give a spurious impression of exactness when in reality they merely indicate the broad category in which the person being tested should be placed. In addition, non-professionals sometimes try to indicate more than the presence of a predisposition, belief, or trait in Alter: the attribute is formulated implicitly in quantitative form through the use of an adverb, such as "strongly," 'fully," "completely" (Cattell, 1965, pp. 54–55). Thus I know not only that you believe man's fate is more likely to be determined by external factors than by his own decisions but also that this is one of the strong beliefs you hold with great confidence.

Characterization on a secondary level can be considered an extension of the ascription occurring on the primary level (Pathway 5.b); but the interpretation is likely to be more general, perhaps therefore more subtle and complete. It may be relatively easy to note that Alter eats very quickly: at any meal he always finishes before everyone else even though his portions are as generous as theirs. As a first approximation, Ego may ascribe some trait like gluttony to him, but additional reflection may suggest the need for more facts. With these facts Ego may be able to decide whether gulping food means that Alter is anxious, eager, or fixated on an oral level. Or any observer may agree that Alter blinks his eyes whenever he is questioned, but disagreement arises when secondary judgments concerning the significance of this non-verbal symbol are passed. Does Alter deliberately blink in order to cope with some of his problems, to show that he is attentive, to shut out reality, to displace nervous energy; or is his blink an expression, somehow, of the deeper layers of his personality (Allport, 1961, pp. 462–63)?

There is also a temporal relation involved in secondary judgments. Ego's original judgment motive may have been to determine one of Alter's traits (such as his ability) on the basis of his behavior (such as his perceived achievement) and then, having observed the behavior, Ego utilizes one of his principles from the past to judge that trait. Or wittingly or unwittingly he observes Alter's behavior, then for some reason he judges that behavior by invoking a principle in order to ascribe a trait to him. *But is there not a causal relation between be-*

havior and the attribution of traits? I wish I knew the answer—all I can point to is individual variability in this respect. *No generalization at all?* Well *perhaps* extremely high *or* low motivation is attributed to American college students by their peers when there is a discrepancy between the grades they receive and their intelligence-test scores (Kepka & Brickman, 1971); but then again apparent diligence *may* be considered a better index of motivation than a measure of such a discrepancy (Usual; Williams, 1976).

At any rate it is not surprising that two Egos may characterize Alter differently on the basis of the same evidence or that they may arrive at the same characterization on the basis of different evidence. One juryman finds the defendant innocent, the other guilty, even though both have been attentive throughout the trial. Or they both declare him innocent, the one juror because he believes the defendant's testimony, the other because he distrusts the witnesses for the prosecution. Even the simplest judgment may emerge from different bases; in our society, for example, children *may* judge the relative age of two persons on the basis of height, but Sarawak children in Malaysia *may* use the additional criteria of strength and fatness for reasons inherent in their culture (U.S. & Malaysia, children; Looft et al., 1972). The statement of this problem, however, may be a bit too glib. Evidence has been called "the same" only from an objective standpoint. *Whose standpoint?* That of another person who is not one of the Egos passing judgment. They themselves, however, may have perceived that evidence quite differently and hence for them it was not the same source of information. Or two persons may use the same word to characterize Alter while having different feelings about him or judging him with varying degrees of certainty. *More solipsism?* Yes. (Pathway 3.1).

At any given moment or over time, as noted in connection with variability (Pathway 6.c), Alter seldom provides Ego with a single bit of information or with bits of information that are congruent or that easily fall into place. In addition, Ego himself may or should seek out additional information to obtain an adequate sample of Alter's potentialities or actualities (Pathway 1.2). The speech of Alter may fit into one category, as we once agreed (Pathway 3.b), but his features, the position of his eyes, his activity, the reports about him, and Ego's own prejudgments based on experience with him or other persons fit into one or more other categories. How, then, can the available pieces be integrated in order to characterize Humpty-Dumpty—and this time I use your phrasing—as he really is? "No matter how large a file of tests, personal documents, interviews, and what-not is compiled on a person, and no matter how well the sources agree," one professionaal suggests, "the data do not pull themselves together." And then he immediately adds: "To synthesize such materials is something of an art, and doubtless always will be" (Holt, 1969, p. 723). The general outline of the procedure professionals employ should be noted because as a model it can function as an advisable pathway (Postscript 7.1: Professional Approaches to the Humpty-Dumpty Problem).

One of the popular, intriguing naturalistic pathways being explored by the professionals involves another phase of the Humpty-Dumpty problem: how in fact do Egos put together pieces of information, especially when they repeatedly rate, rank, or generally describe utterly hypothetical Alters? *I like the name Humpty-Dumpty—but do you mind if I skip this paragraph which I rather think is not going to be my cup of tea?* Facing us—or rather me alone now that my devil's advocate has skipped ahead—are four "models" (viz., conceptualizations or procedures in less jargonistic terms) whose partisans advance arguments favoring one or another model above the rest and who also design microscopically new wrinkles in experiments to support their view. The problem clearly involves the combining of information: what happens when a new item of information is added to existing items or is part of a collection of items? Suppose, for example, Ego has two bits of information, both of which give him a very favorable impression of Alter, and suppose then a third bit is added which is only weakly favorable; what does Ego do? A theorist with an additive model (e.g., Greece and U.S., university students; Triandis & Fishbein, 1963) maintains that the third bit (after being weighted or not) is added to the other bits and hence increases slightly the favorable impression. Professionals with an averaging model (e.g., Usual; Weiss, 1963; Anderson, 1966) demonstrate that the third bit would be averaged in with the other two bits with the result of a slight decrease in the favorable impression. A multiplicative assumption (e.g., U.S., college & medical students; Howe, 1962) suggests another kind of reaction. One's impression of a feminine Alter who has been labelled "kind and beautiful" changes if the adverb "somewhat" is added to the description. Or if the value of the additional information is negative, the product decreases: "She is tolerably kind and beautiful," poor lass. An investigator with the fourth or integrative model (e.g., Usual; Anderson, 1965) would, perhaps sensibly, refuse to discuss the issue in an abstract manner; it would depend upon the nature of the third piece of information and the way it relates to the other two, so that the ensuing impression could be more or less favorable than that derived from the two pieces alone, or it could be unaffected by the addition (Germany; students; Schümer et al., 1968). Disagreement among the experts is especially marked when they would describe the Humpty-Dumpty process mathematically (Usual; Thayer & Schiff, 1969).

Do come back now into the conversation, for I would make two points about these models that may be of interest to you. First, almost all carefully designed experiments have utilized only trait names to designate the bits of information Ego is asked to organize. In real life, however, Ego may be confronted not merely with words describing Alter but also with data about him that he himself obtains from firsthand observations in which the role requirements of situations interact with one another and also with his own conceptualization of Alter's traits (Pathways 0.1, 1.3, & 5.b). *Not very interesting, just another way to point out the artificiality of well-controlled experiments.* Then I am convinced that the last of the four approaches mentioned above seems most reasonable and inviting because it is eclectic, and eclecticism is what is called for. Whether there is addition, averaging, multiplication, or something else depends upon the information available concerning Alter; there is no inevitable consequence as new data are perceived; the controversy can never be conclusively settled (Hendrick, 1968). Alter has a harmless hobby, Ego discovers; then he learns either that Ego works on the hobby every night or that he works on it whenever he wants to escape from one of his responsibilities. In the first instance, more information leaves the judgment unchanged, in the second, it changes the evaluation quite markedly. In addition, Ego may assemble Humpty-Dumpty by means of his own implicit or explicit theory of personality (Pathway II.c). That theory enables him to put discrete bits together and also to infer the existence of some bits from the presence of others, although he *may* believe he can decide whether or not pairs of adjectives can occur in the same person only by referring them to a specific individual (Usual; Hanno & Jones, 1973). The argument favoring eclecticism, moreover, becomes overwhelming when other variables are taken into account: the credibility of the sources providing contradictory information and the order in which they supply the information (Usual; Rosenbaum & Levin, 1968a); or the extent to which Ego perceives the new information as similar or dissimilar to the old (Chalmers, 1969); or indeed the extent to which one bit supplements or virtually replicates another bit (Usual; Schmidt, 1969). And factors such as these must be taken into account in real-life situations (Postscript 7.2: Miscellaneous Factors Affecting the Humpty-Dumpty Problem).

Ego, I imagine, must almost always make peace with himself to justify the Humpty-Dumpty he creates or recreates. As Ego-expositors, the professionals have sought to explain the justifications. They refer to a strain toward consistency, equilibrium, or balance (in contrast, respectively, with dissonance, disequilibrium, and imbalance) achievable through true or false rationalizations, plain forgetting, or repression (Postscript 7.3: Rationalizing Humpty-Dumpty).

The presence of Humpty-Dumpty must also be noted in connection with the judgment of Group Alters. Suppose, for example, you are asked to compare the friendliness of two groups of faces presented to you in photographs. One group displays three very friendly faces, the other, three equally friendly ones plus one that is not unfriendly but not quite as friendly as the rest; which group as a whole do you consider more friendly? The first contains less total friendliness because there are only three faces, whereas the second contains more friendliness as a result of the increment added by the fourth face. But you could also say that the average friendliness of the first picture is higher than that of the second if you add all the faces together and divide by the number in each. Yes, I am serious, for this has been done, and the outcome *may* favor the one with the higher mean friendliness rather than the absolute total, more especially when the faces belong to females rather than males (Usual; Rosnow & Arms, 1968). Convincing? Helpful? *Definitely not.*

In fact what advisable pathway becomes visible after this interminable discussion of Humpty-Dumpty—can you put the pieces together? No, not really, for here, if ever, is an instance in which the advisable cannot be derived from the naturalistic. Ego should know that the pieces can be assembled in various ways, but it is impossible to say whether his Humpty-Dumpty will turn out to be a threatening monster or a delicate jewel. The emerging synthesis or hodgepodge must be judged not by how the pieces have been assembled but by the independent validating criteria to be discussed on Pathway 8. Ego, however, can try to make one decision to help resolve the Humpty-Dumpty problem: weight the items of information regarding Alter and eliminate the trivial. This must be done with great care, if only because judging a trait to be central rather than peripheral within Alter (Pathway I.6) *may* have a profound effect upon Ego's total impression (probably

Usual; Knotts, 1966). When such a central tendency is located, it can be used as a basis for integrating the discrete bits. Experience can also be helpful (Pathway 6.a), especially when it concerns a particular Alter. While it may be true, for example, that there is in general no certain way to choose between words and non-verbal behavior which may convey conflicting information, Ego may learn that the words of one Alter or of several Alters in a given group or society should be weighted much more heavily than gestures or eye movements *except* when Alter is emotionally disturbed.

Without doubt, reflection and secondary judgments are required when Ego tries to characterize Alter's conception of himself. For that is a private matter Alter may seldom be willing to reveal even to the most trusted of confidants and of which he himself may not be completely aware. I suspect than an easy if superficial way for Ego to determine at least Alter's sense of identity is, for once, quite straightforward: ask him who he is. The reply is likely to be phrased in terms of occupation ("I am a plumber"), nationality or ethnicity ("I am an Ibo"), religion ("I belong to the Church of Ireland"), family ties ("I am a mother"), etc. Otherwise, if the direct approach is impossible, considerable insight is gained by determining Alter's demographic attributes; thus, if Ego knows that Alter is a lawyer in American society, he at least establishes the range within which the values of persons with this identity are likely to fall. The catch, however, is the extent of the range. He is a lawyer, yes, but what kind of a lawyer; what role exactly does he think he is performing in his legal activity? Then, if Alter's sense of identity is not clear-cut, a characterization becomes all the more difficult.

Even more elusive than a valid self-characterization is usually Ego's attempt to explain his own behavior. His theory, evoked as he passes secondary judgment upon himself, may or may not correspond to reality. For he may lack insight into himself, however defined, and hence use an invalid theory at the outset. He may never adequately test his theory. He may test the theory but falsely perceive conduct he considers relevant to the test. He may regulate his behavior in accordance with a false theory. Thus he may be selfish and not realize it; he may realize that he is selfish but be convinced that he is only compensating for his own generosity; he may believe himself generous but avoid all opportunities to be generous; he may believe himself generous but be convinced, when someone else labels him selfish, that he is generously acting in only an ostensibly selfish manner for the ultimate welfare of another person; or he may deliberately be generous in various situations, while still clinging to a selfish ethic, to prove to himself that he is indeed generous. On occasion he may judge himself by resorting to virtually the same behavioral criterion he applies to Alter; thus self-perception becomes "a special case of interpersonal perception" (Usual; Bem, 1967). I decide that you do not like snails because you never order them when they are on the menu; I know I like snails because I always do. *Far-fetched: I know instantly that I do not like snails, I do not have to recall that I never eat them.* But do you not have to survey your own behavior when someone asks you whether you are selfish or not? Still your point about not judging yourself like another person is so compelling that the professionals themselves are puzzled by this iconoclastic inversion and they cannot quite decide whether it is sensible or useful (Nisbett & Valins, 1972). At any rate, Ego may or may not be genuinely shocked if ever he discovers that his theory about himself is wrong, for who should know himself, he thinks, better than he? *I keep wondering what it is that provokes Ego to formulate a theory about himself.*

Most of the problems associated with Ego's secondary judgments concerning Alter or himself seem simple in comparison with his effort to pass a reflective judgment upon a Group Alter. Once again the terminology has not been standardized. How, for example, do you characterize a nation or an ethnic group? Almost any term in the language may be employed, but the customary concepts are often anthropomorphic metaphors. A people, an entire people, is thus called immature, paranoid, aggressive, patriotic, untrustworthy, cultured. Paradoxical as it may seem, I think the lack of standardization and the confusion are greater in connection with smaller and observable groups than with larger entities. For with smaller ones the task usually is to judge not only static but also dynamic behavior, and we have no uniform terms for describing or judging interaction; whereas nations are likely to be judged in cruder ways by referring to tradition and structure in the long run or specific leaders in the short run. In either case, it seems essential to include the goals of the group, the rules that are implicitly or explicitly followed, the organization that exists and evolves (including the relation between leaders and followers), the loyalty or esprit de corps that is exhibited, the customs that prevail, and so on. In addition, it would be useful if we could confidently make inferences from the milieu of a Group Alter to the behavior of the persons composing the group. Of course there is a relation: if there is a famine, the tribesmen will starve and therefore. . . . And therefore what? They will experience hunger, yes, but will they also be gentle or aggressive? And it would be equally satisfying to be able to find impressive connections among various behavioral attributes of a group, but even or especially the professionals—in this instance, anthropologists—do not offer us much encouragement (Postscript 7.4: The Anthropology of Group Alters). We must open a Pandora's box, as you know perhaps better than I, when Alter or a Group Alter is not directly observed, when information cannot be obtained from a living informant, and when, instead, only documents are available in the form of diaries, letters, autobiographies, biographies, vignettes, tapes, etc. (Postscript 7.5: Documentary Evidence). *One postscript after the other; do you really think I have the patience to read them, especially when they interrupt the flow of your silvery prose?*

In concluding this section on categories, let us again marvel at the commonplace, matter-of-fact ability of Egos in the clinic or in real life to utilize concepts and procedures provided by professional or nonprofessional outsiders. This ability manifests itself even crossculturally. Naturally it is easier for an African or an Asian to employ his own terms in characterizing Alters and naturally, too, we have to translate ours into his language and sometimes explain them to him; but then he sets to work. We can ask him to give a yes-or-no reply to a simple or complicated question, to rank a group of Alters with respect to a given attribute, or to rate each Alter on a 3-, a 5-, perhaps even on an 11-point scale. The versatility and adaptability of Ego prove, I think, not only that he is willing to cooperate in carrying out sensible or silly assignments but also that he is able to do so because he can categorize Alters in so many different ways and also because he knows that this is so. Of course Egos do not necessarily agree with one another. Is that man in real life or fiction a tragic figure? You might call him that if he suffers and if his suffering seems to spring not from a villain but from his own character; but one critic proposes that an individual should be called tragic only when his actions fulfill the "four elements" of tragedy which, she suggests, are the commission of an "act of shame or horror," consequent "suffering," the generation of "knowledge" on the part of the audience into "man's fundamental nature," and a resulting "affirmation, or reaffirmation, of the dignity of the human spirit and worthwhileness of human life" (Krook, 1969, p. 8). Obviously your use of the category of tragic differs from hers, and I would imagine some difference arises, if less dramatically so, in connection with any category.

We have been discussing, you may or may not recall, the first of three factors affecting categorization. The second has already been referred to again and again: Ego's imaginative ability to project his own impulses upon Alter, to identify with him, to feel sympathetic toward him (Pathway II.5). For a primary judgment, imagination is both advantageous and disadvantageous. It enables or requires Ego to pay close attention to Alter and to try, to the best of his ability, to comprehend him before passing judgment. But simultaneously it leads to error when Ego makes the easy assumption that Alter functions the way he himself did, does, will, or might. As he passes secondary judgment, however, Ego has the opportunity to utilize reflective imagination. He may note similarities between himself and Alter and also differences, and then his categories can be refined. At this point he is like a conscientious psychiatrist or parent who carefully observes Alter without necessarily concluding that the patient or child is a mirror image of himself (Postscript 5.4).

A purely cognitive factor may also affect Ego's imagination: the scope of the categories he employs either in general or while making particular judgments. If you commit the tempting sin of dividing persons into those who are good and those who are bad, as you sometimes do, and if you consider yourself good, as I hope you do, then any Alter has a fifty-fifty chance of being like you. But if you think persons vary in virtue from being good to being despicable, that chance decreases proportionately to the number of steps in the continuum. A tendency to use what has been called overinclusive categories may reflect not simply carelessness on Ego's part but deeper layers of his personality; thus schizophrenics *may* lump the irrelevant and the scattered into single categories with the result that their thought appears inaccurate and vague, though from their standpoint it may have its own logic and consistency (U.S.; Cameron, 1939).

The third factor affecting the characterization of Alter involves the role ascribed to him as he is perceived (Pathway 1.3). *My, you certainly moved rapidly away from the second factor after all those pages devoted to the first one.* Ego need only observe that Alter is a physician, a teacher, a prisoner, a parent, etc., and then he can employ appropriate categories to note how well or faithfully the role is being discharged. Characterizing Alter as conforming or not to the role requirements of a situation may be a significant component of secondary judgments. Insight into Alter *may* increase and more information about him *may* be obtained when his behavior in a given context seems to be unusual or to depart from its cultural expectations (Jones & Davis,

1965, pp. 223–24, 230–32). Pedestrians who do not cross the street against a red light are not likely to be noticed, but those who dash across recklessly usually arouse a judgment motive in a sensible Ego waiting for the light to change. Actually Ego *may* be convinced he can obtain more information and have greater confidence in his judgment when confronted with a non-conforming than a conforming Alter, although the behavior of the conformist, since it fits his categories more neatly, is likely to be recalled more accurately than that of the non-conformist (Jones et al., 1961). Ego *may* employ more concepts and dimensions to describe an Alter whose ethical, religious, inter-personal, and musical views appear inconsistent rather than consistent (Usual; Pyron, 1965), inasmuch as his role is less easy to specify.

The problem of Alter's role raises for Ego a very far-reaching question: is he interested in characterizing Alter segmentally or centrally (Pathway I.6)? If he would appraise Alter's personality as a whole, he must try to separate role-determined from idiosyncratic actions, perhaps by observing how consistently Alter behaves in various situations. But if he wishes only to know how well Alter conducts himself in one kind of role—is he a good chairman, citizen, swimmer, raconteur?—it is both necessary and sufficient to observe him exclusively in that one role. The sampling issue (Pathway 1.2) also arises in connection with evaluating Alter's personality or his ability. Should Ego try to measure his capacity to learn or to solve new problems (general intelligence) or a particular aptitude (skill in the use of tools while working on mechanical problems)? Obviously the answer depends upon Ego's interest in Alter: does he wish to know how Alter is likely to react to a number of challenges or whether he could possibly become a skilled mechanic? Or should Alter be judged when he is undergoing some kind of personal crisis? The case may be argued either way. On the one hand, under such circumstances he is probably displaying atypical behavior: he is anxious, he is not curbing impulses ordinarily under his control, he seems to be without hope, he makes unintelligent decisions, he is a mess. On the other hand, this very behavior of his is revealing since it shows what happens to him under pressure. It would be good to be able to observe him both during and not during a crisis, but that may not be realistically feasible.

As I bid a non-reluctant farewell to this final discussion of categories and concepts, I wish gently to heap mild scorn upon professionals and laymen alike because of the language and theories many but not all of them use. First there is the effort to achieve immortality or notoriety through jargon. It does sound more profound, does it not, to say "superego," "reinforcement," or "dissonance" rather than "conscience," "reward," or "conflict." Then iconoclastic inversions are especially popular: startle your listeners by saying exactly the opposite of what they believe. If men are thought to be rational, then maintain that they are driven by irrational sex. If behavior is explained by a reference to environment, it is exciting and original to stress heredity. If infants are considered protoplasmic and irrational, it is sensational to say they are rational and conduct themselves according to definite strategies. If it is believed that images precede thought, it is newsworthy to uncover evidence proving exactly the reverse. And so maybe you and I as well as the professionals are, after all, no different from philosophers: we can only express old thoughts in new terminology better adapted to our age. *And you said you were going to be scornful.*

7.b Evaluation

I have established to your satisfaction, I hope, that characterization is usually the first step toward evaluation and indeed may be an implicit evaluation or the basis for an evaluation. Call Alter successful in conventional terms and you have both characterized and evaluated him: the notion of success is culture-bound and can be appraised objectively, but the evaluation placed upon achievement may be positive among middle-class Americans and negative among Ojibwa Indians, whose suspicions are aroused by success, which they attribute to the unfair, secret use of a powerful medicine (Jenness, 1935, p. 84). Or if you call Alter dishonest and are yourself not a thief, you have both characterized and stigmatized him. Yet suppose you are told that Alter has an IQ of 105, just slightly above average? By itself this is sheer description; but it could carry a favorable connotation if you had been imagining he ought to be committed to an institution for the feeble-minded, an unfavorable one if you had suspected previously he was a genius capable of great mathematical feats.

In judging others, however, Ego can clearly draw a distinction between the two kinds of judgment; thus members of different ethnic groups *may* describe various out-groups and themselves very similarly but disagree in their evaluations (Chinese & Filipino students, Philippines; Peabody, 1968). When American college students in paper-and-pencil situations are told that a hypothetical Alter has a given trait and are then asked to state whether he also possesses another trait, they *may* be more likely to attribute to him a trait considered descriptively but not evaluatively similar; for example, if Alter is called "modest," they consider him "self-disparaging" but not "confident" (Peabody, 1967).

Evaluation, of course, is one of the most ancient and honorable of the problems that perplex philosophers—"it is the good and the useful that are lovable as ends," Aristotle stated—and, as previously indicated, it is one of the three factors emerging in modern times from the elaborate factor analyses of ratings that have been given to words by thousands of persons in various societies (Osgood, 1969). *Cannot one be "objective" as you would say: is evaluation inevitable?* The tendency to evaluate must be strong; to achieve "the pure void" sought by Zen in which consciousness becomes like a "thoroughly egoless and mindless" mirror (Merton, 1968, p. 6), considerable training and will power are necessary. On both a primary and secondary level, moreover, Ego evaluates Alter in order to know either literally or figuratively whether contact with him has been and hence will be rewarding, punishing, or merely neutral. Characterizations and evaluations spiral: bad persons commit bad deeds and consequently Ego is on the lookout for badness and bad persons. Let us, however, hurriedly, though deliberately, turn the other cheek and state that evaluating Alter may also be an altruistic act performed by Ego not to cope with him more efficiently but to help him. This, of course, is the role of the professional psychiatrist and clinical psychologist, and it is also one that can be undertaken whenever Ego has affection for Alter. Psychiatric characterization need not be employed; thus bits of Alter's behavior may be interpreted for his benefit as being, in Freudian terminology, "secondary gains" enabling him to retain symptoms that are otherwise unpleasant—and in this manner Ego may provide Alter with insight that he has not previously possessed. Were I to dare say to you that you really do not wish to break away from onerous responsibilities not because you would suffer from a feeling of guilt but because you would deprive yourself of a rationale for doing many of the things you like to do, you might deny that this is so and in this manner perhaps confirm my evaluation. But of course I am not sure—and you must believe me when I repeat that I am thinking of your welfare and not of my own. Merely being superficially familiar with a stranger, whether he is evaluated favorably or unfavorably, *may* induce Ego to be more helpful to him than when such familiarity is lacking (Usual; Macaulay, 1975).

Perhaps the most devastating evaluation of all is to consider Alter a non-person. Passengers travelling on a public mode of transportation, especially if the vehicle is crowded, must carefully observe the individuals next to them in order to ignore them: they may not stand too close, they may not stare too brazenly, etc. The one theme that returns again and again in a volume containing a loose series of essays attempting to explain the "sanctions for evil" in the modern world is that atrocities can flourish and cruelty can usually be perpetrated only against non-persons (Duster, 1971, p. 27; Bernard et al., 1971, pp. 105–06); the target person, consequently, is viewed as a category, not a human being, and contact between him and the aggressor is avoided, lest his human qualities be perceived and appreciated.

The values Ego selects, like his categories, come primarily from his society and hence are more or less automatically absorbed (Pathway I.a). What is proper for a respectable human being, according to the Yaghan Indians who live near Cape Horn, is to do what old persons recommend; and "a bad human being behaves badly simply because he is bad; a good human being behaves well because it is his nature to be good" (Gusinde, 1937, p. 1099). *What you have just said is yet another repetition of your deterministic, relativistic philosophy, but I do not think that man has no freedom or just partial freedom of choice.* Characterizing a person as pugnacious is evaluated quite differently, depending on whether the trait or type of behavior is valued by the society or Ego's group (Pathway 4.a). Why is Ego conventional, why does he utilize the evaluation of his fellows? First of all, he has no other values to invoke most of the time; where else do values originate except within society? *I object . . .* But permit me to provide other reasons. Secondly, Ego usually has little incentive to devise a value system of his own: he must adjust to other persons more or less like himself, and hence of necessity he uses the values he knows, or thinks he knows, that they also employ. Finally, the very existence of a value system presupposes some conformity within the society; as a result, the categories Ego borrows from his group or society are likely to provide the best fit between what in fact he perceives and what evaluation he would impose.

Now to your objection. *As my thoughts swirl through the history of philosophy. . . .* And I assume your reference is primarily to Western philosophy, although occasionally you also include some great thinkers of the Middle and Far East. *I would establish two points. First, new values actually do arise, it is part of the profession of philosophers and*

*theologians to invent or discover and to explain and defend them.
What, for example, happens to our system of evaluation when it is
said that "there is no true love save in suffering" inasmuch as "the
moment love becomes happy and satisfied, it no longer desires and it
is no longer love" (Unamuno, 1954, p. 205)? Then we ourselves are
heirs to all, or almost all that has gone before us, so that we have available values from both great and puny thinkers; our choice is almost
limitless and therefore, I conclude, we are not confined only to the
values surrounding us.* I think that much depends upon the "we" of
whom you speak. The vast majority of persons are not creative like
the philosophers or theologians to whom you quietly allude: they have
neither the time nor the desire to create new values, they are content
to absorb modes of judging Alters from their surroundings. A good
library may contain books spilling over with the wisdom of the ages,
but the fact of the matter seems to be that most values from the past
are rejected or ignored. We do not find many Americans applying
Christ's or Kant's standards when they pass judgments upon their
fellow men. On the whole, however, I agree that modes of evaluation
are not a complete reflection of the milieu.

*Whence, then, cometh the evaluations? I have noted the fact that,
each time you stress some form of social determinism, you are able and
willing to be pushed away from a rigid position (Pathway II.2).* Yes,
every individual is somewhat unique, I repeat, and that uniqueness
springs from an interaction between his genetic proclivities and the opportunities afforded and utilized in his particular milieu. Ego, consequently, has a complex series of beliefs concerning the good and the
bad, many of which also interact. It is, therefore, not an intellectual
or emotional hardship for me to proclaim that Ego has a number of
values and hence advisable pathways, not strictly determined by convention, from which to choose. *You say, "from which to choose": does
that suggest the determinism you have been advocating, does that not
sound more like voluntarism or free will?* Almost as ever, I have a
two-fold reply. First, there need not be a difference between phenomenological and deterministic data. You or anyone else may have the conviction, the very precious conviction, that you have in front of you a
wide number of alternatives from which to choose. At the same time,
any investigator, an omniscient deity, or even I myself may feel or even
prove that your choice is predetermined or at least confined within
limits we are able to specify. I am not saying that the feeling of freedom is an illusion because the outcome is more or less predetermined.

I recognize utterly the validity, the force, the necessity of the feeling, and I consider it one of the essential attributes of successful living, at least in our society. *Ah, a qualification.* Yes, but maybe also elsewhere. Similarly, the self-fulfilling prophecy is not always a danger but can be an asset when it produces the desired result. Also, how could most of mankind tolerate their own existence if they did not believe in some form of immortality? I am not being sly when I say that the conviction of choice is one of the factors to be included in the equation enabling me to understand or predict the outcome of your very private, personal deliberations.

After this relatively tangential flurry, we face again the problem of determining the additional naturalistic pathways Ego uses in evaluating Alter. He may be affected by Alter (Pathway 1.a), and the effect includes rewards and punishments with which approval or disapproval is likely to be associated. We cannot, we do not like those who insult, injure, or frustrate either ourselves or the persons or institutions to which we are attached. Immediately, however, we know that other factors are involved. To a certain extent, for example, our tradition suggests that the punishment should fit the crime, and hence our dislike of, and counteraggression against the person who has hurt us should be proportionate to the damage. Standards of equity and inequity, consequently, *may* determine the kind of reciprocity we exhibit in relation to Alter and by implication our opinion of him (U.S., various; Adams, 1965); thus, not absolute deprivation but deprivation relative to others, usually within the same reference group, may turn out to be critical. *Should it?* Yes, let freedom ring—you and Ego must select your own advisable pathway (Pathway 8.c).

Another variable related to Ego's evaluation may be the explanation he gives of Alter's behavior, traits, or whatever category he applies to him (Pathway 5.c). We can see this clearly in the case of legal punishment: the same act committed deliberately ("premeditated," in legal language) receives a harsher evaluation and punishment than one committed without deliberation. Similarly, Ego's estimate of Alter's ability may be highly relevant, although often he feels himself in a quandry when he evaluates Alter in this respect. He may admire a well-developed ability but also feel more kindly toward a clumsy Alter who nevertheless achieves a goal. He may take pity on an Alter who cannot adequately cope with a problem. He may ascribe a motive to Alter if he has the necessary skill to achieve an objective; "it was quite possible to believe that Oswald intended to kill President Kennedy and not Mrs. Kennedy or a secret service man, because he was known to be an expert marksman" (Jones & Davis, 1965, p. 221). He may be eager to reward or praise an Alter, especially one of low ability, who runs risks to achieve an objective whether it is rewarding to himself or not.

The easiest, the slickest, perhaps also the most frequently employed evaluation is simply the reaffirmation of a previous judgment. For various reasons Ego has come to expect Alter to behave in a particular way; and most of his future actions, regardless of how they are described, are ultimately judged in that frame of reference. *That man has lied to me, and I shall never, never trust him, no matter what he says or does.* Or the evaluation may stem from a trusted informant when Alter is unknown to Ego (Pathway 2.1). I have never met a Bushman, but what I have read would affect my characterization and evaluation if I were ever to come in contact with someone from that society. I rather suspect that often, as a result of a previous evaluation of Alter, a secondary judgment motive is less likely to be aroused unless Ego takes really seriously the implications of reflection (Pathway 6).

Reaffirmation of previous evaluations obviously stems from a conservative tendency within all of us. For in normal living, as already indicated in connection with Ego's attitudes (Pathway 4), we need a great deal of stability if we are to go about our affairs or indeed if we are to be happy. Imagine the chaos that would result if everyone we trusted had to be continually evaluated and reevaluated because we imagined they might prove to be untrustworthy. And yet the possibility of change exists, and cannot or should not be ignored (Pathway 6.c).

Ego has a number of impulses he must curb if his pathway to Alter is to produce a valid judgment. Even though the relation between similarity and attractiveness is not at all straightforward (Postscript 5.4), he may be attracted to Alters he finds similar to himself, or he may find them similar because he is attracted to them. He must be wary of his own imagination. He wants his love to be virtually perfect and hence she is perfect, or at least appears so until the first blush has faded. Above all, Ego must be fully aware of the context in which his evaluation is made (Pathway 1.c). You are grateful to him and hence you like him. *Is this really so?* As ever, it depends—and it depends on many factors (U.S., various; Pepitone, 1958). Did he really intend to be helpful; do you value unintentional assistance as much as intentional? Do you consider him the responsible person in the situation, or could it have been someone else who suggested that he intervene? Did the proferred assistance actually turn out to be helpful? You certainly will not have a high opinion of a busybody whose good intentions prevent you from performing well. On top of this is the importance of the task: will you feel as grateful to someone who helps you solve a trivial problem as you would toward someone who intervenes when you consider the task to be of cosmic significance? Thus we have help vs. no help, intention vs. no intention, success vs. failure —the combination of these three factors yields eight real, not theoretical, possibilities, and of course I have only begun to list the combinations. *What about the question of whether you sought assistance at the outset or the obligation you incur or think you incur as a result of Alter's intervention?* Multivariance of course (Pathway II.1), the same phenomenon we encounter again and again as we move around the circle of our chart; it's enough to make us dizzy. Similarly a question may be raised concerning the presumption that you are less grateful to Alter when he helps you by making a small personal sacrifice than when his sacrifice is large. Obviously the effect upon you is the same in either case. Maybe the person making the greater sacrifice is less capable than the one making the lesser one, maybe his motivation to help you is greater.

As I laboriously emphasize multivariance in connection with gratitude, I must wonder whether or not I am being egocentric (Pathway I.4). This dog besides me, whether I share a meager ration with him or simply offer him a microscopic chunk of a huge surplus in my possession, feels equally friendly because I give him food. Presumably he never knows or inquires whether I am making a personal sacrifice as I feed him and so is incapable of experiencing gratitude. *Are there really persons like this who do not inquire into the source of the manna they consume?*

The discussion of evaluation can reach a mild climax by considering the most important and most general evaluation of all: after characterizing Alter, can we call him adjusted, healthy, happy, sane? Here we reach a never-never land between metaphysics or ethics and the disciplines of the professionals, an area which would be even more elusive if we were to carry on by referring to Group Alters. *All right, let us remain on the level of the individual.* The difficulty is that most criteria for distinguishing the healthy from the unhealthy sound so reasonable when they are made explicit. One writer, for example, has proposed that a healthy personality satisfies the five criteria of "ab-

sence of mental disease, normality of behavior, adjustment to environment, unity of personality, and correct perception of reality" (Jahoda,
1950). Another has carefully suggested that the components of such a
person must be the possession of basic trust rather than mistrust, of
autonomy rather than shame and doubt, of initiative rather than
guilt, of a sense of industriousness rather than a feeling of inadequacy
and inferiority, of a compact rather than a diffuse identity. More
specifically, for the adult he proposes intimacy with the other sex and
the avoidance of forces dangerous to the ego rather than self-absorption; providing guidance to the next generation rather than stagnating;
enjoying integrity rather than despair and disgust (Erikson, 1959).
This psychoanalyst also reports that Freud himself gave a very simple
reply when asked to name the attributes of the non-neurotic individual: *lieben und arbeiten,* love and work, he is supposed to have said—
and the Sage really meant a combination of the two, for without one
the other can become meaningless or impossible. I once had the reckless courage to conclude a book by asserting—without wishing to enthrone myself among the immortals—that the goal of planning should
be the development of a "rich personality in a society with diverse
opportunities" (Doob, 1968b, p. 384). I am able, however, to argue the
reverse and maintain that each of the attributes postulated to be part
of the healthy personality can under some circumstances have negative
value. I suppose I would thus only be advancing the ancient, though
probably valid, argument that the creative person, whether he be scientist, citizen, or poet, needs more than a touch of the neurotic to
motivate him to be creative; but then in some ways the creative person
feels healthy during his creative activity or in the retrospective long
run. You and I are not going to be able to settle this problem either
here or throughout our lifetimes. I would claim only that for ordinary
purposes we seldom wish to be associated with persons who are too
unhealthy or too neurotic and that for most tasks to be performed well
we need emotionally stable individuals. It becomes necessary, therefore, to find pathways to identify such persons; we desperately need
but shall never quite agree upon the guides to aid our judgment. *But
the struggle dare not cease.*

7.c Understanding

Sometimes it is sufficient merely to characterize and evaluate Alter
in terms of one or more attributes. When this is done, however, he is

likely to turn out to be a character in fiction, a stranger whom Ego sees once and will never see again, a corpse, or a Group Alter of no significance. More usually, Ego seeks to understand Alter. *And what do you understand by "understand"?* I shall stress the attributes of background and intention (Pathway II): why is Alter the way he is, what will he do in the future? As you anticipate, I believe that any kind of understanding is incomplete: we never know all there is to know about another person, we understand him only when we explore or judge some of the relationships among his numerous attributes.

An almost staggering difficulty confronts Ego when he would account for Alter's behavior: any action, attitude, or feeling can be an expression of so many different motives whose origins are to be found in the past (Pathway 5.c). Only rarely is behavior like the knee jerk attributable with a high degree of certainty to a single cause. Even simple actions, such as yawning or coughing, may spring from different sources. And traits are much more complicated, obviously. Tall, jagged mountains terrify you. You have named the feeling, but why do you have it? Does it reflect experiences on tall mountains during your youth, dissatisfaction with the milieu in which you now live, an aesthetic association with a play you once read, perhaps even an unwitting way of drawing attention to your sensitivity? *I don't really know.* The answer could well be affirmative in all instances, not only because modes of characterizing fear are unstandardized but also because in fact your fear may be an expression of all those feelings or beliefs within you. Similarly I can describe your actions unequivocally, but may be uncertain concerning the motive to which I should ascribe them. I observe you swimming. From the observation I infer that you want to swim, that you are enjoying yourself. Right? *Of course, what other explanation could there be?* Well, you might be trying to strengthen your leg muscles, to attract attention. . . . *Yes, yes, what a silly illustration.*

The motives Ego ascribes to Alter, you may or may not remember, I mentioned in passing while discussing primary judgments (Pathway 5.b) and suggested that Ego's decision requires reflection and hence is part of his secondary judgment. In our society we are convinced that behavior results from so many different causes that we have developed special explanatory disciplines ranging from the social sciences to psychiatry—and I suppose the humanities would wish to be included too. I cannot pause now to review the details, but I mention some of the issues in a postscript (Postscript 7.6: The Ascription of Motives). If you prefer not to read that Postscript, let me mention its highlights concisely. *Really concisely?* First, the cultural point: each society has its own explanatory scheme. Second, the methodological: even though they are addicated to neologisms and anarchy, the professionals use far fewer categories to refer to motives than we when describing human actions or bits of behavior. Thirdly, the big split, the substantive and ancient split about motives is between genetic and environmental explanations. There, haven't I been concise? *Yes, this time.* Let me add two points not in the Postscript which I think useful to note. The inclination to explain human behavior develops gradually as children mature and *may* do so at a rate different from the inclination to explain the actions of physical objects (U.S., kindergarten; Berzonsky, 1973). Then the evaluation of Alter may affect the motives attributed to him (Heider, 1958b, pp. 170–73). You and I consider that semi-learned Alter a bore and therefore find unflattering explanations of why he seeks to dominate social situations with his vacuous speech. You claim he is simply insensitive and has been improperly educated; I believe he is covering his own insecurity with verbiage. I do not know which of us is right, but in the role of Ego-expositor we are thus revealing something about ourselves to another Ego, the reader of these lines.

Can Alter supply valid information about his own motives even when he has no reason to deceive Ego? A philosopher has maintained, a little too glibly, that "man, in effect, is unwilling to remain in ignorance of his motives of his own conduct" (Unamuno, 1954, p. 129). I have my doubts concerning the universality of the proposition when I think of man's frequent efforts to deceive himself in order to avoid facing his own selfish or ignoble impulses (Pathway 1.1). Does Alter engage in vigorous activity to compensate for a recent failure or to leave undisturbed a view of himself that he always comes out on top or close to the top? He may not be able to provide the answer. Perhaps when behavior is segmental rather than central (Pathway I.6)—the color of his shoes, the time he goes to bed at night—Alter can be a reliable informant concerning his own motives, but otherwise I think he faces the same difficulties as Ego. Can you really say why you like to go swimming? *Again swimming, why not ask me about cooking or mountain climbing?*

An Ego wishing to understand Alter may also wish to decide whether a bit of his behavior has been affected by his conscience. For conscience, no matter what it is called—superego, sense of responsibility, character, duty, obligation, categorical imperative—provides the clue to understanding and evaluating many of Alter's actions in the present and in the future. You have one of the strongest consciences on this planet; you would rather be burned at the stake, I think, than commit a deed you consider morally wrong. How do I know that this is so? There is the rub: on occasion you have patiently explained your code to me; I have observed that you almost never yield to temptation and that, when you do, you suffer from guilt; alone, you behave as if the whole world were watching you. I have, you see, very definite criteria on the basis of which I call your conscience strong. *I do not agree with you completely: I feel that fairly often I do not obey my conscience and yet I suffer few if any pangs.* The prophets from Vienna, now residing in New York, would tell you that you are not aware of the impulses your superego represses and hence you may not be giving full credit to it—personification aside, that is a point worth considering. *What, then, do we mean by conscience?* Here is a quick operational definition: a series of beliefs or impulses which, whenever they are salient within an individual, prevent him from giving vent to actions considered taboo either by himself or by influential persons in his milieu. Three items of information are thus required before invoking the concept of conscience: a knowledge of the taboos, of the impulses within Alter that would transgress those taboos, and of the fact that he has not actually transgressed them for reasons to be found within himself. Conceivably you would make yourself follow that code of yours even if you were alone on the moon. Any human being who has risen above the vegetative level of the infant or the moron, whether awake or asleep, is obeying the dictates of conscience at least part of the time; hence Ego's evaluation of Alter is necessarily incomplete unless somehow he has insight into that tremendous force. Attributing Alter's behavior to conscience, finally, is one way of assigning responsibility, a fascinating topic in its own right, though one that takes us slightly off the main path (Postscript 7.7: The Assigning of Responsibility).

Why does Ego try to explain Alter's behavior? I am surprised that you ask this question, unless you wish to see whether you and I give similar explanations. His assessment, I think, serves two functions. It provides another basis for evaluating Alter. Certainly the same person or the same behavior elicits different value judgments when altruism rather than selfishness is invoked as the explanation. One professional has suggested that Ego is more likely to be attracted to Alters whose actions he believes spring from the same causes as his own, a proposition that may indicate why individuals living in the same society and by and large sharing the same explanatory concepts are able to live together peacefully and sometimes even happily (Triandis, 1975). *I wonder.* And so do I, for surely an Ego who is honest enough to frown upon his own reason for some of his actions may feel sympathetic toward an Alter to whom he attributes the same cause-and-effect sequence without necessarily respecting or liking him. Then, secondly, postulating a cause in the past or present may be a way of implying a prediction about Alter's words and deeds in the future.

And so we can turn, not too abruptly this time, from Alter's past to his future, the problem of anticipating or predicting his behavior. Under what conditions does Ego anticipate or predict? To reply, we must first try to discover why a judgment motive has been aroused (Pathway II.a). If Ego is asked by a professional to judge Alter's expression in a photograph, his motive involves only a desire to please the investigator or to avoid making a fool of himself; undoubtedly he will not try to anticipate how the person in the photograph would behave in some situation or other; why should he? But if Ego wonders whether his son is ambitious or lazy, his very judgment, motivated by a concern for the boy's welfare, contains a component of expectancy. In fact, any characterization of Alter *may* imply a prediction about him (Usual; Griffitt, 1969a): saying the boy is ambitious suggests that he will never be a pauper. The advisable pathway is to be aware of the reason for the prediction and then to suspect that it contains a bit of wishful thinking or some other unrealistic tendency.

In fact, prediction is usually the goal to which the pathway of understanding is likely to lead. When Ego challenges himself to decide whether he is certain or uncertain about his opinion of Alter, he is in effect asking whether he will hold the same opinion in the future or whether Alter is likely to change in that respect (Tiberghien, 1971). Educators seek to discover talent in children at an early age in order to encourage those allegedly possessing it, or at least not to discourage them. The discovery is motivated by the assumption that future creativity can be predicted on the basis of behavior in the present. The adolescent trying to plan his life imagines the occupation or profession that will bring him satisfaction or whaever other rewards his self-image craves. The man and woman contemplating marriage wonder whether their companionship can survive the mundane existence likely to be theirs after the waning of initial passion. You judge the expression on his face because you would infer what his inner feelings are, and you are interested in those feelings because they provide, you believe, a basis for knowing what he is actually going to do.

Prediction in a strict sense refers to a formal system of implication based upon a principle or proposition that has been induced or adduced concerning Alter or a group of Alters, usually by a professional (Warr & Knapper, 1968, pp. 140–46). It may also be used to include, at the other end of a continuum, any feeling about future behavior. Ego believes that Alter is going to behave in a particular way: he expects him to speak a specified language, to gesture distinctively, to be pleasant, to be capable of achieving some goals and not others. In a sense any organism follows a principle even after being subjected to the crudest kind of conditioning (a reinforced primary judgment): a dog that is friendly toward some Alters and unfriendly toward others in a metaphorical sense knows what to expect.

The most informal prediction, moreover, is related to formal methods of passing judgment. Ego uses induction either to establish what Alter has done in the past or present or to postulate a central or segmental trait. The tendency is extrapolated into the future, and on an actuarial basis Ego predicts that Alter will continue to behave more or less in the same manner or to exhibit a more or less similar trait. Or having postulated the trait, Ego deduces that as a consequence Alter will behave in accordance with attributes of the class or category: Alter is an honorable man and therefore we can trust him not to break his promise, not to drink the ungarded bottle of gin, not to rape a 14-year-old girl, not to fail to acknowledge in a footnote his indebtedness to the authors whose ideas he has shamelessly borrowed, and so on through a long list of specific tidbits which in our society, I am told, are not the attributes of a gentleman. Conceivably, Egos differ with respect to their unstated or deliberate preference for induction or deduction. I have visited Delphi and there the oracle told me that scientists lean toward induction, humanists toward deduction. *On the way there, if you came from Athens, you must have passed through Lebadea: which well did you drink from, the one producing total remembrance of the past or the one leading to total forgetfulness?* I see you escape from logic by going off on a tangent, but I drive you back to it. *Why?*

There is no reason why a good Hegelian or Marxist should not employ dialectic logic in his effort to predict what Alter will do. If I know that you have been reared as a good Christian (thesis) and that in your community you were also confronted with pagan ideas running somewhat contrary to Christian beliefs (antithesis), I must predict that you have incorporated a bit of the pagan into your Christianity and have emerged with a somewhat original set of beliefs or practices (synthesis). The Ego-Alter relation (Pathway I.c) can also be thrown into this form. Beneath the pleasant face of that woman, you infer, lurks evil intentions; somehow you reveal your suspicion; and that revelation, or at least her belief in your revealed suspicion, makes her behave in a manner further strengthening your suspicion. Another spiral of course (Pathway 4.b), a self-fulfilling hypothesis. I have selected an unpleasant illustration, but the same logic can be used in analyzing mutual or interpersonal trust.

Care must be exercised in making deductions concerning behavior from what appears to be the outcome of "the essential features of the evidence at hand," for the evidence may not of course be reliable and may not really indicate the statistical probability of what should be expected—and Egos *may* indeed thus mislead themselves (Usual; Kahneman & Tversky, 1973). Prediction derived from a knowledge of social factors also has its hazards. If competence is defined in socially acceptable terms—intelligence, education, occupation, employment history, and marital status—then perhaps you might expect the more competent to feel more secure and even more content than the less competent. Actually, the reverse may be true: highly competent psychiatric and normal patients *may* be convinced that there is a greater disparity between their own self-image and either their ideal image or their beliefs concerning what other people think of them than do less competent patients (U.S., adult; Achenbach & Zigler, 1963). Or you might make the reasonable prediction that the attitudes of stutterers toward their parents ought to be different from those of non-stutterers on the assumption that parents play a role, a disruptive role, in the genesis of the difficulty, but this *may* not be so, at least when attitudes are measured on a paper-and-pencil basis (U.S., children; Bourdon & Silber, 1970).

Are you not merely saying again that we should not predict some dispositions on the basis of others? I am, and I am not. Once more the challenge: would you anticipate more or less dishonesty, of a petty or a serious sort, among those whose self-esteem is high rather than low (Usual; Graf, 1971)? We cannot always judge each person in his own right, we have to be actuarial and guide ourselves by probabilities and not by certainties; yet we must simultaneously anticipate nuances in a particular Alter. Yes, with such an approach our prediction may turn out to be wrong in the individual case either because the combination of traits within Alter produces a person transcending the norms or because factors in the external milieu play a decisive role. There is confusion on this point, even among the professionals who analyze personality. "Suppose," my own respected, humanistic mentor used to say in various forms, "that 70 percent of the boys" with a particular demographic background—poor family, criminal father, rejecting mother, marginal neighborhood—become criminals; then suppose that John comes from exactly such a background. "Does this mean that John himself has a 70 percent chance of delinquency?" And the reply: "Not at all," because of his uniqueness (Allport, 1962). Of course the actuarial figure of 70 percent applies to groups of boys and not to the Alter named John; but surely, if we are to make a prediction about unhappy John and all we know about him are the above mentioned demographic facts, we would have to say that the odds favor his becoming delinquent. We would not specify the exact probability, we could not make a prediction "for sure" without additional data (Meehl, 1954, p. 20), but that does not mean we should be ungrateful for preliminary insight of an actuarial nature. Yes, every object, every person, is unique, though each may share one or more attributes with others which on occasion may be stressed or indicated with a quantitative designation: "those who object to assigning the same score to two introverts because their introversion is distinguishable should in all consistency object to saying that two men have the same income since one of them works and the other steals" (Thurstone cited by Meehl, 1954, p. 130). The advisable pathway is thus brightly lit: we should salvage what we can from statements of probability and apply that wisdom carefully to the individual case.

A knowledge of Alter's logic is itself a way of predicting his behavior if Ego can assume that certain modes of thinking, believing, and acting follow from one kind of logic and not from another. Your tendency to overgeneralize is a case in point: it may be confidently predicted that you will induce a premise from very few observations or experiences. The categories Ego employs are likely to be affected by whether he is addicted to personifications, metaphors, similes, allegories, or parables rather than matter-of-fact descriptions or narrations. Perhaps it can be forecast that a follower of the Hegelian or Marxian dialectic will be better able to tolerate contradictions, because he believes they are inevitable and will eventually contribute to a new synthesis.

One form of simple logic has a very high probability of providing a clue to Alter's judgment: he may behave similarly toward two persons he considers similar in some respect (England, presumably students; Bender, 1968) and hence his behavior regarding one of them, if known, provides a valuable clue to his behavior toward the other. This is really another instance of simplification (Pathway II.1) based on past experience (Pathway 6.a) and it ignores the second Alter's individuality.

In this discussion of prediction, I have been gradually abandoning a reluctance to recommend historical pathways to Alter. I still maintain that one can never have a complete history and hence an arbitrary limitation must be invoked; the past is irrelevant if one has a measure of the present (Pathway I.3). From a practical standpoint, however, some propositions more often than not turn out to be useful only when historical data are available. Some clinicians, particularly behavior therapists and many amateurs, self-consciously assert that Ego or Alter should be known by fruits rather than by roots—and often they are right (Postscript I.3)—but the fact remains that one of the useful ways, sometimes the only way, to learn about fruits is to trace them to roots. It is too facile to assert, for example, that a well-established trait, or belief, is likely to be strong and hence, it may be predicted, to endure or to determine Alter's future behavior. For many reasons, a measure of that strength may be impossible to obtain. If Ego knows its history, he may be able to weight it heavily in formulating a prediction. We hear the shrill cry of a very young child; how else are we to know whether it is unusually intense or to assert that in the future he may be expected to express his anguish or pain in such a manner under some conditions and not under others unless we are acquainted with his relevant past history? In this instance only the mother or guardian can provide the reply which must be of a historical nature. Here is another reason for Ego to obtain an adequate sample of Alter's behavior (Pathway 1.2) not from a cross section at a given moment but from a sequence over time; and here also is a partial explanation for the possibility that Ego *may* be able to predict the behavior of his friend in some situations and not in others, or his responses to some questions and not to others (Usual; Bender & Hastorf, 1950).

On a historical level, however, we face the problem of probability and hence uncertainty. The professionals, for example, have tons of evidence indicating the importance of socialization: the parent's treatment of Alter has some sort of lasting effect upon him. The difficulty is that both the treatment and the effect cannot be specified with any degree of exactness: out of an apparently unhappy home can come happy children and vice versa, although we may believe that neither of these is likely. All the cross-cultural studies of socialization practices and adult personality or social institutions, all the comparisons of the early upbringing of delinquents or creative persons and non-delinquents or non-creative individuals, all the case histories, biographies, and auto-biographies always yield a significant tendency *and* an area of doubt.

A related form of historical prediction involves the reverse of inferences concerning present tendencies from historical data: Ego perceives one or more traits or bits of behavior and then infers that they have come into existence as a result of experiences in Alter's past. Some of these deductions are likely to be valid, but they usually turn out, I think, to be more sociological or anthropological than psychological or psychiatric. If Alter speaks English with a slight accent, I must assume that English was not the first language he encountered as a very young child. On the other hand, if he were a communist and if I were to try to account for that fact I could say very little about his previous experience: I simply have no relevant theory at my disposal (Postscript 7.8: Backward Predictions).

Another basis for prediction rests on the assumption that Alter, like any other human being, will be consistent, but only up to some point, for he will also change (Pathway 6.c). Predictably he plays different roles throughout his existence. If he is now a young boy, not even the most devout devil's advocate would deny that he has never been an adolescent, has never been a husband, has never been an old man; hence his past behavior as such is not a guide to what he will do in the future, even though some consistency may remain. But from the role requirements of these stages various crude forecasts about Alter can be made (Pathway 1.3). It seems likely, moreover, that Ego's own judgments become less consistent as he progresses from early childhood to adulthood. For at the beginning he can afford, as it were, to make oversimplified black-or-white judgments about people: do they or do they not feed him, are they or are they not friendly toward him, do they or do they not help him solve problems? Later, finer discrimination may be necessary, for he may learn that for most purposes it is better not merely to try to apprehend the extremes of a continuum but also to place individuals somewhere in between. When mature, Ego will undoubtedly be less likely to utilize new categories or even to change his judgments.

The roles of Alter also depend upon changes in his milieu, a knowledge of which may be an essential component in predicting his behavior. Some of those changes may depend upon the business cycle; will his job in the future be the same as the one he has now or different, or will he be unemployed? *Surely as Ego passes secondary judgment, you cannot expect him to use the principles or insights of economists or businessmen to forecast that cycle.* But that is really what he must do if he is to make a precise prediction. The influences of the milieu, however, cannot be calculated with dispatch (Pathway 4.a). An adolescent's peers can change the direction in which the parents have bent the twig. The young man destined to be a lawyer because his interests roughly correspond to those of successful lawyers may become a chemist after being inspired by his college instructor in a course taken unwillingly to discharge a science requirement. Alter cannot jump out of his skin, and hence will demonstrate some consistency throughout his life, but the specific prediction may turn out to be invalidated by a war, a depression, a religious conversion, or a stroke of good or bad luck. An Ego who recognizes the inevitable pathway of ignorance (Pathway I.3) may be just a little less disappointed and frustrated when his prediction turns out to be faulty.

For me—and I think for you too—the most intricate, the most intriguing challenge comes from Ego's judgment concerning his own future. Some, many, most, even all of his judgments in this respect are of a primary kind: he experiences himself quite directly and knows, or thinks he knows, whether he is hungry, honest, or heaven-bound. *Why the variation from some to all?* There must be a continuum ranging from the very young and innocent child who reacts with little or no reflection to the neurotic who evaluates every one of his own actions. Since the advent of thought, or at least of transmitted thought, as I have been reminding us explicitly throughout our discussions (Pathway I.1), men have probably advised one another to know themselves; and almost without exception, I think, they are in agreement, first, that self-knowledge is essential or desirable for some ethical or psychological reason and, second, that it is very difficult to attain. The difficulty arises from the fact that the immediate impression of oneself, the first impression, the primary judgment, is likely to be superficial in a given situation; then, when a secondary judgment is attempted, there are too many and too few data available to make an adequate or satisfying revision. There are too many data for the very reason that Ego is or can be an almost constant observer of himself as well as an erratic observer of that constant observer: he knows more or less what he does or thinks, he remembers a great deal from the past, he is forever contemplating either the profound or the trival in the future. It is not easy, unless we equip ourselves with the dogma of a philosopher, to decide what is significant or insignificant, what is related or unrelated, to the real self. There are also too few data because Ego is often a puzzle to himself: he has sudden moods, he loses his temper, he dreams, he does something against his better judgment, he is deeply moved when he knows that what is moving him ought to be considered trivial. Indeed, the most severe and puzzling judgment of all that Ego can pass against himself is, you will agree, to be intrigued by the ever approaching ledge and to commit suicide; and here, my foes and friends, is a topic we do not have the courage to pursue. *Are you by any chance morbid?*

We move away from that ledge and agree that often we feel unable to predict what we will do in a situation with whose details we may or may not be acquainted. You are convinced that you will not like this person to whom I shall introduce you, but you are uncertain which facade you will erect around yourself both to conceal and subtly to express some of your feelings. And yet your uncertainty always functions within limits: you know you will shoot him, you anticipate you will not be cordial, you are confident you will not lose your temper when you meet him—only the details are lacking. Similarly, after the fact you may be surprised by what you do, or you do the opposite of what you have predicted, but again I think such invalid or incomplete predictions are the exceptions. It is also reasonable to guess that many of the exceptions arise because the circumstances are exceptional or have not arisen in the past. You might be surprised by what you would do if the roof of your house were suddenly to cave in, but not every bit of your behavior would be unanticipated: the bases of your reactions are within you and you do have a clue to some of them.

Left alone, Ego would have trouble enough with himself. In our society, perhaps in any society, he is frequently prodded or he prods himself to discover what someone else calls his own "true" self. The pathways open to him to achieve that knowledge may or may not be numerous, but they all lead to an undermining of his confidence in primary judgments. It is also assumed that a real self can be discovered if only the proper pathway is uncovered. In our time and especially in the West, we have witnessed alienation not only from the values of our society and its people but also from ourselves, or "self-distantiation" which is "the experience that I am a stranger to myself, or rather that I can be more or less close to myself" (Mannheim, 1956, p. 209).

And so there have arisen or increased in popularity doctrines or creeds which purport to help Ego come closer to his real self. Most professionals, for example, have imbibed at least a touch of psychoanalysis: through the guidance of the analyst who gently seeks to have the analysand become aware of his repressions and the functioning of his unconscious, Ego begins to understand the background of some of his difficulties or his apparent irrationalities, and this realization is supposed to facilitate relief, release, and the kind of organization required by self-knowledge.

Other therapists and laymen suggest that Ego can secure insight into himself by observing and analyzing what happens when he interacts with others. Indeed we do not have to become pathologically dissociated to watch ourselves: even our most unreflective friends sometimes admire or despise what they themselves are doing or have done. I sometimes think that self-understanding and self-prediction can be improved if Ego deliberately puts into words and sentences the bitter and the sweet fruits of his experience, for then they are likely to be stored efficiently or more efficiently, at least, than unexpressed feelings; the advantage here may outweigh the inevitable oversimplification inherent in verbalization.

Through self-reflection, the abnegation of material desires, and the acquiring of a belief in a force pervading mankind, it is said, Zen and its variants should enable a cooperative Ego to feel a sense of detachment within himself and thus to come closer to apprehending his true self as well as the cosmic force within that self. A quotation is essential to catch the flavor:

> Since Mind alone exists, and since all apparent differentiation between this and that, I and you, is contained within it, where else could the deities (Lha) reside? The mind of every being is as broad and deep as the cosmos itself. It is the entire cosmos, not a part but the whole—call it what you will. . . . [Zen] leads to a direct perception of Reality in *this* life, enabling us to transcend duality and go straight to the One Mind. This One Mind, otherwise known as our Original Nature, belongs to everybody and everything. But the method is very hard—hard even for those who practise it night and day for years on end. How many people are prepared or even able to do that? (Blofeld, 1959, pp. 47, 88).

Similarly, I think, the zealots and the priests of the major religious orders, when they devote themselves to theology and to leading the way of life their god or gods embody, try to probe their own depths to find wisdom and goodness there. This they are able to do, they report, by following the instructions and, above all, the example of a loving, respected teacher, who may or may not be an official in an institution and who may be alive or dead (but, if dead, represented by an apostle and by an oral or written creed), so that they come willingly and joyously to subscribe to a set of beliefs and then rigorously adhere to a prescribed regimen and to imposed rituals. Each pathway, in addition, offers evidence to induce and sustain the faith: cures, partial or total, in the case of psychoanalysis; extrasensory or esoteric incidents or other phenomena not presumably explicable through the so-called laws of chance or contemporary science in the case of Zen and similar systems; meditation or exercises that lead to temporary relaxation and detachment; or the historical miracles or prophecies wrought by the believer's god or gods and embodied in books or legends called holy or sacred. To the initiated and the believer, such evidence appears convincing or, at a minimum, compelling; to the outsider, it may seem to be a form of sincere, sophisticated superstition; unproven or unprovable hocus-pocus; or attractive, creative legend.

What these varied doctrines all seek to achieve, it seems to me, is a variant of the adjusted or happy individual we mentioned at the conclusion of Pathway 7.b: an Ego so well-integrated that internally a sense of harmony is experienced; all or almost all his own actions consciously stem from a social philosophy; the actions of others arouse imaginative understanding and never an unreflective hostility. Contradictory and diverse goals are eliminated as far as possible, the self is predictable. Presumably there are no or few surprises, there are no temper tantrums, there is little or no aggression against other human beings other than against evil itself, there is frequent contemplation of the self and its relation to the rest of mankind and to the universe. When or if such a condition is achieved, Ego then not only understands himself but also is receptive to currents—ideas and feelings—that are not experienced by those not similarly inclined and that are related, it is further averred, to metaphysical sources. The pathways from Ego to Alter, therefore, cannot be easily discovered and may not be lightly traversed; but, when discovered, they enable Ego to understand Alter and himself. Here, if ever, is the consistent person, freed, in large measure, from his past and from the currents prevailing in his milieu. *Come, come, you sound a little too lyrical; is such a pathway really discoverable and, if so, is it advisable?*

Postscripts

7.1 *Professional Approaches to the Humpty-Dumpty Problem*

The professionals first try to assemble all the pieces and view them squarely more or less simultaneously. They may construct what they call a clinical profile before hazarding a diagnosis or prognosis: the strengths and weakness of the patient or subject, in comparison with those of his peers or others used in whatever groups have provided the norms, are presented compactly on a single sheet of paper or on a graph, such as a histogram, so that they can be grasped conveniently. The conclusions drawn from such a formal or informal profile can of course be wrong, dreadfully wrong—the carefully assessed undercover agent collapses when the pressures become too great—but the complete record I believe would show that psychiatrists and other professionals are more often right than wrong. The lay Ego of course can only approximate this procedure: he does not, he cannot assemble the bits of information he has acquired concerning Alter, and lay them out on a tidy graph. He cannot accurately compare the weights he informally assigns Alter's attributes because he has no formal records at his disposal; but he has had experience with other human beings (Pathway 6.a) and in his mind (as again with the method of absolute judgment in psychophysics previously discussed at the outset of Pathway 5) he has standards which enable him, however impressionistically, to make some kind of comparison.

Some professionals show dissatisfaction with their instruments and even with their own psychograms by adding a personality sketch which is usually their qualitative impression of the individual derived from observing him and interviewing him about his past. They are not reluctant to admit that some of the subtler categorizations of persons escape their measurement net and can be grasped only qualitatively. We see this especially when an effort is made to characterize Alter by means of a significant but less conventional category. Is he creative or not? Creativity in our society, no doubt everywhere, is a highly valued characteristic, but there simply is no sure-fire way to measure it. Perhaps creative persons, in comparison with the general population, *may* be more self-appreciative, sensitive, broad-gauged, introverted, etc. (U.S., architects; McKinnon, 1962)—but sampling and measuring problems limit the value of any such fling at generalization. What all of us must do, for the moment, perhaps forever, is to draw upon a list of qualities we think a person must possess if he is creative in a particular field or generally creative, and then somehow determine whether the person of interest to us has not only the qualities but also a personality enabling him to integrate those qualities into a functioning whole. *Functioning whole?* No, not jargon, but an assumption, admittedly by me: the impulses of a truly creative person must be well-organized because otherwise he could not function effectively. *Again, you have stated a problem without resolving it, more intellectual anarchism.* Surely confusion results when two persons use the concept of creativity: I am simply pointing out the existing state of affairs.

To assess personality by means of the ink blots represented on the ten Rorschach plates, three steps are necessary. Alter looks at each blot, reports what he sees, and is asked to indicate the location on the blot of what he sees and perhaps his reason for seeing it there. This first step is quite objective. Then the professional studies the record and counts the number of times Alter has mentioned color and movement, has referred to the entire blot, has pointed to the white spaces, etc. At this point some disagreement arises, for the experts use different categories and ways of counting. The disagreements, however, are few in comparison with the differences in their secondary judgments concerning the significance of the scores thus obtained. Rorschach himself, for example, wrote that the color responses "represent the affectivity" of the individual—what we might now call his emotionality—and that the space responses "always signify a kind of spirit of opposition-negation (Rorschach, 1924). It is to be doubted, however, whether his interpretation is valid for all persons, especially for those living in non-Western societies (Doob, 1960a, pp. 60–66). Any Rorschach expert, including Rorschach himself, climaxes this procedure by giving his total impression of Alter derived not only from the scores but also from Alter's incidental behavior while responding and, in addition, from qualitative hunches that have not been objectively scored. *Is this a model for non-professionals to adopt?* Obviously not, in terms of the details, but it is clear-cut in one respect: a procedure is followed and we know exactly when objective scoring ends and when the pieces of Humpty-Dumpty are interpreted subjectively.

7.2 Miscellaneous Factors Affecting the Humpty-Dumpty Problem

Even judging facial expressions may raise the spectre of Humpty-Dumpty. The professionals have noted that the human face is capable of registering two or more emotions simultaneously (Ekman, et al.,

1972, pp. 25–26, 46), which means that an accurate judgment must take into account both or all of the emotions thus expressed, or somehow combine them. "People rarely see a face alone without any context" and therefore they are often compelled somehow to decide, when the facial expression suggests an emotion different from what they would expect the context to provoke, how to reconcile the two bits of information. A small amount of available research, based upon photographs and motion pictures, suggests that either face or context can be the more salient influence and that the outcome *may* depend upon the clarity of each as well as upon the emotions associated with them and their relation—whether concordant or not—to each other (U.S. & Netherlands, presumably students; Ekman, et al., 1972, pp. 135–51, 177).

Then, various attributes of Ego, such as his age and even his ethnic background (U.S., children; Maddock & Kenny, 1973), his tendency to think in concrete or abstract terms (Usual; Ware & Harvey, 1967), or his personality (France, presumably students; Louis-Guérin, 1972–3) *may* influence the degree to which he integrates or wishes to integrate contradictory information, the speed and certainty with which he organizes such information, and the degree of discrimination associated with the categories he actually employs. Ego's attitude toward the component bits of information may cause him to weight some more heavily than others. You value honesty so much that its inclusion or exclusion among the characteristics attributed to Alter inevitably has an overwhelming effect upon your judgment, sometimes almost regardless of what his other attributes happen to be. All of us usually value or, if I may say so, should value the actual product of an artist or the performance of a musician without being influenced by the information supplied beforehand or afterwards by critics or even by the individual himself.

The same Humpty-Dumpty problem arises when canny investigators present Ego with demographic information (income, occupation, education) and ask him to judge Alter's social class. What should Ego say about a hypothetical janitor with little formal education but with a fantastically large annual income? Averaging *may* be the procedure to be followed by and large in dealing with contradictory information, but addition may be employed when the information is reasonably consistent (Usual; Himmelfarb & Senn, 1969).

How the pieces fall into place depends also upon their nature. *Perhaps* negative information about Alter is more influential than positive information—or at least there is evidence to that effect not only from the usual American source (Richey et al., 1967) but also, miraculously, from other countries (Denmark, university students & adults; Gray-Little, 1973. Germany & Ecuador, not specified; cited by Richey et al., 1975). Lists of Alter's attributes *may* have an effect upon Ego different from the one produced by a narrative about him (Usual; Cusumano & Richey, 1970).

Ego's total potential may be involved. Not unexpectedly, the way in which he puts the pieces together as he judges Alter *may* be related to the way in which he utilizes any kind of concept (Postscript I.6); if he reconciles conflicting information concerning Alter, he may also find relations between abstract terms such as Buddhism, fascism, capitalism, and Christianity (Usual; Gollin & Rosenberg, 1956). Social factors may also be relevant. Thus Ego's way of handling information *may* be affected by whether Alter is or is not a member of the group to which he himself belongs (Canada; high school students & adults; Aboud & Taylor, 1971), or by whether Alter is playing a role similar or dissimilar to his own (Canada, presumably high school students; Aboud et al., 1973).

A few professionals have given ingenious twists to the Humpty-Dumpty problem: instead of supplying Ego with consistent or contradictory bits of information about Alter, they have commanded him to observe Alter evaluating a peer and then they have asked him to decide whether he likes that Alter or not. It first appears as if Ego as guinea pig *may* be attracted to an Alter who initially gives a negative opinion that is followed by a positive one than he is to one who gives two positive opinions, presumably because the mixture of opinions makes Alter appear more credible (Usual; Aronson & Linder, 1965). But here, too, other variables intervene; the effect *may* appear only when Ego believes either that Alter's opinions about the peer are based upon careful discrimination (U.S., grade school boys; Mettee, 1971b) or that Alter's first opinion relates to a matter of minor importance and the second to one of major importance, rather than vice versa (Usual; Mettee, 1971a).

7.3 Rationalizing Humpty-Dumpty

Do American college students like Alters who comply with other persons' suggestions? In hypothetical situations involving a harmless topic, an Alter who does or does not comply may be found to be more attractive when his status is high and less so when it is low (Ring, 1964). Some assimilate the two bits of information, compliance and high status, by considering the high-status complier generous since his status could enable him, presumably, to refuse to comply. Or what kind of judgment does Ego make when Alter's performance fluctuates over time; does he consider him bright or stupid? *Perhaps* his judgment depends upon the kind of task Alter is performing. If he thinks a basic ability is involved, his first impression *may* be more influential than his last; hence an Alter performing well at the outset and then less well thereafter may be considered bright because it is tolerantly assumed that the performance of capable individuals fluctuates somewhat, whereas one performing poorly at first and subsequently better may be judged less bright because his later performance is believed to be only a deviation from the initially perceived norm (Usual; E. E. Jones et al., 1968). If he is convinced that trial and error learning is involved, however, he *may* be more impressed with the later than with the earlier performance since he believes that an intelligent person improves as a result of experience, a dullard grows worse (Usual; R. G. Jones & Welsh, 1971). He *may* possibly attribute a successful performance to Alter's ability and effort more readily than he does one involving failure; and consistent success or failure he *may* ascribe to Alter's ability and the nature of the task, inconsistency to effort and good or bad fortune (presumably Usual; Frieze & Weiner, 1971). And so on.

Postscript 7.4   The Anthropology of Group Alters

One anthropologist has seized upon 400 societies and, when data are available, has ingeniously programmed a computer to search for relations among the 480 attributes of culture, institutions, and behavior that social scientists have more or less systematically investigated throughout the world. Each of the 480 is taken one at a time, and its relation to the other 479 is determined. *I am afraid to ask, but give me one example.* Let us take "boastfulness." Below are given the other attributes with which it tends to be significantly related from a statistical standpoint (i.e., the relation could arise by chance no more frequently than 5 times out of 100). The first figure in the parenthesis is the number of societies on which the generalization is based, and the second is the degree of association that can range from 0 (no relation) to 1.00 (a perfect relation):

Slavery is present (89; .23)
Invidious display of wealth is strongly emphasized (88; .24)
Age of males at marriage is 20 or over (39; .35)

Composite fertility level is high (12; .49)

The early aggression satisfaction potential is high (44; .31)

The consistency of reduction of the infant's drives is low (44; .33)

The total positive pressure toward developing self-reliant behavior in the child is high (54; .31)

The total positive pressure toward developing achievement behavior in the child is high (46; .33)

The child's inferred anxiety over non-performance of achievement behavior is high (45; .32)

Warfare is prevalent (32; .46)

Military glory is strongly or moderately emphasized (85; .40)

Bellicosity is extreme (86; .37)

Killing, torturing, or mutilating of the enemy is strongly or moderately emphasized (83; .37)

Supernatural sanctions for morality, having an effect on individual's health, are present (29; .35)

The role of religious experts is conducive to the development of the individual's need to achieve (25; .42)

Composite narcissism index is high (89; .56)

Sensitivity to insult is extreme (87; .25)

The abandonment or killing of old people is unimportant or absent (16; .51)

According to the same computer, however, boastfulness is not significantly associated with hundreds of other attributes (Textor, 1967, category 474). Results such as the above are both encouraging and discouraging in the search for advisable pathways. They show that relations exist; hence Ego can make tentative inferences from one generalized form of behavior or one condition in a society to other behavior. Indeed, there are other cross-cultural studies suggesting more dramatic and potentially useful associations than those recorded in the last paragraph, such as correlations between social structure and the relations members of a society consider incestuous (Murdock, 1949), between child-training practices and theories of disease (Whiting & Child, 1953), between the complexity of a society and the restrictions placed upon sexual activities (Caputo, 1973). But, as the illustration of boastfulness suggests, qualifications are many. First, the established relations, though significant statistically, do not approach perfection, which is another way of saying that there are exceptions to the generalizations. Then the established relations are far fewer than those which have not emerged, so that the process of inference is circumscribed. Those emerging, moreover, seem reasonable enough, but ones equally plausible do not turn out to be significant; thus one might expect a relation between boastfulness and an emphasis on "exhibitionistic dancing" or "degree of insobriety," but the expectation is not supported by the available information. In addition, and finally, the relations are ones known only to the professionals; lay Egos may have hunches concerning possible clusters, but hunches provide perilous pathways.

7.5   Documentary Evidence

When the contents of documents are so numerous that they cannot be grasped at a glance, the professionals often depend upon what they call Content Analysis. The technique offers a standardized procedure to reduce the errors that may arise when a document is informally appraised. A set of categories is selected and then each sentence or thought unit, or a representative sample chosen from each, is assigned to one of the categories; reliability or objectivity is ascertained by comparing the categories of two analysts who work independently of each other; and the resulting tallies are thrown into statistical form so that the total content can be comprehended and trends determined. Although this formal procedure is not followed by laymen—it is both time-consuming and very tedious—it is another advisable, if ideal, model which at least serves as a warning that a trustworthy impression of Alter's documents cannot easily be attained before judgment is passed upon them (Pathway 0.1).

It is useless, however, to analyze a document carefully unless its originator, whether Alter himself or another person, can be trusted (Pathway 2.1). Conscious or unconscious deceptions are not detected by statistical manipulation or computers. Guidelines for using documents have been formulated (Dollard, 1935; Allport, 1942), and each craft—history, psychiatry, literary criticism—has its own rules-of-thumb that are not standardized and that are constantly revised. Obviously, attention must be paid to establishing the authenticity of the material, the circumstances under which it was composed, and supplementary information from other documents or from a knowledge of the milieu in which the Alter lived. One point is especially compelling: it is absolutely essential to know why Alter wrote the document or spoke into the tape recorder or, if a second party has compiled the record, the nature of his motivation and his relation to

Alter. Perhaps the task of comprehending Alter through documents or tapes appears easier when he is dead: the number of facts about him at Ego's disposal is then limited and may never be increased, so that Ego may pass secondary judgment with some confidence that at least he will not suddenly be disturbed by new or contradictory information. "Psychohistory," as it is sensationally called, has become a popular academic sport, for the brilliance of one's neologisms and interpretations can be attacked only in the flimsiest literary tradition of I-just-don't-agree-with-you. But of course, either literally or figuratively, there may be attics or archives from which additional second-hand data may some day emerge and require a change in what has been written or spoken. In any case, documents have one questionable advantage: they may be analyzed leisurely which is not often the case when an Alter is confronted face-to-face.

Similar problems arise when we would or must characterize either a society or living persons by examining archaeological remains or the consequences of their behavior or of previous decisions. Those consequences may include the kinds of houses in which they choose to live, if they have a choice, the style of clothing they wear, the varieties of food and drink they consume, the ways in which they spend their money or its equivalent, etc. (Doob, 1961, pp. 110–20). In all these instances, Alter himself is or may be absent, and Ego's judgments are based on traces whose meaning can seldom be intuitively grasped but must be laboriously evolved on a secondary level.

7.6 The Ascription of Motives

The cultural: Anthropologists often provide neat summaries of the explanations allegedly current in a given society. Of the Wolof in West Africa, for example, it is reported that "some men are . . . said to be exceedingly cruel, parsimonious, unjust, or jealous" and "their incorrigible misconduct is variously explained as the will of God, as the possession of a very jealous personal spirit, or even as the result of poor training by parents when the deviant was young" (Ames, 1953, pp. 134–35). You and I do not know the Wolof, yet I must be skeptical concerning the completeness of such an inventory. For in our own society, if I may be ethnocentric, even the most myopic or well-organized person is seldom so completely consistent that he attributes everything that any Alter does to a single cause or set of causes. He may use one explanation more frequently than any other, but on occasion he moves out of the groove. *Maybe the Wolof are different from us.* Allow me also to guess

that a modal belief in the West may be that an unselfish act is more to
be praised than a selfish one; that an effect achieved through chance or
happenstance is to be judged differently from one deliberately planned
and executed; and that a damaging action of Alter is judged less harshly
when Ego believes that action to be justified rather than unjustified.
What, no reference to Usual or some investigation? Sometimes, I agree
with you, a guess is as good as a study; still somewhere I am quite
certain that that kind of evidence is at hand (Kelley, 1972).

The methodological: When Englishmen and others under the influence of Darwin (during the first quarter of this century) postulated
the instincts of man, their lists were never very long; scattered acts
could be included under a finite number of categories. Some of their
more daring French contemporaries imagined that a single impulse,
such as *élan vital* or *égoïsme*, gives rise to all behavior. You and I need
not enter into the ancient controversy; it is sufficient to note that
motives have been codified more easily than the human actions found
in an unabridged thesaurus. Of course, any schema of motives must be
an oversimplification to some extent. Whether we think that Alter's
behavior demonstrates he is striving for financial success or for approval by his peers, we necessarily must overlook nuances (Postscript
I.6). His striving is different from the striving of other Alters, although
it resembles theirs in some respects; it is different from his strivings of
yesterday or tomorrow, although it likewise resembles them in many
ways. But Ego is thereby reaping the benefit of abstraction by conveniently grouping diverse behaviors under a single category, while
simultaneously suffering the disadvantage of disregarding some or
many of the details. This truly is our destiny: we can profit from experience only by lifting ourselves out of the concrete, but we dare not
overlook the concrete since what confronts us in real behavior is not an
abstraction, but nasty, compelling particulars (Pathway II.1).

The substantive: The professionals offer a rich menu of motivational
systems from which to choose explanations. There are monistic assumptions stressing single factors, such as sex, mastery, or achievement. There are eclectic systems providing an array of instincts or
drives propelling us hither and yon. Among the latter there is a
division of opinion: some believe the multiplicity of impulses should
be traced back to a small number of motives or a single one—ultimately, for example, adolescent and adult motives are said to have
their origin in the one drive of sex, broadly defined—whereas others
claim the multiplicity has been present from birth. The devotees of

multiplicity may suggest that a few basic drives maintain or reinforce the more recently acquired ones or they may assert that motives, once established, tend to persist and require no reinforcement from the motives originally giving rise to them (Postscript I.3). Most professionals simply unfold their chosen motive or set of motives and thereafter strive to fit selected facts of clinical experience or common sense into the frame of reference; and a few claim an impressive authority for their categories, such as an "analysis of historical and contemporary writings of theologians, philosophers, and social scientists" (Wrightsman, 1964). In the final analysis . . . . *Whatever that means.* The basic issue involves the conflict between genetic and environmental explanations (Pathway 5.c). Individual psychiatrists and psychologists may employ both assumptions but for different illnesses, some of which are then called organic, the others functional. Each alternative must then be refined. Instead of simply referring to the general milieu in his background to account for Alter's traits or behavior, for example, the professional may delve into his family, his peers, the dominant culture, a particular group to which he belongs, some influential friend, or the Zeitgeist—in short, the total potential.

7.7 The Assigning of Responsibility

Assigning responsibility to someone assumes that what he does depends upon his volition and not upon another person. I presume, as do others who have considered the question (Asch, 1952, p. 206), that—at least under normal circumstances—Ego's initial hypothesis, as he passes primary judgment, is to consider Alter the sole responsible agent. Only when he reflects is he likely to shift that responsibility to circumstances beyond Alter's control (parents, business cycle, illness, etc.) and then perhaps back again to Alter's conscience. The catch in the analysis is the determination of when "circumstances" are "normal" (Pathway I.7). An Alter who is miserable because his home has been blown away by a tornado is not likely to be blamed for the catastrophe —unless Ego believes he was foolish to live in a tornado-prone area in the first place or not to build a tornado-proof dwelling. For most behavior, the locus and the degree of responsibility attributed to Alter are likely to depend very broadly upon Ego's own philosophy or psychological assumptions, both of which may be affected by Alter's actions and their outcome. On the one hand, a doctrine of complete social determinism suggests that the individual is never responsible for what he does: his parents are to blame because they have passed on to him a genetic constitution or because they have reared him in a particular way; "society" is to blame because "it" has or has not offered him certain opportunities, etc. On the other hand, the proponent of free will asserts that ultimately Ego is responsible for his own destiny. Prosaically, however, Ego *may* judge Alter's responsibility by referring not only to his activity per se but also to its consequences as well as to its relation to possible causal factors in Alter's milieu (U.S., children & adults; Shaw & Sulzer, 1964).

Is there an advisable pathway for Ego to follow as he seeks to assign responsibility? I begin with the naturalistic suggestion (Heider, 1958b, pp. 151–56) that Alter is likely to be considered responsible when his mood, feeling, or behavior fluctuates while external conditions remain more or less unchanged, and that he is not responsible when the reverse is true. If a particular symphony depresses Alter, we are not in a position to know whether the depression results from his mood or the composition. If the symphony always depresses him, it may be called responsible; if it depresses him only sometimes but causes him at other times to feel elated or unmoved, he is responsible. I would guess that this criterion is useful in our society, but not universal, for I can imagine —without data—societies in which responsibility for conformity is given to Alter's parents, and for non-conforming, to evil spirits or himself. Also it is far too simple. Alter must be assigned responsibility when he himself alters the environment: he listens not just to that one symphony but also only to many other symphonies that make him sad. Then Alter is absolved of responsibility if others react similarly to an environmental condition or if it is inconceivable that he could have acted otherwise. A blind man is not held responsible for failing to see an obstruction in his way, nor is a fellow passenger blamed for stepping on your toes in a crowded train or bus that suddenly lurches or comes to a halt.

Assigning responsibility usually leads to an appropriate evaluation (Pathway 7.b). You praise me more when you think I am responsible rather than not responsible for bringing you joy. You condemn me less if I hurt you inadvertently than if you consider my action deliberate. *But am I responsible for my unconscious?* This question, I think, indicates a pathway leading into an impenetrable jungle.

Another phase of responsibility involves a question Ego may pose to himself: on what basis, he may ask, have I passed judgment, what in Alter or myself is responsible for that judgment? I would guess again that Ego's first impulse is to ascribe responsibility to Alter: what Alter does or says, what is reported about him, must be the explanation, rather than any prejudice, mood, or predisposition within himself. Again and again Ego may find some way to avoid assigning responsibility to himself for those judgments of his that run counter to other significant beliefs to which he also subscribes. Persons adhering to an egalitarian ideal must somehow explain away their denigrating attitude toward minority groups when they consider them inherently worthless, primitive, or inferior (Dollard, 1937, pp. 363–88).

7.8 Backward Predictions

In making backward predictions, Ego once more faces a problem also baffling to professionals: is present behavior sustained by the basic drives from which it is derived or does it become self-sustaining in its own right (Postscript I.3)? Fancy terms for the difference are "reductionism" and "functional autonomy." At the present time, psychiatrists, psychoanalysts, and others seriously concerned with healing mental ills are fairly sharply divided on this issue: to help a person must we return to the fundamental source, presumably in childhood, or can we deal satisfactorily with the distressing symptoms being exhibited at the moment? I suspect that laymen, whether sophisticated or not, vacillate between these two extremes and certainly are not consistently adherents of one rather than the other view. Your mood now may be affected by a headache, but yesterday your feelings may have been due to a personal problem, arising out of your scattered youth. There is, then, no advisable pathway to offer an Ego seeking to understand Alter's life history, rather there are too many pathways, as many as the theories of professionals and non-professionals concerning the genesis of motive, and we have no way to select the best or the better ones. Still a selection, however arbitrary, is often highly desirable for the sake of tolerance: knowing or guessing why Alter behaves as he does as a result of a particular past or a momentary drive makes him seem a little less ridiculous, a little more human, perhaps also a little less responsible for what he feels, thinks, or does.

Another kind of backward prediction is ordinarily considered an exercise in validation, a topic to be discussed more fully as Pathway 8.a: for research purposes Ego in the role of subject seeks to match a collection of personality sketches or known facts about real persons with some kind of expressive record, such as handwriting, that they have produced. Here, for example, are 1,000 protocols obtained by administering the Rorschach blots, half to delinquent and the other half to non-delinquent adolescents; can a Rorschach expert identify which protocols come from one group rather than the other? *Well, can he?* Yes, one did, far above chance expectancy (Schachtel, 1950). Although the outcome is known in advance by the investigator, the Ego whose skill is being tested must try to predict backward the particular individuals who would write or react to the blots in specified ways. The task is like that of locating a person from his fingerprints. It involves essentially the assumption that certain traits or bits of behavior tend to cluster into syndromes and that hence one trait can be successfully inferred from the presence or absence of one or more of the others. The Ego who can successfully match the expressive records and the persons originally producing them, moreover, may or may not be able to indicate the bases for his performance: he may look at details or he may examine the entire configuration, but be powerless to verbalize either to himself or to others the precise method he has employed. There is nothing sinful about this inability—let us be grateful for every success —rather it is to be regretted: a real science is able to indicate not only what occurs but also why it occurs, so that the skill can be transmitted to and mastered by others.

The culminating pathway, the final circle on the circumference of our chart, has now, at last, been reached. Even if he is a professional, Ego must live in a real world. *But you have been compulsively maintaining that he is solipsistically encased* (Pathway 3.1). His judgments about Alters, Group Alters, and himself are judged by others and by himself. Are his judgments true or false, useful or useless, ethically right or wrong? These three queries have already permeated our discussion, but usually only implicitly. At this point we must grapple with them directly.

The dimensions to be appraised are infinite in number. To appreciate this, we need only recall the first problem confronting Ego as he passes primary judgment on a basic level: how shall he describe Alter's actions? He must select some concept, some category (Alter is "looking up" at the sky); and then he may, if he wishes, qualify the description (he is looking "intensely"). From there he may go on to other aspects of the primary judgment (he is looking to see whether it is going to rain because he believes you can see a storm coming from the west). After reflection, he may refine the description, the ascription, and the postulation of beliefs by characterizing, evaluating, and seeking to understand Alter on the basis of what he seems to have been doing. Each of these gyrations can be appraised in its own right: is he really looking at the sky, is he looking intensely, does he believe that weather always originates in the west?

Other complications may intrude, especially when Ego and Alter communicate with each other and a spiral makes one of its frequent appearances. With or without direct communication, there is always the possibility of an infinite regress. Consider a boy and girl in love who are thinking about themselves and each other. Each has an opinion of himself, of his beloved, and of that beloved's opinion of himself. The boy considers himself dependable, he thinks the girl is only somewhat dependable, and he believes she considers him most dependable; but the girl, although she also considers herself dependable, has grave doubts about the boy's dependability, and she feels she has no clue to the boy's opinion of her own dependability. Thus the boy's opinion of his own dependability is not shared by the girl, and her opinion of herself is only partially shared with him; the boy's opinion of the girl's view of himself is not correct, the girl cannot decide what his opinion of her is; and the boy is confident that his opinion of himself is shared by the girl, whereas the girl feels in the dark on that score. Should the two get married even though there are these differences between them, or should they first find pathways to clear up the difference? *In spite of all this, a decision is made, and somehow we survive, don't we?* Yes, of course, but let us see how.

8.a   Validity

The criterion of validity involves the straightforward procedure of science and ought to cause no great difficulty: can we verify with a sense impression the proposition that is the primary or secondary judgment? When a professional reviews the methods his colleagues have employed to test "the ability to judge people"—we have mentioned them all in passing: emotional expressions in photographs, drawings, and motion pictures; the rating or ranking of traits; the description of personalities; the matching of personalities; and prediction of behavior from life-history material (Taft, 1955)—he immediately indicates the validating criteria against which each method is appraised and thus correctly assumes the existence of such criteria. As we all know and as you say again and again, however, the utilization of science in human affairs is never simple. The judge of Ego's judgment may require the assistance of other persons, although eventually he himself must function in that role. You are convinced that a given writer is third-rate—and you use that expression or its equivalent again and again with reference to most of our contemporary writers. We must first disentangle what you mean by the statement; I presume you think his skill is such that what he writes has been, is, and always will be third-rate. Is your statement true? As your Ego-expositor I am confronted with a number of alternatives. I could ask other persons their opinion: do they think he is third-rate too? If they agree that he is, your original judgment is true in one limited sense. But you may not respect *their* opinions, nor may I; and perhaps you are more likely to dismiss my consultants if they disagree with you and consider him a first-rate writer. Then we would have to say that your statement is false with reference to criteria in which you have no or little confidence. You thus judge the judges. Instead of consulting other persons, I might test your implied prediction and determine whether one of the future books or poems of this writer turns out to be third-rate; but here again I would be dependent on your judgment, my own, or that of other persons with whom once more you might not agree. *What are you claiming?* To test Ego's judgments concerning Alter we must consider that we or someone else is functioning as another Ego who is judging him and that we or they have followed conscientiously all the best pathways to arrive at an objective, or at least at the best possible, assessment of him. For unless we—the outside judges—really know Alter, we have no way of determining the truth or falsity of Ego's judgments about him. *Now* you *speak of what Alter "really" is.*

We usually face similar uncertainty whenever we employ truth as the validating criterion. I use again the well-worn illustration of an intelligence-test score. Assume that Alter receives a very high score—for example, 150—on a standardized test, as a consequence of which we might predict he will perform excellently in a variety of situations. Is the judgment valid? If he receives an equally high score on another intelligence test, we might begin to have greater confidence in our judgment; and yet there is the possibility that both tests may be measuring not intelligence but "a superior memory span" (Warr & Knapper, 1968, p. 95). If he receives a lower score on the second intelligence test, we could say that either the original or the second test is faulty. If he shows a marked aptitude for mathematics but not for botany, we might conclude that our judgment has been partially validated: the kind of intelligence tested by the test, we would presume, contributes more to mathematics than it does to botany; or perhaps mathematics has tapped his intelligence but, because he lacks interest in plants or genetics, botany has not. Clearly what is needed is a criterion with which the prediction can be compared. If we were completely convinced that only an individual with a test score between 145 and 155 could reply to a riddle within 14 seconds, our judgment concerning Alter's intelligence could easily be tested: does he or does he not solve the riddle in that period of time? But the fact of the matter seems to be that we do not have such clear-cut criteria. Professionals face the same kinds of difficulties when they would validate Ego's or their own judgments (Postscript 8.1: Professional Validation).

Matching the verbal descriptions of emotions given by Alter and Ego points to another problem that arises in the search for criteria. You feel genuinely anxious, let us assume, or at least that is how you describe your mental state. Can I diagnose that state of yours on the basis of your facial expression or your actions? *But you and I have different notions of anxiety.* Yes, exactly, and I shall drive home this banal point with a bit of academic research. Fifty college graduates in New York City, a relatively homogeneous group if ever there were one, were once asked to indicate their reactions to 50 common words describing emotions (ranging alphabetically from "admiration" and "affection" to "solemnity" and "surprise") by checking for each of them those items in a checklist of 556 statements concerning emotion that seemed applicable. *You really mean 556, isn't that a typo?* No, 556 judgments for every one of the 50 words. *Horrors—50 × 556 = 27,800 judgments— who ever does that in real life?* The first item on that list of 556 is "weakness across my chest" and the last "the feeling seizes me, takes over, I don't know how to stop the feeling." One of the 50 words happened to be "anxiety." In fact, only 23 percent of the 556 items were considered by one-third or more of the 50 college graduates to be applicable to "anxiety," only 3 percent of the items were checked by 50 percent or more as being among the connotations of that same word (Davitz, 1969, pp. 7–14, 36). This may be angels-on-the-head-of-a-pin counting; still it is fair to ask how, with so little agreement among these young men and women, can anyone anticipate that two persons, like you and me, will ever use the designation *anxiety* in a similar manner? You call your mental state "anxious," and my judgment of that same state may be one of the following:

1. "anxious," with meanings similar to yours
2. "anxious," with meanings not similar to yours
3. some other word like "fearful," with meanings similar to yours
4. some other word like "fearful," with meanings not similar to yours.

Now which of my judgments shall we consider valid? If the criterion is the use of the same word, then Numbers 1 and 2 qualify; if the criterion is meaning, then Numbers 2 and 3 qualify; if both the designation and the meaning must be the same, then only Number 1 qualifies. Perhaps it is highly unlikely, as the cited academic research suggests, that our meanings will be similar or sufficiently similar; besides, if I must quickly decide whether you are anxious or not, I may not have the opportunity to ascertain the meanings either of us attach to the word *anxiety*.

Most of us use a subjective criterion we equate with validation: new information about Alter arrives, as a result of which we suddenly feel we understand him. It then "makes sense" for us to pass judgment, and we are convinced we are right. Professionals call this "face validity," and they mean of course that the judgment appears true on the face of it. Merely describing the process is sufficient to suggest its lurking peril: apparent intelligibility is not the same as validity. The real test is to determine whether Alter's future behavior can be either anticipated or fitted into the frame of reference indicated by Ego. An adequate criterion, moreover, can give a misleading impression of the judgment's validity. The expression on Alter's face may be called one of "disgust" and Alter may in fact feel disgusted; but virtually the same facial configuration may be elicited by "smelling sulfuric acid" or by "the reaction to a morally repulsive story" (Netherlands, young adults; Frijda, 1969, p. 190).

Again, I suggest, we never precisely know what Ego or Alter "really" is. . . . *Now you are back on the well-worn track again.* And Ego and we pass judgments that do not necessarily agree. What is the color of a person's eyes? That question can "really" be answered by observing the color and then comparing it with the known distribution of colors, like that produced in the ordinary spectrum. But for traits and behavior we have neither a standard mode of measurement nor a standard for purposes of comparison, at least standards that are universally accepted either by the professionals or by any particular Ego. We must depend upon catch-as-catch-can measures. What evidence do you need in order to decide that a person is trustworthy, elegant, boring, perceptive, perspicacious? Obviously you would have greater confidence in a judgment concerning his eye color than you would in judgments concerning any of those attributes, provided you have had an adequate opportunity to observe his eyes and make the necessary comparison.

But why do you keep avoiding the problem of deciding what Alter "really" is; why continue endlessly to give good reasons why Alter cannot be grasped? For the last time I restate my view: I see no way of reaching the fictitious goal of what a person "really" is and I accuse you of a romantic lack of detachment when you suffer from the delusion that the situation can ever be otherwise. Alter is so many different things, and the things can be conceptualized in so many different ways that it is futile to adopt a God's eye view of him and to try to set him down for all eternity in a way which will be approved by all Egos, whether they are Americans or bush Africans, psychiatrists or persons with common sense. Most deliberately I say again, and I am surprised that you have been unwilling to grasp my view: no one ever understands another person completely or can break through the solipsistic wall of fire; we do the best we can with the categories available to us and the insight we have into ourselves (Pathway 6.b). You need not puncture this view, I admit I do not have complete confidence in what I have just said, I do believe that in rare moments of love or trust, sometimes through the arts or sheer luck, we break out of the prison in which we live, or at least we have the cosmic feeling that we do. *And that is why you, who do not believe in understanding, keep insisting that I should be able to understand you or at least your understanding of understanding?*

A subtle problem concerning Alter's "real" nature arises in connection with sincerity. Ego may attribute that virtue to Alter, and Alter himself may agree that what he is saying or doing he "really" believes. But his statement may represent self-deception. Unconsciously he may be seeking one goal—and achieving its opposite. As the writer of a monograph on ingratiation has suggested, popularizers of the capitalistic ethic, such as Dale Carnegie, may in effect argue that "a person will come to believe his insincere remarks and therefore he will cease being insincere" (Jones, 1964, p. 108); thus dissonance dissipates. Under these circumstances the criterion of validity cannot be based upon what Alter says or believes but must involve a deeper level of his personality.

The professionals themselves readily admit that their favorite tests or modes of diagnosis may sometimes be in error. They refer, for example, to false positives and false negatives: attributing an attribute to subjects when in fact they do not have it, or not attributing it when actually they do. Unquestionably, however, complete validation can sometimes be obtained either by Ego himself or any honest investigator, but then ascription must be based upon overt behavior that can be objectively observed and not easily feigned. How can I be certain that I am correct when I say that Alter cannot play a musical instrument? With his cooperation I could ask him to try to play a piano or a cello. He might be able to beat a drum, but then I would have to give a precise definition of "play a musical instrument." Also I can have confidence in my objective criterion only by assuming that he does not wish to conceal his musical talent. *If your nihilism prevents you from being certain about Alter's musical ability, then how can you ever validate a judgment about one of his traits or values?* Exactly—have I finally converted you?

The same question can be raised in a more specialized form: who is to judge the truth or falsity of Ego's self-judgments? He himself ought to be able to do so, presumably he has all relevant information at his disposal. Somerset Maugham has argued that for this very reason we are more tolerant toward ourselves than we are toward others because we are better acquainted with the circumstances ostensibly compelling us to act as we do (cited by Ichheiser, 1970, pp. 146–47). But for good Freudian reasons, we all know, self-deception is possible, rather probable. Ego is swayed by unconscious impulses of which he is unaware; he *may* consider an evaluation of himself "excellent" or "good" rather than "poor" or "very poor," whether it be given by an expert or a peer, provided it is favorable and, like a horoscope, vaguely worded: "You have a strong need for other people to like you and for them to admire you; you have a tendency to be critical of yourself . . ." (Usual; Ulrich et al., 1963). Ego, in short, is likely to be biased in his own behalf and therefore cannot be trusted. *Cannot be trusted by whom?* Ah, there is the rub, Ego tends to trust himself except when he miraculously concludes on the basis of unfavorable experiences that he really is not completely trustworthy. To validate his judgment, Ego needs another Ego such as a friend, a lover, or even a psychiatrist. That second Ego must then be submitted to the same scrutiny we have just accorded any Ego who is judging Alter or himself. Eventually, however, we end up in the same place except that we have now made the situation a bit more complicated: Ego judges Ego 1, Ego 2 judges Ego 1's judgment of himself, and at length Ego 1 judges Ego 2's judgment of Ego's initial judgment of himself. I could express this a bit more simply, if simplicity were my aim. . . . *Would that it were.* How could you decide, were you to consult a psychiatrist (which I do not advise), whether you agree with him when he tells you that you do or do not have insight into yourself? Have you?

Allow me to be concrete without sending you to a psychiatrist. I think you will agree that among close friends, very close ones, you have a penchant for self-criticism. At this point we have no problem: you, your chosen friends, and I (also one of those friends) all have the same sense perceptions about you and therefore from one standpoint your judgment has been validated. But the moment we probe a bit more deeply our accord may disappear. You say you criticize yourself because you are honest and sincere, and the pursuit of honesty and sincerity is one of the cardinal principles around which you organize your life. A few of those friends, just a few, and I, however, account for your motivation a trifle differently. You try to be honest and sincere in your self-criticisms, yes, but perhaps only because you want to protect yourself from the criticism of others. If you criticize yourself, others may not do so; or indeed the others, being polite, may say that you are unjust to yourself and hence you are a much better character than you yourself think or say—and such words bring pleasure to you. In fact, were I cruel, as indeed I am not . . . . *But how do you know you are not cruel, why should I have any confidence in your self-judgment?* If I were cruel, I might say that you are not really self-deprecatory, but rather that you are conceited: you have such a high opinion of yourself that you know your disarming self-criticisms are either untrue or insignificant. Now, I ask, who is to say whether your analysis or my nasty or semi-nasty one is valid? You may not accept mine and I then may not accept your non-acceptance of mine, and so on. *Oh, you are right and I am wrong, of course, of course.* Of course.

How, then, can we interpret a disagreement between Ego's self-judgment and that of someone else? *Perhaps,* for example, there is less discrepancy between the self-description of husbands and the ways they are described by their wives when the men are not alcoholic than when they are (England; Drewery & Rae, 1969). The sensible interpretation is to blame the alcoholic husbands and to declare their self-judgments invalid; the disability makes them poor judges of themselves or leads to behavior that provides misleading or inadequate information to their wives. If they have insight which they have badly communicated, however, their wives' judgments should not be the validating criteria. It is only socially useful to blame the aberrant husbands. Over and over, Ego is dependent upon the judgment of others if he is to judge himself and evaluate his own behavior accurately; his friends, his acquaintances, and his enemies as well as counsellors, parents, clergymen, physicians, and psychiatrists *may* perform this function for him (Usual & adults; Valins & Nisbett, 1972). In general, however, I can find no a priori advisable pathway enabling me to choose between Ego and his judges; the skill of each (Pathway II) and their relation to each other (Pathway I.c) must be appraised. Ego should follow the same advice and not necessarily prefer his own judgment.

It is especially difficult to appraise Ego's judgment when he ascribes Alter's behavior to unconscious motives. For if the unconscious is defined as "what we do not communicate to ourselves or to one another," Ego must use the concept of the unconscious to suggest that he is making an inference concerning Alter's experience as well as his unawareness of some or all the components of that experience (Laing, 1969, pp. 6, 17). By definition, Alter's unawareness makes it impossible to go to him for verification or an appraisal. Even if he agrees and says, "Yes, the inference makes sense to me, I had never thought of that," Ego and we are still on unsafe ground. Alter may be, if I may use a very old-fashioned word, suggestible and he may be trying to please Ego, an attempt which itself may be unconscious. *Here we go again into another infinite regress.* Although the concept of the unconscious is slippery and hence should never be glibly evoked, the evidence supporting the existence of unconscious processes is so overwhelming that it cannot be circumvented or abandoned. Aside from caution, one other pathway is advisable, viz., that of prediction (Pathway 7.c). If ascribing Alter's actions—or some of them—to the unconscious provides more accurate predictions concerning his behavior than not ascribing them, Ego would have some evidence justifying the utilization of the concept. *Not necessarily: this is like saying that ancestors affect us through direct intervention because the Egos subscribing to this belief are more sensitive judges of their peers than those who reject the belief.*

In an effort to achieve objectivity, psychometricians sometimes give the protocol from Alter to another person who knows nothing about him, and they seek from him an unbiased diagnosis or analysis. A lay Ego can attempt to duplicate this laudable procedure (Pathway 0.1) by describing to a second person whatever data or impressions he has about Alter; the description obviously must be as factual as possible; the second person can then provide his own categorization, evaluation, or prediction. The skill of the second person and the relation between him and Ego must be questioned. That relation may in turn involve another Ego-Alter interaction. (Pathway I.c) in which the consultant becomes Ego 2 who may wonder why Ego 1 has consulted him and may thus in turn pass judgment on Ego 1. The original Ego may have glimpsed the unvarnished truth and have been driven from that glory by his own desire to conform or by a more forceful peer who may provide erroneous information.

The validity of the information assembled by Ego and others de-

pends upon the capability of the persons collecting it and the extent
to which it is representative of Alter's repertoire. Collectors, of course,
vary in sensitivity (Pathway II.b); and their own status may be important (Pathway 2.b). Sometimes, but not always, for example, the
leaders of a group, whether formally designated or informally elected,
may be able more accurately to judge the opinions of their followers
than the followers themselves (U.S., high school students, teachers,
adults, naval personnel; Gage, 1953). Perhaps their position gives
leaders a greater opportunity than mere members have to perceive the
opinions of others, perhaps they occupy those positions because they
have perceived their fellow men more sensitively and frequently and
hence have risen or been chosen. Three competent professionals (Sarbin et al., 1960, pp. 166–68) have suggested that information, when it
is not *false*, may be *valid* (a long description of Alter's past history as
observed over time by many competent persons), *misleading* (his behavior on New Year's Eve or some other holiday), *ambiguous* (a liking
for Mozart or martinis), or *insignificant* (the color of his hair or shoes).
The distinctions seem sound, if banal, but I question your glib illus-
trations in parentheses. People who like Mozart, for example, may pro-
vide unambiguous clues to their conscious wish to retreat into a sweet
past and to avoid what they consider to be the cacophony of electronic
music. And the color of her hair is quite significant, for she is a blonde
and blondes are so much preferred that she has less difficulty in solving
some of her problems than she would have if she were a brunette. Good
for you—I was too glib; forgive the parentheses, but use the distinction
as another advisable pathway. *Perhaps.* Fine.

Sometimes Ego wishes to determine how Alter reacts to aspects of
his environment, which suggests that he ought to be able to follow the
advisable pathway of experimentation (Pathway 0.1). In real life, however, the use of the method is sadly restricted (Postscript 8.2: Experimentation). To compensate for his inability to use experimentation, an
alert Ego must impose upon himself a number of restraints. First, he
must be aware, as I have already indicated a number of times, of the
perils arising from stereotypes. He may simplify his own experience
(Pathway 6.a) and be misled by past successes. If he believes that it is
essential to observe samples of Alter's behavior in order to make accurate predictions, for example, he may indeed use such experience to
predict quite accurately how Alter will respond to imaginary or real
situations; but, investigation *may* reveal, his predictions might have
been just as valid, perhaps even more valid, if he had merely known

the identity of Alter's subcultural group and had not had the opportunity to observe him in action (Usual; Gage, 1952).

Next there is the danger of pseudo-validity: confusing validity and reliability or objectivity. Suppose, for example, you were to believe in phrenology. You examine the bumps on Alter's head and you arrive at certain conclusions concerning his character. Then if after an interim you repeat the procedure and adhere to the same method of deducing character from bumps and if you have made your measurements carefully the first time, you will undoubtedly arrive at a similar conclusion the second time; both conclusions, therefore, are reliable. Someone else who belongs to your school of phrenology and who therefore measures the bumps as you do and associates them with identical personality traits or behavior could be asked to examine Alter, and undoubtedly he would draw the same or at least very similar conclusions as you; this pathway, therefore, also possesses objectivity. Such reliability and objectivity, however, contribute zero to validation. Your initial measurements may agree with others taken by you subsequently or by someone else, but the conclusions you both draw may be wrong, utterly wrong. I do not have faith in a light meter which gives a constant reading under identical conditions when the pictures I take with my camera are always overexposed; I rightly conclude that it is consistently faulty. Achieved consensus, however, even though incorrect, may be of extreme interest in its own right: it suggests that Alter has impressed people similarly. It is true, moreover, that you cannot test the validity of a measurement or observation unless you know that it is reliable; otherwise what you think is true or false may reflect only the imperfection of the way the data about Alter have been obtained.

The proposition whose validity is being appraised must be stated in a form that can in fact be tested and, when tested, explained. Let me return to one of your quirks, your curious interest in astrology; you are of the opinion that much or some of Alter's behavior and character can be determined by consulting his horoscope. Many of the characterizations and predictions, especially those appearing—alas, throughout the world—as syndicated newspaper features or as inexpensive pamphlets, are so vaguely expressed that non-believers find it impossible to eke out propositions that can be definitively validated. I am not referring here to the proclivity of the faithful to count the hits and ignore the misses of the astrological sages and their commercializers, but to the flabbiness of their statements. Thus if it is asserted that an "important event" is to occur during the next ten days for those born under a particular constellation, we shall never know whether the extraction of a wisdom tooth, the death of a grandmother, advancement in one's profession, finding a valuable gem in the middle of a gutter, meeting an astronaut who once visited the moon, announcing or breaking off an engagement to a beloved constitutes the validating operational definition of that event. Similarly, many of the trait names attached to Alter, beginning with the aberrant and ending with the zany, are in themselves ambiguous and, when functioning in propositions, misleading. If Ego uses one of these concepts or accepts a vaguely stated proposition as true, however, he may attach specific meaning to it and then validate the characterization through his own behavior, which appropriately affects Alter (Pathway I.c). Ego, let us assume, is really convinced that a person is gracious—because of a head bump; a horoscope; the words of a crystal-gazer, tea-leaf or coffee-grounds reader, diviner, or vestal virgin; the position of dice, bones, or animal entrails; the symbols emerging from cards or an Ouija board; the muffled sounds of a deceased maternal uncle at an ancestral shrine or during a seance in a fashionable flat; or the diagnosis seriously transmitted by a professional. *Halt—you have made the point.* Whatever his reason for calling him gracious, it is highly likely that he will treat him as if he were just that and, indeed, he may thus induce him to become more gracious as a result of the treatment.

A characterization or prediction, in addition, may never be tested not because it is untestable but because the opportunity to conduct a test does not arise. I suspect that under conditions of extreme deprivation your character would not change appreciably, but it makes me happy to think that such conditions are not likely to mar your existence. Similarly, each of us has our breaking point from a psychiatric standpoint, though we may never know whether our own or anyone's propositions concerning that point are valid or not. Ego himself, moreover, may prevent the conditions that would test his own prediction from coming into existence. A psychiatrist refuses to release a patient from an institution when he thinks the man is dangerously paranoid and might try to kill people, and so he and we shall never know whether the prediction is correct, for clearly the risk involved in validation would be too great.

Judgments concerning Alter's inner feelings are more difficult to validate than those that can be more or less objectively perceived (Ichheiser, 1970, p. 24). Competent persons may disagree concerning the degree of "intelligence" Alter has revealed in a series of challenges, and they are likely to disagree even more when they are asked to judge the feelings he experiences in those situations. For intelligence there are somewhat uniform criteria prevalent within the society that give rise to relatively uniform modes of judgment; but for feelings there is, of course, much less standardization and the hedonic state is not directly observable (Pathway I.7).

The time elapsing between Ego's contact with Alter and his judgment may have a profound effect upon that judgment and hence its validation (Pathway II.3). The "sleeper effect"—that tendency perhaps to forget the source of a communication more rapidly than its content (Pathway 2.b)— may produce a secondary judgment more or less valid than the initial primary judgment. In addition, when new information about Alter is available, Ego's judgment of him *may* grow more polarized; he comes to think of him as exceedingly rather than moderately attractive (Usual; Sadler & Tesser, 1973). An Ego with an unfavorable view of Alter may consciously or unconsciously isolate himself from new information (Newcomb, 1947) and thus may decrease the validity of his original judgment.

Even though data elicited from Alter about himself, as previously noted, must be cautiously appraised, some beliefs can be directly and validly ascertained through direct inquiry. Public-opinion surveys in the West generally predict the outcome of elections successfully by asking a sample of persons for whom they intend to vote. If you think Alter is a Protestant, simply question him about his religious beliefs and under normal circumstances—again in the relatively uninhibited West—you are likely to learn whether you are right or wrong. A waiter in a restaurant does not use a projective instrument or a panel of professionals to decide whether the customer prefers soup or fruit juice for the first course. Similarly, "If we want to know how people feel: what they experience and what they remember, what their emotions and motives are like, and the reasons for acting as they do—why not ask them?" (Allport, 1942, p. 37). In fact there *may* be a significant relation between Ego's own comments about himself and the scores he receives on a professional's paper-and-pencil questionnaire, although the agreement *may* be far greater when the category in question is social recognition than when it is achievement (Usual; Merrens, 1975). It is reported (Allport, 1962), but without substantiating evidence, that "the best predictive question" for screening candidates for the armed service of the United States during World War II was the straightforward question, "Do you feel you are emotionally ready to enter military service?" Before he points the x-ray machine or pokes around, the dentist asks the patient which tooth hurts, and the patient is nearly always right. *But in all these instances Ego is motivated to respond truthfully?* Yes. *But often he will not or cannot be truthful.* Yes, again —but surely you have noticed that repeatedly we must depend upon Alter's verbal utterances as significant sources of information concerning himself in general (Pathway 1.a), his conscious feelings (Postscript 1.3), his identification and intentions (Pathway 3.a), his beliefs (Pathway 5.c), and his motives (Pathway 7.c) as well as the validity of Ego's opinion about him (Pathway 3.b). *Yes.*

This question of Alter's deceit we are not facing for the first time: we have mentioned deception (Pathway 1.1) and ways to reduce deception (Postscript 1.3) as well as ingratiation (Postscript 1.2). Here we need only recall three points. First, Alter may convey the partial or whole truth from his own standpoint but not from that of his peers. An Azande is likely to attribute a misdeed he commits to witchcraft, but others may hold him responsible and attribute his action to carelessness, ignorance, or stupidity (Evans-Pritchard, 1937, p. 78). The others presumably are less biased. Secondly, less so in the area of beliefs, more so in the areas of conduct and traits, it is often true that Alter, even if he does cooperate, may be powerless to reveal the complete truth about himself. Not exactly self-deception but self-unawareness characterizes many of the mentally disturbed. An hysterical individual may not appreciate the gratification his symptoms are bringing him, in fact he may deny the satisfaction. The schizoid person may claim he is being gratified when other impulses within him or the central core of his personality remains frustrated. Again and again you have had the experience, I am sure, of listening to someone describe himself in ways you consider absolutely false. He is deceiving himself, you have thought, or he lacks insight, or he is pompously trying to create a favorable impression for nasty or naive reasons.

Then, thirdly, whatever Alter says about himself is valuable, at least after it has been interpreted. From him alone can we discover his dreams, daydreams, images, private thoughts, beliefs, free associations. In addition, the very nature of some situations requires that Alter be asked what his judgment is or has been. If you want to know what I think about you at this very moment, there usually is really no other way to obtain this precious information except by asking. I in turn may wish to discover, for some sensible or perverse reason, whether my guess as to what you think I am thinking about you is correct or incorrect—on some level you simply must obtain information from me and I from you. Ridiculous? No, not quite, for the problem arises whenever there is a reverse judgment (Pathway II); then there *may* be some relation between the accuracy with which a job applicant judges the impression he has made upon an interviewer and that interviewer's impression of how well the applicant has behaved during the interview (Usual & adult; Barocas & Vance, 1972). Alter may lie, deliberately or unconsciously, at the outset of a contact with Ego because he is ill-at-ease, and then later be quite truthful. When and if we discover the truth, we are confronted with the fascinating problem of why he lied, the solution to which may in its own way provide significant insights into him.

Is Alter paying attention, Ego often asks, does he understand what I am saying? Before asking him, if you are face-to-face with Alter, you probably use some form of intuition: you note whether he is looking at you, the expression on his face, the posture of his body. You may also ask him. But what do you do when you distrust your observation or his reply, when you are convinced that he is thinking of something else while looking right at you or that he gives you the reply he thinks you want or he considers polite? If it's your speech you want him to perceive, you may ask him to repeat what you have just said; but repetition as such is not always equivalent to comprehension. Like an instructor on an examination, you may ask him to explain what you have said and, if he uses words or illustrations different from yours but equivalent to what you said, you may rest content. Eventually, however, you may be satisfied only with an objective demonstration: he shows he understands you by doing what you have suggested. But even here there are problems, for the non-doing may connote not lack of comprehension but merely an inability or unwillingness to carry out your suggestion.

An Ego who communicates his judgment about Alter to him may stimulate him to deny, affirm, or modify that judgment. Alter seems depressed, and Ego knows there are many reasons why he should feel that way; the expression on his face confirms the impression. When Ego expresses sympathy, therefore, Alter may say in effect that Ego is wrong, it is not depression but just fatigue that he observes. In this kind of interaction, however, there is no reason why Alter should respond more or less truthfully to Ego's judgment about himself than he would to an open-ended question which asks him to describe his own mood. Then we must wonder again concerning the circumstances under which Ego is likely to make his judgment known to Alter; but here is another Pandora's box we keep tightly shut except to say quickly that Ego may deliberately refrain from expressing to Alter what he really thinks for a variety of reasons, ranging from wanting to spare Alter's feelings, if the judgment is harsh, to conveying a false impression in order in yet another way to goad or inspire Alter to reveal more information about himself. Alter's reactions to Ego's judgment in turn may or may not verify Ego's judgment of him. You are naughty, the mother says, and the child may accept the judgment. Then he becomes naughty or more naughty, thus validating falsely his mother's characterization. *Why falsely?* An anthropologist reports as of the time he was studying the Zande: "It is difficult to judge from a man's public behavior his real feeling" when he is accused of being a witch. For "even if he is certain of his innocence," he performs a simple, traditional ceremony to convince his accuser that he has made the witchcraft innocuous; "it is the proper thing for a gentleman to do" in a society obsessed with a belief in witchcraft (Evans-Pritchard, 1937, pp. 123–24).

A direct, head-on approach is usually neither possible nor profitable when Ego is judging a Group Alter. There may be too many persons to interview: we cannot speak to everyone in a football stadium, a modern corporation, an army, or a nation. Even if we could, we would obtain only partial information from each person, and we would have no guarantee that the bits from each would add up to the total objective Ego's judgment he or someone else is attempting to test. A sampling technique eliminates some of the difficulties but does not necessarily produce an overview of whatever interactions there are to observe (Pathway 1.2). We know, to our grief, how unreliable we ourselves as well as expert witnesses can be (Pathway 2.1), and both our and their reliability may decrease proportionately to the size of the group or the significance of the judgment being assessed. All of us at a game, including the players, can agree which side has won, but we might disagree concerning which team played more skillfully, especially if the victory is a narrow one. I shift to a loftier illustration: neither laymen nor professionals have achieved consensus when they seek valid ways to characterize Germans or to compare them with Italians or Frenchmen. But the Ego who questions the validity of his judgment has at least placed himself upon an advisable pathway: he is less cocksure of his immediate judgment, perhaps he must modify it. In addition, he as well as psychologists and journalists might well hold before themselves the model of competent anthropologists (Pathway 0.1): know the group so well (literally or figuratively by living among them) that at least their modal tendencies can be grasped, formulated, and then tested on the members themselves.

Obtaining information from Alter about himself and his peers raises another issue that is ordinarily not a matter of direct concern in psychological or psychiatric analysis as such but that confronts us in these times, the question of privacy. For various reasons, it may seem essential to investigate Alter: is he disloyal, does he smoke marijuana, does he pay his bills promptly, is he emotionally stable? There are, of course, ways to secure such information when Alter is unwilling to reveal it or when Ego does not wish Alter to know that he is being surveyed. Telephones are tapped, detectives or spies are set to work, associates are bribed, deception is used during an interview or experiment. Quite obviously privacy is thus invaded, and the ethical-political issue is whether the value sought by Ego (e.g., national security, the prevention or detection of crime, or an advance in scientific knowledge) outweighs the deprivation or loss of freedom then suffered by Alter. Almost everyone agrees that some pathways to Alters must be blocked, such as the use of torture, brainwashing, and many forms of the third degree, and also that some must be open, such as confidential information about income for the purpose of taxation or about inoculations for the prevention of epidemics. But we are not quite sure, are we, just where the line must or should be drawn.

Suppose Alter willingly allows his privacy to be invaded? He consults a psychiatrist in order most deliberately to express highly guarded beliefs and impulses. He exposes himself voluntarily to an interview by journalists. This, then, is his affair, we say on a naive level. We quickly realize, however, that in many instances the issue is not so simply settled. Children, persons under the influence of drugs, and the seriously insane, we say, must be protected from themselves. Assent by them is usually meaningless. Also there are borderline cases. Suppose an ostensibly normal person suffers a personal reverse, is temporarily depressed; should he be permitted to allow his privacy to be invaded when you and I know perfectly well that, in another mood, he would refuse permission? There is no glib reply, is there?

Considerable information is usually needed to validate Ego's explanation, if he offers one to himself or to others, about why he has passed judgment. The interaction between the factors affecting Alter and those affecting Ego's perception of Alter must be analyzed separately and then somehow brought together. You seem sad to me and I attribute my impression to your facial expression. But how much of my own sadness have I projected upon you (Pathway II.5)? Even if I agree that I am in a happy mood and you agree that you are in fact sad, videotape might reveal that my opinion is correct but my reason for it incorrect. A painstaking analysis of the tape could show that you have exactly the same expression when you are sad, sleepy, or even reflective. Perhaps my impression has been derived from a sign or verbal intonation I have scarcely noticed. In less personal terms: ordinarily Ego is not in a position either to utilize or to observe research designs sufficiently subtle to validate more or less conclusively his own reasons for passing judgments (Campbell & Stanley, 1963). Ego, for example, judges Alter on the basis of a particular cue, and then Alter behaves in a manner congruent with that judgment; has Ego validated his own use of the cue? No, not at all. The judgment may have stemmed from another cue of which Ego was unaware; the cue Ego used may have been fortuitous or irrelevant; or Alter's behavior may have arisen for quite different reasons. Ego's explanation can perhaps be validated only when, again and again, there is an almost invariable connection between the cue and behavior: one follows the other. Or the sequence must be observed in many Alters, though this is not necessary if Ego's interest is only in a particular Alter. As a control it must be shown that in the absence of the cue Alter does not reveal the behavior, or that most Alters do not. *Does this mean you can never explain anything?* No, caution is needed; Ego must keep trying to validate the reasons for his hits and his errors, otherwise he is less likely to profit from experience (Pathway 6.a).

8.b   Utility

Naturally the most useful judgment is a valid one: Ego sets up within himself expectations that are verified. Such a judgment is useful, not merely because it brings Ego the satisfaction that he has judged wisely and well, but also because it enables him, perhaps, to adjust to Alter by seeking him out, by avoiding him, or by some actions in between. The spectators at a play and the readers of a novel make similar judgments and enjoy similar satisfactions: they obtain insight into a character and hence are pleased, presumably, when he is portrayed more or less in accordance with their anticipations. *More or less?* Yes, for the fulfillment of expectation, either in life or in art, can also be a bore. You want the real or imaginary character also to reveal behavior that you have not expected and that, though unexpected, still cannot be completely surprising, for then the action would be "out of character" and hence unreal or disturbing.

Ego has innumerable naturalistic pathways at his disposal to convince himself, partially or completely erroneously, that a judgment of his is valid (e.g., Pathways I.2, I.4, II.5, 1.1, etc.). He may also influence Alter in order, wittingly or not, to create the same impression (Pathway I.c). In fact, the sources of satisfaction are as numerous as the impulses belonging to Ego's behavior potential. Thus his judgment may be gratifying when he believes that he and no one else is sufficiently acute or perspicacious to make the judgment. Only you know, you think, that beneath that woman's pleasant facade lurks a very sly person. Or Ego is pleased when he convinces himself that the Alter whom he respects also has attributes he respects. Among his peers Ego may have the reputation for judging leniently or harshly; then he will be delighted when he can justify that reputation by continuing to pass judgments of a similar nature.

The subjective utility of a judgment can be assessed only by reference to the goal of the judgment motive originally instigating Ego to perceive Alter through a particular channel, to pass primary judgment, and—though not always—to revise or reflect upon that judgment (Pathway II.a). The employer must discover empirically whether his prior assessment of the applicant really gave him both valid and useful cues to the man's capabilities and performance. The participants in an encounter group wonder afterwards whether the *Sturm und Drang* they experienced during the long weekend was worth the trouble: did they secure insight into themselves, do they now cooperate more efficiently with their fellows? A judgment of mine that nomads in Africa and elsewhere barely maintain themselves at a subsistence level but gain deep satisfactions from their way of life was initially motivated by a theoretical aim to understand these people; and so the goal I ultimately attain from this judgment is to feel well-informed on at least one score, which is something.

The judgment motive and the judgment concerning Alter usually lead to appropriate behavior by Ego, by Alter, or by both of them, and it is the rewarding or punishing value of this behavior that ultimately determines the utility of the judgment to Ego. If Alter renders Ego a favor, Ego's judgment about him may be affected and hence—and hence what? Will he then feel obligated to reciprocate? In our society

we can anticipate what research by and large has demonstrated: there
will be some form of reciprocation. But the matter is not so simple, for
reciprocation *may* depend upon Ego's opinion concerning Alter's original motive for bestowing the favor; if the motive is suspect, there
may be no reciprocation (Usual; Schopler & Thompson, 1968). In any
case, Ego's characterization of Alter is useful in mediating appropriate
action, and what is considered appropriate depends, as ever, upon the
conditions under which the favor has been granted. Advisable pathways
concerning the effects of behavior upon judgment cannot be codified:
from experience in general or with specific Alters, Ego adds whatever
wisdom he can to his understanding potential (Pathway II) and he reflects upon that experience in future situations (Pathway 6); and then
he attempts to salvage whatever he can.

Sometimes the utility of Ego's judgment may be appraised without
considering its validity. I may believe that you are disturbed by a
personal problem when in fact this is not so. My belief, however, induces me to treat you with extra kindness, which thus strengthens our
relation, a good value in its own right. Misunderstandings between two
persons, especially a man and wife, can result from faulty communication and *may* be alleviated when each can be shown what the other
person thinks of him and what that other person thinks the first person
thinks of him; in retrospect, either Ego or Alter may explain that "if I
had only known how you felt, it would have made a great difference"
(England, adults; Laing et al., 1966, pp. 18, 86–91).

A loud cry has been raised in behalf of imagination (Pathway II.5)
when it has been argued that anthropomorphic terms should be used
to describe the emotions of animals: "a complete rejection of all concepts derived from experience with man would leave a vacuum" in
comprehending their behavior, since we have no other terms except
those applicable to human beings. Comprehending human beings, the
same argument continues, functions similarly and hence in a sense must
also be anthropomorphic (Hebb, 1946). On occasion, moreover, we
likewise personify objects and environmental forces: the sea is angry,
the sun is merciless, the wind is erratic, the mountain is cruel—and we
may or may not recognize such metaphors, though we continue to use
them. On a superorganic level we may personify an abstraction when
we characterize crowds, tribes, or nations as cruel or cunning. These
anthropomorphic, personifying, or metaphoric concepts may be useful
because they provide the comforting conviction that nature, animals,
and Group Alters are intelligible. Intelligibility, however, is not equiv-

alent to validity. Animals, for example, may not experience or have the same motives as human beings, and so anthropomorphism, though psychologically useful in the short run, may prove misleading in the long run. Similarly, my sympathy for another person may convince me that he behaves like me and hence my forecasts concerning him may be correct most of the time—but then suddenly this pathway may lead me astray.

A judgment concerning a Group Alter can be useful from a practical standpoint. In fact, the discipline called sociometry provides a standardized technique applicable to friends, neutrals, and enemies: each member of a group is asked privately to choose from among his peers those he likes, respects, has as friends, and would have as a leader, as well as those he does not like, etc. By thus investigating concretely the popularity or unpopularity of each individual, the investigator can discover the "stars" and "isolates" in a particular group: he combines and compares all the choices and rejections by means of a diagram called a "sociogram" which thus reflects the judgments of all the group members. These pooled judgments are useful because, for example, if they like one another, individuals *may* work together more efficiently than if they do not (U.S., various adolescents & adults; Fiedler, 1958).

8.c Ethics

In a flash I anticipate a final dose of relativism as I view this heading. You are quite correct. Obviously ethical principles are relative, and ethical principles lurk in the foreground of judgments involving the good or the bad. Who, then, is to decide whether Ego's judgment is good or bad? And good or bad for whom? Either Ego or some other person, including Alter, may make the decision. Ego, for example, distrusts or has no respect for an important political leader. He realizes that it would be preferable to have a favorable opinion: he thus partially condemns his own judgment. Or another person tells him that the leader merits trust and respect; for that matter, the leader himself, if he were acquainted with the judgment, obviously would voice the same sentiment. In each case, the judgment depends upon an ethical standard, viz., the attitude one should have toward a public official. The standard employed by Ego, moreover, may not correspond to the one Alter himself employs to evaluate his own behavior. On the surface, Alter may appear to be successful because he has the attributes associated with success in his society. Internally, however, he may despise these accomplishments because he once sought objectives he has failed to attain. And who is right, Ego or Alter?

To the extent that ethical standards are relative, the judgment of goodness remains arbitrary. If you call someone crafty, you and others may consider the judgment bad in a society or group that places a low value on that attribute, but good when it is highly valued. *Nonsense, there are standards, maybe even universal standards, for praising or condemning the goodness or badness of judgments concerning our fellow men.* Calling them our fellow men, I say, is perhaps the key. We are all in this vale of tears together, and great thinkers, teachers, and writers everywhere, whether they be philosophers, prophets, priests, judges, or indeed psychiatrists, are struggling, it appears, to give voice to a common set of values. Loving thy neighbor as thyself is one of these dicta; and if we do, our judgments about him must be benevolent, no matter what we think his weaknesses are. When Ego loves Alter, moreover, he tries to help him; and helping in turn usually requires that he be understood correctly and that valid predictions be made about him. Our knowledge about others may be tentative and uncertain, but it is essential.

It is essential, as I emphasized at the outset in the Prologue, because otherwise we could not live together, we could not appreciate each other's assets and avoid or mitigate our liabilities. Somewhere in this state of affairs, good ethical principles must emerge. We could not find adventure and experience fulfillment in meeting and comprehending other persons if this were not so. We never do or should rest content with what we understand about the Alters with whom we are enmeshed. This person we think we know so well may violate, for better or worse, our expectation. We suddenly climb out of our rut and find a steep pathway to a stranger, whether friend or foe. And yet, as our long conversation throughout these pages has tried to show and as I have insisted again and again, especially in response to your critical thrusts, we can never be certain of anything because we cannot succeed in stepping out of ourselves, so securely and inevitably are we solipsistically imprisoned. Our best, or at least our most frequently traversed, pathway, you must have observed, is a common culture which, however, provides no safe or clear escape. Yes, we derive some comfort from the multiplicity of clues to Alters and to Group Alters that confront us and that can lead to understanding when and if, as a result of past experience, we guide primary judgments sagaciously into secondary ones. Even then we have our doubts, you and I may never be able to understand a scientist who suddenly solves an intricate problem, a poet who turns an incredible phrase, or a statesman who miraculously prevents a war. But we may, if we wish, draw somewhat closer. We are perpetual explorers, encountering thrills and sorrows as we move up and down the numerous direct and devious pathways to persons and groups we never quite reach. *Never?* Never; still deep satisfaction can be attained, as Browning proclaimed, when that reach exceeds the grasp.

POSTSCRIPTS

8.1   *Professional Validation*

Let us begin by glancing at a straightforward procedure employed by many professionals who would test whether Ego "understands" other persons. It seems very simple: those others answer questions about themselves on a personality schedule, and Ego tries to reply to the same questions as he imagines they would reply. Obviously tons of data can be collected in this manner, and computers just ache to process them. But a moment's reflection or a devastating critique of this procedure by a competent technician (Cronbach, 1955) alerts us to the possibility that there are at least a baker's half-dozen ways of collecting the data (how narrow or wide should the scale of judgments be?) and analyzing them (how should the difference between Alter's response and Ego's guess be calculated?). The identical procedure can be followed to discover whether Ego's self-appraisal is true or not, an illustration of which are studies using the so-called Q-sorting technique (Block, 1961). Ego is given 100 statements (e.g., "is fastidious," "is self-indulgent," "is personally charming," "tends to proffer advice") and he eventually sorts them into nine piles ranging from those he thinks most clearly describe himself to those he believes are not true of himself. The collection can also be sorted in the same way by others who know Ego, and then a comparison can be made between their judgments and his. But who is to say whether a group of Alters understands Ego better than he understands himself?

In carrying on research, it is necessary to determine the validity of Ego's judgment inside the laboratory or the clinic: do his judgments agree with this kind of circumscribed reality which may be operationally defined by Alter's own judgment or the judgment of presumably competent observers or investigators? Such "internal validity" must be distinguished from "external validity" (Campbell & Stanley, 1963, p. 5) which uses real-life criteria outside the laboratory or the clinic. An Ego

who can match some non-verbal measure like a collection of photographs and verbal descriptions of the expressions allegedly portrayed
may or may not be able to judge accurately the expressions of his relatives or peers; his judgments would have internal but not necessarily
external validity. Or when he is asked to identify the emotion being
portrayed on Alter's face, what should his frame of reference be? It
could be either Alter's intention or the situation provoking the facial
expression (Ekman et al., 1972, p. 18), quite different criteria.

Both in England and the United States, large institutions like governments and corporations have established assessment centers in which
candidates for various positions are measured and observed in a large
number of ways through standardized tests, interviews, games, and
other forms of interaction, sometimes over a period of days. Even such
heroic, expensive, time-consuming efforts, however, may have limited
success. For it may be impossible to foresee one or more of the crucial
situations for which the assessments are made. Thus Alter may be
judged a sturdy character in the assessment center, and he may generally be just that in his normal existence, but may later demonstrate a
weakness in a particularly difficult situation with which he had never
been confronted either in the center or in that existence. In addition, the
future assessment of the past assessment may not be valid or reliable:
the Ego who makes the original judgment concerning Alter may be
better qualified than the Ego whose subsequent judgment serves as the
validating criterion. The individual *may* be judged normal and dependable by his peers, by professionals, and by himself; but he may be
called neurotic by a neurotic Ego who becomes his supervisor (U.S.,
adults; OSS Assessment Staff, 1948, p. 431).

8.2   Experimentation

When the professional investigates large groups of subjects in order
to determine, for example, whether a communication is effective or not,
he randomly or deliberately splits them into two equivalent groups, an
experimental and a control group. Both groups are measured twice, that
is, they reply to questionnaires or are observed on two occasions: an
initial measurement before any communication is delivered; a second
measurement after the experimental but not the control group receives
the communication. The change in the experimental group, if any, is
compared with that, again if any, in the control group; if the former
change is greater than the latter and if in terms of probability theory
it is unlikely to be due to chance, the conclusion may be drawn with

some confidence that the communication has been effective. Why? If the two groups were randomly selected or made equivalent at the outset, they did not differ appreciably with respect to the factor being measured. The magnitude of the change in the experimental group, if the communication has been effective, must exceed that within the control group, this latter change must be common to both groups and reflect the imperfect measuring instrument, the effect of repeated measurement, or events having little or nothing to do with the communication as such. The initial equivalence of the two groups ensures they have undergone roughly similar experiences in real life between the two measurements. An effective experimental method thus enables us to take methodological error into account and provides real assurance that the other things assumed to be equal have in fact been equal. The only, or only probable, explanation for the obtained difference between the two groups must be the communication.

But can a simple Ego, not a professional, employ such an experimental method in judging whether Alter has "really" changed and in attempting to establish the reasons for that change? The answer has to be a flat no, it would seem, if the model is to be followed: Alter may be an individual, not a group, and hence there is no easy way to assess the effects of measurements or observations (Pathway 0.1). An effort can be made, however, to treat him in a quasi-experimental manner by noting, for example, how he reacts in the presence and also in the absence of a critical variable. But then a complication may be introduced by the order in which the measurements are made: the first measurement may affect Alter and hence distort his reaction to the subsequent presence or absence of the variable, whichever one comes second. This difficulty can be somewhat satisfactorily overcome by repeated presentations of both the experimental and the control conditions. If Ego wishes to determine whether Alter reacts more favorably to lawyers than to surgeons, he may observe him again and again in the presence of each. Even if this simple experimental approach were to yield clean-cut results, it would be necessary to randomize the order in which lawyers and surgeons appear. Randomization in real life is difficult or impossible, and that is why serious investigators prefer to observe their subjects in the laboratory, where they can control the presentation of the critical stimuli (rather than leaving this temporal factor to chance, as happens under normal circumstances) but where the artificiality of the simulated conditions may make Alter self-conscious or ready to please or deceive. An alert Ego, nevertheless, can view the experimental

method as an ideal advisable pathway when he would pass judgment
on a changing Alter or a Group Alter: he cannot reach the perfection
achievable through the use of a control and a measuring instrument,
but the knowledge of the nature of perfection provides him with another reason to hesitate before passing final judgment.

0.1 Ideal Model
I. Behavior potential
  I.1 Self-knowledge
  I.a Culture
  I.2 Ethnocentrism
  I.b Personality
  I.3 Limitation
  I.4 Egocentrism
  I.5 Situational empiricism
  I.6 Centrality
  I.c Ego-Alter relations
  I.7 Normality

II. Understanding potential
  II.1 Simplification and
       multivariance
  II.a Judgment motives
  II.2 Determinism
  II.3 Timing
  II.4 Salience
  II.b Sensitivity and skill
  II.5 Imagination
  II.c Convictions

1. The stimulus
  1.a Alter
  1.1 Deception
  1.b Behavior
  1.2 Sampling
  1.c Context
  1.3 Role

2. Channels
  2.a Attributes

2.b Credibility
2.1 Informants
2.c Restrictions

3. Perception
  3.a Speech and language
  3.1 Solipsism
  3.b Non-verbal symbols
  3.c Indices

4. Attitudes
  4.a Groups
  4.b Spirals
  4.c Change

5. Primary judgment
  5.a Description
  5.b Ascription
  5.c Imputation

6. Reflection
  6.a Experience
  6.b Detachment
  6.c Variation

7. Secondary judgment
  7.a Characterization
  7.b Evaluation
  7.c Understanding

8. Appraisal
  8.a Validity
  8.b Utility
  8.c Ethics

Aboud, Frances E. and Donald M. Taylor. 1971. Ethnic and role stereotypes. *Journal of Social Psychology*, 85, 17–27.

Aboud, Frances E.; Donald M. Taylor; and Robert Doumani. 1973. The effect of contact on the use of role and ethnic stereotypes in person perception. *Journal of Social Psychology*, 89, 309–10.

Achenbach, Thomas and Edward Zigler. 1963. Social competence and self-image disparity in psychiatric and nonpsychiatric patients. *Journal of Abnormal and Social Psychology*, 67, 197–205.

Adams, J. Stacy. 1965. Inequity in social exchange. *Advances in Experimental Social Psychology*, 2, 267–99.

Aderman, David and Leonard Berkowitz. 1970. Observational set, empathy, and helping. *Journal of Personality and Social Psychology*, 14, 141–48.

Alker, Henry A. 1972. Is personality situationally specific or intrapsychically consistent? *Journal of Personality*, 40, 1–16.

Allen, Bem P. 1973. Perceived trustworthiness of attitudinal and behavioral expressions. *Journal of Social Psychology*, 89, 211–18.

Allgeier, A. R. and Donn Byrne. 1973. Attraction toward the opposite sex as a determinant of physical proximity. *Journal of Social Psychology*, 90, 213–19.

Allport, Floyd H. 1933. *Institutional behavior*. Chapel Hill: University of North Carolina Press.

Allport, Gordon W. 1937. *Personality*. New York. Henry Holt.

Allport, Gordon W. 1942. *The use of personal documents in psychological science*. New York: Social Science Research Council.

Allport, Gordon W. 1954. *The nature of prejudice*. Cambridge, Mass.: Addison-Wesley.

Allport, Gordon W. 1958. What units shall we employ? *In* Gardner Lindzey (ed.), *Assessment of human motives*. New York: Rinehart, pp. 239–60.

Allport, Gordon W. 1961. *Pattern and growth in personality*. New York: Holt, Rinehart and Winston.

Allport, Gordon W. 1962. The general and the unique in psychological science. *Journal of Personality*, 30, 405–12.

Allport, Gordon W. and Henry S. Odbert. 1936. Trait names. *Psychological Monographs*, 47, no. 211.

Allport, Gordon W. and Leo Postman. 1947. *The psychology of rumor.* New York: Henry Holt.

Allport, Gordon W. and Philip Vernon. 1933. *Studies in expressive movement.* New York: Macmillan.

Allport, Gordon W.; Philip E. Vernon; and Gardner Lindzey. 1951. *The study of values.* Boston: Houghton Mifflin.

Altman, Irwin and Elliott McGinnies. 1960. Interpersonal perception and communication in discussion groups of varied attitudinal composition. *Journal of Abnormal and Social Psychology, 60, 390–95.*

Ames, David Wason. 1953. Plural marriage among the Wolof in Gambia. Ph.D. dissertation, Northwestern University.

Anderson, Norman H. 1965. Averaging versus adding as a stimulus-combination rule in impression formation. *Journal of Experimental Psychology, 70, 394–400.*

Anderson, Norman H. 1966. Component ratings in impression formation. *Psychonomic Science, 6, 279–80.*

Anderson, Norman H. 1968. Application of a linear-serial model to a personality-impression task using serial presentation. *Journal of Personality and Social Psychology, 10, 354–62.*

Argyle, Michael and Marylin Williams. 1969. Observer or observed? *Sociometry, 32, 396–412.*

Aronson, Elliot and Darwyn Linder. 1965. Gain and loss of esteem as determinants of interpersonal attractiveness. *Journal of Experimental Social Psychology, 1, 156–72.*

Aronson, Elliot and Philip Worchel. 1966. Similarity versus liking as determinants of interpersonal attractiveness. *Psychonomic Science, 5, 157–58.*

Asch, Solomon E. 1952. *Social psychology.* New York: Prentice-Hall.

Asch, Solomon E. 1958. *In* Renato Tagiuri and Luigi Petrillo (eds.), *Person perception and interpersonal behavior.* Stanford: Stanford University Press, pp. 86–94.

Atzet, Jon Edward. 1969. Perceptual and physiological correlates of accuracy in interpersonal perception. *Dissertation Abstracts, 29, 3215A–6.*

Ayer, A. J. 1963. *The concept of a person and other essays.* New York: St. Martin's Press.

Bailey, Roger C; Phillip Finney; and Bob Helm. 1975. Self-concept support and friendship duration. *Journal of Social Psychology, 96.*

Baker, Bela O. and Theodore R. Sarbin. 1956. Differential mediation of social perception as a correlate of social adjustment. *Sociometry, 19, 69–83.*

Baldwin, Clara P. and Alfred L. Baldwin, 1970. Children's judgments of kindness. *Child Development, 41, 29–47.*

Bannister, D. and J. M. M. Mair. 1968. *The evaluation of personal constructs.* London: Academic Press.

Barnlund, Dean C. and Carroll Harland. 1963. Propinquity and prestige as determinants of communication networks. *Sociometry, 26, 467–79.*

Barocas, Ralph and Forrest L. Vance. 1972. Interpersonal performance and placement interview decisions. *Journal of Social Psychology, 86, 23–28.*

Barron, Frank. 1955. A case study of a residual. *In* Arthur Burton and Robert E. Harris (eds.), *Clinical studies of personality.* New York: Harper, pp. 668–93.

Bartmann, Theodor. 1963. Der Einfluss von Zeitdruck auf die Leistung und das Denkenvarhalten bei Volksschülern. *Psychologische Forschung, 27,* 1–61.

Beloff, Halla and Simpson Coupar. 1968. Some transactional perceptions of African faces. *British Journal of Social and Clinical Psychology, 7,* 169–75.

Bem, Daryl L. 1967. Self-perception. *Psychological Review, 74,* 183–200.

Bender, Irving E. and Albert H. Hastorf. 1950. The perception of persons. *Journal of Abnormal and Social Psychology, 45,* 556–61.

Bender, Irving E. and Albert H. Hastorf. 1953. On measuring generalized empathic ability (social sensitivity). *Journal of Abnormal and Social Psychology, 48,* 503–06.

Bender, M. P. 1968. Does construing people as similar involve similar behaviour towards them? *British Journal of Social and Clinical Psychology, 7,* 303–04.

Benedict, Ruth. 1934. *Patterns of culture.* Boston: Houghton Mifflin.

Benjamin, Harry. N.d. *Basic self-knowledge.* London: Health for All Publishing Company.

Berkowitz, Leonard and Richard G. Goranson. 1964. Motivational and judgmental determinants of social perception. *Journal of Abnormal and Social Psychology, 69,* 296–302.

Bernard, Viola W.; Perry Ottenberg; and Fritz Redl. 1971. Dehumanization. *In* Nevil Sanford, Craig Comstock, and Associates (eds.), *Sanctions for evil.* San Francisco: Josey-Bass, pp. 102–124.

Berscheid, Ellen; David Boye; and John M. Darley. 1968. Effect of forced association upon voluntary choice to associate. *Journal of Personality and Social Psychology, 8,* 13–19.

Berscheid, Ellen and Elaine Hatfield Walster. 1969. *Interpersonal attraction.* Reading, Mass.: Addison-Wesley.

Berzonsky, Michael D. 1973. Some relationships between children's conceptions of psychological and physical causality. *Journal of Social Psychology, 90,* 299–309.

Bickman, Leonard. 1971. The effect of social status on the honesty of others. *Journal of Social Psychology, 85,* 87–92.

Birdwhistell, Ray L. 1970. *Kinesics and context.* Philadelphia: University of Pennsylvania Press.

Block, Jack. 1961. *The Q-sort method in personality assessment and psychiatric research.* Springfield: Charles C. Thomas.

Blofeld, John. 1959. *The wheel of life.* London: Rider.

Bodelev, A. A. 1970–1. Individual and developmental differences in interpersonal understanding. *Soviet Psychology, 9,* 157–69.

Bodelev, A. A.; V. N. Kunitsyna; et al. 1972. New data on the problem of social perception. *Soviet Psychology, 11,* 126–31.

Borke, Helene. 1971. Interpersonal perception of young children. *Developmental Psychology, 5,* 263–69.

Bourdon, Karen H. and David E. Silber. 1970. Perceived parental behavior among stutterers and nonstutterers. *Journal of Abnormal Psychology, 75,* 93–97.

Boyd, J. Edwin and Raymond P. Perry. 1972. Quantitative information differences between object-person presentation methods. *Journal of Social Psychology, 86,* 75–80.

Brandt, Lewis W. 1967. The phenomenology of the self-concept. *Existential Psychiatry, 6,* 422–32.

Breed, Warren and Thomas Ktsanes. 1961. Pluralistic ignorance in the process of opinion formation. *Public Opinion Quarterly, 25,* 382–92.

Brickman, Philip. 1969. Predicting behavior from first impressions of a T-group member. *International Journal of Group Psychotherapy, 19,* 53–62.

Briscoe, Mary E.; Howard D. Woodyard; and Marvin E. Shaw. 1967. Personality impression change as a function of the favorableness of first impressions. *Journal of Personality, 35,* 343–57.

Brislin, Richard W. 1971. Interaction among members of nine ethnic groups and belief-similarity hypothesis. *Journal of Social Psychology, 85,* 171–79.

Brislin, Richard W.; Walter J. Lonner; and Robert M. Thorndike. 1973. *Cross-Cultural research methods.* New York: Wiley.

Britton, J. H.; Jean O. Britton; and Carol Finn Fisher. 1969. Perception of children's moral and emotional behavior. *Human Development, 12,* 55–63.

Bronfenbrenner, Urie. 1958. The study of identification through interpersonal perception. *In* Renato Tagiuri and Luigi Petrillo (eds.), *Person perception and interpersonal behavior.* Stanford: Stanford University Press, pp. 110–30.

Brown, Robert D. 1970. Experienced and inexperienced counselors' first impressions of clients and case outcomes. *Journal of Counseling Psychology, 17,* 550–58.

Bruner, Jerome A.; David Shapiro; and Renato Tagiuri. 1958. *In* Renato Tagiuri and Luigi Petrillo (eds.), *Person perception and interpersonal behavior.* Stanford: Stanford University Press, pp. 277–88.

Bull, Andrew; Susan E. Burbage; et al. 1972. Effects of noise and intolerance of ambiguity upon attraction for similar and dissimilar others. *Journal of Social Psychology, 88,* 151–52.

Byrne, Donn. 1961. Interpersonal attraction and attitude similarity. *Journal of Abnormal and Social Psychology, 62,* 713–15.

Byrne, Donn. 1971. *The attraction paradigm.* New York: Academic Press.

Byrne, Donn; Glen Dale Baskett; and Louis Hodges. 1971. Behaviorial indicators of interpersonal attraction. *Journal of Applied Social Psychology, 1,* 137–49.

Byrne, Donn; Fran Cherry; John Lambert; and Herman E. Mitchell. 1973. Husband-wife similarity in response to erotic stimuli. *Journal of Personality, 41,* 385–94.

Byrne, Donn and William Griffitt. 1966. Similarity versus liking. *Psychonomic Science, 6,* 295–96.

Byrne, Donn; William Griffitt; and Carole Golightly. 1966. Prestige as a factor in determining the effect of attitude similarity-dissimilarity on attraction. *Journal of Personality, 34,* 434–44.

Byrne, Donn; William Griffitt; William Hudgins; and Keith Reeves. 1969. Attitude similarity-dissimilarity and attraction. *Journal of Social Psychology,* 79, 155–61.

Byrne, Donn and Oliver London. 1966. Primacy-recency and the sequential presentation of attitudinal stimuli. *Psychonomic Science,* 6, 193–94.

Byrne, Donn and Don Nelson. 1964. Attraction as a function of attitude similarity-dissimilarity. *Psychonomic Science,* 1, 93–94.

Cameron, Norman. 1939. Schizophrenic thinking in a problem-solving situation. *Journal of Mental Science,* 95, 1012–35.

Campbell, Donald T. and Julian C. Stanley. 1963. *Experimental and quasi-experimental designs for research.* Chicago: Rand McNally.

Campbell, John D. and Marian R. Yarrow. 1961. Perceptual and behavioral correlates of social effectiveness. *Sociometry,* 24, 1–20.

Cantril, Hadley. 1957. Perception and interpersonal relations. *American Journal of Psychiatry,* 119–27.

Capon, Noel and James Hulbert. 1973. The sleeper effect—an awakening. *Public Opinion Quarterly,* 37, 332–58.

Caputo, G. Craig. 1973. Sexual restrictions, social complexity, and cultural achievement. Ph.D. dissertation, Yale University.

Cattell, Raymond B. 1965. *The scientific analysis of personality.* Baltimore: Penguin Books.

Cautela, Joseph R. and Patricia Wisocki. 1969. The use of imagery in the modification of attitudes toward the elderly. *Journal of Psychology,* 73, 193–99.

Chalmers, Douglas K. 1969. Meanings, impressions, and attitudes. *Psychological Review,* 76, 450–60.

Chance, June Elizabeth and Wilson Meaders. 1960. Needs and interpersonal perception. *Journal of Personality,* 28, 200–09.

Child, Irvin L. and Leonard W. Doob. 1943. Factors determining national stereotypes. *Journal of Social Psychology,* 13, 475–87.

Chomsky, Noam. 1972. *Language and mind.* New York: Harcourt Brace Jovanovich.

Christensen, Larry. 1970. Person perception accuracy as a function of ethnic group and familiarity. *Perceptual and Motor Skills,* 31, 510.

Clement, David E. and Dale W. Sullivan. 1970. No risky shift with real groups and real risks. *Psychonomic Science,* 18, 243–45.

Cline, Victor B. and James M. Richards. 1961. A comparison of individuals versus groups in judging personality. *Journal of Applied Psychology,* 45, 150–55.

Cohen, Akiba and Randall P. Harrison. 1973. Intentionality in the use of hand illustrators in face-to-face communication situations. *Journal of Personality and Social Psychology,* 28, 276–79.

Cohen, Arthur R. 1957. Need for cognition and order of communication as determinants of opinion change. *In* Carl I. Hovland et al., *The order of presentation in persuasion.* New Haven: Yale University Press, pp. 79–97.

Cole, C. W.; E. R. Oetting; and R. W. Miskimins. 1969. Self-concept therapy for adolescent females. *Journal of Abnormal Psychology*, 74, 642–45.

Coleman, J. C. 1969. The perception of interpersonal relationships during adolescence. *British Journal of Educational Psychology*, 39, 253–60.

Collins, Barry E. and Harold Guetzkow. 1964. *A social psychology of group processes for decision-making*. New York: Wiley.

Collins, Corliss. 1972. Effects of a self-improvement course on self-concepts of adolescent female clients. *Journal of Psychology*, 80, 81–87.

Conn, Lane K. and Douglas P. Crowne. 1964. Instigation to aggression, emotional arousal, and defensive emulation. *Journal of Personality*, 32, 163–79.

Cooley, Charles Horton. 1902. *Human nature and the social order*. New York: Scribner.

Couch, Arthur and Kenneth Kenniston. 1960. Yeasayers and naysayers. *Journal of Abnormal and Social Psychology*, 60, 151–74.

Cozby, Paul C. 1973. Self-disclosure. *Psychological Bulletin*, 79, 73–91.

Cranach, M. von; H. G. Frenz; and S. Frey. 1968. Die "angenehmste Entfernung" zur Betrachtung sozialer Objekte. *Psychologische Forschung*, 32, 89–103.

Crandall, James E. 1969. Self-perception and interpersonal attraction as related to tolerance-intolerance of ambiguity. *Journal of Personality*, 37, 127–40.

Crassweller, Peter; Mary Alice Gordon; and W. H. Tedford. 1972. An experimental investigation of hitchhiking. *Journal of Psychology*, 82, 43–47.

Crawford, Jeffrey L. and Daniel C. Williams. 1974. Contingent reinforcement and response constraints as confounding factors in attitude attribution. *Journal of Social Psychology*, 94, 95–102.

Crockett, Walter H. 1965. Cognitive complexity and impression formation. *Progress in Experimental Personality Research*, 2, 47–90.

Cronbach, Lee J. 1955. Processes affecting scores on "understanding others" and "assumed similarity." *Psychological Bulletin*, 52, 177–93.

Crow, Wayman J. 1957. The effect of training upon accuracy and variability in interpersonal perception. *Journal of Abnormal and Social Psychology*, 55, 355–59.

Crow, Wayman J. and Kenneth R. Hammond. 1957. The generality of accuracy and response sets in interpersonal perception. *Journal of Abnormal and Social Psychology*, 54, 384–90.

Cusumano, Donald R. and Marjorie H. Richey. 1970. Negative salience in impressions of character. *Psychonomic Science*, 20, 81–83.

Dahl, Robert A. 1970. *After the revolution?* New Haven: Yale University Press.

Danielian, Jack. 1967. Psychological and methodological evaluation of the components of judging accuracy. *Perceptual and Motor Skills*, 24, 1155–69.

Darwin, Charles. 1872. *The expression of the emotions in man and animals*. London: J. Murray.

Davis, James H.; Ruth Kalb; and John P. Hornseth. 1966. Stability of impression formation and implications for emergent group structure. *Sociometry*, 29, 104–20.

Davis, William L. and E. Jerry Phares. 1967. Internal-external control as a determinant of information-seeking in a social influence situation. *Journal of Personality*, 35, 547–61.

Davitz, Joel R. 1969. *The language of emotion*. New York: Academic Press.

Davitz, Joel R.; Michael Beldoch; et al. 1964. *The communication of emotional meaning*. New York: McGraw-Hill.

Dibiase, William J. and Larry A. Hjelle. 1968. Body-image stereotypes and body-type preferences among male college students. *Perceptual and Motor Skills*, 27, 1143–46.

Dickey, Lois Edith. 1968. Projection of the self through judgments of clothed figures and relation to self-esteem, security-insecurity, and to selected clothing behaviors. *Dissertation Abstracts*, 29, 1080–1B.

Dittes, James E. 1959. Attractiveness of group as a function of self-esteem and acceptance of group. *Journal of Abnormal and Social Psychology*, 59, 77–82.

Dittmann, Allen T. 1971. (Review of Birdwhistell, q.v.). *Psychiatry*, 34, 334–42.

Doise, Willem. 1969. Autoritarisme, dogmatisme et mode d'approche. *Journal de psychologie normale et pathologique*, 66, 35–53.

Doise, Willem and Marisa Zavalloni. 1970. The generality of social perception characteristics. *Acta Psychologica*, 34, 521–24.

Dollard, John. 1935. *Criteria for the life history*. New Haven: Yale University Press.

Dollard, John. 1937. *Caste and class in a southern town*. New Haven: Yale University Press.

Dollard, John and Frank Auld. 1959. *Scoring human motives*. New Haven: Yale University Press.

Doob, Anthony N. and Alan E. Gross, 1968. Status of frustrator as an inhibitor of horn-honking responses. *Journal of Social Psychology*, 76, 213–18.

Doob, Leonard W. 1958. Behavior and grammatical style. *Journal of Abnormal and Social Psychology*, 56, 398–401.

Doob, Leonard W. 1960a. *Becoming more civilized*. New Haven: Yale University Press.

Doob, Leonard W. 1960b. The effect of codability upon the afferent and efferent function of language. *Journal of Social Psychology*, 52, 3–15.

Doob, Leonard W. 1961. *Communication in Africa*. New Haven: Yale University Press.

Doob, Leonard W. 1964. *Patriotism and nationalism*. New Haven: Yale University Press.

Doob, Leonard W. 1968a. Facilitating rapid change in Africa. *In* Arnold Rivkin (ed.), *Nations by design*. Garden City: Doubleday, pp. 333–86.

Doob, Leonard W. 1968b. *The plans of men*. Hamden: Archon Books.

Doob, Leonard W. 1968c. Tropical weather and attitude surveys. *Public Opinion Quarterly*, 32, 424–30.

Doob, Leonard W. 1971. *Patterning of time.* New Haven: Yale University Press.

Drewery, J. and J. B. Rae. 1969. A group comparison of alcoholic and non-alcoholic marriages using the interpersonal perception technique. *British Journal of Psychiatry,* 115, 287–300.

Duncan, Starkey, Jr. 1969. Nonverbal communication. *Psychological Bulletin,* 72, 118–37.

Duster, Troy. 1971. Conditions for guilt-free massacre. *In* Nevil Sanford, Craig Comstock, and Associates (eds.), *Sanctions for evil.* San Francisco: Josey-Bass, pp. 25–38.

Dymond, Rosalind F. 1949. A scale for the measurement of empathic ability. *Journal of Consulting Psychology,* 13, 127–33.

Edney, Julian. 1973. Territory and control. Ph.D. dissertation, Yale University.

Edwards, Allen L. 1957. *The social desirability variable in personality assessment and research.* New York: Holt, Rinehart and Winston.

Ehrlich, Howard J. and Carol Lipsey. 1969. Affective style as a variable in person perception. *Journal of Personality,* 37, 522–40.

Eiser, J. Richard and Alistair J. Smith. 1972. Preference for accuracy and positivity in the description of oneself by another. *European Journal of Social Psychology,* 2, 199–201.

Ekman, Paul. 1965. Communication through non-verbal behavior. *In* Silvan Tomkins and Carroll E. Izard (eds.), *Affection, cognition, and personality.* New York: Springer, pp. 390–442.

Ekman, Paul; Wallace V. Friesen; and Phoebe Ellsworth. 1972. *Emotion in the human face.* New York: Pergamon.

Ekman, Paul; E. Richard Sorenson; and Wallace V. Friesen. 1969. Pancultural elements in facial displays of emotion. *Science,* 164, 86–88.

Eliot, T. S. 1958. *The cocktail party.* London: Faber and Faber.

Ellsworth, Phoebe C. and J. Merrill Carlsmith. 1968. Effects of eye contact and verbal content on affective response to dyadic interaction. *Journal of Personality and Social Psychology,* 10, 15–20.

Ellsworth, Phoebe C. and J. Merrill Carlsmith. 1973. Eye contact and gaze aversion in an encounter. *Journal of Personality and Social Psychology,* 28, 280–29.

Endler, Norman S. and J. McV. Hunt. 1968. S-R inventories of hostility and comparisons of the proportions of variance from persons, responses, and situations for hostility and anxiousness. *Journal of Personality and Social Psychology,* 9, 309–15.

Erickson, Jeanne M; Blair W. McDonald; and E. K. Eric Gunderson. 1971. Reliability of demographic and job related information. *Journal of Personality,* 79, 237–41.

Erikson, E. H. 1959. Growth and crises of the "healthy personality." *Psychological Issues,* 1, 50–100.

Ertel, Suitbert. 1964. Kategorien der Personwahrnehumung und ihre kulturelle Bedigheit. *Psychologische Forschung,* 27, 475–540.

Evans-Pritchard, E. E. 1937. *Witchcraft, oracles, and magic among the Azande.* Oxford: Clarendon Press.

Evans-Pritchard, E. E. 1962. *Essays in social anthropology.* London: Faber and Faber.

Exline, Ralph V. 1957. Group climate as a factor in the relevance and accuracy of social perception. *Journal of Abnormal and Social Psychology,* 55, 382–88.

Exline, Ralph V. 1960. Effects of sex, norms, and affiliation motivation upon accuracy of perception of interpersonal preferences. *Journal of Personality,* 28, 397–412.

Exline, Ralph V. and David Messick. 1967. The effects of dependency and social reinforcement upon visual behavior during an interview. *British Journal of Social and Clinical Psychology,* 6, 256–66.

Eysenck, H. J. 1954. *Psychology and politics.* London: Routledge and Kegan Paul.

Eysenck, H. J. and S. Rachman. 1965. *The causes and cures of neurosis.* San Diego: Robert R. Knapp.

Fancher, Ralph E. Jr. 1966. Explicit personality theories and accuracy in person perception. *Journal of Personality,* 34, 252–61.

Fancher, Raymond E. Jr. 1967. Accuracy versus validity in person perception. *Journal of Consulting Psychology,* 31, 264–69.

Fancher, Raymond E. Jr. 1969. Group and individual accuracy in person perception. *Journal of Consulting and Clinical Psychology,* 33, 127.

Farina, Amerigo; Charles H. Holland; and Kenneth Ring. 1966. Role of stigma and set in interpersonal attraction. *Journal of Abnormal Psychology,* 71, 421–28.

Feldman, Robert S. and Vernon L. Allen. 1975. Determinants of the primacy effect in attribution of ability. *Journal of Social Psychology,* 96.

Festinger, Leon; Stanley Schachter; and Kurt Back. 1950. *Social pressures in informal groups.* Stanford: Stanford University Press.

Fiedler, Fred E. 1958. Interpersonal perception and group effectiveness. *In* Renato Tagiuri and Luigi Petrillo (eds.), *Person perception and interpersonal behavior.* Stanford: Stanford University Press, pp. 241–57.

Fiedler, Fred E. and Edward L. Hoffman. 1962. Age, sex, and religious background as determinants of interpersonal perception among Dutch children. *Acta Psychologica,* 20, 185–95.

Fiedler, Fred E.; Edwin B. Hutchins; and Joan S. Dodge. 1959. Quasi-therapeutic relations in small college and military groups. *Psychological Monographs,* 73, no. 473.

Flesch, Rudolf. 1948. A new readability yardstick. *Journal of Applied Psychology,* 32, 221–33.

Fletcher, Alice C. and Francis La Flesche. 1911. *The Omaha tribe.* Washington: Government Printing Office.

Flugel, J. 1930. *The psychology of clothes.* London: Hogarth.

Foa, Uriel G. 1958. Empathy or behavioral transparency? *Journal of Abnormal and Social Psychology,* 56, 62–66.

Fortes, Meyer. 1949. *The web of kinship among the Tallensi*. London: Oxford University Press.

Foulds, G. A. 1961. Personality traits and neurotic symptoms and signs. *British Journal of Medical Psychology, 34*, 263–70.

Foulkes, David and Susan Heaxt Foulkes. 1965. Self-concept, dogmatism, and tolerance of trait inconsistency. *Journal of Personality and Social Psychology, 2*, 104–110.

Fowles, John. 1965. *The Magus*. Boston: Little, Brown.

Franklin, Billy J. 1973. The effects of status on the honesty and verbal responses of others. *Journal of Social Psychology, 91*, 347–48.

Frauenfelder, Kenneth J. 1974. A cognitive determinant of favorability of impression. *Journal of Social Psychology, 94*, 71–81.

Freud, Sigmund. 1953. *Beyond the pleasure principle*. New York: Bantam Books.

Friedland, Seymour J.; Walter H. Crockett; and James D. Laird. 1973. The effects of role and sex on the perception of others. *Journal of Social Psychology, 91*, 273–83.

Frieze, Irene and Bernard Weiner. 1971. Cue utilization and attributional judgments of success and failure. *Journal of Personality, 39*, 591–605.

Frijda, Nico H. 1953. The understanding of facial expression of emotion. *Acta Psychologica, 9*, 294–362.

Frijda, Nico H. 1969. Recognition of emotion. *Advances in Experimental Social Psychology, 4*, 167–223.

From, Franz. 1971. *Perception of other people*. New York: Columbia University Press.

Fry, P. S. 1976. Children's social sensitivity, altruism, and self-gratification. *Journal of Social Psychology, 98*.

Gage, N. L. 1952. Judging interests from expressive behavior. *Psychological Monographs, 66*, no. 350.

Gage, N. L. 1953. Explorations in the understanding of others. *Educational and Psychological Measurement, 13*, 14–26.

Gahagan, Lawrence. 1933. Judgments of occupation from printed photographs. *Journal of Social Psychology, 4*, 128–34.

Garland, Howard and Bert R. Brown. 1972. Face-saving as affected by subjects' sex, audience's sex, and audience expertise. *Sociometry, 35*, 280–89.

Gergen, Kenneth J. and Edward E. Jones. 1963. Mental illness, predictability, and affective consequences as stimulus factors in person perception. *Journal of Abnormal and Social Psychology, 67*, 95–104.

Gibson, James J. 1951. Social perception and the psychology of perceptual learning. *In* Muzafer Sherif and M. O. Wilson (eds.), *Group relations at the crossroads*. New York: Harper, pp. 120–38.

Gibson, James J. and Anne D. Pick. 1963. Perception of another person's looking behavior. *American Journal of Psychology, 76*, 386–94.

Gifford, Robert K. 1973. Informative properties of descriptive words. Ph.D. dissertation, Yale University.

Goffman, Erving. 1959. *The presentation of self in everyday life*. Garden City: Doubleday Anchor.

Goffman, Erving. 1961. *Encounters.* Indianapolis: Bobbs-Merrill.

Goldberg, Lewis R. 1959. The effectiveness of clinicians' judgments. *Journal of Consulting Psychology, 23,* 25–33.

Goldstein, Alvin G. and Edmund J. Mackenberg. 1966. Recognition of human faces from isolated features. *Psychonomic Science, 6,* 149–50.

Gollin, Eugene S. and Sheldon Rosenberg. 1956. Conception formation and impressions of personality. *Journal of Abnormal and Social Psychology, 52,* 39–42.

Goodman, Norman and Richard Ofshe. 1968. Empathy, communication efficiency, and marital status. *Journal of Marriage and the Family, 30,* 597–603.

Gottheil, Edward and Robert J. Joseph. 1968. Age, appearance, and schizophrenia. *Archives of General Psychiatry, 19,* 232–38.

Gottman, John M. 1973. N-of-one and n-of-two research in psychotherapy. *Psychological Bulletin, 80,* 93–105.

Graf, Richard G. 1971. Induced self-esteem as a determinant of behavior. *Journal of Social Psychology, 85,* 213–17.

Graf, Richard G. and Jeanne C. Riddell. 1972. Helping behavior as a function of interpersonal perception. *Journal of Social Psychology, 86,* 227–31.

Gray-Little, Bernadette. 1973. The salience of negative information in impression formation among two Danish samples. *Journal of Cross-Cultural Psychology, 4,* 193–206.

Griffitt, William. 1969a. Attitude evoked anticipatory responses and attraction. *Psychonomic Science, 14,* 153 and 155.

Griffitt, William. 1969b. "Object" evaluation and conditioned affect. *Journal of Experimental Research in Personality, 4,* 1–8.

Griffitt, William and Russell Veitch. 1971. Hot and crowded. *Journal of Personality and Social Psychology, 17,* 92–98.

Gruenfeld, Leopold and Jack Arbuthnot. 1969. Field independence as a conceptual framework for prediction of variability ratings of others. *Perceptual and Motor Skills, 28,* 31–44.

Gruner, Charles R. 1967. Effect of humor on speaker ethos and audience information gain. *Journal of Communication, 17,* 228–33.

Gusinde, Martin. 1937. *Die Yamana.* Mödling, Austria: Anthropos-Bibliotek (available in English, Human Relations Area Files).

Guthrie, George M. and Pepita Jimenez Jacobs. 1966. *Child rearing and personality development in the Philippines.* University Park: Pennsylvania State University Press.

Haire, Mason and Willa Freeman Grunes. 1950. Perceptual defenses. *Human Relations, 3,* 403–12.

Hall, Edward T. 1959. *The silent language.* Garden City: Doubleday.

Hamid, Paul N. 1969. Changes in person perception as a function of dress. *Perceptual and Motor Skills, 29,* 191–94.

Hamid, Paul N. 1972. Some effects of dress cues on observational accuracy, a perceptual estimate, and impression formation. *Journal of Social Psychology, 86,* 279–89.

Hammond, Kenneth R.; Marilyn M. Wilkins; and Frederick J. Todd. 1966.

A research paradigm for the study of interpersonal learning. *Psychological Bulletin*, 65, 221–32.

Hanno, Mildred Sara and Lawrence E. Jones. 1973. Effects of a change in reference person on the multidimensional structure and evaluations of trait adjectives. *Journal of Personality and Social Psychology*, 28, 368–75.

Hansson, Robert O. and Fred E. Fiedler. 1973. Perceived similarity, personality, and attraction to large organizations. *Journal of Applied Social Psychology*, 3, 258–266.

Hartshorne, Hugh and Mark A. May. 1928. *Studies in the nature of character: I. Studies in deceit.* New York: Macmillan.

Harvey, John H. and David R. Kelley. 1973. Effects of attitude-similarity and success-failure upon attitude toward other persons. *Journal of Social Psychology*, 90, 105–114.

Hastorf, Albert H.; Stephen A. Richardson; and Sanford M. Dornbusch. 1958. The problem of relevance in the study of person perception. *In* Renato Tagiuri and Luigi Petrillo (eds.), *Person perception and interpersonal behavior.* Stanford: Stanford University Press, pp. 54–62.

Hastorf, Albert H.; David J. Schneider; and Judith Polefka. 1970. *Person perception.* Reading, Mass.: Addison-Wesley.

Hathaway, Starke R. 1956. Clinical intuition and inferential accuracy. *Journal of Personality*, 24, 223–50.

Hays, William L. 1958. An approach to the study of trait implication and trait similarity. *In* Renato Tagiuri and Luigi Petrillo (eds.), *Person perception and interpersonal behavior.* Stanford: Stanford University Press, pp. 289–99.

Hebb, D. O. 1946. Emotion in man and animal. *Psychological Review*, 53, 88–106.

Heider, Fritz. 1958a. Perceiving the other person. *In* Renato Tagiuri and Luigi Petrillo (eds.), *Person perception and interpersonal behavior.* Stanford: Stanford University Press, pp. 22–26.

Heider, Fritz. 1958b. *The psychology of interpersonal relations.* New York: Wiley.

Heiss, Jerold S. 1963. The dyad views the newcomer. *Human Relations*, 16, 241–48.

Hendershot, Gerry and Kenneth W. Eckhardt. 1971. Social perception of liberals and conservatives. *Journal of Social Psychology*, 85, 251–60.

Hendrick, Clyde. 1968. Averaging vs. summation in impression formation. *Perceptual and Motor Skills*, 27, 1295–1302.

Hendrick, Clyde. 1969. Preference for inconsistent information in impression formation. *Perceptual and Motor Skills*, 28, 459–66.

Hendrick, Clyde and Arthur F. Costantini. 1970. Effects of varying trait inconsistency and response requirements. *Journal of Personality and Social Psychology*, 15, 158–64.

Hewitt, Jay. 1969. Interpersonal attraction as a function of the accuracy of personal evaluations. *Psychonomic Science*, 17, 95–96.

Hicks, Jack M. 1972. The validation of attractiveness judgments as an indirect index of social attitude. *Journal of Social Psychology*, 88, 307–08.

Hilgard, Ernest R. 1949. Human motives and the concept of the self. *American Psychologist*, 4, 374–82.

Himmelfarb, Samuel and David J. Senn. 1969. Forming impressions of social class. *Journal of Personality and Social Psychology*, 12, 38–51.

Hjelle, Larry. 1969. Personality characteristics associated with interpersonal perception accuracy. *Journal of Counseling Psychology*, 16, 579–81.

Hoeth, Friedrich and Hannelore Gregor. 1964. Guter Eindruck und Persönlichkeitsfragebogen. *Psychologische Forschung*, 28, 64–88.

Hollender, John. 1973. Self-esteem and parental identification. *Journal of Genetic Psychology*, 122, 3–7.

Holt, Robert R. 1962. Individuality and generalization in the psychology of personality. *Journal of Personality*, 30, 377–404.

Holt, Robert R. 1969. Assessing personality. *In* Irving L. Janis (ed.), *Personality*. New York: Harcourt Brace, pp. 573–801.

Horowitz, Eugene L. 1935. Spatial localization of the self. *Journal of Social Psychology*, 6, 379–87.

Hovland, Carl I.; Enid H. Campbell; and Timothy Brock. 1957. The effects of "commitment" on opinion change following communication. *In* Carl I. Hovland (ed.), *The order of presentation in persuasion*. New Haven: Yale University Press, pp. 23–32.

Hovland, Carl I.; Irving L. Janis; and Harold H. Kelley. 1953. *Communication and persuasion*. New Haven: Yale University Press.

Hovland, Carl I.; Arthur A. Lumsdaine; and Fred D. Sheffield. 1949. *Experiments on mass communication*. Princeton: Princeton University Press.

Howe, Edmund S. 1962. Probabilistic adverbial qualifications of adjectives. *Journal of Verbal Learning and Verbal Behavior*, 1, 225–42.

Hunt, J. McV. 1965. Traditional personality theory in the light of recent evidence. *American Scientist*, 53, 80–96.

Hunt, William A. 1941. Recent developments in the field of emotion. *Psychological Bulletin*, 38, 249–76.

Hutt, Corinne and Christopher Ounsted. 1966. The biological significance of gaze aversion with particular reference to the syndrome of infantile autism. *Behavioral Scientist*, 11, 346–47.

Ichheiser, Gustav. 1970. *Appearances and realities*. San Francisco: Jossey-Bass.

Ingersoll, James W. 1972. The effect of feedback in reducing constraining verbal behavior in small, short-term training groups. *Dissertation Abstracts*, 32, 5546a–7a.

Irwin, Marc; Tony Tripodi; and James Bieri. 1967. Affective stimulus value and cognitive complexity. *Journal of Personality and Social Psychology*, 5, 444–48.

Ittelson, William H. and Charles W. Slack. 1958. The perception of persons as visual objects. *In* Renato Tagiuri and Luigi Petrillo (eds.), *Person perception and interpersonal behavior*. Stanford: Stanford University Press, pp. 210–28.

Iverson, Marvin A. 1964. Personality impressions of punitive stimulus persons of differential status. *Journal of Abnormal and Social Psychology*, 68, 617–26.

Izzett, Richard R. and Walter Leginski. 1971. Efficacy of associative versus dissociative strategies in producing affective ratings of a stimulus person. *Psychonomic Science*, 24, 161–62.

Izzett, Richard R. and Walter Leginski. 1972. Impression formation as a function of self versus other as source of the information. *Journal of Social Psychology*, 87, 229–33.

Jackson, David J. and Ted L. Huston, 1975. Physical attractiveness and assertiveness. *Journal of Social Psychology*, 96.

Jackson, Douglas N.; Samuel J. Messick; and Charles M. Solley. 1957. A multidimensional scaling approach to the perception of personality. *Journal of Psychology*, 44, 311–18.

Jacoby, Jacob. 1971. Interpersonal perceptual accuracy as a function of dogmatism. *Journal of Experimental Social Psychology*, 7, 221–36.

Jahoda, Marie. 1950. Toward a social psychology of mental health. *In* M. J. E. Senn (ed.), *Symposium on the healthy personality: II. Problems of infancy and childhood*. New York: Macy Foundation, pp. 211–98.

James, William. 1890. *The principles of psychology*, Vol. 1. New York: Henry Holt.

Jenness, Diamond. 1935. The Ojibwa Indians of Parry Island. *Bulletin of the Canada Department of Mines*, no. 78.

Johnson, Charles D. and Anne V. Gormly. 1975. Personality, attraction, and social ambiguity. *Journal of Social Psychology*, 97.

Johnson, Wendell. 1946. *People in quandaries*. New York: Harper.

Johnston, Shawn and Richard Centers. 1973. Cognitive systematization and interpersonal attraction. *Journal of Social Psychology*, 90, 95–103.

Jones, Edward E. 1964. *Ingratiation*. New York: Appleton-Century-Crofts.

Jones, Edward E. and Keith E. Davis. 1965. From acts to dispositions. *Advances in Experimental Social Psychology*, 2, 219–66.

Jones, Edward E.; Keith E. Davis; and Kenneth J. Gergen. 1961. Role playing variations and their informational value for person perception. *Journal of Abnormal and Social Psychology*, 63, 302–10.

Jones, Edward E. and Eric M. Gordon. 1972. Timing of self-disclosure and its effects on personal attraction. *Journal of Personality and Social Psychology*, 24, 358–65.

Jones, Edward E. and Victor A. Harris. 1967. The attribution of attitudes. *Journal of Experimental Social Psychology*, 3, 1–24.

Jones, Edward E. and Richard E. Nisbett. 1971. *The actor and the observer*. Morristown: General Learning Corporation.

Jones, Edward E.; Leslie Rock; Kelley G. Shaver; George R. Goethals; and Lawrence M. Ward. 1968. Patterns of performance and ability attribution. *Journal of Personality and Social Psychology*, 10, 317–40.

Jones, Edward E. and John W. Thibaut. 1958. Interaction goals as bases of inference in interpersonal perception. *In* Renato Tagiuri and Luigi Petrillo (eds.), *Person perception and interpersonal behavior*. Stanford: Stanford University Press, pp. 151–78.

Jones, Edward E. and Gary A. Wein. 1972. Attitude similarity, expectancy violation, and attraction. *Journal of Experimental Social Psychology*, 8, 222–35.

Jones, Robert G. and James B. Welsh. 1971. Ability attribution and impression formation in a strategic game. *Journal of Personality and Social Psychology*, 20, 166–76.

Jones, Stanley E. 1971. A comparative proxemics analysis of dyadic interaction in selected subcultures of New York City. *Journal of Social Psychology*, 84, 35–44.

Jones, Stephen C. 1966. Some determinants of interpersonal evaluation behavior. *Journal of Personality and Social Psychology*, 3, 397–403.

Jones, Stephen C.; Dennis A. Knurek; and Dennis T. Regan. 1973. Variables affecting reactions to social acceptance and rejection. *Journal of Social Psychology*, 90, 269–84.

Jones, Stephen C. and J. Sidney Shrauger. 1968. Locus of control and interpersonal evaluation. *Journal of Counseling and Clinical Psychology*, 32, 664–68.

Jourard, Sidney M. and Jacquelyn L. Resnick. 1970. Some effects of self-disclosure among college women. *Journal of Humanistic Psychology*, 10, 84–93.

Jourard, Sidney M. and Jane E. Rubin. 1968. Self-disclosure and touching. *Journal of Humanistic Psychology*, 8, 39–48.

Jung, C. G. 1928. *Contributions to analytical psychology*. London: Kegan Paul, Trench, Trubner.

Jung, C. G. 1959. *The archetypes and the collective unconscious*. New York: Pantheon.

Junod, Henri A. 1927. *The life of a South African tribe*, vol. 2. London: Macmillan.

Jurovsky, Anton. 1971. The functionality of interpersonal proximity in adolescents. *European Journal of Social Psychology*, 1, 5–94.

Kahneman, Daniel and Amos Tversky. 1973. On the psychology of prediction. *Psychological Review*, 80, 237–251.

Kanouse, David E. 1972. Language, labelling, and attribution. *In* Edward E. Jones et al., *Attribution*. Morristown: General Learning Press, pp. 121–35.

Kasl, Stanislav and George F. Mahl. 1965. The relationship of disturbances and hesitations in spontaneous speech to anxiety. *Journal of Personality and Social Psychology*, 1, 425–33.

Katz, Phyllis and Edward Zigler. 1967. Self-image disparity. *Journal of Personality and Social Psychology*, 5, 186–95.

Kaufman, Harry. 1966. Hostility, perceived similarity, and punitivity under arousal condition. *Journal of Personality*, 34, 538–45.

Kauranne, Urpo. 1964. Qualitative factors of facial expression. *Scandinavian Journal of Psychology*, 5, 136–42.

Kelley, Harold H. 1950. The warm-cold variable in first impressions of persons. *Journal of Personality*, 18, 431–9.

Kelley, Harold H. 1967. Attribution theory in social psychology. *Nebraska Symposium on Motivation*, 14, 192–240.

Kelley, Harold H. 1972. Attribution in social interaction. *In* Edward E. Jones et al., *Perceiving the causes of behavior.* Morristown: General Learning Press, pp. 1–26.

Kelly, George A. 1955. *The psychology of personal constructs.* New York: W. W. Norton.

Kelman, Herbert C. (ed.). 1965. *International behavior.* New York: Holt, Rinehart and Winston.

Kendon, Adam. 1967. Some functions of gaze-direction in social interaction. *Acta Psychologica,* 26, 22–63.

Kenner, Hugh. 1962. *Flaubert, Joyce, and Beckett.* Boston: Beacon Press.

Kepka, Edward J. and Philip Brickman. 1971. Consistency versus discrepancy as clues in the attribution of intelligence and motivation. *Journal of Personality and Social Psychology,* 20, 223–29.

Kiener, Franz and Hinrich Ahrens. 1973. Nicht bewusste Lernvorgänge bei Personwahrnehmung. *Psychologische Rundschau,* 24, 153–60.

King, M. G. 1970. Sex differences in the perception of friendly and unfriendly interactions. *British Journal of Social and Clinical Psychology,* 9, 212–15.

Kipnis, Dorothy M. 1961. Changes in self concepts in relation to perception of others. *Journal of Personality,* 29, 449–65.

Kirscht, John P. and Ronald C. Dillehay. 1967. *Dimensions of authoritarianism.* Lexington: University of Kentucky Press.

Kissen, Morton. 1968. A demonstration of certain effects of emotional states upon perception. *Dissertation Abstracts,* 29, 1836B.

Kleiner, Robert J. 1960. The effects of threat reduction upon interpersonal attractiveness. *Journal of Personality,* 28, 145–55.

Klemperer, Edith. 1968. The body image of the "other" in hypnoanalysis. *American Journal of Clinical Hypnosis,* 11, 63–68.

Kluckhohn, Clyde and Dorothea Leighton. 1946. *The Navaho.* Cambridge: Harvard University Press.

Knotts, A. Frank. 1966. Centrality and meaning in impression formation. *Dissertation Abstracts,* 26, 6158–59.

Koech, Regina and George M. Guthrie. 1975. Reciprocity in impression formation. *Journal of Social Psychology,* 95, 67–76.

Koenig, Frederick and Jerroll Seaman. 1974. Vigilance and justification as explanations of complex cognition. *Journal of Social Psychology,* 93, 75–80.

Kramer, Ernest. 1964. Personality stereotypes in voice. *Journal of Social Psychology,* 62, 247–51.

Krech, David and Richard S. Crutchfield. 1948. *Theory and problems of social psychology.* New York: McGraw-Hill.

Kreines, David C. and Karen Bogart. 1974. Defensive projection and the reduction of dissonance. *Journal of Social Psychology,* 92, 103–08.

Krook, Dorothea. 1969. *Elements of tragedy.* New Haven: Yale University Press.

Laban, Rudolf. 1950. *The mastery of movement.* London: MacDonald and Evans.

Laing, R. D. 1969. *Self and others.* London: Tavistock.

Laing, R. D.; H. Phillipson; and A. R. Lee. 1966. *Interpersonal perception.* London: Tavistock.

Lampel, Anita and Norman H. Anderson. 1968. Combining visual and verbal information in an impression-formation task. *Journal of Personality and Social Psychology, 9,* 1–6.

Landis, Carney and William A. Hunt. 1939. *The startle pattern.* New York: Farrar and Rinehart.

Landy, David and Elliot Aronson. 1969. The influence of the character of the criminal and his victim on the decisions of simulated jurors. *Journal of Experimental Social Psychology, 5,* 141–52.

Larken, P. M. 1926-7. An account of the Zande. *Sudan Notes and Records,* 10, 1–55, 85–135.

Laumann, Edward E. 1969. Friends of urban men. *Sociometry, 32,* 54–69.

Lay, Clarry H. and Gordon Thompson. 1968. Sensitivity to the generalized other with control for assimilative projection. *Psychonomic Science, 12,* 351–52.

Lazar, Eve. 1969. Children's perception of other children's fears. *Journal of Genetic Psychology, 114,* 3–11.

Lazarus, Richard S. and Elizabeth Alfert. 1964. Short-circuiting of threat by experimentally altering cognitive appraisal. *Journal of Abnormal and Social Psychology, 69,* 195–205.

LeBon, Gustave. 1921. *The crowd.* New York: Macmillan.

Lefcourt, Herbert and Jerry Wine. 1969. Internal versus external control of reinforcement and the deployment of attention in experimental situations. *Canadian Journal of Behavioural Science, 1,* 167–81.

Leginski, Walter and Richard R. Izzett. 1973. Linguistic styles as indices for interpersonal distance. *Journal of Social Psychology, 91,* 291–304.

Lerner, Melvin J. and Rosemary R. Lichtman. 1968. Effects of perceived norms on attitudes and altruistic behavior toward a dependent other. *Journal of Personality and Social Psychology, 9,* 226–32.

Lerner, Melvin J. and Carolyn H. Simmons. 1966. Observer's reaction to the "innocent victim." *Journal of Personality and Social Psychology, 4,* 203–10.

Lerner, Richard M. 1969. Some female stereotypes of male body-build behavior relations. *Perceptual and Motor Skills, 28,* 363–66.

Lerner, Richard M.; Stuart A. Karabenick; and Joyce L. Stuart. 1973. Relations among physical attractiveness, body attitudes, and self-concept in male and female college students. *Journal of Psychology, 85,* 119–29.

Leventhal, Howard. 1957. Cognitive processes and interpersonal predictions. *Journal of Abnormal and Social Psychology, 55,* 176–80.

Leventhal, Howard and Elizabeth Sharp. 1965. Facial expression as indicators of distress. *In* Silvan S. Tomkins and Carroll E. Izard (eds.), *Affect, cognition, and personality.* New York: Springer, pp. 296–318.

Leventhal, Howard and David L. Singer. 1964. Cognitive complexity, impression formation, and impression change. *Journal of Personality, 32,* 210–26.

Levitt, Eugene. 1959. A comparison of parental and self-evaluations of psychopathology in children. *Journal of Clinical Psychology*, 15, 402–04.

Levy, Leon H. 1961. The conditioning and generalization of changes in social perception dispositions. *Journal of Abnormal and Social Psychology*, 63, 583–87.

Levy, Leon H. 1964. Group variance and group attractiveness. *Journal of Abnormal and Social Psychology*, 68, 661–64.

Levy, Leon H. and Martin L. Richter. 1963. Impressions of groups as a function of the stimulus values of their individual members. *Journal of Abnormal and Social Psychology*, 67, 349–54.

Levy, Nisim and Harold Schlossberg. 1960. Woodworth scale values of the Lightfoot pictures of facial expression. *Journal of Experimental Psychology*, 60, 121–25.

Lévy-Schoen, Ariane. 1964. *L'image d'autrui chez l'enfant*. Paris: Presses universitaires de France.

Lewis, William A. and Wayne Wigel. 1964. Interpersonal understanding and assumed similarity. *Personnel and Guidance Journal*, 43, 155–66.

Lindskold, Svenn; Ronald Price; et al. 1974. The perceptions of individual and group stability. *Journal of Social Psychology*, 93, 211–18.

Little, Kenneth B. 1968. Cultural variations in social schemata. *Journal of Personality and Social Psychology*, 10, 1–7.

Loh, Wallace D. and Harry C. Triandis. 1968. Role perceptions in Peru. *International Journal of Psychology*, 3, 175–82.

Looft, William R.; Jack R. Rayman; and Barbara B. Rayman. 1972. Children's judgments of age in Sarawak. *Journal of Social Psychology*, 86, 181–85.

Loprieno, M.; F. Emili; and R. Esposito. 1967. Rapporti fra valutazione di sé e degli altri e ruolo sociometrico. *Securitas*, 52, 97–112.

Lott, Albert J. and Bernice E. Lott. 1965. Group cohesiveness as interpersonal attraction. *Psychological Bulletin*, 64, 259–309.

Louis-Guérin, Christiane. 1972–73. Perception d'autrui. *Bulletin de psychologie*, 26, 814–30.

Lovie, A. D. and Ann D. M. Davies. 1970. An application of Bayes' theorem to person perception. *Acta Psychologica*, 34, 322–27.

Luchins, Abraham S. 1958. Definitiveness of impression and primacy-recency in communication. *Journal of Social Psychology*, 48, 275–90.

Luchins, Abraham S. and Edith H. Luchins. 1961. Social influences on impressions of personality. *Journal of Social Psychology*, 54, 111–25.

Luchins, Abraham S. and Edith H. Luchins. 1968. The effect of massing or spacing communications on primacy effect. *Journal of General Psychology*, 79, 191–99.

Luchins, Abraham S. and Edith H. Luchins. 1970. Effects of preconceptions and communications on impressions of a person. *Journal of Social Psychology*, 81, 243–52.

Luft, Joseph. 1950. Implicit hypotheses and clinical predictions. 1950. *Journal of Abnormal and Social Psychology*, 45, 756–59.

Macaulay, Jacqueline. 1975. Familiarity, attraction, and charity. *Journal of Social Psychology*, 95, 27–37.

Maccoby, Eleanor and William Cody Wilson. 1957. Identification and observational learning from film. *Journal of Abnormal and Social Psychology*, 55, 76–87.

McCollough, Celeste. 1961. Forming and acting on impressions. *Journal of Psychology*, 52, 63–75.

McGuire, William J. 1961. The current status of cognitive consistency theories. *In* Shel Feldman (ed.), *Cognitive consistency*. New York: Academic Press.

McKinnon, Donald W. 1962. The nature and nurture of creative talent. *American Psychologist*, 17, 484–95.

McLuhan, Marshall. 1964. *Understanding media*. New York: McGraw-Hill.

Maddock, Richard C. and Charles T. Kenny. 1973. Impression formation as a function of age, sex, and race. *Journal of Social Psychology*, 89, 233–43.

Maehr, Martin L.; Josef Mensing; and Samuel Nafzger. 1962. Concept of self and the reaction of others. *Sociometry*, 25, 353–57.

Mahl, George F. 1968. Gestures and body movements in interviews. *Research in Psychotherapy*, 3, 295–346.

Mannheim, Karl. 1956. *Essays on the sociology of culture*. London: Routledge and Kegan Paul.

Manz, Wolfgang and Helmut E. Lueck. 1968. Influence of wearing glasses on personality ratings. *Perceptual and Motor Skills*, 27, 704.

Maracek, Jeanne and David R. Mettee. 1972. Avoidance of continual success as a function of self-esteem, level of esteem certainty, and responsibility for success. *Journal of Personality and Social Psychology*, 22, 98–107.

Maslow, A. H. and N. L. Mintz. 1956. Effects of esthetic surroundings. *Journal of Psychology*, 41, 247–54.

Matkom, Anthony. 1963. Impression formation as a function of adjustment. *Psychological Monographs*, 77, no. 5.

Maucorps, Paul and René Bassoul. 1958. Conscience d'autrui et empathie des relations interpersonnelles. *Psychologie française*, 3, 286–306.

May, Mark A. and Leonard W. Doob. 1937. *Competition and cooperation*. New York: Social Science Research Council.

Mead, George H. 1934. *Mind, self and society*. Chicago: University of Chicago Press.

Mead, Margaret. 1928. *Coming of age in Samoa*. New York: Morrow.

Mead, Margaret. 1930. *Social organization of Manua*. Bishop Museum Bulletin, no. 76.

Mead, Margaret. 1952. *The changing culture of an Indian tribe*. New York: Columbia University Press.

Meehl, Paul E. 1954. *Clinical versus statistical prediction*. Minneapolis: University of Minnesota.

Mehryar, A. H. 1969. Generality of social perception. *Journal of Social Psychology*, 78, 91–98.

Melbin, Murray. 1972. *Alone with others*. New York: Harper and Row.

Merrens, Matthew R. 1975. The relationship between personality inventory scores and self-ratings. *Journal of Social Psychology*, 97.

Merrens, Matthew and William S. Richards. 1970. Acceptance of generalized versus "bona-fide" personality interpretation. *Psychological Reports, 27,* 691–94.

Merton, Thomas. 1968. *Zen and the birds of appetite.* New York: New Directions.

Mettee, David R. 1971a. Changes in liking as a function of the magnitude and affect of sequential evaluations. *Journal of Experimental and Social Psychology, 7,* 157–72.

Mettee, David R. 1971b. The true discerner as a potent source of positive affect. *Journal of Experimental Social Psychology, 7,* 292–303.

Mettee, David R.; Edward Hrelec; and Paul C. Wilkens. 1971. Humor as an interpersonal asset and liability. *Journal of Social Psychology, 85,* 51–64.

Mettee, David R.; Shelley E. Taylor; and Stuart Fisher. 1971. The effect of being shunned upon the desire to affiliate. *Psychonomic Science, 23,* 429–31.

Mettee, David .R. and Paul C. Wilkens. 1972. When similarity "hurts." *Journal of Personality and Social Psychology, 22,* 246–58.

Mischel, Walter. 1968. *Personality and assessment.* New York: Wiley.

Montagu, Ashley. 1971. *Touching.* New York: Columbia University Press.

Moos, Rudolf H. 1968. Situational analysis of a therapeutic community milieu. *Journal of Abnormal Psychology, 73,* 49–61.

Morse, Stanley J. 1972. Help, likeability, and social influence. *Journal of Applied Social Psychology, 2,* 34–46.

Munroe, Robert L. and Ruth H. Munroe. 1972. Population density and affective relationships in three East African societies. *Journal of Social Psychology, 88,* 15–20.

Munsinger, Harry and William Kessen. 1964. Uncertainty, structure, and preference. *Psychological Monographs, 78,* no. 9.

Murdock, George Peter. 1949. *Social structure.* New York: Macmillan.

Murray, Robert P. and Hugh McGinley. 1972. Looking as a measure of attraction. *Journal of Applied Social Psychology, 2,* 267–74.

Murstein, Bernard I. 1958. Some determinants of the prediction of hostility. *Journal of Consulting Psychology, 22,* 65–69.

Nacci, Peter; Richard E. Stapleton; and James T. Tedeschi. 1973. An empirical restatement of the reciprocity norms. *Journal of Social Psychology, 91,* 263–71.

Nash, Jeffrey and Darwin L. Thomas. 1973. Code elaboration and self-concept states. *Journal of Social Psychology, 90,* 45–51.

Newcomb, Franc Johnson. 1940. *Navajo omens and taboos.* Santa Fe: Rydal Press.

Newcomb, Theodore. 1947. Autistic hostility and social reality. *Human Relations, 1,* 69–86.

Nidorf, Louis J. 1968. Information-seeking strategies in person perception. *Perceptual and Motor Skills, 26,* 355–65.

Nidorf, Louis J. and Walter H. Crockett. 1964. Some factors affecting the amount of information sought about others. *Journal of Abnormal and Social Psychology, 69,* 98–101.

Nisbett, Richard E and Stuart Valins. 1972. Perceiving the causes of one's own behavior. *In* Edward E. Jones et al., *Attribution.* Morristown: General Learning Press, pp. 63–78.

Norman, Warren T. 1963. Toward an adequate taxonomy of personality attributes. *Journal of Abnormal and Social Psychology, 66,* 574–83.

Obitz, Frederick W. and L. Jerome Oziel. 1972. Varied information levels and accuracy of person information. *Psychological Reports, 31,* 571–76.

Ogden, C. K. and I. A. Richards. 1936. *The meaning of meaning.* New York: Harcourt, Brace.

O'Neal, Edgar, and Judson Mills. 1969. The influence of anticipated choice on the halo effect. *Journal of Experimental Social Psychology, 5,* 347–51.

Opler, Morris Edward. 1943. Navaho shomanistic practice among the Jicarilla Apache. *New Mexico Anthropologist, 6,* 13–18.

Ortega y Gasset, José. 1957. *Man and people.* London: Allen & Unwin.

Osgood, Charles E. 1969. On the whys and wherefores of E, P, and A. *Journal of Personality and Social Psychology, 12,* 194–99.

Osgood, Charles E.; George J. Suci; and Percy H. Tannenbaum. 1957. *The measurement of meaning.* Urbana: University of Illinois Press.

Osofsky, Joy D. 1971. Children's influence upon parental behavior. *Genetic Psychology Monographs, 83,* 147–69.

OSS Assessment Staff. 1948. *Assessment of Men.* New York: Rinehart.

Paivio, Allan. 1972. The role of imagery in learning and memory. *In* Peter W. Sheehan (ed.), *The function and nature of imagery.* New York: Academic Press, pp. 253–79.

Passini, Frank T. and Warren T. Norman. 1966. A universal conception of personality structure? *Journal of Personality and Social Psychology, 4,* 44–49.

Pastore, Nicholas. 1952. The role of arbitrariness in the frustration-aggression hypothesis. *Journal of Abnormal and Social Psychology, 47,* 728–31.

Payne, R. W.; W. K. Caird; and S. G. Laverty. 1964. Overinclusive thinking and delusions in schizophrenic patients. *Journal of Abnormal and Social Psychology, 68,* 562–66.

Peabody, Dean. 1967. Trait inferences. *Journal of Personality and Social Psychology Monographs, 7,* no. 644.

Peabody, Dean. 1968. Group judgments in the Philippines. *Journal of Personality and Social Psychology, 10,* 290–300.

Pedersen, Darhl and Kenneth L. Higbee. 1969. Personality correlates of self-disclosure. *Journal of Social Psychology, 78,* 81–89.

Pedersen, Darhl and Loyda Shears. 1973. A review of personal space research in the framework of general system theory. *Psychological Bulletin, 80,* 367–88.

Pepitone, Albert. 1958. Attributions of causality, social attitudes, and cognitive matching processes. *In* Renato Tagiuri and Luigi Petrillo, *Person perception and interpersonal behavior.* Stanford: Stanford University Press, pp. 258–76.

Perry, Raymond P. and J. Edwin Boyd. 1972. Communicating impressions of people. *Journal of Social Psychology*, 86, 95–103.

Perry, Raymond P. and J. Edwin Boyd. 1974. The effect of message length, motivation, object person information on communicating personality impressions. *Journal of Social Psychology*, 92, 115–25.

Pesso, Albert. 1969. *Movement in psychotherapy*. New York: New York University Press.

Piaget, Jean and Bärbel Inhelder. 1969. *The psychology of the child*. New York: Basic Books.

Poe, Charles A. and David H. Mills. 1972. Interpersonal attraction, popularity, similarity of personal needs, and psychological awareness. *Journal of Psychology*, 18, 139–49.

Pollack, I.; H. Rubenstein; and A. Horowitz. 1960. Communication of verbal modes of expression. *Language and Speech*, 3, 121–30.

Posavac, Emil J. and Stanley J. Pasko. 1971. Interpersonal attraction and confidence of attraction ratings as a function of number of attitudes and attitude similarity. *Psychonomic Science*, 23, 433–35.

Posavac, Emil J. and Stanley J. Pasko. 1973. Risk taking and the set-size effect in interpersonal relations. *Journal of Social Psychology*, 90, 137–40.

Posavac, Emil J. and Stanley J. Pasko. 1974. Attraction, personality similarity, and popularity of the personality of a stimulus person. *Journal of Social Psychology*, 92, 269–75.

Potter, David A. 1973. Personalism and interpersonal attraction. *Journal of Personality and Social Psychology*, 1973, 28, 192–98.

Pound, Ezra. 1968. *The spirit of romance*. New York: New Directions.

Prince, Morton. 1906. *The dissociation of a personality*. New York: Longmans, Green.

Pruitt, Dean G. 1971. Choice shifts in group discussion. *Journal of Personality and Social Psychology*, 20, 339–60.

Pyron, Bernard. 1965. Accuracy of interpersonal perception as a function of consistency of information. *Journal of Personality and Social Psychology*, 1, 111–17.

Quereshi, M. Y.; Ann H. Leggio; and Frederick Widlak. 1974. Some biosocial determinants of interpersonal perception. *Journal of Social Psychology*, 93, 229–44.

Rabinowitz, William. 1956. A note on the social perceptions of authoritarians and nonauthoritarians. *Journal of Abnormal and Social Psychology*, 53, 384–86.

Raush, H. L.; A. T. Dittmann; and T. J. Taylor. 1959. Person, setting, and change in social interaction. *Human Relations*, 12, 361–78.

Raymond, Beth J. and Rhoda K. Unger. 1972. "The apparel oft proclaims the man." *Journal of Social Psychology*, 87, 75–82.

Regula, C. Robert and James W. Julian. 1973. The impact of quality and frequency of task contributions on perceived ability. *Journal of Social Psychology*, 89, 115–22.

Richey, Marjorie H.; Robert J. Koenigs; Harold W. Richey; and Richard

Fortin. 1975. Negative salience in impressions of character. *Journal of Social Psychology*, 97.

Richey, Marjorie H.; Lucille McClelland; and Algimantas Shimkumas. 1967. Relative influence of positive and negative information in impression formation and persistence. *Journal of Personality and Social Psychology*, 6, 322–27.

Riesman, David. 1950. *The lonely crowd*. New Haven: Yale University Press.

Ring, Kenneth. 1964. Some determinants of interpersonal attraction. *Journal of Personality*, 32, 651–65.

Robbins, Lillian Cukier. 1963. The accuracy of parental recall of aspects of child development and child rearing practices. *Journal of Abnormal and Social Psychology*, 66, 261–70.

Rodin, Miriam J. 1972. The informativeness of trait descriptions. *Journal of Personality and Social Psychology*, 21, 341–44.

Rodin, Miriam J. 1975. The effect of behavioral context on information selection and differential accuracy in a person perception task. *Journal of Social Psychology*, 97.

Rogers, Carl R. 1947. Some observations on the organization of personality. *American Psychologist*, 2, 358–68.

Rokeach, Milton. 1960. *The open and closed mind*. New York: Basic Books.

Rommetveit, Ragnar. 1960. *Selectivity, intuition, and halo effects in social perception*. Oslo: Oslo University Press, 1960.

Rorschach, Hermann. 1924. The application of the interpretation of form to psychoanalysis. *Journal of Nervous and Mental Diseases*, 60, 225–48, 359–79.

Roscoe, John. 1911. *The Baganda*. London: Macmillan.

Rose, Arnold M. 1962. A systematic summary of symbolic interaction theory. *In* Arnold M. Rose (ed.), *Human behavior and social process*. Boston: Houghton Mifflin, pp. 3–19.

Rosenback, Dvora. 1968. Some factors affecting reconciliation of contradictory information impression formation. *Dissertation Abstracts*, 29, 1957A.

Rosenbaum, Milton E. 1967. The source of information in impression formation. *Psychonomic Science*, 8, 175–76.

Rosenbaum, Milton E. and Irwin P. Levin. 1968a. Impression formation as a function of source credibility and order of presentation of contradictory information. *Journal of Personality and Social Psychology*, 10, 167–74.

Rosenbaum, Milton E. and Irwin P. Levin. 1968b. Impression formation as a function of the relative amounts of information presented by high and low credibility sources. *Psychonomic Science*, 12, 349–50.

Rosenkrantz, Paul; Susan Vogel; Helen Bee; and Inge Broverman. 1968. Sex-role stereotypes and self-concepts in college students. *Journal of Consulting and Clinical Psychology*, 32, 287–95.

Rosenthal, Robert. 1966. *Experimenter effects in behavioral research*. New York: Appleton-Century-Crofts.

Rosenthal, Robert and Ralph L. Rosnow. 1969. *Artifact in behavioral research*. New York: Academic Press.

Rosnow, Ralph L. and Robert L. Arms. 1968. Adding versus averaging as a stimulus-combination rule in forming impressions of groups. *Journal of Personality and Social Psychology,* 10, 363–69.

Rotter, Julian B. 1966. Generalized expectancies of internal versus external control of reinforcement. *Psychological Monographs,* 80, no. 1.

Rozelle, Richard M. and James C. Baxter. 1975. Impression formation and danger recognition in experienced police officers. *Journal of Social Psychology,* 95.

Ruble, Thomas L. 1973. Effects of actor and observer roles on attributions of causality in situations of success and failure. *Journal of Social Psychology,* 90, 41–44.

Rudin, Stanley A. 1959. Application of the methods of bisection and equal appearing intervals to the perception of persons. *Psychological Reports,* 5, 99–106.

Ryle, Gilbert. 1949. *The concept of mind.* London: Hutchinson.

Sackett, Gene P. 1966. Monkeys reared in isolation with pictures as visual input. *Science,* 154, 1468–73.

Sadler, Orin and Abraham Tesser. 1973. Some effects of salience and time upon interpersonal hostility and attraction during social isolation. *Sociometry,* 36, 99–112.

Sager, Eric B. and Leonard W. Ferguson. 1970. Person perception as a function of perceiver's position on a cold-warm dimension. *Psychological Record,* 20, 321–25.

Sapir, Edward. 1921. *Language.* New York: Harcourt, Brace.

Sarbin, Theodore R.; Ronald Taft; and Daniel E. Bailey. 1960. *Clinical inference and cognitive theory.* New York: Holt, Rinehart and Winston.

Scarlett, Helaine; Allen N. Press; and Walter H. Crockett. 1971. Children's descriptions of peer. *Child Development,* 42, 439–53.

Schachtel, Ernest G. 1950. Some notes on the use of the Rorschach test. *In* Sheldon Glueck and Eleanor Glueck, *Unraveling juvenile delinquency.* Cambridge: Harvard University Press, pp. 363–85.

Scheflen, Albert E. 1972. *Body language and the social order.* Englewood Cliffs: Prentice-Hall.

Scherer, Klaus R. 1972. Judging personality from voice. *Journal of Personality,* 40, 191–210.

Schmidt, Charles F. 1969. Personality impression formation as a function of relatedness of information. *Journal of Personality and Social Psychology,* 12, 6–11.

Schopler, John and Vaida Diller Thompson. 1968. Role of attribution process in mediating amount of reciprocity for a favor. *Journal of Personality and Social Psychology,* 10, 243–50.

Schümer, Rudolf; Rudolf Cohen; and Dirk R. Schwoon. 1968. Einige Bemerkungen zur Problematik linearer Modelle der diagnostischen Urteilsbildung. *Zeitschrift für experimentelle und angewandte Psychologie,* 15, 336–53.

Scodel, Alvin and Maria Livia Freedman. 1956. Additional observations on the social perceptions of authoritarians and nonauthoritarians. *Journal of Abnormal and Social Psychology,* 52, 92–95.

Searles, Harold F. 1959. The effort to drive the other person crazy. *British Journal of Medical Psychology*, 32, 1–18.

Sears, Pauline S. and Vivian S. Sherman. 1964. *In pursuit of self-esteem*. Belmont: Wadsworth.

Sears, Robert R. 1963. Dependency motivation. *Nebraska Symposium on Motivation*, 10, 25–64.

Secord, Paul F.; Carl W. Backman; and H. Todd Eachus. 1964. Effects of imbalance in the self-concept on the perception of persons. *Journal of Abnormal and Social Psychology*, 68, 442–46.

Secord, Paul F. and William Bevan. 1956. Personalities in faces. *Journal of Social Psychology*, 43, 283–88.

Secord, Paul F.; William F. Dukes; and William Bevan. 1954. *Genetic Psychology Monographs*, 49, 231–79.

Secord, Paul F.; William F. Dukes; and William Bevan. 1958. Personalities in faces. *In* Renato Tagiuri and Luigi Petrillo, *Person perception and interpersonal behavior*. Stanford: Stanford University Press, pp. 300–15.

Secord, Paul F. and John E. Muthard. 1955. Individual differences in the perception of women's faces. *Journal of Abnormal and Social Psychology*, 50, 238–42.

Sewell, Alan F. 1973. Person perception as a function of the personal consequences and immediacy of a decision. *Journal of Psychology*, 85, 157–64.

Sewell, Alan F. and James T. Heisler. 1973. Personality correlates of proximity preferences. *Journal of Psychology*, 85, 151–55.

Shah, Saleem Alam. 1960. Predictive ability in mental hospital personnel and university students. *Journal of General Psychology*, 63, 185–97.

Shapiro, M. B. 1961. The single case in fundamental clinical psychological research. *British Journal of Medical Psychology*, 34, 255–62.

Shaw, Marvin and Jefferson L. Sulzer. 1964. An empirical test of Heider's levels in attribution of responsibility. *Journal of Abnormal and Social Psychology*, 69, 39–47.

Sheehan, M. A. 1975. The relative salience of negative information in lifelike situations. Cited in Marjorie H. Richey et al., Negative salience in impressions of character. *Journal of Social Psychology*, 97.

Sheldon, William H. 1949. *Varieties of delinquent youth*. New York: Harper.

Sigall, Harold and David Landy. 1973. Radiating beauty. *Journal of Personality and Social Psychology*, 28, 218–24.

Signell, Karen A. 1966. Cognitive complexity in person perception and nation perception. *Journal of Personality*, 34, 517–37.

Siipola, Elsa M. and Vivian Taylor. 1952. Reactions to ink blots under free and pressure conditions. *Journal of Personality*, 21, 22–47.

Simon, William E. and Edward Bernstein. 1971. The relationship between self-esteem and perceived reciprocal liking. *Journal of Psychology*, 79, 179–201.

Singh, Ramadhar. 1973. Attraction as a function of similarity in attitudes and personality characteristics. *Journal of Social Psychology*, 91, 87–95.

Skinner, B. F. 1957. *Verbal behavior*. New York: Appleton-Century-Crofts.

Soucar, Emil and Joseph P. DuCette. 1972. A re-examination of the vigilance hypothesis in person perception. *Journal of Social Psychology*, 88, 31–36.

Spranger, Eduard. 1928. *Types of men.* Halle: Niemeyer.

Squier, Roger W. Jr. 1971. The effect of feedback information and behavior consistency on accuracy of social prediction. *Journal of Social Psychology,* 83, 255–64.

Stapert, John C. and Gerald L. Clove. 1969. Attraction and disagreement-produced arousal. *Journal of Personality and Social Psychology,* 13, 64–69.

Stapleton, Richard E. E.; Barry L. Nelson; Vincent T. Franconere; and James T. Tedeschi. 1975. The effects of harm-doing on interpersonal attraction. *Journal of Social Psychology,* 96.

Steiner, Ivan D. and Homer H. Johnson. 1963. Authoritarianism and "tolerance of trait inconsistency." *Journal of Abnormal and Social Psychology,* 67, 388–91.

Stroebe, Wolfgang; Chester A. Insko; Vaida D. Thompson; and Bruce D. Layton. 1971. Effects of physical attractiveness, attitude similarity, and sex on various aspects of interpersonal attraction. *Journal of Personality and Social Psychology,* 18, 79–91.

Sullivan, Harry Stack. 1953. *Conceptions of modern psychiatry.* New York: W. W. Norton.

Taft, Ronald. 1955. The ability to judge people. *Psychological Bulletin,* 52, 1–23.

Tagiuri, Renato. 1958. Social preference and its perception. *In* Renato Tagiuri and Luigi Petrillo (eds.), *Person perception and interpersonal behavior.* Stanford: Stanford University Press, pp. 316–36.

Tagiuri, Renato. 1968. Person perception. *In* Gardner Lindzey and Elliot Aronson (eds.), *The handbook of Social Psychology,* v. 3. Cambridge, Mass.: Addison-Wesley, pp. 395–449.

Tajfel, H. 1959. Quantitative judgment in social perception. *British Journal of Psychology,* 50, 16–29.

Taylor, Shelley E. and Davis R. Mettee. 1971. When similarity breeds contempt. *Journal of Personality and Social Psychology,* 20, 75–81.

Terry, Roger L. and Jane E. Evans. 1972. Class versus race discrimination attributed to self and others. *Journal of Social Psychology,* 80, 183–87.

Terry, Roger L. and William G. Snider. 1972. Veridicality of interpersonal perceptions based upon physiognomic cues. *Journal of Psychology,* 81, 205–08.

Tesser, Abraham. 1971. Evaluative and structural similarity of attitudes as determinants of interpersonal attraction. *Journal of Personality and Social Psychology,* 18, 92–96.

TeVault, R. Kent; Gordon B. Forbes; and Henry F. Gromoll. 1971. Trustfulness and suspiciousness as a function of liberal or conservative church membership. *Journal of Psychology,* 79, 163–64.

Textor, Robert B. 1967. *A cross-cultural summary.* New Haven: HRAF Press.

Thayer, Stephen and Lewis Alban. 1972. A field experiment on the effect of political and cultural factors on the use of personal space. *Journal of Social Psychology,* 88, 267–72.

Thayer, Stephen and William Schiff. 1969. Stimulus factors in observer judgment of social interaction. *American Journal of Psychology*, 82, 73–85.

Thomas, Alexander; Herbert G. Birch; et al. 1963. *Behavioral individuality in early childhood*. New York: New York University Press.

Thornton, G. R. 1944. The effect of wearing glasses upon judgments of personality traits of persons seen briefly. *Journal of Applied Psychology*, 28, 203–07.

Tiberghien, Guy. 1971. La certitude. *Psychologie française*, 16, 67–87.

Tomé, Hector J. Rodriquez. 1967. Unité et diversité de l'image de soi chez des adolescents. *Psychologie française*, 12, 114–23.

Touhey, John C. 1972. Attribution of person concepts by role accessibility and interaction outcomes. *Journal of Social Psychology*, 87, 269–72.

Touhey, John C. 1973. Attitude similarity and attraction. *Journal of Social Psychology*, 90, 251–57.

Triandis, Harry C. 1975. Culture training, cognitive complexity, and inter-personal attitudes. *In* R. W. Brislin, S. Bochner, and W. J. Lonner (eds.), *Cross-cultural perspectives on learning*. San Francisco: Sage, pp. 39–77.

Triandis, Harry C. and Earl E. Davis. 1965. Race and belief as determinants of behavioral intentions. *Journal of Personality and Social Psychology*, 2, 715–25.

Triandis, Harry C. and Martin Fishbein. 1963. Cognitive interaction in person perception. *Journal of Abnormal and Social Psychology*, 67, 446–53.

Triandis, Harry C.; Vasso Vassiliou; and Maria Nassiakou. 1968. Three cross-cultural studies of subjective culture. *Journal of Personality and Social Psychology, Monograph Supplement*, 8, no. 4.

Triandis, Harry C.; David Weldon; and Jack M. Feldman. 1974. Level of abstraction of disagreements as a determinant of interpersonal perception. *Journal of Cross-Cultural Psychology*, 5, 59–79.

Ulrich, Roger E.; Thomas J. Stachnik; and N. Ransdell Stainton. 1963. Student acceptance of generalized personality interpretations. *Psychological Reports*, 13, 831–34.

Unamuno, Miguel de. 1954. *Tragic sense of life*. New York: Dover Publications.

Uno, Yoshiyasu; Judith H. Koivumaki; and Robert Rosenthal. 1972. Unintended experimenter behavior as evaluated by Japanese and American observers. *Journal of Social Psychology*, 88, 91–106.

Valins, Stuart and Richard E. Nisbett. 1972. Attribution processes in the development and treatment of emotional disorders. *In* Edward E. Jones et al., *Attribution*. Morristown: General Learning Press, pp. 137–50.

Vernon, Philip E. 1933. Some characteristics of the good judge of personality. *Journal of Social Psychology*, 4, 42–58.

Vernon, Philip E. 1964. *Personality assessment*. New York: Wiley.

Vielhaber, David P. and Edward Gottheil. 1965. First impressions and subsequent ratings of performance. *Psychological Reports*, 17, 916.

Walker, Crane; E. P. Torrance; and Timothy S. Walker. 1971. A cross-cultural study of the perception of situational causality. *Journal of Cross-Cultural Psychology*, 2, 401–4.

Wallace, John. 1967. What units shall we employ? *Journal of Consulting Psychology*, 31, 56–64.

Walster, Elaine; Vera Aronson; et al. 1966. Importance of physical attractiveness in dating behavior. *Journal of Personality and Social Psychology*, 4, 508–16.

Waltzer, Herbert. 1968. Depersonalization and self-destruction. *American Journal of Psychiatry*, 125, 399–401.

Ware, Robert and O. J. Harvey. 1967. A cognitive determinant of impression formation. *Journal of Personality and Social Psychology*, 5, 38–44.

Warr, Peter B. and Valerie Haycock. 1970. Scales for a British personality differential. *British Journal of Social and Clinical Psychology*, 9, 328–37.

Warr, Peter B. and Christopher Knapper. 1966. The relative importance of verbal and visual information in indirect person perception. *British Journal of Social and Clinical Psychology*, 5, 118–27.

Warr, Peter B. and Christopher Knapper. 1968. *The perception of people and events.* New York: Wiley.

Weinstein, Eugene; Kenneth A. Feldman; et al. 1972. Empathy and communication efficiency. *Journal of Social Psychology*, 88, 247–54.

Weiss, Walter. 1963. Scale judgments of triplets of opinion statements. *Journal of Abnormal and Social Psychology*, 66, 471–79.

Weiss, Walter. 1969. Effects of the mass media of communication. *In* Gardner Lindzey and Elliot Aronson (eds.), *The handbook of social psychology*, v. 5. Reading, Mass.: Addison-Wesley, pp. 77–195.

Wertheimer, Max. 1938. Gestalt theory. *In* Willis D. Ellis (ed.), *A source book of Gestalt psychology.* New York: Harcourt, Brace, pp. 1–16.

White, Robert W. 1960. Competence and the psychosexual stages of development. *Nebraska Symposium on Motivation*, 8, 97–141.

Whiteman, Martin. 1967. Children's conception of psychological causality. *Child Development*, 38, 143–55.

Whiting, John W. M. and Irivin L. Child. 1953. *Child training and personality.* New Haven: Yale University Press.

Whorf, Benjamin Lee. 1956. *Language, thought, and reality.* Cambridge: M.I.T. Press.

Wiener, Morton and Albert Mehrabian. 1968. *Language within language.* New York: Appleton-Century-Crofts.

Wiggins, Nancy; Paul J. Hoffman; and Thomas Taber. 1969. Types of judges and cue utilization in judgment of intelligence. *Journal of Personality and Social Psychology*, 12, 52–59.

Wiggins, Nancy and Jerry S. Wiggins. 1969. A topological analysis of male preferences for female body types. *Multivariate Behavioral Research*, 4, 89–102.

Wild, Cynthia. 1965. Creativity and adaptive regression. *Journal of Personality and Social Psychology*, 2, 161–69.

Willems, Edwin P. 1969. Risk is value. *Psychological Reports*, 24, 81–82.

Williams, Daniel C. 1976. Effects of aptitude, diligence, and performance on the attribution of motivation and ability. *Journal of Social Psychology*, 98.

Willich, Christa; Arthur Fischer; and Enno Schwanenberg. 1972. Sprachlicher Informationstransfer in und zwischen sozialdifferente Populationen mit ausdruckshaltigen Fotos als Bezugsgegenständen. *Zeitschrift für Sozialpsychologie*, 3, 245–61.

Wilson, Godfrey and Monica Wilson. 1945. *The analysis of social change.* Cambridge: At the University Press, 1945.

Wishner, Julius. 1960. Reanalysis of "impressions of personality." *Psychological Review*, 67, 96–112.

Witkin, H. A. et al. 1962. *Psychological differentiation.* New York: Wiley.

Wittmer, Joe. 1971. Perceived parent-child relationships. *Journal of Cross Cultural Psychology*, 2, 87–94.

Worchell, Philip and Stephen D. Shuster. 1966. Attraction as a function of the drive state. *Journal of Experimental Research in Personality*, 1966, 1, 277–81.

Worthy, Morgan; Albert L. Gary; and Gay M. Kahn. 1969. *Journal of Personality and Social Psychology*, 13, 59–63.

Wrightsman, Lawrence S. Jr. 1964. Measurement of philosophies of human nature. *Psychological Reports*, 14, 743–75.

Wyer, Robert S. Jr. 1968. The effects of information redundancy on evaluations of social stimuli. *Psychonomic Science*, 13, 245–46.

Zaidel, Susan F. and Albert Mehrabian. 1969. The ability to communicate and infer positive and negative attitudes facially and vocally. *Journal of Experimental Research in Personality*, 3, 233–41.

Index

The italicized numbers and letters in parentheses after an entry refer to the Pathways as indicated throughout the text and in the Appendix.